NANTUCKET
A NATURAL
HISTORY

To Elizabeth,

NANTUCKET
A NATURAL
HISTORY

Peter B. Brace

[signature]

Distinctive Nantucket Books
Nantucket, Massachusetts
MMXII

Published by Mill Hill Press
An affiliate of the
Egan Maritime Institute
4 Winter Street
Nantucket, Massachusetts 02554

www.eganmaritime.org

Copyright © 2012

All rights reserved.

No part of this book may be reproduced or transmitted in any form or by any means, electronic or mechanical, including photocopying, recording, or by any information storage or retrieval system, without the written permission of the author's agents and the publisher, except where permitted by law.

The trademark Mill Hill Press® is registered in the United States Patent and Trademark Office.

Cover photo by Rob Benchley

Maps by Joseph M. Serrani

Cover design and interior illustrations by Rose Gonnella

Interior book design by Cecile Kaufman, X-Height Studio

ISBN: 978-0-9822668-2-3

Library of Congress Control Number: 201 293 4061

First Mill Hill Press printing 2012

Printed in the United States of America

DEDICATION

This book is dedicated to the Nantucket conservation organizations and those from away, whose collective mission is the protection of our island wilderness, its inhabitants and natural resources. They are the Maria Mitchell Association, Nantucket Land Council, Nantucket Conservation Foundation, Madaket Land Trust, 'Sconset Land Trust, Nantucket Islands Land Bank, the Trustees of Reservations, the Massachusetts Audubon Society and the U.S. Fish & Wildlife Service.

CONTENTS

PREFACE	ix
ACKNOWLEDGMENTS	xiii
A Laurentide Junk Heap	1
Instant Island: Just Add Life	23
An Unlikely Garden at Sea	39
Birds—Naturals and Accidentals	75
Feral Kingdom	103
Wetland Creatures	129
It's a Bug's Island	147
Water: Salt and Fresh	177
A Backyard Ocean	229
Erosion, the Reaper	259
Epilogue	281
ENDNOTES	283
BIBLIOGRAPHY	307
GLOSSARY	317
INDEX	325

PREFACE

Look around Nantucket, at the people who live here and visit the island, and then think about the surprising diversity of living things here, so far from the mainland. You'll quickly begin to realize the metaphor our mashup of a population becomes for the wildlife that shares these 47.8 square miles with us humans. Plants, birds, mammals, reptiles, amphibians, arthropods and marine life survive here for a world of varied and specialized reasons, just as people do.

Like Nantucket's summer residents, many species migrate here every year and then move on after a few months. The island's day-trippers, weekenders and short-term visitors, like the species passing through, need food, beverages and shelter before they continue on. There are those islanders who, like birds, were blown here off-course and found the island to their liking, staying much longer than they intended. And then there are the year-rounders. Much like the permanent wildlife here that has adapted to the limited resources of these islands, Gulf Stream–skewed seasons, the ever-changing impacts of weather at sea, poor soils, sometimes harsh living conditions, and loss of their habitat to human development, they've adjusted to an intense seasonal work period, limited options for year-round jobs, biannual housing swaps, staggering real estate prices and expensive living costs.

Still, so enamored are they with this place, that humans and natural world residents alike go to great lengths to remain or adapt to living conditions on the Nantucket Archipelago, just as the first humans did when they arrived at the start of Holocene Epoch, to shape their manmade rookery to their liking—and, within the last two centuries, to the liking of island visitors who, in return, enable so many of them to afford to live here. It is lucky for us that Nantucketers have the intelligence and resourcefulness to wrest an existence out of this place, manipulating our environment to suit our needs. It was how the Native Americans and early settlers living on the island did it, and it is the reason that we have the oddball zoo and arboretum that we do.

We've all heard the calls to arms from island conservation organizations since the first one, the Nantucket Conservation Foundation, thrust out an empty hand for contributions. It was 1963 when the NCF began to ask for help in preserving as much open space as it could from overdevelopment, ensuring the cleanliness of the island's sole-source aquifer and conserving Nantucket's unique collection of ecosystems and species.

They are indeed unique, and they most certainly do warrant our protection, because their continued existence, regardless of origin, relies on human intervention, depending on the particular school of conservation thought to which you subscribe. What I mean is that, in many cases on Nantucket, we're not protecting those remnants of a pristine wilderness at sea that are still untouched by man since the birth of these islands approximately 6,000 years ago. We're not keeping watch over all of the species that have been naturally distributed on our three-island archipelago. We should be charged with caring for and perpetuating an anthropogenically defined ecological unit at sea, because it is the way it is in large part because of the things that humans have done to it.

From its gravelly, sandy, glacial erratic foundation, when it formed naturally and randomly of materials from Canada dragged down through New England and dumped onto our section of the coastal plain, Nantucket developed in its own way. Its birds, amphibians, reptiles, insects, mammals, fish, trees and smaller vegetation became, after the first humans arrived around 10,000 years ago, a composite, a mosaic of life that, to a certain extent, humans played a major role in shaping. Despite our mostly inadvertent—but sometimes intentional—attempts at playing Creator, remaining open space, whether unplundered as yet or too soggy for our use, must still be protected, along with all natural life on these three islands.

Those deer that Nantucketers brought back to the island after hunting them to extinction, the south shore's sandplain grasslands and the maritime heathlands in the moors (both habitats of rare grasses and flowers that wouldn't have existed on Nantucket in their current form without human land-clearing survival efforts), the wind-breaking pitch pines, the ornamental opulence and soil retention of Rosa rugosa around the island and the deciduous trees in the Old Historic District, the domesticated turkeys gone feral and the jackrabbits introduced by a hunt club—all are here by our hand. And all of the island's conservation organizations made the conscious choice to protect intact the rare, endangered, threatened and special concern species living here, whether introduced by humans or naturally occurring.

It's not that they're all part of some diabolical distortion of Eden. It's that the alternative—letting it all go native, letting a natural process of succession of dominant and invasive plant species and an unbalanced faunal hierarchy blank out the species for which federal and state protection is mandatory—is philosophically incongruous with the missions of these organizations. Anthropogenic or not, these organisms are deemed worthy of protection.

How I do know this? Well, I'm not a biologist in any discipline of study within our natural world. Although my aspirations in higher education had me chasing a degree in marine biology or forestry, whichever path kept me outdoors the most, the unforgiving sentries of chemistry and math blocked all advances down those career paths and showed me how I was decidedly right-brained, geared for making it somehow as a creative professional.

In my time on Nantucket, I've been privileged to do just that: I've been the environmental writer for two island newspapers and a contributor of such stories to several other local publications. I spend as much time as I can out exploring the island on foot or bike and by kayak. My first book, *Walking Nantucket*, embodies my spirit. You're more likely to find me paddling up in Coskata Pond or hiking out to Smith's Point or around the moors than shopping for whale pants or barhopping downtown.

We chose the title of this book because, although my editor called for this work to be "definitive," it is not that. My research and writing showed that it can't be, because the natural history of these three islands is still unfolding—and because, of course, it would be impossible to include every last detail on what happened from when the islands were formed through the spring of 2012, when I had my final chances to squeeze in new information.

I agonized over which of the highly knowledgeable islanders would be the best resources for each chapter. I wanted to include every expert I could. And I lamented that I couldn't track down every single book, paper and study on Nantucket's ecosystems to comb through for all facts relevant to this subject. But I think I got to the ones that mattered. I spoke with the folks without whose knowledge this book couldn't exist.

To be clear, though, I'm merely a gatherer, collator and storyteller. I have recounted anecdotal, factual and speculative island natural history, infused with interviews of respected authorities on the various topics in this book. There are myriad people who study and research this stuff for a living, and I've included their voices in my story of the continuing evolution of the Nantucket Archipelago because their knowledge of the physical Nantucket is far superior than mine ever will be. Whenever possible, I consulted with people residing and practicing their craft on Nantucket. Where no expert existed on-island for a particular discipline, I enlisted those elsewhere who were recommended as most knowledgeable by their island peers.

What you'll find in these 10 chapters is the synthesis of what I found in searching for the natural history of Nantucket, Tuckernuck and Muskeget over the three years I spent on this project, supplementing everything I learned during my writing career on Nantucket over the better part of two decades. It is a story of the birth of these islands, their growing pains, their ongoing maturation and their gradual disintegration into the ocean—quite a lot like my own.

I sincerely hope you enjoy reading this book as much as I did researching and writing it!

ACKNOWLEDGMENTS

WRITING THIS BOOK is something I never imagined I could do, but I reveled in its researching and writing, ecstatic about being given such a rare chance to tap into my accumulated Nantucket Island consciousness.

During the summer of 2006, I was sequestered indoors, researching and writing a special publication for the *Nantucket Independent* called "Our Natural World." Shortly after it published in the *Independent* late that August, I heard through the grapevine that the managing editor for this project, Dick Duncan; the late Wes Tiffney's widow, Susan Beegel; and Nantucket author Nat Philbrick were conspiring to get me to write the natural history of Nantucket.

Having spent three months inside on this subject, I realized that I'd just done a warm-up for such a book. The enormity of the task scared me enough to start rehearsing reasons to give them for not wanting to do it. Two years later, Dick and I met, and we ironed out our rough ideas for the book's chronology and its feel. Then I got to work.

My brother is forever telling me I need to leave the island and go do my life's work elsewhere. "Elsewhere" has always been close to wherever he is living, and I understand such sage advice springs from love and his desire for us to live closer to one another. But I can't imagine living anywhere else. And had I heeded his call, I wouldn't have been here to receive the call about this book.

Well, here it is: my biggest, most challenging writing project to date, and I have to thank those three conspirators for thinking enough of my abilities and knowledge of Nantucket to pull it off. There are, however, quite a few others that I can't neglect to thank, as well.

Naturally, for publishing this book, huge thanks go to the Mill Hill Press and the Egan Maritime Institute, including its outgoing executive director, Jean Grimmer; Nantucket historian Nat Philbrick, for supporting Mill Hill's excellent taste in island writers; and I do have to expound on Dick Duncan's contribution to this book project. He had the same vision as I for the importance of telling the story of Nantucket's birth and evolution since its beginnings on the coastal plain upon which its three islands rest. Our working relationship was much more a partnership than that of an editor and writer. For that, and for his patience, humility and enthusiasm, I feel extremely lucky to have been able to work with him. Nancy Martin, whose Faraway Publishing produced my first book, *Walking Nantucket*, gets a big nod also for her encouragement and for being so cool about me writing for another island publisher. Jennifer Ahlborn is to be commended for her imaginative and impeccable copy-editing. Great big thanks, admiration and respect go to my long-time friends and co-workers at several island publications: Rose Gonnella for her illustrations and the design of the cover and Rob Benchley for the cover photo.

I spent a considerable amount of time doing research in the Maria Mitchell Association Science Library. Curator Jascin Leonardo Finger kindly let me borrow books for as long as I needed them, sometimes months at a time, always let me into the Science Library or the basement of Drake Cottage to search the special collection, gave me access to the copier upstairs and generally went out of her way to help me find what I needed. I found great depth in the islands' resource of Andrew McKenna-Foster, the director of the Natural Science Department at the Maria Mitchell, and in general I'm extremely grateful for all the help and support that the Maria Mitchell Association afforded me throughout this project.

Jim Lentowski, executive director of the Nantucket Conservation Foundation and my island friend and source since my first year with *The Nantucket Beacon*, started me off with some examples of books from his collection, which gave me great ideas on how to approach *Nantucket: A Natural History*. The staff and the collection at the Nantucket Atheneum meet their match only at the Maria Mitchell campus on Vestal Street. Like their sadly under-utilized, and under-funded, Science Library, the Nantucket Atheneum is a tremendous island resource that we should all cherish and support.

I have identical allegiance, respect and gratitude for the Nantucket Historical Association and its Research Library, especially for Libby Oldham,

ACKNOWLEDGMENTS

Georgen Charnes, Ralph Henke and Ben Simons, all of whom graciously and selflessly helped me find whatever I was looking for.

Dr. Tom French, Assistant Director of the Natural Heritage and Endangered Species Program at the Massachusetts Division of Fish & Wildlife, was invaluable in his almost infinite historical knowledge of the state's fauna and with his equal parts enthusiasm and patience in sharing it with me. I spent several highly educational afternoons on the phone with retired U.S. Geological Survey geologist Robert Oldale after reading his book on the geology of the Cape and the Islands, extracting information from him and asking the same questions over and over, which he patiently answered each time. Skip Lazell, the reptile/amphibian guy for the Cape and Islands, brought smiles to my face with his fantastic book, *This Broken Archipelago*, and his colorful yet expert answers to all my queries.

My admiration and thanks go posthumously to the late Wes Tiffney, co-founder of the UMass Boston Nantucket Field Station, for all his papers and books on Nantucket, Tuckernuck and Muskeget, and for the many comments he added to articles I wrote for *The Nantucket Beacon*. Thanks also to Susan Beegel, Wes's widow, who allowed me to explore his library of resources in Phippsburg, Maine, and to borrow or copy what papers and books I deemed necessary.

Following Wes as director of the field station was Dr. Sarah Oktay, who remains at her post today. Sarah, you really are the most amazing multi-tasker I've ever known, so I thank you for always having the time to stop what you were doing and answer my questions, and for shooting me follow-up e-mails packed with links to further information.

There are people, on this island and off, who, like myself, have devoted their lives (or large parts of them) to understanding Nantucket's creatures, vegetation and habitat, and moreover to sharing their discoveries with the rest of us. I feel quite fortunate to have been granted audiences with them, including the grand dame of birds on Nantucket, Edith Andrews; botanist Peter Dunwiddie, who promptly answered all of my e-mailed follow-up questions with enthusiasm; and island bird experts E. Vernon Laux, Edie Ray, Ken Blackshaw and Dick Veit.

Thanks to Karen Beattie for her help with island mammals, including bats; to Danielle O'Dell for her passionate spotted turtle lectures; to Bruce Perry for his wetlands vegetation help and for enlightening me on Glacial Lake Sesachacha; and to Cormac Collier for his endless search for the elusive spadefoot toad. Dr. Timothy J. Lepore and Dr. Sam R. Telford, III, dialed me in on everything I ever wanted to know about deer ticks, tick-borne diseases and arthropods in general, adding to the help I got from Andrew McKenna-Foster, Paul Goldstein and Mark Mello.

Kudos go to Blair Perkins, Bill Blount, the late J. Clinton Andrews, Diane Lang, town shellfish biologist Tara Anne Riley, former town biologist Tracy Curley, marine superintendent Dave Fronzuto, Boston attorney Ed Woll, Jr., and David Goodman and Bill Pew for their invaluable help in my understanding of our islands' worlds of water in the ponds, harbors, the Sound and the Atlantic Ocean. For the end of the chapter on erosion, I thank pilot George Reithof, who, with his Nantucket Aerial aerial photography, supplied me with fantastic photos of Tuckernuck Island and Smith's Point.

Finally, I want to thank my friend and unofficial writing coach, Andrea Gollin, for her encouragement and timely advice throughout most of this project.

If there is anyone I've missed, your omission is not a slight. You know how much you helped me with this book.

NANTUCKET
A NATURAL
HISTORY

Nantucket Sound

Muskeget Island

Tuckernuck Island

Eel Point

Madaket Harbor

Smith's Point

Long Pond

Madaket

Clark Cove

Hummock Pond

Dionis

Maxey Pond

Cisco Beach

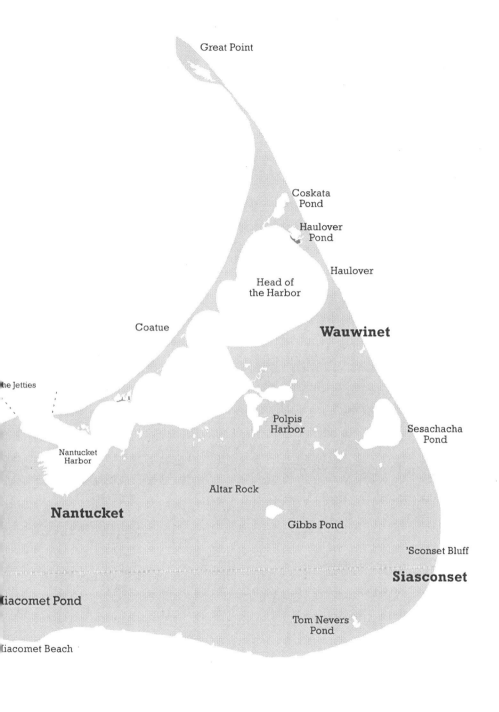

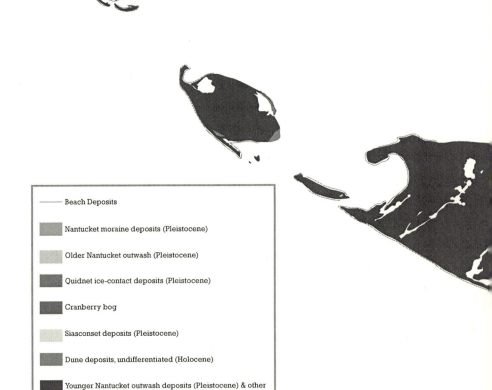

Map courtesy of Robert N. Oldale

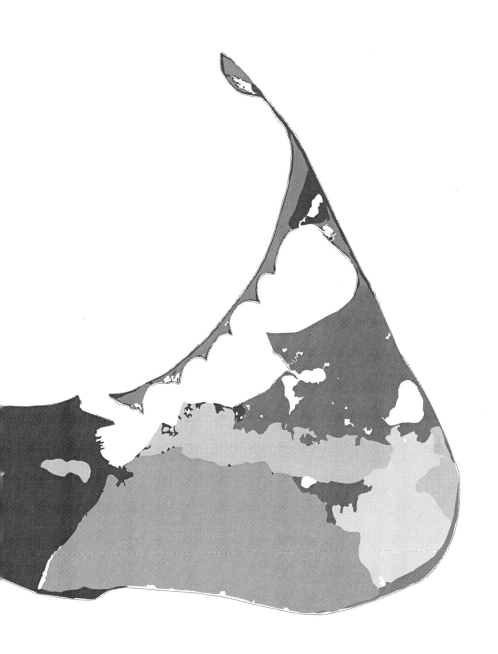

A LAURENTIDE JUNK HEAP

UNDERSTANDING THE PHYSICAL reality of Nantucket Island is as easy as walking up to Altar Rock and surveying the island landscape in all directions. No, don't just read this book; look at a map of the island or, even better, refer to one specifically on the geology of the Cape and Islands. But you can't really learn about the island's physical features without getting out onto the terrain to see it for yourself. A geological trash heap, Nantucket offers some easily identifiable geological forms to anyone willing to poke around. Walk around Altar Rock, bend over and grab some of the stones—most likely basalt, granite and volcanic rock from Nantucket's primordial basement—and some sand from the ground. Roll them around in your hands while you get your bearings and search for what writer John McPhee calls "a sense of where you are." This is a good exercise for those who've succumbed to the claustrophobia of the urban parts of the island, because you should get outside and learn about your surroundings.

The rocks, gravel and sand that you're holding and standing on are some of the ancient material dropped by the glacier that brought them here with the boulders you can see around you, sitting on and around the summit of Altar Rock, some placed there and others unmoved since the ice left them. They came down from Canada or were picked up along the glacier's way through New England before being deposited on this spot that became Nantucket. Some are also fragments of the bedrock on which Nantucket rests, formed during the period stretching from the Precambrian Era to the Mesozoic Era (which includes the Triassic, Jurassic and Cretaceous periods, the age of the Dinosaurs), 66 to 245 million years ago.

Up on this best known of the island's high points—the second highest on the island, next to Folger's Hill—note where you are: the harbor and Nantucket Sound are north, the Atlantic Ocean is to the south and east, Sankaty Head Lighthouse is to the east, and town is in a westerly direction. Then look at the map of the island that you most certainly brought with you, and turn east to Macy's Hill, then look on to Folger's Hill and Quarter Mile Hill beyond. Next, cast your gaze to the west for the lower bumps, the Shawkemo Hills toward town. You are standing at roughly the apex of the Nantucket version of a mountain range, which in this case reaches hypoxia-inducing heights of barely 96 inches over 100 feet.

On your map, you can draw a jagged line from east to west along these hills all the way out to the northern sections of Tuckernuck and Muskeget Islands, and beyond them, on to the south side of Martha's Vineyard, over Block Island, down the length of Long Island and further to the Jersey Shore. Roughly, this regional latitude marks the southern-most reaching edge of the Laurentide ice sheet, named for the St. Lawrence Region (Laurentian) of Canada where this glacier originated during the Wisconsinan Glacial Stage, 10,000 to 75,000 years ago. It was the last glacier to blanket a good portion of North America and to mold northern sections of the Midwest; all of New England, New York, and New Jersey and parts of Pennsylvania, Alaska, Canada and Greenland from 14,000 to 25,000 years ago. At the full extent of its southern advance in New England 21,000 years ago, the Laurentide ice sheet formed an ice mountain more than a mile high over Northern New England, about 1,500 feet tall over Cape Cod and roughly 500 feet over Nantucket.

The glacier and its meltwaters sculpted Nantucket into two distinct sections: a northerly portion composed of rough, gravelly soil, and a southern part composed of soft, sandy dirt. It punched springless ponds in her north side and gouged shallow valleys that later evolved into long, shallow ponds and valleys along her southern shores.

Go walking around the moors with Allen Reinhard, the affable, white-haired, bespectacled Middle Moors ranger for the Nantucket Conservation Foundation since 1990, and you may not even need this book. His knowledge of Nantucket's birth, childhood and continuing evolution is nearly limitless. And he'll surely share with you that you're standing on a geological dump of glacial deposits. Out on the moors—his outdoor classroom for demonstrating the work of the glacier—Reinhard sees his heathland territory and the island as a whole, in multiple dimensions. Point to a geological feature or a rock, soil or sand grain, and he can tell you what geological force in time did the work, why the vegetation growing there took hold, and what its future is. On Nantucket's mere existence, Reinhard clarifies:

> Nantucket would not exist if it were not for the most recent glacier. Actually, over the last 100,000 years, there have been different glaciations that have put down different layers. On top of the bedrock are different layers of glacial till, mixed glacial deposits of sand, gravel, rocks and boulders—basically material pushed here by the glacier. There are different layers of till from different glaciations. The top 500 feet are the result of the most recent glacier that arrived here 21,000 to 25,000 years ago. So Nantucket is the terminal moraine. Nantucket is where the glacier ended. We're essentially a huge pile of rubble that was dumped here by the most recent glaciation.

And beneath that 500-foot layer of sand, gravel and boulders that we call Nantucket are remnants of deposits, on top of the bedrock, left by previous glaciers that moved through the region during the Illinoian (125,000 to 350,000 years ago) and Pre-Illinoian (500,000 to 2.5 million years ago) glacial stages. Visible on the surface today, however, are mostly those deposits left during the Wisconsinan Glacial Stage—though Sankaty Bluff exposes layers left during the Illinoian glacial stage and the Sangamonian interglacial stage (the latter, 75,000 to 125,000 years ago).

The island-making process began for Nantucket around 7,500 to 8,000 years ago when the sea level rose high enough to cover the Georges Bank. Lapping up and out of the upper wall of the mile-deep Labrador Abyssal at the outer ocean edge of the Continental Shelf, seawater flooded the coastal plain that stretched some 75 miles south and 50 miles east of Nantucket, before the glacier began to melt, and spilled into the basins that became Nantucket and Vineyard Sound.[1]

The southernmost edges, sides and bottoms of the three lobes of the Laurentide glacial ice sheet, like fingers pushing through sand, formed Nantucket, Martha's Vineyard and Cape Cod with their extreme downward and forward, although uneven, pressure. The Cape Cod Bay and Great South Channel lobes threw up Nantucket's uneven line of hills, called kames. On its northern portion, it created ponds and dells, called kettles, which today include Sesachacha, Gibbs, Jewel and the Pout Ponds, and its southern ponds and valleys were formed with glacial meltwater raging in torrents down through the outwash plain on the southern side of the island. From Canada and New England north and west of the island, the lobes brought materials, including sand, gravel, rocks and clays, collectively called glacial till, and giant boulders called glacial erratics, so named because of their wide-ranging and random origins in the region and their erratic distribution along the path of the ice sheet. The glacier, acting like an enormous cheese grater with a grading blade in front of it, pushed these materials ahead of it, all the while shaving off new material along the way and carrying it forward.

At the southern end of this ice sheet, the Cape Cod Bay Lobe deposited most of the glacial till on the upland of the coastal plain that became Nantucket, Tuckernuck and Muskeget. The Great South Channel Lobe likely did the same for the eastern edges of the Quidnet and Sankaty parts of the island, including the formation of Sankaty Bluff with the help of the Cape Cod Bay Lobe.

All of this natural sandcastle building happened within the Wisconsinan Glacial Stage, 10,000 to 75,000 years ago. Moving south, its glacier blanketed all of New England by 25,000 years ago, reached its maximum southern limit at 21,000 years ago and left Nantucket ice-free at 18,000 years ago. It stalled along the northern third of what was to become Nantucket, forming its hills about 21,000 to 23,000 years ago, ending as the probable byproduct of a period of global warming—triggered by planet-warming, climate-changing events yet to be identified.[2] But it left behind those hills. Considering that the rest of the island is quite flat, Nantucket truly does have some striking geological features that are often overlooked.

From Quarter Mile Hill (so named because it's about a quarter of a mile from end to end) east to west at its base, to Altar Rock are Saul's Hills, named, along with several ponds, for Old Saul, a Nantucket Native American chief in the 1600s. These hills are part of the terminal moraine that the glacier polished and tweaked. Northwestward, beyond Altar Rock and the bowling-pin-shaped, white aircraft Omni beacon navigation tower on its slopes, are the Shawkemo Hills running northwest along Polpis Road before crossing it to run into the Shimmo area. From there, Nantucket's "mountainous" region continues on the southwest side of town with the Popsquatchet Hills, none of them taller than 100 feet. Running west, first there is Mill Hill, with the Old Mill at its peak, followed by Chicken Hill (christened for the late William G. Egan's chicken farm on its eastern side), with Dead Horse Valley in between and Colt Valley to the north. And finally, there's the lower Prospect Hill, the location of one of the town's cemeteries. (Also part of this end of Nantucket's zigzagging mountain range—though not of its terminal moraine—are Trott's Hills, west of Madaket Road, and several hills in town, including Academy and Sunset.³)

The terminal moraine formed of these hills outlines the southern limit of the glacier, which pushed them up like a bank of snow created by a plow.

And beneath it, the conveyor-belt action brought Nantucket all of its sand, gravel, rocks, clays, silts, sediments and boulders, even while the glacier retreated, extruding this material out of its base at the melting end like an asphalt paving machine. The grading plow action of the glacier fed off both the material dug up by its leading edge and the matter its bottom scraped off the surface of the land, gradually pushing the material forward. Nantucket is not the only rock-and-gravel tailing that remained above water at the southern limits of the Laurentide ice sheet; others include Martha's Vineyard, Block Island, Gardner's Island, Fisher's Island, Long Island and possibly the very eastern and northern edges of Tuckernuck Island. All were once part of the mainland about 7,500 to 8,000 years ago, when the ocean was roughly 300 feet lower than it is now and the coast was 75 miles south of where Nantucket sits at present.

However, although this terminal moraine extends from Quarter Mile Hill down to the Jersey Shore, seemingly in line with the landmasses where Tuckernuck and Muskeget Islands formed, the Cape Cod Bay Lobe traveled ten to 20 miles southward beyond the site of these islands instead of stopping here and creating a moraine as it did with Nantucket. Robert N. Oldale, who wrote *Cape Cod, Martha's Vineyard & Nantucket: The Geologic Story*, the definitive work on Nantucket's geology, believes the Cape Cod lobe of the glacier shaped Tuckernuck as an outwash plain, pushing its payload of till beyond the current location of Tuckernuck and then melting northward, trailing behind it outwash deposits that formed the surface of Tuckernuck. Reinhard agrees that Tuckernuck is carved from eroding outwash, a remnant of a vastly larger formation of till.

Still, there may be evidence on Tuckernuck's northern and eastern edges that these parts of this island are part of the terminal moraine left by the last glacier. There are large boulders (glacial erratics) along these shores, including Great Rock, about 100 feet off the east end of the island, and other boulders partially submerged in shallow water to the north, as well as thicker till on the east end of the island.⁴

The Cape Cod Bay Lobe did the same for the formation of Muskeget: it laid down outwash deposits as the glacier melted and left a high spot for this 292-acre island to grow on. But because its foundation was laid on the gentle west slope of Tuckernuck—all continental islands essentially being hilltops and mountain peaks whose inclines were eventually inundated by seawater—the outwash till deposited was not high enough to give Muskeget an outwash plain that would top out above the ocean after the water stopped rising. It wasn't until sand and gravel, likely collected from Tuckernuck and shoals that are no longer exposed, were carried by ocean currents, waves and wind over thousands of years to the hilltop of outwash material, exposed at low tide, that Muskeget was slowly created. This extra matter gave it barely enough clearance to survive as an island at about ten feet above sea level.[5]

As the glacier slid down over New England, the sheer weight of it had pushed down on the earth's crust. In some places in New England, including the Boston area, the crust had been depressed as much as 150 feet, and that depth was also possible near the front edge of the glacier. But the glacier didn't push Nantucket and the two smaller islands beneath sea level. When the weight of the glacier melted away, the crust of the earth gradually rose back up to roughly where it had been; however, this uplift wasn't enough to help push the young Muskeget Island any higher above the waves.

Oldale believes there is an easy explanation for the genesis of Muskeget:

> The simplest thing is all this happened when sea level was very, very low. The deposits on Muskeget are totally related to marine processes. In other words, all of the deposits there are either dune or beach or marsh or some form like that, and that has to rest on something, and so what those deposits rest upon would be the same types of deposits that we have in Nantucket, and would be glacial deposits and deposits of the last glaciation.

That same material is everywhere on Nantucket—occasionally exposed at the surface, eroding from hillsides and banks, and across much of the island, covered by the layers of poor-quality organic loam soils thinly blanketing the island. To glimpse Nantucket's foundation requires drilling very deep wells down into the bedrock, which is what the U.S. Geological Survey did in 1975 off Russell's Way, one of the lowest points on the island, and out on Great Point.[6] Drilling down 1,686 feet near the center of the island to take a core sample to analyze the Grey Lady's underpinnings, the USGS found fresh water from the water table extending from inches below the surface down to around 500 feet.[7] It also identified various sands, gravels, clays and rocks from the Pleistocene Epoch, the Tertiary Period, the Cretaceous Period and the Triassic Period.

At 1,686 feet, 495 feet below sea level, the USGS found Triassic basalt, volcanic rock created late during the Triassic Period of the Mesozoic Era, around 145 to 213 million years ago, but at around 528 feet, the USGS found fresh water floating on brackish water.

Nantucket's freshwater supply, known as its sole source aquifer because it isn't fed by underground rivers, is the island's only source of potable fresh water. Additionally, contrary to local myths and legends, it isn't the product of melting glacial ice way back when.[8] Instead, Nantucket's aquifer, estimated at about a trillion gallons by the Wannacomet Water Company, is recharged exclusively from precipitation. The average annual rainfall of 43 inches of rain drops 36.1 billion gallons on Nantucket and, of that, 10.8 billion gallons of water goes into the aquifer each year via percolation through the island's sandy soils. The rest that falls on the island each year evaporates back into the atmosphere. About two percent flows into island ponds and streams.

The fresh water beneath the island is floating on the salt water beneath it, because the fresh water is much lighter.[9] The aquifer is roughly in the shape of a squat, oval-shaped ball with its sides spread out at shallow angles, rather than a bowl with steep sides with another resting upside-down on top, as depicted on many maps and drawings of the island's aquifer. Before sea level reached its current elevation, the fresh water was deeper in the ground, but as the ocean level rose, wending its way into the porous, sandy, gravelly soils beneath the landmass, it forced the fresh water upwards.

Between the bottom of Nantucket's freshwater lens and the salt water connected with the ocean is a transition zone of a saltwater-freshwater mix. It is about 130 feet thick, straight down to the very bottom, toward the center of the island, and then it tapers, growing thinner and thinner as it rises to the shore. The groundwater reaches a short distance out under the ocean floor.

Says Oldale, "The salt water is the base for the fresh water to float on and as sea level rises, that interface also rises. As sea level rises, it reduces the amount of freshwater because [as] your reservoir is getting smaller and smaller, it's getting shallower because it's got to float on top of the seawater."

Today, Nantucket's aquifer, resting on the salt water beneath, is held in all around the island's shores by the pressure of the brackish water of the transition zone and the seawater outside of it.[10] You can experience the freshwater-saltwater interface at the surface of the island by wading in the shallow water at low tide along the shores of Monomoy in the summer. During July and August, when the harbor water is at its warmest, you can feel the colder groundwater seeping out of the aquifer along this shore, because at low tide on this part of Nantucket's shoreline, the hydrostatic pressure of the seawater is not great enough to keep the fresh water in. This is essentially a freshwater spring. There are three others on the island worth noting and visiting: Shawkemo Spring on the east side of Folger's Marsh, south of Polpis Road; Eat Fire Spring near the driveway of the Nantucket Island School of Design & the Arts, just off Wauwinet Road on private property; and Sachems Spring, emanating from the Cliff west of Jetties Beach. Each occurs where the aquifer is close enough to the surface of the island to surge out of the ground unaided by a pump. The Wampanoags named Eat Fire Spring for its pure, cold waters and their belief that it had great powers to preserve and restore health. The plaque marking the spring details its dependability. Nantucket relied on it during the Great Drought of 1874, which exhausted many of the island's deepest fresh water wells. During that drought, Eat Fire Spring filled 548 barrels at a rate of 12 gallons per minute every 24 hours.

In an effort to learn the shape, depth and overall make-up of the aquifer and the potential for saltwater intrusion, the Town of Nantucket hired Dr. Mark Person of the University of Minnesota's Computational Laboratory in the Department of Geology & Geophysics to do a three-dimensional model of the aquifer in 2001.

Dr. Person's model showed that the aquifer is closest to the island's surface at its shores and deepest at the center of the island, and that various layers of clays may segment the aquifer into layers of clay and water, all resting on volcanic rock.[11]

Although many of the soils that contain Nantucket's freshwater supply are prevalent on the surface of the island in great abundance, you have to know where to look for examples of the foundational debris revealed at the bottom of the Russell's Way bore hole.

Curious island explorers, searching for evidence of the island's prehistoric foundation, including basalt, granite, volcanic pebbles and rocks scattered around on island ground, would do well to bend over and look down after they've hiked up to Altar Rock, as suggested earlier, and taken in the amazing views in all directions. And there are a couple of other places on Nantucket to examine the island's geomorphology, as well. They include the sand pit at the northern boundary of the Milestone Cranberry Bogs, from which the Nantucket Conservation Foundation mines sand to spread on the bogs at the end of each season for weed control, and the glacial erratics along the road leading to the sand pit.

Layers of drift and till left by the glacier are visible in the exposed faces of the banks of this sand pit. More glacial erratics are visible immediately northwest of Altar Rock and can be seen strewn around the moors.[12] These geologic sites in the Middle Moors are just a few of the many other glacially influenced land features to see around the island. They're out there, both in the interior and around the shores, if you know where to look. When you are standing on Altar Rock with your back to the harbor, Coatue and Great Point, survey the Milestone Cranberry bogs to the southeast, the village of Siasconset further on, Tom Nevers directly south and then the airport and all the land in between. With some rolling hills—kames—mixed in, you're looking at the oldest of Nantucket's outwash plains. For an even more striking view of this interface between Nantucket's terminal moraine and the outwash plains, get over to Bean Hill, the short rise just east of Tom Nevers Road. From the turnout on the south side of Milestone Road or the Nantucket Conservation Foundation's Serengeti parking lot on the north side of the road, the southern border of the terminal moraine is clearly visible, looming 30 to 40 feet over the far northern side of the cranberry bogs.

You can peel back the layers of Nantucket's sandy onion and learn about her past at the exposed bluff below Sankaty Head Lighthouse, called a "marine scarp" by geologists. Here, three Pleistocene Epoch stages are visible. Two glacial stages sandwich an interglacial stage of sediments in a section of the bluff beneath Sankaty Head Lighthouse. The oldest, the Illinoian Glacial Stage, occurred 125,000 to 350,000 years ago; it displays glacial drift materials and is believed to lie lowest down, closest to the beach. Atop that are layers of sediment that were once part of a seabed of

Cliff face erosion

an ocean that existed during the Sangamonian Interglacial Stage, 75,000 to 125,000 years ago. These layers contain fossils of mollusks and Ostracodes, tiny crustaceans commonly called seed shrimp, which are 0.75 to 1.2 inches long and resided on the surface or just beneath the ocean bottom in this area during the Sangamonian Interglacial Stage. A distinctive white layer of these fossils is clearly visible from the beach, and shell fragments, freed by wind erosion, tumble down the bluff face onto the beach below in a steady stream of fine, powdery sand known as glacial flour. Oldale says he also found there the intact shells of mollusks, including soft-shell clams, quahogs, oysters, mussels, whelks and snails.

And atop the Sangamonian layers is the glacial till laid down by the last glacier during the Wisconsinan Glacial Stage, between 10,000 and 21,000 years ago. But these layers of sediment and till are not resting in their original state; the glacier pushed them into standing ripples and wrinkles of layers of glacial drift and till. They resemble a rug being pushed forward onto itself, with each tall wrinkle falling onto the next, scraped from the land surface and gouged out of the ground to be thrust upwards and either on top of or beneath the other exposed layers.

The entire bluff runs about two miles from just south of Sesachacha Pond to the village of 'Sconset, measuring several feet tall just south of Sesachacha Pond to around 100 feet at Sankaty. It came into being, and had these layers exposed, as the surging fingers of the Cape Cod Bay and Great South Channel lobes of the glacier advanced southward side by side. When the glacier receded, the material left behind between the two lobes—including, in the vicinity of the lighthouse, a giant erratic, called an interlobal moraine—became the marine scarp that is Sankaty Bluff. Although a peak once existed on this interlobal moraine after the two glacier lobes melted away, the ocean and wind have long since eaten it westward from the east so that today, Sankaty Head stands on the lower elevation of the western slope of this interlobal moraine. The northern, lower section of Sankaty Bluff, closer to Sesachacha Pond, most likely played another role in the shaping of the eastern side of the island. Oldale and other geologists believe that part of Sankaty Bluff and the Great South Channel Lobe formed the east side of a glacial lake, Glacial Lake Sesachacha, estimated to lie at one time 50 to 60 feet above sea level. It covered a significant portion of this end of the island, including Quaise, Pocomo, Wauwinet, Quidnet, all the land surrounding Polpis Harbor, a portion of the southeast side of Sesachacha Pond, and the underpinnings of the Coskata Woods. The

Cape Cod Bay Lobe of the glacier likely formed the north shore of this lake in the vicinity of Polpis Harbor and Pocomo, while ice and glacial drift contained the south and west sides. Water from the melting ice front of the glacier filled this lake and others in the area, including Glacial Lake Cape Cod, as the glacier gradually withdrew northward.

During the life of Glacial Lake Sesachacha, probably 19,000 to 20,000 years ago, the silty, clay-rich soil found in these areas today, along with glacial till, gravelly sand, gravel (pebble-sized to melon- or basketball-size) gradually tumbled into and settled down to the bottom of the lake from the glacier and formed the soils in this part of Nantucket. As the water leaked from the bottom of the ice-and-drift dam of this lake, roughly between Sankaty Head and Quarter Mile Hill, it fanned out over the part of the moraine found at that end of the island, swirling northwestward into a gap between the southern edge of the terminal moraine and its outwash. There, it formed a backwater where the Milestone Cranberry Bogs and Gibbs Pond are today.

This eddy carved out a foundation below Quarter Mile and Folger's Hills, heading west, and rippled into a canyon-like depression containing the Gibbs Pond kettle, forming a swampy zone where sphagnum moss thrived and creating conditions that eventually turned the soil acidic. These turned out to be ideal conditions for the construction, in the mid-1860s, of the 234-acre Milestone Cranberry Bog, at one time the largest contiguous cranberry bog in the world, before dikes were built within it. As bog conditions progressed, the lake continued to drain toward the ocean over the moraine deposits, spreading out a wide delta of outwash between Siasconset village and Tom Nevers Head.[13]

This youngest of Nantucket's three outwash plains spread in southerly directions from Glacial Lake Sesachacha, forming the Siasconset outwash plain with deposits of gravelly sand called pebble-to-cobble gravel, mixed with silt and till from the receding glacier and similar material eroded from the existing terminal moraine beneath, which the glacier laid down during its arrival on the Nantucket site around 21,000 years ago.

Siasconset's outwash is one of three created by glacial meltwater running south away from the glacier down Nantucket's landmass, across the coastal plain and out to the ocean over the eastern portion of the oldest Nantucket outwash deposits laid down shortly after the glacier arrived. Glacial Lake Sesachacha provided the outwash water that repaved the moraine deposited by the glacier, remodeling that part of the island's landscape with a mixture of original moraine and outwash deposits.

Seeing the remains of the Siasconset outwash plain is easier than one might imagine. Many of us pass right over this delta every day without realizing it. Oldale points to the lower land level immediately south of Sesachacha Pond as a logical sign of where the Glacial Lake Sesachacha's waters broke through and washed out to, and south of, Barnard Valley Road, spreading out to the Nantucket Golf Club land and broadening on toward the ocean south from Siasconset's elevated water storage tank to the LORAN station and on to Low Beach. On its western edges, this runoff lapped at Tom Nevers Head, so notice the relatively steep incline heading up from the west side of the former farmlands there, where rye and potatoes were once cultivated. The outwash plain there contains the U.S. Coast Guard LORAN tower, the Siasconset Sewage Treatment Plant and Tom Nevers Pond.

And driving west out of the village of Siasconset, see how the road reaches a peak coming out of the trees and lawns lining Main Street, then gradually dips down onto a valley that doesn't end until Milestone Road begins to climb Bean Hill just before Tom Nevers Road. That peak is roughly the eastern boundary of the Siasconset outwash; the drop-off is another remnant, as is the northeast slope of the plateau of the Nantucket Conservation Foundation's Serengeti property overlooking the Milestone Cranberry Bogs.

The second of the island's outwash plains, and the oldest, expanded out from the glacier below the moraine south of Polpis Road. It is bounded by the Siasconset outwash plain to the east, on a jagged line just north of Gibbs Pond running roughly northwest-southeast down to just east of Tom Nevers Pond, and to the west from the Creeks south to the ocean, following closely the east side of the Miacomet Pond valley all the way down to the beach on a roughly north-south line. Next to the drumlin exposed at the woods in Sanford Farm, this is believed to be the second oldest section of Nantucket.

The third and most recent outwash begins on the other side of that line and encompasses most of the western half of Nantucket, including Esther Island, Tuckernuck Island and the subterranean underpinnings, many believe, of Muskeget Island.

Want to see more? Nantucket's geological clues aren't confined to its eastern side. Head over to Sanford Farm, off Madaket Road, and follow the main trail from the parking lot out to a barn sitting on top of a hill overlooking Ram Pasture and the ocean beyond. Oldale believes this hill to be part of a drumlin, an elongated, sometimes oval-shaped hill molded of deposits by advancing glacial ice, and the oldest part of Nantucket, regardless of its suspected formation. He says that this drumlin is not part of

Nantucket's easterly moraine but could be a distinctly separate remnant of a moraine made of muddy, gravelly sand that pushed out over the land of Nantucket before the island's primary moraine appeared.[14]

There are kettles, depressions left by buried ice chunks pressed into the ground by the glacier, in this western part of the island. They are not necessarily ponds but low spots, many of them containing wetland plants and even water for at least part of the year. Their existence further supports Oldale's theory. After the Cape Cod Bay Lobe of the glacier retreated back into the Nantucket area, its meltwaters ran toward the ocean, distributing the deposits of the island's youngest outwash over the rest of the island, including Tuckernuck and Muskeget Islands, all west of the Miacomet Pond/Creeks boundary.

Says Oldale:

> If you look at the eastern outwash plain [the Siasconset outwash], which I consider younger, it doesn't have any kettle holes, so there's no evidence of buried ice being there in that outwash plain. It must have been deposited in front of the ice beyond where the ice front was. But now, you get to the west end of the island and that outwash plain is heavily kettled and that means that the ice had to be further south as a sublobe and as the sublobe retreated, it left the ice blocks behind. If you don't have any kettle holes, the ice probably didn't pass there and if you did have kettle holes, the ice had to go by.

Walking back from the Sanford Farm hill overlooking Ram Pasture, you might detour down one of the trails on the east side of the property, which run past a sandy slope overlooking the Head of Hummock. That exposed sand and gravel is part of this youngest outwash plain. Or, to see the edge of the terminal moraine, near the Siasconset outwash, walk west from the intersection of Hoicks Hollow and Polpis Roads, following Barnard Valley Road into the moors, where you'll eventually encounter the Milestone Cranberry Bogs to the south. To the north is the edge of the terminal moraine, which runs on to town, and a little bit beyond.

But for those searching for evidence of glacial activity, the real eye-openers are the tangible, easily identifiable land features that people see every day and can name: Nantucket's ponds and valleys, which were washed out by churning glacial meltwater running south from the softening ice sheet out to the ocean. Nantucketers, year-round and seasonal alike, already know these ancient, former meltwater stream beds by their popular island names, including Madequecham Valley, Miacomet Pond, Hummock

Pond, Long Pond—which almost cuts the island in half—Hither Creek, and the lesser known valleys of Mioxes Pond [my-ox-ese], the Weweeder Ponds, Toupshue Pond [toop-shoe], Forked Pond, and another valley starting at Gibbs Pond, connecting to Phillips Run just west of the Nantucket Golf Club and trailing on to Tom Nevers Pond at the southern end of Low Beach Road below Tom Nevers Head.

These outwash ponds represent one of several kinds of ponds on the island. The ponds on the north side of the island are kettle ponds. Coskata and Haulover Ponds, and East and North Ponds on Tuckernuck, are tidal ponds.

To understand better the formation of the moraine and the outwash plains on a smaller scale, hike into the moors after a heavy rainstorm and find a dirt road where the rainwater has washed down its sandy track. You'll see where the water, running down the road, has formed overlapping layers of different-colored sand and soils. Imagine this on an island-size scale, and you've got the outwash plain concept. In your dirt-road miniature, there will be dried-up channels where the water cut the deepest as it ran down the road. These are good models for the valleys, later to become the ponds mentioned above, that the glacier cut into the outwash. Notice the pebbles left in the flows of sand from the running rainwater, and pick up a few. The depressions they leave are not unlike those, on a grander scale, that filled with water after chunks of ice, covered with outwash deposits, melted on Nantucket's outwash plain, each leaving a kettle pond. The glacier's withdrawal was not a uniform melting; chunks and shards broke off from the main flow and were left behind buried under glacial till. When they gradually melted away, they left kettles that are now low points on the island, ponds fed only by precipitation and/or maintained by the water table. Many people know them as the Wigwam Ponds; the Pout Ponds [poot]; Almanac, Jewel, Gibbs and Donut Ponds; and many other unnamed dents in the landscape.

Walk around the moors enough and you're bound to discover almost all stages of these kettle ponds, which are gradually evolving from depressions that collect water, creating habitat for aquatic birds, amphibians and invertebrates, to swampy areas. They fill in first with wetland plants, but as decomposing organic matter (old plant parts) is gradually converted into peaty soil, upland species eventually take hold when the pond bottoms rise above the water table.

The second largest of these kettle ponds—Sesachacha Pond being the biggest—is Gibbs Pond, situated approximately where the ice of the Cape Cod

Bay Lobe stopped encroaching and began melting. Although a huge chunk of ice, buried beneath layers of till, was the primary excavator of Gibbs Pond, it is likely that a waterfall of meltwater from the glacier, driving down into the start of the outwash plain here, helped hollow it out. This flow of water would also have joined the eddy of the water flowing from Glacial Lake Sesachacha in the area at the foot of the terminal moraine and northeast of the Serengeti, and together, they would have fostered ideal conditions for swampland that would later become the Milestone Cranberry Bogs.

To see this in action, pick a calm day and go to a relatively flat island beach, like Dionis, 40th Pole or an inner harbor beach in Wauwinet, or on Pocomo Point, where few, if any, waves are breaking on the beach. Stand five or six feet from the water's edge and, using the heels of your hands, push up a large, wide and uneven ridge of sand and gravel, several feet wide and long and roughly a foot tall. There. You were just the glacier, making its final advancing movements and bulldozing glacial till (the sand) into a terminal moraine (the ridge). Now, fill a large pail with water, add a few handfuls of pebbles of various sizes, and slowly dump the contents over the ridge top, aiming toward the water's edge. Watch how your poured water churns down into the sand beneath your ridge, carries sand and pebbles away from the ridge, smoothes out the beach between it and the water, and gouges braided channels into the sand that spread out and smooth over the beach. To see how the ponds along Nantucket's south shore were cut into the landscape, slowly dump a few more pails of this watery mixture over your sand ridge and watch the water form braided channels in the sand as it flows toward the larger body of water. You're seeing how, over thousands of years of the glacier gradually melting and retreating northward and growing and re-advancing southward, the valleys were created and later evolved into ponds south of the terminal moraine on Nantucket. As the ocean eroded the shoreline inland, it closed these openings to the sea with sand transported along the shores by littoral drift; thus it formed the south shore ponds, which gradually filled with fresh water.

Although Altar Rock is the premier viewing spot for the island's glacial canvas, Bean Hill—the high spot just east of Tom Nevers Road—is where you can best see the most pronounced example of an end wall of a terminal moraine, an outwash plain (the Serengeti to the west) and the former swampland (now cranberry bogs). While the glacier's advance-retreat-re-advance dynamic tattooed Nantucket with the landforms recognizable in the present day, the island then didn't resemble what we see today.

Nantucket and Madaket Harbors didn't exist yet, and the island did not have its current signature shape until well after the ocean rose up around it but was considerably more oblong. Today's inner harbor shore, running from Jetties Beach out to Wauwinet, was the continuation of the north shore of the island we know today and was fully exposed to the wind and waves of Nantucket Sound and the Atlantic Ocean.

The most famous of the island's sandy extremities—Great Point, extending out from the Haulover and Coskata [coss-kay-tah], which derives from the Wampanoag language as "at the broad woods"—and its westerly dogleg, Coatue [coh-two], which translates to "at the pine woods"—most likely began humbly from a point just above Wauwinet, roughly 1,000 years after Nantucket became an island, and grew with the help of the south-to-north "long shore current" prevalent on this part of the eastern shore of the island. This movement by water up and down beaches is called "littoral drift" or "long shore drift." Its direction and intensity depend on wind, currents and tides. The flowing sand didn't just scatter about on the bottom of Nantucket Sound and ocean. A lot of it built northward, creating a tombolo—a sandbar that joins an island to a main island, the mainland or to another island—that connected Nantucket, at Wauwinet, to the nearest larger island, what is Coskata today.

Nantucket would probably not have its harbor without the existence of the soils beneath Coskata Pond, with its dunes and thick old-growth maritime oak forest, and Great Point, with its high, broad dune fields. Grounded on remnants of Pleistocene outwash deposits beneath the Nantucket moraine, which included erosion-resistant clays, gravel and sand and, later, a still-growing layer of organic loam soils, the Coskata area most likely started as a smaller island just north of Nantucket, once the ocean rose enough to make islands of all the high spots on the coastal plain. This location eventually became an ocean current intersection and, as the currents carried marine deposits northward from south of Wauwinet, sand and gravel were deposited both at Coskata and further north at another pile of gravelly, sandy soils, a small island and former peak on the coastal plain that would become Great Point.

The gradual formation of Nantucket Harbor began when enough glacial meltwater entered the ocean about 8,000 years ago. At its quickest rate, the meltwater raised the ocean 50 feet every 1,000 years. Between the time 7,500 years ago, when seawater entered Vineyard Sound, and 6,000 years ago, when salt water found Nantucket Sound, the ocean filled the lowlands of Nantucket and Vineyard sounds, and the coastal plain high grounds of Nantucket, Tuckernuck, Muskeget, Coskata and Great Point became islands. Dr. Peter Rosen, an associate professor of geology, chair of the Department of Earth & Environmental Science at Northeastern University, and a coastal geologist who wrote his thesis on the formation of Coatue and its six sand spits (geologically known as cuspate spits), has charted this process, and Oldale agrees. Rosen studies the geological dynamics of post-glacial deposits—namely, what happens to barrier beaches, sand spits and shoals when they are hit with powerful storms, erosion and wind. He is an expert in the formation of what today is called the Coskata-Coatue Wildlife Refuge, which includes the Haulover, Coskata Pond, and the woods, the Galls and Great Point, altogether 1,117 acres owned by the Trustees of Reservations.

Says Rosen of these marine deposits, "Coskata was a much larger island, and Great Point was likely an island as well [based on the gravelly shoals all around it now]. Wave refraction around these islands would have caused Coskata to connect to Wauwinet, and Great Point to connect to Coskata."[15]

With these islands just north of Nantucket, the south-to-north littoral drift of sand probably helped the gradual development of a tombolo connecting Wauwinet to Coskata and eventually attaching via tombolo to the island that is now Great Point. Sand migrating via littoral drift south, down the west shore of Great Point and the Galls, is Oldale's best guess and that of U.S. Geological Survey geologist Nathaniel S. Shaler, author of *The Geology of Nantucket*, 1889, for the origin of Coatue and for the series of low ridges—reputed to be the oldest dunes on Nantucket—that are randomly spaced within the Glades, the salt marsh between the northwest side of Coskata Pond and the Cedars on Coatue.[16] Nearly a dozen rows of dunes fill the Glades, the final, furthest northwesterly one probably part of the migration of Coatue toward town.

Oldale tends to agree with Rosen's reconstruction of events:

> You probably had, in terms of Coatue and Great Point, those sediments derived by erosion along the east shore of Nantucket. In other words, the cliff section of Nantucket is applying the sand to make Great Point and Coatue. Quite frankly, what probably really happened was Coatue had to wait until Great Point was built and then the direction of the long shore currents would be entirely different than they would be while Great Point was being built. And you must have had a dominant east-to-west current that picked up the sediment that bypassed Great Point and probably built Coatue.

Coatue, its growth slowed by building tidal currents, surely might have kept growing westward into the 1900s and connected with the north shore of Nantucket, had the town not built the jetties. Construction of the jetties began in 1881 with the west jetty, and it wrapped up in 1910 when Nantucketers finished the east jetty.

Today, west to east, those cuspate spits Rosen studied are known as First, Second, Third, Five-Fingered, Bass and Wyers Points. Linked, they enclose Nantucket's elongated, 5.5-mile harbor. These sand peninsulas, cuspate spits, are rare finds for geologists.

In his thesis, *Evolution of Processes of Coatue Beach, Nantucket Island, Massachusetts: A Cuspate Spit Shoreline*, Rosen explains that winter's northeast winds and summer's southwest winds, striking the inner shores of Coatue at oblique angles, gouge out sand from the bends by erosion, carrying it southeast and southwest along to the ends of the spits, building them outward. Simultaneously, the ebb and flood of the tides redistributes the sand from the points back along the bends. Combined, these coastal geological dynamics hold the six points and their intermittently submerged sandbars at an equilibrium, preventing them from closing off the harbor. (The integrity of the harbor was interrupted only once in the island's history, when the Haulover cut opened in 1896 and remained open for 12 years.) Rosen writes, in his conclusions, "The Nantucket Harbor cuspate spits are a shoreline in dynamic equilibrium where long shore currents, the spit-building agent, approximately equal the destructive tidal currents."

The town has dredged the harbor numerous times to help the tides keep up with the winds for safe boat navigation in the harbor. Two tides daily flush carbon dioxide, marine life wastes, and toxic materials from groundwater and surface runoff, while replenishing oxygen- and food-rich ocean water. But the breach of the Haulover during the December 1896 storm did far more than any hydraulic dredging project ever could in this regard. Recorded as a northeast gale, the "Portland Storm," which cleaved the barrier beach in two, pushed monstrous waves and storm surge into the harbor.

However, the storm had crucial help from cod fishermen. Rather than row their fishing dories across the Chord of the Bay and around Great Point and back again every day, the fishermen hauled their dories over the dunes to the ocean to save time. That repeated transport of their boats back and forth over the beaches and dunes wore a ditch in this barrier beach that invited the nor'easter-driven waves into Nantucket Harbor.

For 12 years after the storm, the opening remained deep enough for fishermen to row through. But the channel didn't stay put. The south-to-north littoral drift, as it did in connecting the island to Coskata some 3,000 to 4,000 years ago, gradually built the beach northward, moving the cut about a mile in that direction. In 1908, the Haulover cut's northward march slowed when its north side met the hard clay and gravelly soils of Coskata. Unable to erode any further, the gradually accreting south side of the cut caught up and joined with the north side of the cut, closing the gap and eventually forming the tidal Haulover Pond.

While that cut remained open and Coatue, Coskata and Great Point existed as a temporary island, the tidal flow dropped off significantly, Rosen says, causing the six cuspate spits to grow and approach the southern inner shore of the island because there was little or no tidal current to erode the sand and redistribute it back onto the bends.[17]

With littoral drift on the western end of the island flowing east to west, the same coastal geological machine that grew the northeast post-glacial parts of Nantucket made Smith's and Eel Points. But currents flowing between Nantucket and Tuckernuck have kept Eel Point a stunted knurl of a peninsula. Rosen believes this land began eroding rapidly when the new cut opened up between Nantucket and Esther Island during the Patriots' Day nor'easter in 2007. On April 19, that storm plowed through the roughly 200-foot-wide barrier beach that, between the ocean and Madaket Harbor, connected Nantucket to Esther Island. Rosen couldn't wait to get down to the island to see the new cut in the beach. Right away, he developed a theory for its opening, one equally valid for the Haulover cut's opening in 1896: "That water wants to go there. It's the one place that keeps opening repeatedly, so it seems to be an area that, were it not for the extreme long shore drift, would stay open because it looks like the tidal hydraulics are such that the water wants to go through. It is a place that's been open for many years in the past and presently is very deep; it has the potential for staying open for a substantial amount of time."

The east-west long shore drift current that created Smith's Point off the west end of Nantucket didn't stop where Smith's Point ends today.[18] At one point, as recently as 1868, that peninsula extended over to and just offshore along the south side of Tuckernuck Island, and to just beyond Muskeget Island, protecting both from the Atlantic Ocean's destructive wave-driven erosion.

As Tuckernucker Edward Wayman Coffin detailed in his book, *Nantucket's Forgotten Island: Muskeget*, from about 1700 on, sand borne by the tides and the east-to-west longshore current built a fragile barrier beach of Smith's Point, extending from Nantucket parallel with Tuckernuck's south shore. By 1860, this elongated peninsula stretched for five miles. While remaining intact from the west end of Nantucket out to just beyond Muskeget, this peninsula was called Great Neck.[19] But this greatest western extremity of Nantucket wouldn't last. On September 8, 1869, a strong gale, which Coffin described as changing direction from the southeast to the southwest, blew a hole in this barrier beach that never repaired itself.

The western section of Great Neck then became known as Smith's Island, which attached itself to the southwestern side of Tuckernuck. Tuckernuckers dubbed it Bigelow's Point, after Dr. Jacob Bigelow from Boston, who regularly hunted inland bird species on Tuckernuck. That point eventually wrapped around to the north, forming a second North Pond that tenuously persists today. In 1872, what was, at low tide, a land bridge used by livestock owners to herd their animals over to Tuckernuck for grazing, washed out completely during a particularly strong tide, disconnecting Nantucket from Tuckernuck for good.

Around 1880, the eastern section of the former Smith's Island fused with Tuckernuck Island, just west of where the Humane Society house was located on Smith's Island before it was moved inland on Tuckernuck. By the 1890s, that barrier beach arced around to the north, eventually forming Great South Pond, which has since disappeared. Remnants of Great Neck continue to exist today. A long sandbar in the vicinity of the Gravelly Islands, in between Tuckernuck and Muskeget and around where the western end of Great Neck stretched to beyond Muskeget, is now visible and stays dry even during the highest tides. And what's left of the east end of Great Neck, known as Whale Island, attached itself to Tuckernuck in the summer of 1975.[20]

Since the Haulover cut healed in 1908, there have been no breaks in this barrier beach protecting Nantucket Harbor, other than washovers by storm waves. The severing of Great Point from the Galls in 1984, during the storm that toppled the Great Point lighthouse with hurricane-force winds, was the second-to-last time, to date, that such a cut occurred on the eastern side of the island, the most recent being a brief opening in the Galls during the No-Name Storm, the "Perfect Storm," on October 29 and 30, 1991.

Defiantly, at just that spot and only 21 years after the cut was healed, Arthur Norcross, in 1929, built for Lester Kafer the largest house in North Wauwinet. Narrow as this beach is, the house still stands, despite the giving and taking that the winds and tides work on the island. As reverent as the Kafers and their neighbors are that they have landed in such an extraordinarily beautiful yet fragile spot for their summer lives, none is foolish enough to believe that his time on this finger of sand and beach grass is anything but a fortunate coincidence in the scheme of geologic time. Just as steadily as it was formed some 2,000 to 5,000 years ago, this post-glacial addition to Nantucket is being taken away by sea levels rising at a rate of 2.95 millimeters per year. However, Nantucketers like Peter Kafer, Lester Kafer's grandson, feel privileged to be a part of the geologic sculpture, the work-in-progress that is Nantucket. What is happening around them, and to the whole island, is the relentless erosion-accretion dynamic that has been going on for tens of thousands of years, in which erosion is steadily winning by leaps and bounds during winter storms. Yes, the shores of Nantucket, Tuckernuck and Muskeget return to some form of normalcy during the quieter late spring and summer months, but from September to October, the later months of hurricane season (officially June 1 through November 30), through the late fall and winter nor'easters, the Atlantic Ocean helps itself to the easily digestible sand of the eastern and southern shores of these islands. The late Wes Tiffney, Jr., former director and co-founder of the UMass Boston Nantucket Field Station, put Nantucket's life expectancy at 1,200 years, based on the historical average erosion rate of 15 feet per year. But Tiffney qualified that prediction by factoring in the effects of global warming and said that sea level rise predictions of three times that rate would put Nantucket underwater in 400 years.

Peter Kafer, having spent every summer of his life but one at his family's house since his birth in 1955, sounded like he understood what this process means, when he talked with conviction about living on the beach at the Haulover, several years ago. "Wauwinet villagers, as I'm sure you have observed, are warm, giving, helpful and accommodating to strangers, and as fatalistic as the ancient Greeks in our respectful obedience to the god Poseidon. It's just part of our charm."

INSTANT ISLAND: JUST ADD LIFE

SANFORD FARM, 767.5 acres of conservation land owned jointly by the Nantucket Conservation Foundation and the Nantucket Islands Land Bank, sits bounded by Madaket Road, Hummock Pond, Barrett Farm Road and the ocean. On the trails that crisscross this extraordinary property, you can explore many of the habitat types found on Nantucket: upland meadows, sandplain grasslands, low forests, beach-dune systems, barrier beaches, ponds, wetlands, ocean and marshlands. For those seeking a glimpse of Nantucket's past, these are essential, educational hikes through the island's living history.

But before embarking on an exploration of this tract, you must realize where Nantucket exists on the planet, on the East Coast, in New England and on the southeastern coast of Massachusetts. We have nearly everything but rivers, mountains, volcanoes and deserts here. Adaptation to, and tolerance of, harsh conditions is key to survival on Nantucket.

Chemical oceanographer Dr. Sarah Oktay, managing director of the UMass Boston Nantucket Field Station and the Grace Grossman Environmental Center, has her own read on Nantucket's biodiversity:

> What's different about Nantucket—[different] from I think pretty much anywhere else in the United States—is its location latitudinally and longitudinally, the fact that we're on a north-south floristic division. So we've got the furthest southern reach of many northern species and the furthest northern reach of many southern species, the influence of the warm Gulf Stream that brings a lot of creatures up here, the influence of the buffering of having ocean water around us that means a lot of northern species are able to be here and be comfortable at our location.

And at 50 square miles, I can't think of anywhere else, certainly [in] the United States, maybe [in] the world, where there are so many habitats in such a small area.

Before the Laurentide ice sheet slid down over it, the piece of coastal plain that would become Nantucket was forested with hardwoods and conifers, dotted with ponds and lakes, and sliced up by streams, brooks and rivers. That terrain, though, would have been barely recognizable once the last glacier had bulldozed the northern third of our future islands' landscape and glacial meltwater had smoothed out the southern portions of this landmass. Life on the coastal plain had been erased by the scour and grind of glacial ice as much as a mile thick, but after it retreated, around 18,000 years ago, new micro-ecosystems began to emerge.

To a large extent, the life that first developed on Nantucket, Tuckernuck and Muskeget after the glacier receded mirrored what would sprout and spawn on the Cape and Martha's Vineyard. But it was an odd grouping of life forms that would ultimately come to cohabit on these three islands. Vegetation sprang from plant seeds and spores blown onto the plain from non-glaciated areas and washed down onto it by meltwater. A medley of wildlife moseyed into the area as it could, depending on food availability, predators and tolerance of the ever-warming climate.

What these islands are today is definitely not what they were when they were simply uplands on the coastal plain, so things really didn't get interesting until the rising ocean separated them from the mainland. Later, humans arrived and started altering the landscape and utilizing its life forms for their own survival. Then, around 6,000 years ago, rising seawater inundated the land bridges and fixed the roster of our island arks for the time being—at least until the arrival of those that could fly, swim, boat or plane to the islands, solo or with the help of humans.

As an overview of the types of life forms found on Nantucket, this chapter is a precursor to all the chapters to come, which will detail how life developed on the geologic stage set 25,000 years ago. To say that Nantucket is an enigma is only to scrape the surface. Here begins your decoder for a deeper probe into the mysterious unknown of island natural history.

First upon the barren ground and boulders of Nantucket, there were tundra plant communities, then spruce and pine forests followed by maritime heath lands growing from the human-altered terminal moraine, which formed where the glacier had stopped in what today are the moors in the central and northern sections of the island. The terminal moraine reaches from Sankaty over to Monomoy, supplemented by a small patch just west of town (or a larger one running all the way out to Eel Point, if you subscribe to Shaler's assessment of glacial impact on Nantucket), and a sliver of the northern section of Tuckernuck. Stranded, buried under glacial till, ice chunks melted and morphed into ponds such as Sesachacha, Gibbs, the Wigwam and Pout ponds. Smaller, shallower such depressions gradually filled in with decomposing organic material. Now they support miniature groves of black tupelo, sassafras and red maple known as hidden forests.

On the outwash plains, glacial meltwater ran south to the ocean and scoured out valleys that later became Miacomet, Hummock and Long Ponds, as well as ponds in the now seasonally dry Toupshue, Forked Pond and Madequecham Valleys, where prairie-like sandplain grassland has established itself. Coves, inlets and creeks on what was once the continuation of Nantucket's north shore between town and Wauwinet—including Polpis Harbor, Folger's Marsh, Shimmo Creek, the inlet at Abram's Point, the Creeks and the now-filled tidelands north from the Creeks to Jetties Beach—siphoned sediment from tidal currents, slowly building a shallow medium for today's salt marshes.

And the island's post-glacial marine deposits, scattered around the island in the form of shoals, beaches, dunes, bluffs and coastal banks, became the Haulover, Coatue, Great Point, Eel and Smith's Points; Bigelow Point; the Gravelly Islands; Great South Point; and, later, Whale Island on Tuckernuck Island and all of Muskeget Island.

Most of the coastal plain highlands first had to go through a period nearly devoid of vegetation, from the melting of the glacier 18,000 years ago to perhaps 13,800 years ago, before tundra plants took hold. They gave way to boreal forest species, including jack, red and white pine, and spruce, starting around 13,000 years ago.[1]

A warming trend led to the gradual shrinking of the glacier, beginning around 75,000 years ago at the start of the Wisconsinan Glacial Stage. Most of the heating came during the final advance of the Laurentide ice sheet, which is what invited life back into the region, despite a 1,400-year cool-off period between 11,500 and 12,900 years ago.[2]

And so, after the melting glacier raised the level of the ocean high enough to make continental islands—those that were once part of the nearby continent—out of Nantucket, Tuckernuck and Muskeget around 6,000 years ago, their inventory of crawling, walking, running and freshwater pond wildlife and vegetation was sealed—for that moment in time. How the rest of Nantucket's plant and animal species got here depended as much on the motivation and abilities of the various latecomers as it did on the random chance of their arrival by human and natural means.

For instance: in the winter of 2008–2009, several island naturalists discovered and confirmed signs of river otters at Clark Cove and Hummock Pond, including tracks, sliding marks and the white, jelly-like substance that river otters secrete from glands around their anus as a means of communication with other otters. How did they get to a place where they may have existed historically but no longer inhabited?[3] At the time, there was a growing population of river otters, one still documented today, on Martha's Vineyard, Nomans Land and the Elizabeth Islands. It's certainly possible, then, that these freshwater cousins of the sea otter swam to Nantucket or were blown over in some storm.

Another instance: mucking around in a sphagnum moss swamp in the southwest corner of Sesachacha Pond in October 2009, Maria Mitchell Association Director of Natural Science Andrew McKenna-Foster discovered the four-toed salamander for the first time on Nantucket. Nantucket was the last of Massachusetts's 16 counties to confirm the existence of this salamander, which means either this species somehow found its way out to Nantucket before it became an island and McKenna-Foster was the first to find it, or it found its way here by other, most likely modern, means, such as stowing away in firewood logs.

A more dramatic example occurred before Thanksgiving in 2008, when Nantucketer Joyce Godfrey returned to her home near Quidnet to find three squawking turkeys tearing up her yard and defecating all over everything. Her description of what happened next is comical, though the experience must have been frustrating:

> I came home one day and parked my van, and I heard what I thought was squeaking springs from my car. I got out of my car and I couldn't find what it was, and [then] I saw three turkeys in my fenced-in yard. I had one of the dogs in my car and thought my dog could flush them out, but the dog didn't want to flush them because they were bigger than my dog.
>
> I ended up flushing them off, and two of them flew off [on their own], and the other one flew into our screened-in porch and it landed on our chandelier and it was swinging from it.

The turkey rattled Godfrey's chandelier around, breaking off the glass globes and smashing them on the floor as it tried to keep its balance and stay out of reach of Godfrey's broom, all the while defecating on her porch. Godfrey eventually shooed the errant turkey off the chandelier, sending it scuttling behind her gas stove. She finally caught this icon of the classic American fall holiday and flung it out into her yard, and her dogs chased it off her property; however, the three turkeys returned the next day.

Turkeys alleged to be wild turkeys—probably the same perpetrators at the Godfrey residence—were sighted again and photographed in August of 2009 by Nantucketer Andrew McCandless. Although turkeys are indigenous to Massachusetts, they usually grace Nantucket in any great number only during the holidays, and then only on Styrofoam trays and wrapped in cellophane, but McCandless had found the birds out in the far reaches of Polpis Road. A few others were also spotted that year at the west end of the island, on Jackson Point in Madaket. A member of the Gallinaceous bird family—heavy-bodied, ground-feeding domestic and game birds, including quail, pheasant, grouse and chickens—the Eastern wild turkey is known to be in every town on Cape Cod, all the way to Provincetown, on Martha's Vineyard and all over the state, but they had never been known to be on Nantucket after it became an island. They cannot sustain flight for more than a mile, typically using their wings only to fly up into trees to roost at night. These domesticated, heritage breed turkeys, transported to the island to live on farms, had escaped their owners and gone feral.

In a more independent migration, the second coming of the island's white-tailed deer population is widely believed to have begun with Old Buck, the male deer found swimming across the Muskeget Channel between Nantucket and Martha's Vineyard in 1922. He was pulled aboard a fishing vessel traveling to Nantucket, where he was released and later provided with imported does. White-tailed deer had roamed this coastal plain area before the glacier moved into the region, and they repopulated the island following its retreat, but the species had disappeared again, this time extirpated by hungry Native Americans and European settlers.

Other rumors of human-aided species distribution on Nantucket include the report that Eastern gray squirrels hitched a ride on the 'Sconset Woodman's firewood shipments from Maine, and the Nantucket Hunt Club's 1926 introduction of jackrabbits to the island for their hunts. Jackrabbits were considered preferable to foxes, which posed a threat to the poultry industry on the island.

Nantucket does not have most of the middle mammals of the mainland: skunks, possums, woodchucks, raccoons, coyotes, black bears, muskrats, beavers, porcupines, minks, weasels, fishers, and bobcats. Neither does it have such ungulates as moose, elk and caribou. White-tailed deer, Eastern gray squirrels, Eastern cottontail rabbits, jackrabbits and snowshoe hares, however, somehow found their way out to Nantucket or had survival instincts that allowed them to adapt quickly to a temperate climate evolving from the arctic one of the young Nantucket. Anything with wings, fins or sufficient lightness to be carried by the wind or the ocean—birds, insects, mammals and fish—all found Nantucket on their own, just as many soils, bacteria and plant seeds did.

Karen Beattie, a plant ecologist and manager of science and stewardship for the Nantucket Conservation Foundation since 1991, is an apt guide for all of those hoping to learn what makes up Nantucket's living universe. Like Oktay, Beattie has found in her research that Nantucket's evolution into the confluence of north-south species' ranges during the Wisconsinan Glaciation of Cape Cod and the Islands was key to the genesis of our special three-island preserve. She explains:

> Nantucket has a very rich biodiversity because of the unique combined influences of natural and cultural history, location, and climate. The species that occur here have to be adapted to harsh weather conditions (wind, salt spray), and nutrient-poor, sandy soils. Some of these species are at the southern limits of their range, because glaciers were in the nearby vicinity only 10,000 to 15,000 years ago and the climate was much colder. Other species are at the northern limits of their range because this is currently one of the mildest climates in New England, due to the moderating influence of the ocean. The lack of natural ground predators that occur on the mainland (raccoon, fox, coyote, opossum, skunk, etc.) benefits some animal species, particularly ground-nesting birds such as northern harriers, bobwhite and whippoorwill. Although the island is small, there are many different upland and wetland habitat types, which provide varied conditions for a variety of species. The fact that the island is isolated means that some of the invasive species that have severely degraded landscapes and outcompeted native species on the mainland have not become as firmly established here (which means that management, increased vigilance and prevention are very important).

Cultural impacts also contributed to these islands' biodiversity. Native Americans and European settlers burned the land to encourage growth of certain plants, enrich the soil with nutrients and attract game birds. Both also cleared land for agriculture and sheep grazing, which contributed to the creation of our sandplain grasslands. These are composed of low grasses, flowers and shrubs that thrive in nutrient-depleted shallow soils, mixed in with a lot of sand and scant numbers of taller plants and trees. This habitat attracted various birds, mammals and insects that require grassland habitats. As sandplain grassland is now rare on the planet and limited to fewer than 2,000 acres, the fauna depending on this habitat have also become rare species over the years as well.

Beattie says that all of the 27 islands in our waters below the Cape share the natural, cultural and climate conditions that created both island-specific arboretums and uncommon open-air zoological parks comprising species not ordinarily living together in the same numbers and combinations on the continent. In addition, Nantucket, Tuckernuck and Muskeget work as a unique three-island ecological community, due in part to the efforts of local conservation groups. More than 60 percent of Nantucket, portions of Tuckernuck and all of Muskeget are able to exist in their wild states under permanent conservation protection. This means that plant and animal species that might otherwise be extirpated due to development and invasive species, as they have been on the mainland, are able to thrive because they are afforded the protection and preservation of habitats key to their survival. Today, it's estimated that some 4,627 species (not counting bacteria, soil nematodes and other microscopic organisms) populate land and water habitats of Nantucket, Tuckernuck and Muskeget.

Distinct habitats—heathland, grassland, upland meadows, upland shrub, small hardwood forests, pitch pine barrens, old fields, wet meadows, ponds, vernal pools, bogs, freshwater marsh, swamps, barrier beaches, sand dunes, salt marshes, shallow harbor waters, tidal ponds, and open ocean—all exist on and around Nantucket. Oktay and Beattie describe the island as one of most important areas in the state for protecting rare and endangered species, due to the high percentage of these habitats preserved as open space by conservation organizations and town, state and federal agencies.

Nantucket's most famous rodent, the Muskeget vole, is one of those animals, and as the only endemic species in the Commonwealth of Massachusetts, it is the poster child for biological diversity on Nantucket.[4] It is a product of the marooning of the island's menagerie of species, and it exemplifies what can happen on landmasses separated from the mainland. When it was parted from its mainland relatives, Nantucket's population of meadow vole adapted to a different and very limited food supply.

To avoid overpopulating Muskeget's 292 acres, it did what evolution dictated: produce fewer young, because the island's food supply is extremely limited, and evolve to keep its island population down. It now lives within Muskeget's tight confines of beach and other grasses, low cedar trees, shrubs, beach rose and poison ivy, and it is a classic local example of the adaptation of life cut off from its home ground.

This scenario has played itself out around the world on every patch of high ground that transformed into a continental island as sea levels rose. Continental islands form when rising water separates elevated coastal acres from the mainland. They are populated by those species that occupied the landmass before ocean waters rose, supplemented by those that find their way to the new island by air or water. Oceanic islands—those that have grown from submerged volcanoes on the ocean floor—are populated only by living things that can get there by air or by water after the island is formed, a process biologists call long-distance dispersal.

Cognizant of the island's rich population of known and yet-to-be-discovered species of life, the island's conservation groups in 2004—the Linda Loring Nature Foundation, the Maria Mitchell Association, the Massachusetts Audubon Society, the Nantucket Conservation Foundation, the Nantucket Garden Club, the Nantucket Islands Land Bank, the Natural Heritage & Endangered Species Program of the Massachusetts Division of Fisheries & Wildlife, the Science Department of Nantucket High School, the Trustees of Reservations, the Tuckernuck Land Trust and the University of Massachusetts Boston Nantucket Field Station—were led by the Maria Mitchell Association (MMA) and coordinated by Dr. Bob Kennedy, MMA's former director of Natural Science, to embark on the Nantucket Biodiversity Initiative (NBI). Designed to inventory and study Nantucket's natural world, the NBI invited local and visiting scientists to work within 25-acre biodiversity plots, 25 of them that together represented all of Nantucket's ecosystems, to conduct any research on the island's living denizens that interested them. That first year, the fieldwork began, and the following year, they held a conference to present their findings. Those first two years set the cadence of the Nantucket Biodiversity Initiative: fieldwork and conference on alternating years.

All of the written reports from NBI research are filed in a special library at the Maria Mitchell Association. Ultimately, the gathered information is being used to manage the island's natural resources wisely and to enable us to comprehend better the unique evolutionary process that created Nantucket's non-human inhabitants.

Kitty Pochman, an island woman trained in biology who has immersed herself in the island's living world, first as the Maria Mitchell Association's executive director and presently heading the Linda Loring Nature Foundation off Eel Point Road, remains astounded at the breadth of Nantucket's species and habitat catalogue. Says she:

> Because of the geology, you have the diversity of habitats here. I love the little vernal pools that you kind of stumble upon and the different swamps, the shrub swamps and the kettle hole ponds. They are all here because of our glacial history. Anytime you have lots of different habitats—especially edges, one habitat merging with another—that's also going to increase the biodiversity of an area. There's so much we're still learning about the island, and that's one of the great things with the Nantucket Biodiversity Initiative.[5] They're starting to do some inventorying of things that are not obvious. The trees are really obvious and the flowers are really obvious, but the things that escape our notice—the insects, the fungi, the lichens—they're starting to find out more and more about those. And [because] of all that, it's great to live in an area that has so much to offer.[6]

The Pochmans' 365-day backyard bird observations regularly yield around 100 species. The 50 or so birders who participate in the annual Christmas Bird Count, in its 57th year on the island, always count upwards of 135 species in just one day during the winter, which is one of the best birding seasons of the year. Tens of thousands of long-tailed ducks are counted almost every year, as are 12 to 16 gull species that feed just off of Siasconset, a gang of young snowy owls spotted in 2008, the nine short-eared owls seen all at once on Tuckernuck in 2009 (15 of them in 2011), the yellow rails found in Folger's Marsh, and the American oystercatchers hanging on in Polpis Harbor; in addition, there is the inundation of various warblers seen on just one day around Christmas each year. People who admit to watching birds and who pursue their feathered quarry with some level of dedication are also afforded extraordinary year-round migratory, nesting, fledging, staging and courtship viewing opportunities. Although there are many species of birds residing on Nantucket year-round, many, many more are just passing through, generally having been blown off course or just visiting for their nesting season. Avid birders have no trouble spotting around 150 species of birds on the island every year during Nantucket's Christmas Bird Count.[7]

Although, throughout history, most birds have found the island by their wings—domestic poultry not included—Nantucket's gravity-restricted flora and fauna arrived in Nantucket habitats by whatever means available. Ponder the Eastern prickly pear cactus, with its yellow flowers, found in only a few places on Coatue. As a succulent found thriving not just in the arid climes of New Mexico and Florida, but in most states from Montana eastward in the U.S. and up into southern Ontario, its seeds might have first arrived on island via the Gulf Stream or tucked into feathers, or encased in mud stuck to the feet of birds from hotter biomes where cacti typically thrive. Or perhaps they stowed away on a whaler whose route took it through cactus-covered islands.

Look at the existence of sandplain grasslands. Much of the flora in this magnificent coastal prairie-like habitat is believed to have spread eastward by means of wind, water and migrating critters from the Midwest prairies that penetrated far west into Ohio. Today, most of the total acreage of sandplain grassland left on the planet exists only on Nantucket, Tuckernuck Island and Martha's Vineyard. Likewise, the island's heathlands, its moors on the northern portion of the island where the glacier halted and began melting, were formed not only at the grinding, sculpting hands of the glacier and its runoff, but with the help of the human manipulation and occupation of the island.[8] They are akin to sandplain grasslands in the sense that land clearing, burning and sheep grazing were important factors in their emergence on the island.

A sprinkling of other species, including low-bush blueberry, the Nantucket shadbush, and sharks, simply survived millions of years of evolution. Most notably, the Atlantic horseshoe crab that can be seen gliding along in the

Horsehoe crab

shallows of the harbors, tidal ponds and salt marshes—the larger females piggybacking the smaller males while searching for egg-laying beaches around the full and new moons during May and June—just happened to be around when Nantucket's harbors were formed.

When Maria Mitchell Association spider researchers Cheryl Comeau-Beaton and McKenna-Foster discovered, in 2009 on Tuckernuck, both a northern version of the black widow spider and also the purse web spider, an inch-long cousin of the giant tarantulas of the Southwest, they provided more examples of how species establish themselves on islands. As McKenna-Foster explained at the September 2009 Nantucket Biodiversity Initiative Conference, the black widow and purse web spiderlings begin spinning silk as they soon as they leave their eggs. Like the wispy filaments attached to the seeds of common milkweed, these baby spiders are carried aloft by the wind.[9] Could they have floated over on a southwesterly from Martha's Vineyard or been carried across the country by the Jet Stream and dropped on our islands?

So how did this complex, constantly evolving Petri dish of life get started on the Nantucket archipelago?

During the latter half of the Wisconsinan Glacial Stage, as the ice sheet ground through New England, 500 feet of ice bore down on where Nantucket is today, 1,500 feet covered Cape Cod, and a mile or so buried northern New England. The region's arctic climate drove most life well south of the southernmost reaches of the ice sheet.

During the late Pleistocene and early Holocene Epochs, Georges Bank and the landmass that would become Nantucket, Tuckernuck and Muskeget Islands, in addition to the land continuing well south of this part of the Coastal Plain, had become wildlife and vegetation sanctuaries, known as refugia, for plants and animals displaced from inland New England by arctic conditions. Our three islands owe their dense and widely varied biodiversity in part to that once richly populated dry land fringe of coastal Massachusetts, because repopulation of the upland was simply a matter of some species moving north and west when the climate warmed enough to suit them. In essence, there was enough life in the neighborhood to begin again.

Around 6,000 years ago, the Laurentide ice sheet had melted enough to bring the ocean's elevation up 300 feet to where it is now, rising from its previous level, roughly 50 miles east and 75 miles south of modern-day Nantucket, out at the coastal edge of the Continental Shelf, to submerge the coast of the continent and create islands out of the former peaks of the coastal plain. Until then, all of today's Southeastern New England islands were part of the mainland, and all species of life found on the mainland lived in these outer reaches, moving freely within their ranges south of the glacier.

So, with the glacier's arctic conditions having killed the area's flora and displaced its fauna, it was a combination of the effects of the glacier's presence and those of its retreat that created the conditions for the next phase of life in the region.

A melting glacier will dump its water into splash pools beneath its face. These became depressions in the island, right at the southern end of the terminal moraine, and evolved into salt marshes such as those in Polpis Harbor, the Creeks, Folger's Marsh, Coskata Pond and Madaket Harbor on the Eel Point side. Swampy areas were created as well, including Stump Pond and its swamp; Squam Swamp and the swampy areas around the north head of Long Pond and the cranberry bogs; and the cranberry bogs themselves: Milestone, Windswept and two former bogs, one at the Land Bank's Eilert property at 169 Polpis Road and the other on land owned by the Linda Loring Nature Foundation south of Eel Point Road.

As the glacier continued to melt, it churned out across the ever-evolving outwash plain toward the ocean. While, at first, this water benefited only bacteria—the first organism to capitalize on the glacier's retreat—it carried young soils across the land to the tundra and boreal vegetation. This lean start is hard to believe when one considers the breadth of diversity of life that now flourishes on the island.

The period following the retreat of the glacier was one in which various distinct habitats began to form. When the glacier melted away, at the rate of about a mile per decade, south to north, it exposed the foundations of the heathlands, sandplain grasslands, salt marshes, swamps, bogs, kettle holes and south shore valleys-cum-ponds, allowing sunlight and rain to work their magic. Plant life gradually reemerged shortly after soil formed on the recently exposed glacial deposits. That first soil consisted of mostly drifting sand, silt and beach dune sand. Known as mineral soil, it had been ground into fine grains by the glacier and left behind to become the basis for the island's first soils.

Then seeds were carried to the area by the strong, unrelenting winds and also by migrating wildlife, those birds and mammals that could survive in gradually degrading arctic conditions. They transported the seeds in their fur, hair, feathers and paws and also left them behind in their feces.

As the first plants—tundra sedges and boreal forest plant species—took root in the mineral soils fueled by decomposing bacteria, water and sunlight, their dying and decomposing bodies were converted into the organic matter of soil, which grew gradually in depth and nutrient richness.[10]

Plant ecologist Peter Dunwiddie, former property manager for the Massachusetts Audubon Society's two sanctuaries on Nantucket, is fairly certain what plant species were first to appear on Nantucket after the glacier retreated. Says Dunwiddie, "The best evidence we have is that, initially, there would have been tundra and boreal forest assemblages, the sort of thing you'd see in Northern Canada."

Dunwiddie was stationed on Nantucket for 13 years as Mass Audubon's resident plant ecologist, a researcher of sandplain grasslands and heathlands, and is regarded as one of the major authorities on post-glacial Nantucket plant ecology. While today's sedges, found at the edges of freshwater ponds and in sandplain grasslands, are not the same as the grass-like species that likely took hold as the glacier melted, they resemble their predecessors. In Dunwiddie's words:

> Those types of species would have persisted in areas of retreating ice. Where and for how long is speculative, and presumably there were a lot of species moving around on the landscape at that time, so there could have been rather novel assemblages of species, some of which would have looked like tundra or boreal forest, but maybe with a different abundance of what you see in either the tundra or [the] boreal forest.

Following this early post-glacial vegetation, the best guess by Dunwiddie and others is that spruce and jack pine sprouted at least 11,000 years ago. Between 9,300 and 9,500 years ago, oaks, beech, red maple, black tupelo, chestnuts, ash and hickory made the scene, along with white and pitch pines, which replaced the jack pine. He also speculates that grassy heathlands covered the outwash plain on the southern half of the island, which had been formed by the glacial meltwater flowing southward to the ocean.

Even while this new combination of plant species was developing, animals began returning to the area—but, as with the vegetation, the new animal populations were a mixture of old and new. At that time, around 18,000 years ago, still 8,000 years from the end of the Pleistocene Epoch known as the Late Pleistocene that eventually gave way to the current geological period, the interglacial Holocene Epoch around 10,000 years ago, and about 3,000 years after the start of the retreat of the glacier, large mammals dominated the North American Continent as they had also during the Laurentide glaciation.

Events in Nantucket's Natural History

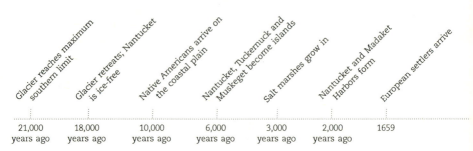

Before the coastal plain of the East Coast was immersed, extending out to the then-dry Continental Shelf, megafauna roamed the arctic tundra-like landscape: mammoths, mastodons, saber-toothed cats, glyptodons, ground sloths, native horses, moose, caribou, camels and short-faced bears.[11,12] This is known because fishermen, dredging for sea scallops and drag-netting for groundfish in the shifting shoals on the Continental Shelf and on Georges Bank off Nantucket, have found fossils of these mammals, including teeth and tusks, in their fishing gear.[13]

But with the glacier retreating, these species began to disappear. In fact, 35 to 40 mammal species, including some of those living on the Northeast region of the continent, became extinct between 10,000 and 12,000 years ago.[14] They were replaced by some of the warm-blooded species currently populating Nantucket: smaller mammals, including rabbits and wood, field and kangaroo mice; migratory birds; and larger, more mobile mammals, such as white-tailed deer. These species adapted better than their predecessors to the loss of habitat and scarcity of food, and they expanded their range northward again with the warming of the planet that exposed more and more suitable habitat.

It was around this time, about 10,000 to 11,000 years ago, that the Paleo-Indians of the Lithic Period moved into the region after migrating across North America, followed by the Early and Late Archaic Indians of the Archaic Period around 8,000 years ago. The Paleo-Indians were the first humans to live in the Cape and Islands area after the glacial retreat. They had come to North American from Europe via Beringia, the land bridge connecting Asia with the U.S., around 20,000 years ago. Beringia is now submerged beneath the Bering Sea, the Chukchi Sea and the Bering Strait running between Alaska

INSTANT ISLAND: JUST ADD LIFE

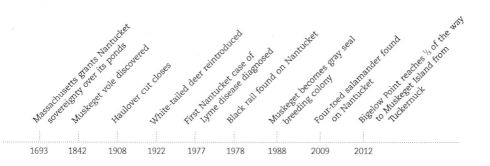

and Siberia. The Wampanoags, believed to be the descendants of the Late Archaic Indians, were the Native Americans that coexisted with Nantucket's first Europeans settlers, eventually morphing into several sub-tribes on Nantucket: the Nantucket, Polpis, Miacomit, Sasacaskeh, Shaukimmo, Siasconset, Squam, Talhanio and Tetaukimmo Island tribes.

With humans living on the coastal plain where Nantucket emerged disconnected from the mainland about 6,000 years ago, our zoo at sea, our island Petri dish, was stocked for the future, and island life as we might recognize it commenced. From a barren and nearly sterile plain immediately following the retreat of the glacier, the island, by all the means that nature provided, was on the way to its current natural state. Today, as estimated by the Maria Mitchell Association, Nantucket boasts 4,627 species. They break down into the following groups:

Vascular plants:	1,265
Fungi:	approx. 200
Insects:	2,317
Moths:	182
Spiders:	250
Salamanders:	2
Turtles:	3
Snakes:	6
Earthworms:	7
Mammals:	21
Marine life:	114
Sharks:	5
Whales:	5
Birds:	250

Biologists don't yet know all the entities that live on these three islands off the coast of Massachusetts. They don't know every species on the mainland or the planet, either, but zoologists, botanists, entomologists, herpetologists and ornithologists maintain a much clearer picture of the mainland than they do of Nantucket, because her three islands are so young. Some island scientists say we know more about the surface of the moon than we do about Nantucket. However, through the continuing research of Nantucket's world-class conservation organizations, the documentation efforts of the Nantucket Biodiversity Initiative and the Maria Mitchell Association, and the curiosity of an enlightened populace with eyes and hearts aimed at the natural world around them, full knowledge of our island ecosystems is only a matter of time.

AN UNLIKELY GARDEN AT SEA

SPOROPOLLENIN IS NOT a Native American name on Nantucket for a place, a long dead-sachem or a spiritual belief, although, reading this book full of strange, localized anthropological titles and descriptions, you might assume it was.

Instead, sporopollenin is one of the main reasons that botanists know anything at all about what plants first grew on the upland portions of the coastal plain that became Nantucket, Tuckernuck and Muskeget Islands and the succession of vegetation that followed.

Specifically, it is a biopolymer, an organic adhesive that is the main component in the super-tough outer wall of pollen grains, and it is extremely resilient in warding off destruction of the pollen grain. Although scientists are unsure of its precise composition, they speculate that it is a molecular soup of primarily long-chain fatty acids combined with phenylpropanoids, phenolics and small amounts of carotenoids to form a protective shell around a plant's essential reproduction vessel. Scientists do know this nearly indestructible bio-defense structure is an anti-disintegration mechanism guarding against strong chemical reagents and enzymes: it keeps pollen grains from decomposing. Because of it, the grains are built to last, which benefits not only their particular species, but also inquisitive humans. They are one of the key tools botanists use to determine the presence of plant species in a given area. Collected by core sampling—where one end of a pipe is forced deep into the ground—pollen grains, because their shape, size and appearance are unique to each species of plant, can be easily tracked through time, like fingerprints down the length of the sample removed from the pipe.

Dunwiddie and other biologists have taken such core samples from bogs and ponds around the island in an attempt to discern the history of island vegetation. It is partially by speculation that we know that tundra and boreal species—those that grow in northern climate zones where cold winters and warm summers are the norm—were the first vegetation to take root on Nantucket as the glacier receded, but it is by the reading of pollen grain samples, written accounts, survey records and diaries, that the sowing of Nantucket's garden is really known.

In writing his paper entitled "Forest and Heath: The Shaping of the Vegetation of Nantucket Island," published in the July 1989 issue of the *Journal of Forest History*, Dunwiddie employed all of these research methods. But he learned the most about Nantucket's plants through core samples he took from the middle of Donut Pond, a kettle hole in Middle Moors sitting immediately north of Pout Pond Road and the namesake ponds just to the south, and from Tawpawshau Bog about a quarter of a mile west from Donut Pond on the north side of Pout Pond Road.

Both water bodies are ideal for this kind of research because they are suspended above sea level and the level of groundwater by layers of clay, which are themselves formed of many layers of sediments that trap and hold pollen grains more or less intact. Tawpawshau Bog is some 42 feet above sea level and 30 feet above the groundwater that could certainly have washed the pollen grains out of the soil if the bog were at a lower elevation.

From the center of Donut Pond, Dunwiddie extracted a core sample 1.5 meters (nearly five feet) long and, near the center of Tawpawshau Bog, another five meters (16.4 feet) in length. From these cores of sediments, soils and sand, he was able to identify a fairly reliable picture of local plant life, starting about 11,000 years ago when sediments began accumulating in the bog. What he found was that spruce and jack pine were then the dominant species blanketing the landmass that became Nantucket.[1] Around 2,000 years later, the post-glacial climate warmed enough for pitch pine, white pine, oaks and birch to push out the spruce and jack pine. This shift in tree species dominance manifested itself in a fossil pollen profile that held true into the Holocene Epoch while Nantucket was still part of the continent. Dunwiddie believes that oaks, likely white and black, along with a smattering of white and pitch pines, and beech, tupelo, maples and hickory, which all still grow on the island today, essentially covered Nantucket's upland plot of the coastal plain, which would have been quite similar to sections of present-day Martha's Vineyard and Cape Cod. On the ground, this pollen record reveals, bayberry and sweet fern were part of the undergrowth; both still grow out in Nantucket's moors, along with low bush blueberry.

This is the clearest possible picture of early vegetation on Nantucket's acres of the coastal plain, but none of it existed until there was a medium to germinate in, since the glacier had scraped off what was there previously. That post-glacial substrate, the first soil, began as mineral deposits left by the glacier. Rocks of many varieties, pulverized into sand grains by the glacier and shoveled southward onto the coastal plain into piles of glacial drift and late-glacial Aeolian (wind) deposits—called parent materials—formed the basis for Nantucket's soils along with dune sand, nutrient-rich clays and silt.[2] Known as mineral soil, this first medium also contained some decomposed plants forming organic matter. Mineral soil genesis, Oldale and others believe, coincided with the start of the retreat of the glacier around 18,000 years ago. This crude potting soil for the planting of Nantucket's special, hardy garden of plants became richer and richer with each season's passing. Plants died and decomposed. Melt water from the withering glacier and atmospheric precipitation trickled down through the new mineral soil, carrying with it organic matter, minerals and compounds.

This relatively young soil was called podzol, usually a term for a type of soil found in arctic regions, because the colder climate that prevailed during this time limited chemical and biological activity. Eating their way through the podzol were worms and insects, including ants and grubs. They ingested the soil and defecated richer organic matter that supercharged it with nutrients including nitrogen; this, in turn, encouraged the growth of still more plant life on the surface.

Most plants use their water for growth. Lichens, a nearly flat, moss-like plant and one of the first plants to grow on the recently exposed rocks and boulders, because they retain water, slowly helped to improve the soil. Known to survive under the harshest conditions on earth, including on rocks in the Arctic and Antarctica; on the upper ramparts of the tallest and coldest mountain peaks on the planet; in the hottest, most arid climates; and everywhere in between, lichens were almost certainly among the first vegetation to colonize the bare rock ground that eventually became our three islands.

Spreading on fixed surfaces, like a rash, sometimes greenish gray, sometimes yellow-orange, but also many shades in between, lichens grow on gravestones, glacial erratics and other rocks, tree trunks, branches and twigs and cedar-shingled house roofs, exterior cedar-shingled sidewalls and sidewalks—essentially any stable, non-moving surface. They are actually a symbiotic organism consisting of both fungi and algae, typically blue-green or cyanobacteria, which, along with some mosses, break down rock, and wood over hundreds and thousands of years. The spores of the fungi part of the lichens, and the algae, would have reached this part of the coastal plain via wind, on birds (or possibly in bird guano, because some birds use lichens for their nests), and also perhaps in outwash streams flowing from the glacier.

To live, most lichens are half green algae relying on photosynthesis to use the sun's energy to convert carbon dioxide and hydrogen into carbohydrates (food) for both the algae and the fungi, and they supplement this food with water and minerals from dust and the air. In turn, the fungi provide physical structure for both organisms and retain moisture for the plant.

Today, a total of 148 lichen species exist on Nantucket. Some of these were most likely on the coastal plain areas shortly after the glacier receded, according to amateur lichenologist Elizabeth Knieper and botanists Peter Dunwiddie and Bruce A. Sorrie, authors of *The Vascular and Non-Vascular Plants on Nantucket, Tuckernuck and Muskeget Islands.* Lichens probably found the large glacial erratics left by the glacier a good place to live because they grow so slowly and require their growing medium to stay put. Walk up to Altar Rock and spot an erratic in the moors, and you're likely to find a patchwork of lichens on these boulders. Likewise, take a stroll through any of the island's cemeteries, and you'll find lichens plastered on many of the headstones.

Says Knieper of rock lichens: "The mineral content, the texture and the acid/base levels in the rocks influence the lichen species assemblages on the rocks, as [do] the humidity, light levels, temperature and competition from bryophytes [seedless, nonvascular plants including mosses, liverworts and hornworts] and vascular plants."

An abundance of lichens in a given location means several things. It indicates the absence of sulfur dioxide in the form of acid rain (which is a byproduct of the burning of fossil fuels), good sunlight, humidity and plenty of tree bark or stone to grow on.

While some believe that Nantucket's lichen species grow only on north-facing roofs, walls and other substrates, lichen growth surfaces depend on the amount of light the plants require. Heavily light-dependent lichens, including the smaller encrusting microlichens, will not grow on north-facing surfaces.

Just as lichens remain on the island for us to discover, the three layers of podzol are visible to anyone looking along Nantucket's South Shore or in the inner harbor. Find a part of this island shoreline undergoing erosion where whole chunks of the land are calving off onto the beach below, and you should be able to see the clearest definition of Nantucket's soil profile. It is as if you sliced a cross section of the island off to look at. Almost anywhere along the South Shore, including Cisco Beach on to the east of the end of Hummock Pond Road, Madaket Beach in either direction, and the exposed bluffs of the inner harbor, are places where you can get close enough to the top of a coastal bank or bluff face to see podzol layers. The top layer, or horizon, of the ground surface is a thick light to dark brown or black sandwich of plant parts, called organic litter, in various stages of decomposition; below the horizon, a blended layer of mineral soil and humus is followed by a final whitish layer of all-mineral soil that is the result of water percolating down through it. The second horizon is red-brown in color from the iron-laden soils above washing down into this part of the ground. Below this layer is the lower horizon of all parent material, the till that the glacier left behind.

The pollen grains trapped in these layers of soils, clays and sediments over thousands of years are not the only clues to the island's vegetational past. Botanists like Dunwiddie and fellow Nantucket researcher Dorothy Peteet, a paleoecologist with NASA/Goddard Institute for Space Studies, New York, and Lamont Doherty Earth Observatory, Palisades, New York, also depend for distribution information on some organic remnants, called macrofossils, of seeds, leaves and twigs, which are large enough to see with the naked eye.

Peteet's research, which she began in 2009, aimed to ascertain the true age of plant pollen and macrofossils preserved in the sediments beneath ponds and bogs along the edge of the long terminal moraine stretching from Nantucket to Martha's Vineyard down past Block Island, Rhode Island, to Long Island, New York, and into New Jersey, so she could paint a clearer picture of both when the glacier did recede, and what plants began growing right afterwards. On Nantucket, that meant coring in wet spots including No Bottom Pond (immediately north of the dirt trail section of Grove Lane), Donut Pond and Tawpawshau Bog in the moors, and then analyzing this data.

What made Peteet's post-glacial vegetation research challenging is that there are several schools of thought around fossil dating. The common belief is that the Laurentide ice sheet, whose Great South Channel and Cape Cod Bay lobes sculpted the Grey Lady, retreated from Nantucket around 18,000 years ago, although Oldale believes it began retreating 21,000 years ago. Scientists who used radiocarbon dating of rocks and soil deposit samples to determine the age of long-dead living organisms 500 to 50,000 years old used this dating method to determine when the glacier began its retreat.

But Peteet believes there are more accurate methods of dating:

> The reason why most people think it's 18,000 is that in the old days, people would take a big chunk of the bottom of a lake sediment, which was clay, and they would take like 20 centimeters worth and send that to a radio carbon lab, and it would give you a mixture of ages that would come out anywhere from 18,000 to 22,000. That was the old way of radiocarbon dating.[3]

Around 1990, accelerator mass spectrometry came on the scene. It uses a particle accelerator to date the actual carbon-14 atoms that are decaying by weighing them, dramatically reducing the testing time from several weeks or months to just a few minutes, and allowing much smaller samples to be measured. This leap in carbon-dating technology meant that Peteet could determine that the macrofossils she found in clay soils were much younger than she had thought when they were dated using radiocarbon dating.

Peteet's moraine study of post-glacial vegetation was further complicated by another method of ascertaining age called beryllium-10 dating that, upon its introduction around 1985, turned the fossil-dating world on its proverbial stamen.[4] The beryllium believers think of Nantucket as the oldest part of the terminal moraine in Peteet's study area, followed closely by Martha's Vineyard, and they say that the glacier actually left the island 28,000 years ago, which contradicts her ice-retreating dates of between 14,000 and 15,000 years ago.

Peteet dated her core samples with the greatest accuracy she could muster, and she found that her pollen data mirrored Dunwiddie's after she compared her pollen dates with the ages of the seeds she found in the near-surface clays at her ten sites. These seed dates are not disputed by anyone, she says, and she feels confident in her theory that the glacier retreated from Nantucket 3,000 to 4,000 years later than the common wisdom of 18,000 years ago.

But not everyone is convinced. Those subscribing to the beryllium-10 dating method believe that it was too cold for any plants to germinate and grow right after the glacier left the area. Peteet doesn't agree, citing evidence of tundra vegetation and other plants along the ice edge in Pennsylvania and New Jersey. Still, she admits that a big mystery remains: why beryllium ages are so old and why carbon ages are so young. However, regardless of Peteet's theory on glacial retreat and the one held by the beryllium-10 dating community, the common belief is that the glacial retreat occurred 18,000 years ago.

From coring work on Nantucket in October 2009, Peteet and one of her students at Columbia University, Kathryn Sears, made some discoveries about what the climate and vegetation may have been like on Nantucket just west of town at the time it became an island. In a core they collected from No Bottom Pond, Peteet and Sears found evidence of sand layers that they believe indicate drought conditions and a drier climate overall. Peteet and Sears also found signs of pitch pines more than 6,000 years old, "which were previously believed to be absent on Nantucket prior to European impact." Also within this core were plentiful macrofossils, nearly all seeds of emergent plants that grow in shallow water, including native swamp loosestrife and three-way sedge, and what, to Peteet and Sears at the time, looked like sections of deeper water plants: pond lilies and watershield.

In comparable sites southwest of Nantucket along the moraine within the ice margin, Peteet sometimes finds evidence of spruce, larch and, once in a while, jack pine. The pollen from these species is mixed in with large amounts of pollen blown in from south and west of the moraine, but most of the pollen Peteet finds from around the time the glacier left is that of tundra plants such as dwarf birch, blueberry and a lot of sedges, including bulrushes and low, grass-like tussocks in the wetland areas, which Dunwiddie also found in his core samples taken on Nantucket.

Working in Alaska for 20 years, Peteet learned how the ground-up clays are packed with the kind of nutrients that some plants require for survival. Others grew in quickly on their own, including ferns, which have both male and female genetic components, and alders, which are nitrogen-fixing plants that can process atmospheric nitrogen for food. Conditions on Nantucket at the time of glacial recession, she says, were probably similar. "This is an island, but the sea level was lower, so my guess is that you had birds and plants, you had sources not that far away—and the wind blows.

Even in cracks in rocks, if there's a little bit of algae or moss or something, a seed can sprout. So it's actually not that bad of an environment for plants to start up."

And grow they did. Before humans arrived on Nantucket—Paleo-indians from the Litchic Period, probably around 11,000 years ago—the coastal plain acreage destined to become the islands of Nantucket was blanketed in forests of varying densities and species distributions, all the way out to the edge of the continental shelf. Most likely this forest consisted of all of the trees I have mentioned earlier detected in the pollen samples, taking root as the climate warmed inexplicably about 10,000 years ago and replacing spruce as the dominant species. Following Arctic vegetation of tundra plants and lichens immediately trailing the glacier, tree species familiar to New Englanders—white, red and black oaks; white and pitch pines; beech; tupelo; maples; and hickory that Dunwiddie theorizes eventually took root on Nantucket—all moved northward and westward from the refugia where they had withdrawn during the glacial period. These refugia were areas that avoided the drastic climatological impact of the advancing Laurentide ice sheet. According to John O'Keefe, Harvard University Forest Fisher Museum and Educational Programs director, and David R. Foster, director of Harvard Forest, in their article, "Dynamics In The Postglacial Era," they likely included the southern Appalachians, the Eastern coastal plain, including what is now known as Georges Bank, and the edge of the Continental Shelf.

The first trees to arrive were the boreal forest species, the primary Northern conifers of spruce and jack pine.[5] But what parts of the island were covered with all the dense stands of trees, following the demise of jack pine and spruce, encountered and used at will first by the Archaic and Wampanoag Indians and later by the European settlers? The answer is: not very many, considering the brief time it took the settlers to go through their supply of island trees. The details are reported during the first eight years of island settlement in the early Nantucket County Record and Nantucket Public Record, and they are set forth in the "Essay on Nantucket Timber" by Elizabeth Little in the Nantucket Historical Association's "Nantucket Algonquian Studies No. 1–No. 8":

> 1659: Thomas Mayhew bought the 'Plains' between Hummock Pond and Long Pond and the 'use of the meadow and to take wood for the use of him. . . .'

1660: The proprietors bought the west end of the island, as well as meadow, pasture, and 'free liberty for timber and wood' on any part of the island.

1662: Tradesmen were to have 'half a share of land and meadow, wood and timber.'

1663: No man shall fall and make use of any Timber on Coatue (without liberty of the town) except it be for building houses . . . and . . . to make folds for sheep or goats.

1664: A woodland at the west end of 'the plains at Wesquo.'

1664: 'If any land on any part of the island be set to by any Indian so that the land or grass be Burnt to any considered value as to a quarter of a mile or more the Indians in whose jurisdiction so ever it shall be fined 20 pound, except it be in the month of April.'

1666: All considerable woodland on Nanahuma's Neck [the Long Woods], the grate swamp only, was to be laid out in 25 shares. Until then no one was to fell 'timber' within the tract.

1667: 'There shall be no more green wood fallen in the Long Woods until all the old that is to say already cut down be spent that is fit for firewood. Also, it is concluded that no more Timber shall be fellen for rales and posts except only for boards of the like. . . . An order was made that hence fourth no Timber shall be fellen for building on any part of the Island at any time of the year Except it be in May and the first week in June. . . .'

Historically documented forests on Nantucket include the "Broad Woods," the mature maritime forest of white and black oaks on Coskata Pond's east shore, as well as another dense forest of scrub, white, black and dwarf chestnut oaks in the northern center of Tuckernuck Island, where these trees are squat with wide trunks and far-reaching branches; the "Beech Woods" around Stump Pond; the "Long Woods" in Ram Pasture, where firewood, rails, posts, boards and timber were available; and other heavily forested parts of Nantucket, including just west of Wesco, at Pocomo, Quaise, Polpis and on Coatue, according to Little in her 1981 "Essay on Nantucket Timber" for the Nantucket Historical Association. "From 1667 on, the English rules for harvesting time were increasingly restrictive and reflect overuse of a limited natural resource," Little says. "Details from the county records give a feeling of just how limited the native wood supply was."

Further select entries from the town and county records bear this out:

1668: Coffin and Swain were allowed to fence their land on Nanahuma's Neck, but the wood and timber were to remain common.

1677: Permission granted for the cutting of 18 trees at Coatue.

1688: No pines should be cut down and carried away from Coatue.

1709: Order was made 'to stop & prohibit ye cutting of any more wood of any sort of from Coatue.'

1741–1747: According to the English, their Squam tract was 'so over run with Briars and other Rubbish' that they enclosed it for pasture of sheep, cattle and horses. Although they allowed the Indians who had been living there 'to cut wood on Our Lands,' the Squam Indians appear to have gone to the Gibbs Pond region, inhabited by Sakedan Indians, for wood. The Sakedan Indians then wrote letters to Boston complaining that '. . . these other Town Indians come in upon us daken away our wood away from our land. . . .'

As Little describes, John Woolman, a Quaker visiting Nantucket in 1743, remarked on how barren the island was, noting that "timber, fences and firewood were being imported from the mainland."

All of these forested areas on Nantucket, save two, are on the northern side of the island, the moraine, where the moors developed. And in this part of the island, the true hidden forests for which the private beech grove off the west side of Almanac Pond Road is named, are abundant. These forests—groves, really—are deemed hidden because they germinated in former kettle ponds sunken lower than most of the land around them, partially or completely hiding them from view. These ice chunk dents were gradually filled in by lesser vegetation, and eventually trees sank their roots into organic matter consisting of centuries of decomposed plant materials.

Wind- and salt-stunted groves of red cedar still exist on Coatue, as do the white and black oaks, Eastern red cedar and black tupelo in the Coskata Woods, on Tuckernuck Island and a stand of white oaks along the west side of Somerset Lane between its southern end and Catherine Lane. To a certain extent, stands of beeches are also found in the Nantucket Conservation Foundation's Masquetuck property on the west side of Polpis Harbor and in its Squam Swamp property. Naturally, there are plenty of maples, sassafras and black tupelos in the moister areas of the island.

The so-called Hidden Forest, tall, mostly American beech trees really hidden from public view only by "no trespassing" and "private property" signs amongst red maples and ferns, is atop a rise, instead of growing out of a depression in the moors. It borrows its name, but not its habitat and topography, from the many true stands of hardwoods (including sassafras and black tupelo) growing and partially obscured from view in the kettles, but has unjustifiably gained notoriety as the only remaining forest on the island because it is a stand of tall, mostly American beech trees "hidden" on private property.

"The northeastern portion of Nantucket is currently the most forested area of the island because the retreating glacier left behind many poorly drained depressions that developed rich, peaty organic soil," reads NCF's "Natural Habitats of Nantucket" on its website. "Here, forest trees can grow to be 30 to 40 feet tall before they are impacted by high winds and salt. These wooded areas are locally referred to as hidden forests because they tend to occur in depressions that are surrounded by hills, which reduces salt exposure and makes them somewhat hidden when viewed from a distance."

Tupelo

Possible evidence of what might have grown elsewhere on the island, in the way of wide-girth tall trees left over from the heavily forested coastal landscape, is found in bogs once mined for peat to be used as stove fuel. These include Eastern red and Atlantic white cedar trees with trunks up to 12 inches in diameter, reports Bassett Jones, an electrical engineer with a passion for all things natural on Nantucket who summered on the island all of his life, eventually purchasing a year-round house in Wauwinet.

However, from his 1935 paper detailed in the April 1967 *Historic Nantucket*, the Nantucket Historical Association's magazine, entitled "Was Nantucket Ever Forested?" Jones argued that, despite the discovery of wide cypress trunks, Nantucket's poor soil conditions, salt spray and relentless strong winds meant that such dense forestation of Nantucket never existed to the extent historically described. The rich, deep quality of loam soil needed for stands of oaks, maples, hickories, beeches and other hardwoods exists only in limited quantities trailing from town south to between Miacomet and Hummock Ponds, and in moister portions of Polpis, Wauwinet, Squam and Quidnet.

Stated Jones on his disbelief of house construction lumber coming out of Nantucket trees:

> The soil of such forests is not here, nor are there any traces of it. So, I am forced to conclude that the probabilities are much in favor of such soil never having existed. If the soil did not exist, neither did the forest exist. The only argument I have ever heard in favor of the speculative pristine Nantucket forest of such very large trees, from which such very 'sticks' could be cut, is the discovery of 'stumps' of old trees in peat bogs. But, to my knowledge, with a single reported example . . . I shall mention hereafter, no stump has yet been found belonging to any such large trees. None that I have seen, or dug myself, were more than 10 inches or, at the outside, 12 inches in diameter. Most of these stumps are much smaller. Furthermore, I can show you living wild trees on this island with 'stumps' larger than this—but these same living trees have boles or 'trunks' but a few feet tall at the most, and the whole tree is not over 20 to 25 feet tall. Certainly no such timber was ever cut from these trees.

However, Jones's explorations of the island probably did not include a visit to Naushon Island, the largest of the Elizabeth Islands archipelago just west of Martha's Vineyard across Vineyard Sound, privately owned to this day, where exists a great example of the climax forest for the Cape and Islands portion of the coastal plain. It is the only piece of land in the Cape and Islands region that was left almost entirely alone, nearly all of its trees left standing and never leveled for building lumber, its lands never cleared for farming.

Beech trees standing 100 feet or more dominate the island and are what botanists say were among the last in a succession of tree species to establish themselves after the glacier melted away. Beeches were also present on Nantucket prior to human habitation and many, detailed above, still grow tall on Nantucket, strongly challenging Jones's assertion. And his research did not include taking core samples from Nantucket's bogs and dating the pollen grains found in the soils beneath island ponds and bogs, so with just ancient stumps and anecdotal accounts, he was not evaluating the more complete picture that Dunwiddie, Peteet and other botanists were afforded in reaching their conclusions.

Besides, strong ocean winds capable of stunting trees with their relentless force, laden with salt spray, would not be felt on this part of the coastal plain until maybe around 6,000 to 7,000 years ago, when the ocean rose high to make islands of the coastal plain uplands. This, at the latest, was at least 2,000 years after Native Americans were said to have arrived where Nantucket is today. There was plenty of time for them to chop down what they needed for cropland and building materials, the odd wide stump ending up in a bog near where it was felled. As the ocean gradually moved closer and closer, inundating coastal plain lowlands as it rose, this certainly drew the strong salty winds toward the edge of whatever coastal forest grew here. All botanists agree that these winds substantially pared back large and tall woody plant growth on the young island.

Out in the moors, I challenge you to find but a handful of tree groves, hidden forests and pitch pines excepted, rising taller than the sea of scrub oak blanketing this part of the island. For examples of windswept, salt-stunted trees, check out the pines on the south side of Madaket Road just before the Sanford Farm parking lot, stand at the entrance to Island Lumber on Polpis Road to observe the tops of the pines in the State Forest, or see the cedar trees on Coatue and examine the canopy of the maritime oak forest at its western edges from Coskata Pond. Once the ocean got within striking distance of the new island, gradually eating up the sylvan windbreak with wind, waves and salt, trees that remained were forced to bow to these relentless elements and grew not taller but at a more horizontal angle away from the direction of prevailing winds.[6]

From a plant community perspective, the Nantucket and Tuckernuck we see today largely didn't exist until after Native American islanders and European settlers had impacted the island vegetation. They cleared from the land the trees that did exist as they needed them for crops and pasture, they burned selected tracts to control certain species and stimulate new growth of others, and they harvested what they needed to burn as fuel and to build houses and boats. Muskeget doesn't really figure into this equation because its marine deposits of sand and gravel have never been enough to support anything taller than low cedar trees, beach grass, poison ivy, bayberry, goldenrod, several grasses and flowers, and other dune community vegetation also found in beach plant communities on Coatue, the Haulover and Eel Point on Nantucket.

However, botanist W. L. McAtee, in his paper, "Winter Flora of Muskeget Island, Massachusetts," listed 59 plant species on the smallest sandy island in Nantucket's archipelago, while Dunwiddie found a total of 160 vascular plants on Muskeget.[7]

Today, as in the early years of the island, trees and other island vegetation grow where the proper nutrients, water sources and conditions allow for that particular species. Salt-tolerant plants thrive in salt marshes and at the ends of ponds biannually opened to the ocean and on beaches and dunes. Freshwater aquatic vegetation grows in and along the edges of ponds, near and in swamps. Upland species adapted to the poor soil conditions of Nantucket's sandy, gravelly ground grow in the moors—the moraine—and on the southern section of the island, the outwash plain.

Not wanting to live without the shade and beauty of trees to which they were accustomed on the mainland, many Nantucketers in the two primary urban zones of the island—Nantucket town and Siasconset—began planting trees along streets and in their yards in the downtown around 150 years ago. Today, the island's densest tall-tree forest is man-made, existing because of aesthetic desires, not natural selection or succession, in its old historic districts, which are replete with elms, redwoods, lindens, sycamores, willows, catalpas, locusts, yellow poplars, chestnuts and maples.

Although the post-glacial garden of plant species of Nantucket and its two neighboring islands began to germinate 11,000 years ago with plenty of time to establish itself, this flora continued to expand, as the island did, in number and species variety. The island's marine deposits (geologists' parlance for the sand, gravel and soils that compose the beaches and barrier beaches grown seaward as appendages of the islands) were the last major land additions to Nantucket, Tuckernuck and Muskeget as they became islands.

Currents, wind and waves shifted this mostly sand mix from nearshore shoals and beaches to sculpt the various appendages. And so, into existence between 2,000 to 6,000 years ago came Smith's Point, Eel Point,

Tuckernuck Island's ever-changing—vanishing and reappearing—sand spits, including Whale Island (once part of Great Neck) off of its southeast end, Bigelow Point and the barrier beach on its northwest end that protects North Pond, and the one forming East Pond, Low Beach and its massive dune field, the Haulover, Coskata, Coatue, the Galls and Great Point. On these marine deposits, a dynamic growing medium developed for vegetation able to withstand salt spray, ocean overwash, near-constant wind and barren growing, low nutrient conditions.

The lush pale green sand cover of American beach grass is a perfect example. It probably first reached Nantucket via migrating birds, wind and ocean currents. Lacking any semblance of decent soil from which to extract food, beach grass collects its nutrients, along with moisture, from salt water, blown and washed in. It also gets moisture from rain. Sending rhizomes deep down into the beach and then horizontally within the dunes, beach grass roots sprout new stems from which the plant's blades grow. They trap blowing sand, which gradually builds up the height, width and length of the dunes, into which more beach grass grows. With beach grass providing bulwarks for the beach plant community and holding the base of the future growing medium in place, other salt- and wind-tolerant plants began building a foundation of soils on top of the decidedly unreceptive basis of

Beach grass

the beach. These salt-tolerant shrub plants, which can thrive in poor soil conditions, include bayberry, goldenrod, Rosa rugosa (beach rose), salt-spray rose, groundsel tree, black huckleberry and low-bush blueberry, and several lichens. They shed their leaves each fall, in addition to contributing other plant parts such as branches and whole plants throughout the year, and a richer soil of these decomposing organic materials began to build up.

Historically, as this enriched beach loam increased in depth, it allowed the establishment of Eastern red cedar, predominantly in the Coskata Woods, along the length of Coatue and in a dense concentration at the east end of Coatue. Other small tree species took hold in these beach plant communities of the island, including black cherry, black oak and beach plum. And out on Smith's Point and in the vast and wide dune system of Low Beach, a few small groves of pitch pines eventually got going, taking root among the other beach and dune vegetation.

As the Haulover, Coskata and Coatue grew, their beach plant communities filled in while the beaches themselves expanded. Combined, the sand and roots of this vegetation gradually gave Nantucket a true harbor, just as Eel and Smith's Points did for the west end of the island, forming enough of a protective cove for Madaket Harbor to exist. These post-glacial marine deposits also provided enough of the proper protection from the open ocean for another of Nantucket's signature plant communities, the salt marsh, to germinate and thrive. They grew along the ocean-inundated valleys and kettle holes opened up by erosion along this eastern section of the north shore that evolved into the inlet-like mini harbor of Polpis; in the massive marsh areas of Folger's Marsh and Shimmo Pond; in the cove between Pimney's and Abram's points; in the Creeks and around Hither Creek in Madaket; and in the marsh area northwest of Warren's Landing in Madaket on the south side of Eel Point.

Before the Haulover and Coatue extended north and west, respectively, to create Nantucket Harbor, the island's north shore continued from Jetties Beach out to where Wauwinet is today. That meant that waves from the northwest, north, northeast and east all broke on what is now the inner harbor shore from Brant Point all the way out to Wauwinet. At that time, without the Haulover, Coskata and Coatue, these shores of the now-inner harbor were part of the exposed, above-the-water backside of the terminal moraine left by the glacier, and that wave action combined a constant erosion with the rapid movement of sand and sediments, with little chance for them to be left in one place to build up enough for salt marsh vegetation to take root.

The salt marsh ecosystem is an amazing community of plants, animals, birds, fish and crustaceans that produces around ten tons of organic material per acre annually. It is vital to the protection of inland areas, with its ability to absorb ocean storm surge, and its plants and bacteria converting toxins and pollution into food they can use to grow, and then into beneficial waste for other salt marsh organisms. But it requires specialized growing conditions. It grows best with the relatively gentle tidal exchange found in protected bays and inlets where the salt marsh can accumulate the necessary elevation of mud and sand so it can take hold and prosper.

The daily moderate to severe erosion sustained by exposed ocean beaches, then, is not conducive to salt marsh growth. The continuous rise of the ocean, and the rebounding of the submerged land upward once it was released from the massive downward pressure of the Laurentide ice sheet, didn't give salt marsh plant communities in more exposed locations, such as the inlets and creeks along the inner harbor, a good chance to grow.

Sea level rise eventually slowed enough to allow salt marsh vegetation to get going. With the islands' post-glacial deposits protecting its young harbors from the wave action of Nantucket Sound and the Atlantic Ocean (the primary salt marsh areas in the harbor having been essentially carved out before the Haulover and Coatue halted the erosive action of the ocean), sediments were able to accrete enough for salt marsh vegetation to germinate and stay just ahead of the rising sea level.

These salt marshes are found in Medouie Creek, Pocomo Meadows, Polpis Harbor, Folger's Marsh, around Abram's Point, Pimney's Point and Shimmo Creek and the Creeks, the former seven areas likely collapsed kettle holes formed by massive ice chunks left behind by the glacier. Other inlets that formed along the newer parts of the island and proved receptive to salt marsh vegetation include Coskata Pond and the Glades between the northwest side of the pond and Coatue, on the protected sides of First, Second, Third and Five-fingered Points on the south side of Coatue, around the nearly freshwater lagoon on Great Point, the south side of Eel Point, in Hither Creek, the west end of East Pond on Tuckernuck, the east and north sides of North Pond on that island, and in the small lagoon on the south end of Muskeget Island.

Salt marsh growth in Folger's Marsh probably began around 3,000 years ago, and it's highly likely that other young inlets along this inner harbor shore began filling in with salt marsh plant species around this time as well.[8] This was roughly 2,000 years after the Haulover tombolo began gradually growing northward to connect with Coskata, forming the protective sand spit and dune system between the open ocean and that part of the island's then-north shore. During the accretion of this tombolo, salt marsh proliferation probably accelerated gradually, spreading faster when the tombolo connected with the hard clay and gravels of Coskata and continuing to gain in acreage as Coatue began growing westward, slowly forming today's harbor and locking out significant wave action from hitting the inner harbor shores.

Oldale says, in general, the regional Cape and Islands formation period of salt marsh deposits—when sand bottoms and mud flats increased to intertidal elevations, allowing salt marsh cord grass to remain, at least part of the daily tidal cycles, above water, in bays and inlets—formed as early as 4,000 to 6,000 years ago.[9] For Nantucket, that is likely to have been around 3,000 to, at the earliest, 4,000 years ago, when melting-glacier-induced sea level rise slowed just enough for the rate of growth of mud flats and sandbars upward in elevation to allow salt marsh cord grass the chance to take root and keep pace.[10]

Salt marsh cord grass, one of two primary salt marsh grasses, is viable in this quasi-saltwater environment only because it sprouts with greatest success in a habitat where there is a fresh water source—a river, stream or creek—flowing into the salt water. With none of these waterways present on Nantucket in their true mainland forms, the requisite fresh water both falls on the marsh as precipitation and seeps out of the ground from the island's sole source aquifer in the intertidal zone.

Fresh water is one of two ingredients needed for salt marsh cord grass seed germination, the first being mud or sand flats. From these conditions sprang Nantucket's salt marshes, say John and Mildred Teal in their book, *The Life and Death of the Salt Marsh*. With mud and sand flats allowed to accumulate in the waters of these areas, the essential salt-tolerant plants of the marsh, saltmarsh cord grass and salt meadow grass, were able to root themselves into the soggy bottoms.[11]

Anyone with even a passing interest in Nantucket's harbors and inner shores knows a salt marsh when they encounter one. That inescapable pungent, salty, earthy smell of the muddy honeycomb base of the marsh flooding the air with its heavy aroma of life; the abundance of shorebirds wading in the shallows hunting the fish, snails, mollusks and insects that live in this unique ecosystem; and the neon green cord grass glistening with briny moisture—that's the salt marsh.[12]

As beach rose bushes and American beach grass roots gradually formed a bulwark of sand dunes, the roots of these salt marsh grasses formed a web that held the intertidal sediments in one place. That is what builds, as the Teals describe it, a peat-like soil netting of organic detritus created with the movement of the tides. With each season's grass parts and animals dying and decaying, the marsh grows incrementally over time. Over the last 3,000 years or so, upward and outward expansion of salt marsh peat formation has been more or less able to grow in step with the gradual rise of sea level, forming a medium for salt marsh plants and a muddy honeycomb of living spaces for fin fish, snails, worms, shellfish, birds and other marsh animals.

Low tide, during the late spring through early fall, is the perfect time to observe this partially submerged ecosystem from mudflat to upland meadow's edge. The salt marsh is really two marshes grounded in the two cord grass species above. Salt marsh cord grass, which has adapted to saltwater submersion during twice-daily high tides, makes up the low marsh that is barely visible at the peak of high tide. Seaweeds also grow in this zone and can form clusters around the grass's exposed roots where ribbed mussels sometimes collect. Just above the wrackline, the highest reach of the water during high tide, is the beginning of the high marsh held together by the other major grass, salt meadow cordgrass. It is accompanied by sea lavender, spike grass and black grass mixed in with seabeach knotweed, salt marsh aster, seaside goldenrod and common reeds. Also known as phragmites, these tall reeds are an invasive species that force out all other plants while forming dense thickets in wetland areas.

The transition zone at the upland edges of the high marsh, bordering on drier inland ecosystems, contains plants rooted in drier soils, along with others, including marsh alders and groundsel tree (also called high tide bush), that grow with some of their roots in infrequent saltwater inundation during astronomical high tides.

As easy as it is to imagine such a fertile area growing in quickly, its seeds had to *get* to the island in order for the accumulating salt marsh deposits to serve as a soggy soil for the marsh plants. Nantucket had become an island before its salt marshes developed. So, unlike the spruce and jack pine that first covered the island after the glacier receded and, later, the hardwood species that followed when Nantucket was a part of the mainland, the germination of the salt marsh vegetation had to happen either by air or by water. "By water" meant seeds washed ashore from other salt marshes, probably from the nearby mainland marshes along the coast of what are now Cape Cod and Southeastern Massachusetts. Because the salt marsh grass seed coats are built to withstand salt water, it's highly likely that they drifted across Nantucket Sound and were carried into the island's estuaries on the incoming tides. Shorebirds, and to a certain extent insects such as honeybees, bumblebees and other plant nectar feeders, were probably Nantucket's best salt marsh farmers, handling the inadvertent harvesting of seeds, transportation to Nantucket, distribution, and even fertilization via defecation if they ingested the seeds. Also, birds' bodies and legs could have easily been encrusted with mainland salt marsh mud sprinkled with seeds, or their feathers dusted with piggybacking seeds.

Birds played a large role in the broadcasting of seeds, not only in the marshes but for dominant plant communities on the maritime heathlands of the northern portion of the island, the terminal moraine, and the sandplain grasslands and coastal plains. Nantucket's plant ecologists, including Dunwiddie and Peteet, believe that much of the early sandplain grassland and heathlands vegetation came from the prairies of the Midwest, which at one time extended as far east as Eastern Ohio and into westernmost Pennsylvania in a habitat formation known as the Prairie Peninsula, an extension of western prairie habitat, during the Xerothermic Period.[13]

The Xerothermic Period, more commonly known as the Hypsithermal, was, to date, the warmest part of the Holocene Epoch, our current interglacial stage. Some believe the warming was related to increased solar activity that may have contributed to the initial melting of the Laurentide ice sheet. Although the Northwest experienced its peak heat wave 9,000 to 11,000 years ago, the Northeast didn't get warmest until about 4,000 years ago. Well before this warming period in the Northeast topped out, the Prairie Peninsula, many botanists believe, began stabbing eastward, expanding into ice-free corridors and refugia leading into New England as the glacier retreated from the warming air. The soils gradually became more arid as the Prairie Peninsula finally reached its furthest extension in our direction around 5,500 years ago, Peteet and Dunwiddie believe. Foster theorizes that the drought of this warm period was the main cause for a major die-off of hemlock, a species that requires moist conditions to grow. And that climate change may have paved the way for the seeds and pollen of prairie species, which thrive in drier, warmer conditions, to reach our coastline landmass. Leslie J. Mehrhoff, in her research essay, "Thoughts on the Biogeography of Grassland Plants in New

England," says the lowlands of central New York state were the most likely route for some of these prairie plants to migrate northeast, populating the coastal grasslands from the Jersey Shore to Long Island, Block Island, Martha's Vineyard, Tuckernuck Island and on to Nantucket.

The seeds still had to travel 500 or 600 miles to reach Nantucket. Although the primary modes of seed migration transport were wind, water, mammals and birds, it wasn't one exclusive leap to the southern portion of Martha's Vineyard and Nantucket for this Midwestern agrarian cargo. The eastward distribution of these plants was much more like a relay race, with avian, mammalian and insect species in one area carrying and depositing seeds to the easternmost extent of their own ranges. The plants then established themselves and the process of range expansion (mobile species–aided migration) repeated itself.

Says Dunwiddie, "They also don't necessarily migrate in a single, wave-like, unidirectional manner. They may move in jumps, tongues, and lobes, with some areas skipped over for centuries and millennia by some species. We tend to think of these community types moving as a wave across the continent, but that almost assuredly is wrong." Operating parallel to this prairie vegetation dispersal system were the wind and waterways, which augmented the easterly movement of these plants by means of walking and flying critters, until eventually a carpet of grasslands extended from the northern part of the Jersey Shore up along Long Island to Martha's Vineyard and on to Tuckernuck and Nantucket, populating both the northern section of Nantucket (the heathlands) and the south of the terminal moraine in the outwash plain (the sandplain grasslands) with vascular plants.[14]

Dunwiddie speculates that, although some grass-like species were probably on the island around 8,000 years ago, Nantucket and Tuckernuck were likely the last of the coastal areas to begin to support this type of habitat, because it was the farthest north and therefore the last to warm up. The more cold-tolerant species of the oak forest took hold first, he believes, while other, warmer climate species followed.

Sandplain grassland species began arriving on Nantucket and Tuckernuck when the rising ocean started flooding the lowland basins of Vineyard Sound and Nantucket Sound in the coastal plain around 7,500 years ago, after the arrival of Native Americans. The process continued through the time when our three islands became separated from Martha's Vineyard and the mainland via Monomoy Island approximately 6,000 years ago, and it went on for an unknown length of time. Sandplain grassland species found the islands' soils of fine sand, glacial outwash and debris ideal for germination, and the majority of plant ecologists estimate that most of the first such species that appeared here were different from the goldenrod, yarrow, pearly everlasting, field pussytoes, multiple varieties of asters, bluets, trailing arbutus, little bluestem grass, bearberry and false indigo that grow today. All agree that the optimum growing conditions for the sandplain grasslands plant species lie on Nantucket and Tuckernuck's southern sides and in the coastal heathlands on their northern sections, and that these conditions are the result of human influences, including burning off land to encourage growth, clearing land for crops of edible and fruit-bearing plants, harvesting trees for building houses and boats, and later, grazing sheep. In essence, it was not natural plant distribution and succession but human interference that ushered in sandplain grassland plant species on Nantucket and Tuckernuck. From the perspective of these prairie plants, the clearing of the island landscape of most of the larger plants and trees had to happen, because the species that inhabit these two ecosystems require copious amounts of sunshine and little or no competition for nutrients.

By the time these species began to find their way here, the earliest Native Americans who had settled the coastal plain between 8,000 and 11,000 years ago had already, inadvertently, conditioned the outwash plain of our islands for these species. The repeated controlled burning of these grasslands over hundreds of years by Native Americans kept larger woody plants and shrubs from crowding out and shading the sandplain grassland and heathland species. This fire treatment of the landscape also deposited layer upon layer of charred plant parts, the thatch, litter and woody plant parts that would otherwise have been released slowly by decay. Nutrients were released directly into the soil from the ashes. The fires also burned off the leaves and thinner branches of the taller plants and low trees, including scrub oaks, which decreased the shading impact of these bigger, canopy-like plants over the sandplain plants.

Today, the Nantucket Heathlands Partnership, a working research collaborative of the island's conservation organizations and the Nantucket Fire Department, continue the legacy of maintaining these man-made habitats by conducting regular controlled burns during the spring and fall on selected plots of their properties around the island. These burns serve both to further sandplain grassland and heathland management research and to keep invasive species at bay. Sandplain grassland was once considered a proper biome for the breadth of its range and its thousands of acres of coverage south of the moraine along the coastal portions of New Jersey to Long Island and up to Martha's Vineyard and Nantucket. Now a mere one percent of the original sandplain grasslands habitat remains, but Martha's Vineyard, Tuckernuck and Nantucket retain, on estimate, more than 90 percent, according to Jennifer M. Karberg and Karen C. Beattie in their report, "Effectiveness of Sheep Grazing as a Management Tool on Nantucket Island, MA." Nantucket alone contains 620.8 acres of the 1,900 total acres left. Most of Nantucket's patch lies west of Miacomet Pond in the Smooth Hummocks area, east of the village of Madaket, and on Tuckernuck Island along the length of most of its south side, wrapping around northward to the east of its old growth maritime oak forest. But it remains confined to certain sections of the southern halves of Nantucket and Tuckernuck because of their sandier, drier soils, salt-drenched winds that severely stunt the growth of taller plants, and human development of surrounding land. Much of the sandplain grasslands are corralled in the Moorlands Management District, a 600-acre prairie-like preserve for the short-eared owl, between Miacomet Pond and Cisco that is owned by the Nantucket Islands Land Bank and largely protected from most future development by the requirement of ten-acre minimums for new lots.

By contrast, Nantucket's coastal heathlands, found mostly in what Nantucketers call the moors, are contained within Milestone and Polpis Roads and primarily owned by the Nantucket Conservation Foundation, the Nantucket Islands Land Bank, the Massachusetts Audubon Society, and some private property owners. They are grounded in the low nutrient content of the larger-grain sand and gravel soils found along the edge of, and just south of, the line where the glacier ended its aggregate bulldozing in New England. While the glacial melt water had washed the finer, lighter soil granules of pulverized rocks toward the ocean, creating Nantucket's three outwash plains, the heavier, larger particles remained behind to form the heathland growing medium.

In their paper, "Nantucket's Endangered Maritime Heaths," Wes Tiffney, Jr., and Doug E. Eveleigh listed some plants still found in the moors: the Nantucket shadbush, butterfly-weed, St. Andrew's cross, aster, Conrad's broom crowberry, bearberry, purple cudweed, bushy rockrose, creeping St. John's wort, little bluestem grass, flax, prickly pear, beak-rush and little blue-eyed grass. And the NCF has found shrubs that include black huckleberry, lowbush blueberry, bayberry and pasture rose in big clumps in the moors. All are relative newcomers to the island heathland plant community. Before it became an island and until the Paleo-Indians of the Lithic Period arrived on the island 8,000 to 11,000 years ago, the land area that Nantucket occupied was heavily forested, and these plants were nearly nonexistent. They took root only after the humans leveled the vegetation down to open land conducive to heathland and grassland species.[15] And as the ocean rose, drawing closer to what is now Nantucket, a colder maritime environment intensified, featuring ocean winds heavy with salt vapor. This ensured the domination of low-growth vegetation in the island's maritime heath, which covered much of the northern section of the eastern half of the island. Tiffney, Eveleigh and other top botanists believe that, at the peak of island growth of maritime heath, the most abundant plant was the common bearberry, a low-growing, trailing evergreen shrub producing white or whitish pink-tinged bell-shaped flowers and red berries. It shared its dominance with black huckleberry, golden heather, late sweet blueberry, early sweet blueberry and, in certain areas, Conrad's broom crowberry, Pennsylvania sedge, wiregrass, common hairgrass and red fescue.

Among these low-growing heathland species was a shrub growing 6.5 to ten feet high that still thrives on Nantucket and Tuckernuck today; the Nantucket shadbush. It likely survived in refugia in the coastal plain and

Nantucket shadbush

all the way out to the edge of the exposed continental shelf, including Georges Bank, as the glacier melted northward. The Nantucket shadbush, up until 2011 a distinct member of the shadbush family distinguished by being lower-growing than its mainland cousins and by its whitish-cream-colored five-petaled flowers, is thought by some to have diverged into its own species classification because of those same conditions of wind, salt spray and, when white-tailed deer arrived in the early 1920s, food-browsing.

Bruce Perry, property manager for the Nantucket Islands Land Bank, is the prescribed "burn boss" for the Massachusetts Audubon Society and the Nantucket Islands Land Bank. Hardly ever in the Land Bank's Broad Street offices, Perry is more likely found at the wheel of a tractor mowing and brush-cutting Land Bank properties to maintain specialized habitats. From this rather heavy-handed position of habitat preservation and through his voluminous prior wetlands protection duty, Perry knows Nantucket's vegetation and, naturally, is fluent in Nantucket shadbush knowledge.

Says Perry:

> I think that as the glacier receded, it was probably here and it got isolated and because our soils are so poor and you get salt spray [and], over time, you get shorter plants that survive better than the taller shadbushes, so you're going to end up with shorter plants that can take browsing and, nowadays, mowing and that kind of stuff. To have to survive versus the taller shadbush that can't take the browsing and mowing, that's a 5,000-years kind of thing.
>
> Has it [evolved] enough to be its own species? Developers want to say that it hasn't, of course, and the Massachusetts Natural Heritage & Endangered Species Program says that it has enough and that it's distinct enough, but no one's sat down and spent tens of thousands of dollars to do the genetics on it. The way you can tell the Nantucket shad from any other shad is the flower. You get down and count petals and the size of petals.

Actually, the Massachusetts Natural Heritage & Endangered Species Program did spend a bit of money examining the validity of the endemic status of the Nantucket shadbush. As a result, in the fall of 2011, it was in the process of delisting this shrub as endemic to Nantucket and as a state-listed species partly because it had been discovered elsewhere: from Long Island to interior parts of Connecticut and Massachusetts, and on bare mountaintops in Massachusetts.

The Nantucket shadbush, so named because its blossoms are said to coincide with the spawning shad charging up into mainland waterways in the springtime, has survived, to the delight of naturalists, but to the chagrin of developers hoping not to have to shrink their buildable land at the behest of watchful island conservation organizations. But many heathland species have not lasted on Nantucket as protected heathland species. Tiffney and Eveleigh noted that needlegrass, tick-trefoil, gerardia, fox-tail club-moss, false gromwell, chaffseed, nut-rush and good-night green-briar no longer exist in Nantucket's moors because of a variety of natural selection and human-influenced reasons. It is the latter that led to the emergence and eventual dominance of invasive, woody plant species over most of the island's heathlands and some of the sandplain grasslands. Most of these dominant species, primarily scrub oak, dwarf chestnut oak, and black huckleberry, began their ascension to vegetative superiority near the end of the 19th century. Eastern pitch pine was brought to the island by European settlers in 1847, and the Japanese black pine followed some time later. Even though the whaling industry dominated the Nantucket economy for 150 years, it didn't deplete the ranks of shepherds enough to keep the animals from grazing from one end of the island to another. In 1846, near the end of whaling's reign but at the height of island agriculture, 15,000 sheep were grazing all over the island on 22,676 common grazing shares of collectively owned Nantucket pastureland.

Obed Macy, in his *History of Nantucket: Being a Compendious Account of the First Settlement of the Island by the English, Together With the Rise and Progress of the Whale Fishery; and Other Historical Facts Relative to Said Island and its Inhabitants*, recounts how the island's original 27 proprietors, after purchasing the island from the Wampanoag Indians, divided its acreage up into shares commonly owned by each of the proprietors for agricultural use. Popularly known as sheep common shares, they were for raising farm cattle, including sheep, or planting crops, to the extent that each share was cleared of trees. When entirely cleared of trees and brush, each share could contain 720 sheep, which meant, according to the proprietors agreement, the island could support 19,440 sheep. Whether the proprietors ever reached that cap is not known, but the number of sheep common shares eventually reached 22,676.

The sheep certainly kept the shares cleared of vegetation. Historic photos of the island from the 1880s show a Nantucket mostly devoid of any vegetation other than grass, low shrubs and a smattering of trees, with much of the island visible from the various high spots. With the exception of the remaining forested pockets around the swamps and residential areas, Nantucket was nearly all grasslands, an organic smorgasbord of grasses, flowers and green shoots of would-be dominant plant species. And it was a menu for the sheep, which ate down each attempt by a tree or shrub to send new shoots of life up through the thin layers of soil. These four-legged brush cutters conditioned the landscape for heathland and grassland plants by preventing the larger vegetation from growing tall enough and spreading out enough to shade out the sunlight and take up the nutrients required by the grasses, low shrubs and wildflowers.

Efficient as the sheep were at invasive species control, they were no match for the vagaries of the economic engines driven by their shepherds and humans on the mainland. Sheep farming did continue uninterrupted right up until around 1890, but it had been declining rapidly since the mid-1800s when four isolated historical events had effectively killed the island whaling economy, drastically reducing Nantucket's population from a high of 10,000 down to an eventual low of around 3,500 and, as a result, shrinking sheep grazing island-wide. The culprits were the shoaling up of the mouth of Nantucket Harbor to the point that even the barges that were rigged for ferrying whale ships over the growing sandbar couldn't make it into the harbor themselves; the discovery of crude oil in Titusville, Pennsylvania, quickly sparking the refining of kerosene and effectively ending the need for whale oil; the start of the California gold rush in 1848; and, later, the onset of the Civil War in 1861.

As sheep numbers dropped and their dominance of the island's open spaces waned, the door opened for the next evolutionary, albeit human-assisted, wave of successional plants. Scrub oak, dwarf chestnut oak, black huckleberry and eventually pitch pine moved out of the borders of the pastureland. Suspected of helping this invasion along were plants such as bayberry and sweet fern, which are nitrogen-fixers, meaning that, with the help of symbiotic soil bacteria, they break down nitrogen gas at the molecular level into food for the plants."[16] Although scrub oak does not utilize nitrogen-fixing, the decomposition of vegetation around these shrub-trees, along with its own leaves and other parts, did provide a nutrient source, which gradually built up organic matter on the ground, creating soil that eventually retained water and nutrients. And with bayberry and other shrubs making room for scrub oak, another food-processing method, mycorrhiza, gave the scrub oak a sharp survival edge. Like the symbiotic bacteria, which benefit from the forming of nodules with plant tissue, a mycorrhizal cooperation involves a fungus that helps scrub oak roots gather water, zinc, phosphorus, copper and manganese from the soil. The fungus helps ward off disease and plant-eating animals while it absorbs the food it needs to live.

Lacking a trunk and, instead, wrapped with a huge root collar inches below the soil surface, scrub oak is actually classified as a shrub because of its multiple stems. They grow up from a base that sends out hundreds of quiescent buds when activated by fire, browsing animals or brush-cutting.

If you haven't already, get out to Altar Rock now. From the top of Altar Rock, Folger's Hill or any second-floor deck in Tom Nevers West, you can see a good portion of the dominion of scrub oak on Nantucket that, together with Eastern pitch pine, forms what are also known as barrens. Bring a copy of Dunwiddie's *Nantucket Wildflowers* with you and take your time exploring the moors to learn to identify its rare plants. Notice that there is far more scrub oak than pitch pine, and there is still a good portion of the moors open enough for the rare and endangered plant species to grow. West of Tom Nevers Road, the scrub oak is incredibly dense; except for a few groves of pitch pine, it smothers the landscape. Another excellent observation spot for continuing this lesson in Nantucket plant succession is Quarter Mile Hill. Find it by taking the dirt road opposite Hoicks Hollow Road off of Polpis Road. The unmarked dirt road on the west side of Polpis Road, called Barnard Valley Road, runs into the Eastern Moors. Follow it about 0.7 of a mile in, passing a proper four-way intersection and then a road running north off the right side of this dirt track. By then, you'll see Quarter Mile Hill. From this hill, look south toward the Nantucket Golf Club. Notice the open fields and meadows to the east, but also the varied shrub clusters working their way into the open grassland.

Although the Eastern pitch pine played a successional role, along with scrub oak, in gradually crowding out heathland plants in the eastern portion of the island over time, botanists had long considered it not to be an indigenous tree like the oak. Then Peteet found, in a 2009 core sample from No Bottom Pond, macrofossils that were evidence of Eastern pitch pine growing on Nantucket 6,000 years ago. This discovery was confirmed by Dunwiddie, who found, in a pollen grain core sample, that the Eastern pitch pine was indigenous to Nantucket around 10,000 years ago.[17] Nonetheless, early Nantucketers did reintroduce the two species of pine in the mid- to late 1800s.

The Nantucket Conservation Foundation, in its website description of island habitats, says that, in 1847, Josias Sturgis planted Eastern pitch pine seedlings along Milestone Road to grow a windbreak, especially for Bean Hill. This initial planting spread Eastern pitch pines down most of the length of Milestone Road on both sides, eventually propagated the State Forest between Milestone Road and Polpis Road and west of Lover's Lane, and blanketed much of the Miacomet and Surfside areas and parts of mid-island, with sprinklings in Ram Pasture.

The Japanese black pine, Tiffney and Eveleigh report, found its way to the island in 1895 and then spread to areas including Low Beach in Siasconset, Quidnet, around the western half of the island at the end of Hummock Pond Road and in the vicinity of Moth Ball Way, and near the stone house on Madaket Road overlooking the Head of Hummock Pond. Japanese black pine also spread to certain locations on Tuckernuck from the late 1930s through the 1960s and '70s.

Today, the ocean, roads and developments corral the island's sandplain grasslands and heathlands, keeping them from expanding into other parts of the island. And the prescribed burning and mowing of these lands is preventing the proliferation of invasive, dominant species, at least on land owned by the Nantucket Islands Land Bank, the Nantucket Conservation Foundation and the Massachusetts Audubon Society.

Considered the evil weed by all island conservation organizations, scrub oak stands little chance of running unchecked over the entire island. However, should the burning and mowing cease on these barrens, the NCF's belief is that tall hardwood and coniferous forest trees would, over time, again dominate these parts of the island as they did before people arrived here.[18]

Nantucket is ever an island in flux, and its dry uplands are not the only plant habitats in evolutionary motion. In fact, the changing mosaic of wetland vegetation varies greatly from year to year, even seasonally, due to the vagaries of drenched or drought conditions as influenced by meteorological forces. The sand-gravel-clay relief left behind by the glacier was not, of course, perfectly flat; instead, it was punctuated with a kettle-and-kame topography on the northern and northeastern portions of Nantucket and Tuckernuck, dotted with some kettles and kames on the western portion, plowed into wide, shallow glacial outwash valleys in its southern section, and then pockmarked throughout with random depressions and dells. All of these low spots came to be collectors of water ideal for widely specialized gardens of wetland vegetation depending on soil type and water level. In some, the water table—where groundwater intersects the elevations of some of these depressions—serves as the source of liquid life for coastal plain pond shores around kettle hole ponds such as Almanac, and the Wigwam and Pout Ponds.[19] Plants growing there today are not likely to be the same complement that first sank roots into the soggy soils before and after the glacial presence. Many likely existed on our portion of the coastal plain before the sea level rise sequestered Nantucket in its current position away from the mainland. But they disappeared when the advancing ice sheet brought arctic climate conditions to the area.[20] Those conditions included permafrost, which prevents roots from growing down into the soils. Obviously the wetland plants, many of them less hardy than the larger woody plants such as large shrubs and trees, wouldn't have survived. But as the glacier melted away and the climate continued to warm, wetland plants gradually repopulated their respective ecosystems.

Among the more common kettle hole pond plant species of St. Johnswort, sundews and several sedges, there are some of Nantucket's rarest plants, including two sedges. Again, it's a good bet that these species, and others growing today in and around the island's kettle hole ponds, are not the original aquatic and wetland plants to germinate near these ice-chunk water holes. Because ducks and waterfowl, in general, tend to prefer the open water of ponds and lakes over swamps and bogs that are typically snarled with wetland vegetation, the complement of plants in and on the shores of Nantucket's kettle hole ponds probably changed over time. This process would have depended on the origin of the water birds that dropped into the ponds with plant seeds attached to their feathers, mud plastered to their legs and feet, or passed out of their systems as waste, and thereafter on the adaptability of the plant species.

Others (including the swampy areas of the island and the ponds along the south shore, Hummock, Miacomet, and Long Ponds and the former ponds of Madequecham, Forked Pond and Toupshue Valleys, and the Slough on Tuckernuck's eastern end), were too large to have been pressed into shape by giant ice chunks and, instead, were carved out by glacial melt water or movement of the glacier over the land. Surrounding watersheds flowed into each valley or swamp and so determined their contents. Over the span of hundreds—maybe even thousands—of years, water, always present in these ponds and swamps (unlike kettle hole ponds) has been able to move through these habitats, diluting the acidity of their soils and making them more stable while attracting a wider array of vegetation. By comparison, bogs, including cranberry bogs, usually have acid conditions because they are closed hydrological systems allowing acidic soils to build up.

On the edges and banks of the south shore ponds, including the Slough on Tuckernuck, a wetland trough running north-northeast and south-southeast on the eastern end of the island, reedy species grew into an inland habitat that Dunwiddie calls "freshwater marsh." It is populated by narrow- and wide-leaved cattails, common reeds, water parsnips and woolgrass. Closer to the ocean, some of these ponds, including Long, Squam and Sesachacha Ponds, eventually supported one or a mixture of fresh water, salt and brackish marsh species, including American beach grass, freshwater cordgrass, salt meadow grass and rose mallow.[21] All of these were likely planted by migrating and visiting water birds.

The island's larger, shallower wetlands with clay, silt, gravel and sandy soils beneath them, mostly on the eastern half of Nantucket, became "swamp variations." This is a broad, generalized term Dunwiddie says botanists use to describe several different types of shallow wetlands.[22] They include Squam Swamp and the swampy area on the southerly and easterly fringes of Stump Swamp, Burnt Swamp, Trot's Swamp and the cattail-ridden swampy area immediately southwest of Sesachacha Pond on the south side of Polpis Road.

While the glacier's movement carved out depressions in the land where these future wetlands—called shrub and forested swamps, wet meadows and sphagnum bogs on Nantucket—undoubtedly filled with meltwater as the ice shrank away to the north, their water content was maintained by the soils beneath them, by groundwater levels in their part of the island and by water flowing in from one side and exiting out another. Water from Stump Pond and Swamp flows into the shrub swamp between them and Windswept Cranberry Bog all year long, and in a larger flow during the cranberry harvest in October, when the Nantucket Conservation Foundation's cranberry bog crews use this water to flood the bogs to float the berries off of their plants to be collected. NCF uses Gibbs Pond for the same purpose for Milestone Cranberry Bog.

Clay and silt, and marine and freshwater bog, as well as glacial deposits on the eastern side of the island left behind by the glacier and Glacial Lake Sesachacha, also help slow the draining of water away from the wetlands, allowing swampy areas—including Squam Swamp, Stump Pond and its swamp—to remain wet and stave off the filling in of wetlands by upland vegetation. The movement of water prevents the soils from becoming too acidic. Taking root in the moist medium of shrub swamps were high bush blueberry, winterberry, bayberry, poison ivy, sweet pepperbush and swamp azalea. In forested swamps, which often overlap with shrub swamps, there are red maple, black tupelo and sassafras, ferns and sphagnum moss.

Although some forms will survive intact longer than others, evolution of the island's wetlands began immediately after the glacier gouged out these freshwater vessels and depressions. Since then, all of Nantucket's wetlands, with widely ranging speeds, are gradually, steadily morphing into dry land habitat.[23] The reason is that both wetland and shoreline species' roots catch dead and decomposing plant parts, slowly forming enough soil for upland plant species to move in and take over the pond. As the pond water shallows and its surface area shrinks, this opens the door for sphagnum moss, which survives by holding up to 25 times its weight in water and living on top of the water while dangling its roots into soggy soils developing below. Over time, the presence of sphagnum moss in ponds and wetlands continues the process of drying them out, because the upper stems and branches keep growing, increasing the weight of the plant beneath the surface, which, when denied necessary sunlight, withers, dies and decomposes. Over thousands of years, former ponds and wetlands become vast caches of peat formed under the pressure of an endless growth cycle of sphagnum moss living, dying and breaking down above.[24] This transformation from duck refuge to deer bivouac, however, is dependent on pond and wetland size, depth, underlying soil composition, vegetation in and around, water source and its movement, and annual precipitation.

Want some examples? Kettle ponds that have already been mentioned are the Pout Ponds, which at times are nearly dry, similar to Almanac Pond. The Wigwam Ponds and Jewel Pond are younger in the hidden forest creation process and contain water year-round. An older—or maybe shallower, and therefore possibly older—kettle pond showing signs of becoming one with its upland perimeter is in the eastern moors at the edge of a large field. Find it by taking Barnard Valley Road, opposite Hoicks Hollow Road on Polpis Road, and heading west into the moors. At the first proper four-way intersection, go left (south) and then take the first right. This road eventually runs along the northern slope of this kettle pond, which is easy to access on foot, because there is no dense brush on this side preventing access.

Notice how the vegetation is really growing in toward the center of this pond. Try to visit Jewel and Almanac Ponds and the Pout Ponds beforehand for a good comparison. Also, north across Pout Pond Road from the Pout Ponds is Donut Pond, from which both Dunwiddie and Peteet have extracted core samples. This pond gets its name from being almost entirely consumed by vegetation, which fills in the pond with a narrow moat of water ringing it, forming a donut shape. Kettle ponds are a great living example of plant succession on Nantucket, and we're fortunate to have so many of them in the various stages, from pond to bog to hidden forest. Like the kettles out in the moors and other parts of the island, the swamps, too, are gradually transforming into upland areas, but much more slowly.

The cranberry bogs, Windswept and Milestone, are not evolving, because the NCF maintains them in their current state in order to cultivate cranberries, but they do owe their genesis to a soil-changing evolutionary process that began with an eddy of glacial meltwater. About 19,000 to 20,000 years ago, it spun off to the northwest from the outwash water leaking from the drift and till dam at the south end of Glacial Lake Sesachacha. That backwater's currents seem to have eroded out a depression in the land to form the area where Milestone Cranberry Bog is today. The foundation for Windswept, and probably to a certain extent Milestone, is believed to have been excavated by meltwater cascading off the glacier and plunging down into the head of the outwash plain.

In the depressions that would become cranberry bogs in the mid-1800s, botanists believe, sphagnum moss joined other wetland plants and eventually took hold in the wetlands, helping condition the soil as acidic for the cranberry plants. Like the steady encroachment of upland and wetland plants into kettle ponds that eventually produced a perfect medium for sphagnum moss, the lands of the cranberry bogs also went through a plant successional process before cranberry plants could take root in these areas. Sphagnum moss probably led the way, with its ability to form mats floating on the surface of open water and its roots running down into the soggy soils mingling with roots of other plants.

The Conservation Foundation's description of ponds and bogs on the Habitats page of its website reads: "As Sphagnum accumulates in a bog, acids that are produced during the process of plant decay build up. The thick layers of peat further serve to isolate the surface of the bog from the groundwater and its minerals and nutrients. Most plants cannot tolerate these acidic, nutrient-poor conditions, with the exception of a few species that have developed special survival adaptations."[25] Those that can live amongst the sphagnum moss, subsisting on the bare minimum of nutrient content in the soil, include what the Foundation calls "carnivorous bog plants," such as the pitcher plant. This unusual plant uses nectar, produced by specialized glands, to entice insects into a water chamber amongst its inner leaves and body. Once its prey is in the water cavity, digestive enzymes break the insect down into usable food for the plant. Likewise, the leaves of sundew plants are packing "sticky glandular" hairs capable of snagging insects, as flypaper does, and digesting them as is.

Other plants that rough it in acidic, nutrient-deprived soils include bog rosemary, sheep laurel and leatherleaf, all of which the NCF classifies as woody shrubs that survive by growing energy-efficient evergreen leaves and employing fungi in their root hairs to glean oxygen and nutrients in a manner similar to the mycorrhizal cooperation used by scrub oaks.

After the glacier had shrunk far enough north to allow a suitably warm climate, these wetland plants began to reestablish themselves. They then began their epoch-spanning progression of transforming the wetlands and ponds. The sphagnum moss and the other bog plants processed decomposed vegetation into acidic soils that were on course to produce a perfect foundation for cranberry plants. The cranberry, incidentally, is one of only three native fruit-bearing plants in the U.S.; the others are the Concord grape and the blueberry. Industrious Nantucketers began cranberry cultivation on the island in 1857, and the Milestone Bog was built and planted around 1865.[26] At 234 acres, it was once the world's largest bog until it was segmented by ditches and dikes so that water from Gibbs Pond could be used more efficiently to float the berries for harvesting. Several of the bog workers at Milestone Cranberry, including Fred Maglathlin, built the 105-acre Windswept Cranberry Bog in the early 1900s. Debra A. McManis, in her book, *Town Farms & Country Commons: Farming on Nantucket*, tells how Maglathlin and the other bog builders, to prepare this bog for cranberry plants, removed the peat, the compressed sphagnum moss to be used as heating fuel, and removed other wetland plants and sphagnum moss, as they did for Milestone Cranberry Bog. And in Windswept, they dug out the clay, which is abundant in that part of the island, to reach the porous soils beneath, so that cranberry plant roots would set in the ground, and water percolate through.

In 1937, Maglathlin hired Marland "Red" Rounsville of Cape Cod to work this bog and eventually, Rounsville took it over from Maglathlin. He later sold it to the Foundation, an acquisition that included 205.6 acres of bog, marsh and woodland, on August 19, 1980. Then three of the Foundation's founders, Roy Larsen, Walter Beinecke, Jr. and Arthur Dean, purchased Milestone Cranberry Bog in 1968 from the bog's owner and operator, Nantucket

Cranberries. That purchase included 1,000 acres of bog, heath and outwash plain. Today, NCF runs the bogs itself, operating just 40 acres of Windswept as an organic bog and cultivating 193 of Milestone's 234 acres.

Lest you leave this chapter believing that those who look after Nantucket's wild lands aren't tending to their conservation properties, and are perhaps allowing dominant plant succession to overcome the more delicate, specialized and yet, rarer shrub, grass and flower species, fear not. Diligent conservation measures are employed by the Nantucket Conservation Foundation, the Nantucket Islands Land Bank, the Nantucket Land Council, the Massachusetts Audubon Society, the Madaket Land Trust and the 'Sconset Trust. These include, for some of these nonprofits, regular brush-cutting and prescribed burning, both to control invasive species and to encourage growth of uncommon species; ongoing research; patrol of their properties; and public education.

In addition, there is a higher power watching over Nantucket's special plants: the Massachusetts Natural Heritage and Endangered Species Program, part of the Massachusetts Division of Fisheries and Wildlife, has their back. Yes, humans have manipulated much of Nantucket's habitat since their arrival on the island 8,000 to 11,000 years ago, affording certain plant species ideal growing conditions that would have been otherwise unavailable, had natural succession been allowed to proceed unchecked. But since we have created this special garden, and provided the required conditions for many globally rare and endangered prairie-esque plants and heathland species, we can feel somewhat confident that given the current, local, state and federal environmental protection laws, the prosperity of these plants should continue well into the future.

Sadly though, their prosperity is going to hinge increasingly on the impacts of global warming–induced climate change, which will surely cull some species from the island while enhancing the survivability of those that can adapt to warmer temperatures. This, in turn, is going to affect insect, reptile, amphibian, bird and mammal species in ways we can't even imagine today.

BIRDS—NATURALS AND ACCIDENTALS

Tens of thousands of long-tail ducks spend the colder months of the year wintering in our waters.

Tens . . . of . . . thousands.

Don't believe it? Be out in Madaket any day around three o'clock in the afternoon during the winter, but especially between Thanksgiving and Christmas, and watch the horizon southeast of the island and the sky over the ocean for a loud, steady stream of these birds flying back to Nantucket Sound for the night.

Such daily avian sorties in these staggering numbers are rarely seen anywhere around the globe, except during annual migrations. That long-tail ducks have adopted Nantucket as their winter perch means the ocean's food south of the island is good and plentiful. These black-and-white sea ducks, with their distinctive, elongated tail feathers, live in arctic environs for most of the year, nesting on shallow tundra ponds. They migrate to Nantucket waters for one reason: to feed on shrimp-like crustaceans swarming 30 to 50 miles southeast of Nantucket.[1] These, and other protein-rich sea duck food such as mollusks and small fish, are produced by a combination of ocean currents and the right water temperatures. But the sea ducks, long known also as oldsquaws, have to work for it.

The relatively sheltered geography and sea conditions of Nantucket Sound provide suitable leeside refuge for long-tail ducks, which spend their nights sleeping in massive flotillas, riding the waves in peaceful slumber. Mornings before sunrise find them re-energized for their daily feeding off Nantucket. But a majority of these ducks ignore the Sound's food offerings

Long-tail duck

and fly by the thousands southeast over the western end of the island to feed on the crustacean banquet. Then, in mid-afternoon, they fly back over the sea to the relatively protected waters of the Sound. Witnessing their mass commute, weather permitting, is quite a treat for bird lovers.

Another treat is the seasonal presence of about 16 gull species on the island. During the late fall through early spring, in addition to black-back, herring and laughing gulls, Nantucket birders encounter such species as Bonaparte's, black-headed, little, Icelandic, glaucous and lesser black-back gulls, all feeding on tiny crustaceans and other small food in the surf and waters just off the beach from Sankaty Head down to Low Beach.

Sea birds aren't the only avian show on the island. Inland, prairie-like conditions and the vast grassland habitats of Nantucket, due in unequal parts to the work of island conservation organizations, salt-sodden ocean winds, and the human harvest of timber for boats, houses, fuel, and crop and pastureland, provide a starkly different yet much safer environment for raptors than the mainland. Replete with Northern harriers, red-tail hawks, sharp-shinned hawks, Cooper's hawks, rough-legged hawks, peregrine falcons and kestrels, the relatively exposed, unforested terrain of the island and the amount of conservation land—more than 60 percent of Nantucket—make the island ideal for these soaring and hovering birds of prey.[2]

Once Nantucket lost its connection to the mainland about 6,000 years ago, after glacial meltwater raised the sea level high enough to separate the island from Martha's Vineyard and the mainland, another complement of island birds gained an edge that their mainland counterparts did not have. Ground-nesting water birds, including herring and black-back gulls, great blue herons, and mallard and black ducks, whose eggs are vulnerable to mammal predators on the mainland, are largely spared those losses on

Nantucket. They are threatened only by feral cats, crows, some gulls and the odd errant dog. Ornithologist Dick Veit, a pony-tailed shorebird researcher and biology professor at City University of New York's College of Staten Island who has written scores of ornithological research papers and who performs much of his research on Nantucket, Tuckernuck and Muskeget Islands, knows this from a lifetime of watching the abundant waterfowl and upland species on Tuckernuck. Awarded Nature Conservancy funding from the Orvis clothing company to restore the nearly obliterated nesting roseate and common tern colonies on Muskeget Island from 2000 to 2004, Veit has spent all his summers and early falls on these islands. From his house on the west end of Tuckernuck Island, on land that includes that island's western extremity, Bigelow Point, Veit enjoys a shorebird watcher's dream view of this sandy point jutting out toward Muskeget. The point, coincidentally, is named for Dr. Jacob Bigelow, a Boston doctor who was a frequent upland bird hunter, or gunner, as they were known from the late 1800s into the early part of the last century.

Veit says, "One big advantage [of Nantucket] and the other islands is the fact that there are virtually no mammal predators. There are no skunks, no raccoons, no coyotes, and that makes a huge difference for nesting water birds: gulls, herons, ducks. Things like that would otherwise be killed by those predators. So one of the big advantages is the lack of those predators out there. . . . [P]robably the biggest reason that Muskeget used to be the biggest tern colony in North America is the fact that there weren't any mammals there. It was mixed commons and roseates, and there were some arctic terns as well."

Veit was attempting to restore these two of Muskeget's tern species to healthier levels that might someday approach what ornithologist William Brewster experienced on July 3, 1890, when he logged 20,000 common terns, and some 50,000 more later that summer, including fledged chicks on July 30 and 31. That same year, Brewster counted 100 pairs of roseate terns and no arctic terns. Today, although roseate and common terns nest on Muskeget, pairs of least terns are likely to outnumber both those species.

To understand Nantucket's place in avian natural history, it helps to know its location along the Atlantic Flyway, one of four north/south bird migration routes across North America, which runs along the Eastern Seaboard between the Canadian Maritime Provinces and the Gulf of Mexico, the Caribbean and South America.[3] One must also grasp the predominant randomness of bird species distribution on Nantucket rising from weather conditions; food supplies on the mainland and at sea; the changing global climate; and luck, chance or an alternative system of karma. Other than the few dozen resident bird species found on Nantucket, including several gulls, crows, ducks and smaller species, most birds seen on the island are those that migrate to the island to nest, spend the winter here, stop off for a bite to eat, and rest themselves on the way to some place else. Or they're accidentals, birds blown off course or who have flubbed their navigational waypoints and, lacking enough energy to continue their migration, find the island out of exhausted and starved desperation.

The regularity of the random appearances of avian species out of their range on Nantucket is significant because of the ever-changing variety of these wayward birds. In the summer of 2010, birders spotted an American pelican in the lagoon at Great Point, and that September, Hurricane Earl got credit for detouring several black skimmers over to Nantucket. In 2009, a Siasconset resident reported a black-chinned hummingbird, a western mountain states bird that winters in the Southwest and into Mexico, loitering around his bird feeder for a week or so, and he hosted another one in the fall of 2010. The venerable Nantucket birder, Edith Andrews, found a black rail—a rare, likely accidental bird that resides in coastal areas south of New York—around April Fool's Day in 1978. Glossy ibises turn up at the ocean end of Hummock Pond in springtime, when the pond is almost overflowing the beach, even though their year-round range of the New England coast doesn't usually include Nantucket. Said Andrews:

> The first specimen of a black rail was found on the day before April Fool's Day.... Bruce Bartlett found it. It's in the [Maria Mitchell] collection and it's so rare that I kept it in the house in a cigar box, a cedar cigar box (before they had all the cases for the bird collection). And I kept that because it was a rare bird. Anyway, Mass Audubon didn't believe that I identified it as a black rail, so they sent somebody down to see the bird. We were still living at the field station.... I got my famous box, opened it and of course, there was the black rail. I don't know what they thought I had.

Although there are certainly birds diverted by storms, displaced to Nantucket out of their element and not necessarily on the island's regular roster of species, certain factors predispose rare and unlikely bird species to appear in the vicinity. Nantucket is at the southern edge of the range of many northern species and the northern extremity of quite a few southern species' comfort zones. That results in the presence of some unusual birds, joined by others expanding their ranges, translating into new birds showing up all the time. Carolina wrens, cardinals, turkey vultures and American oystercatchers, to name a few, are all examples of southern species that have found Nantucket's climate and terrain suitable for survival beyond their home ground. As of the end of 2010, the common eider duck population, which typically nests in the Arctic, had grown significantly. And the red-breasted robins that swarm all over the island during fall through early spring are not a resident population, but robins from northern climes whose southern exodus for the winter terminates on Nantucket, Martha's Vineyard and Cape Cod. Along with abundant food supplies, Nantucket enjoys weather conditions strongly influenced by the warm waters of the Gulf Stream, passing through the ocean like a winding river, some 200 to 400 miles south of the island. In addition, Nantucket also possesses widely varied habitats that meet the needs of many different types of birds. Altogether, it is no wonder Nantucket is a magnet for so many odd birds.

Island bird expert Edie Ray, a shorebird monitor for the Nantucket Conservation Foundation (and the town, on occasion) walks her employer's beaches during the nesting seasons of piping plovers, least terns and American oystercatchers, scanning the sands for the birds' arrival in late winter and early spring. She notes the courtship and coupling of these shorebirds, the nests they build, the eggs they lay, the chicks they hatch and fledge, and all details regarding their wellbeing during their time on Nantucket. Her chief concern is the continued safety, the preservation and enhancement of these endangered species. But as her license plate reading "AckBird" belies, her eyes are not so trained on these protected birds as to miss the comings and goings of all other birds on the island. From a feeder right on her bedroom window as a child, to Sunday morning bird walks with Nantucket friends Howard and Carol Crocker and John Sable, to bird walks with the Maria Mitchell Association and lessons in Nantucket bird lore from the grand dame of Nantucket bird knowledge, Edith Andrews, Ray got seriously hooked. And now, when she assesses the island's avian community, particularly those members known as vagrants and accidentals, she has a rule formed through long experience: nothing can be ruled out.

Says Ray with a knowing laugh, "I like to say—it's very corny, but I like to say it—it's like Forrest Gump's box of chocolates: you never know what you're gonna get, and I think that's the exciting thing about birding here. You just never know, and you have to keep your options open. It's like when people call me on the phone and they've seen something, they've mulled on it for a while, they've looked in a couple of bird books and they call me and say, 'I saw a pelican at Great Point.' I never say, 'No, you didn't,' because anything is possible. I say, 'Well, can you describe it? Can you take me to where you saw it? Do you have a picture of it?' You can never say, 'No, you did not see that bird,' because who would have thunk that an African reef heron would have showed up here."

Ray is speaking of birds alive today, even those rarely seen on the islands, that are easily spotted and recorded nowadays because of the ever-soaring popularity of birding. Especially on Nantucket, there exists an enlightened populace and a full complement of year-round and seasonal residents who embrace the conservation movement. Nantucket, with its acreage more than 60 percent preserved as undevelopable open space in perpetuity, imbues a protective nature in many people that is accompanied by a sense of wonder and a drive to learn everything they can about their island wilderness. Hence, the island is crawling with amateur birders toting the latest bird field guides, squinting through pricy binoculars and acting as a loosely organized bird scouting corps that reports unusual and unknown birds to resident experts. Several of the region's leading ornithologists reside on or visit the island regularly. There is a Sunday morning bird walk led by members of the Nantucket Birding Club; the annual Christmas Bird Count on Nantucket and Tuckernuck; numerous bird education courses taught by the Maria Mitchell Association; natural history tours of Great Point, Costaka and the Haulover; and daily marine wildlife charter boat trips during the summer. And there is the Maria Mitchell Association's island bird specimen collection, which contains carefully preserved corpses, called skins, of most of Nantucket's birds for the purposes of documentation and ongoing research.

But for all this present day avifauna observation and historical data, there is very little mainstream historical information dated before the mid-1800s, and thus information is scant regarding what birds first alighted on Nantucket before and after it became an island.

Looking at Saul's Hills, the kettle ponds in the Moors, the ponds along the south shore, soil deposits or the topography of Nantucket, Tuckernuck or Muskeget Islands, geologists were able to say how our islands were formed, and roughly when. Pollen-laced core samples from the bottoms of

Nantucket's ponds and bogs tell botanists, with fair certainty, which plants took root on the island first and also provide credible evidence of the succession of plant growth up through the present day.

But local bird experts and ornithologists don't have these historical research luxuries. They don't have nearly as much hard data on what avian species colonized the coastal landforms that became Nantucket and its outer islands. Not nearly enough birds, with their relatively delicate feathers and hollow bones, just durable enough to last *their* lifetimes, survive the millennia in any recognizably usable form.[4] Researchers cannot discern their age and origin to form a complete record of the evolution of each species unless they're fossilized in sediments or mud, or else flash-frozen in ice. Fortunately, these same bird people say they don't need avian fossils to determine accurately which bird species were living in this area near the end of the Pleistocene Epoch—before the glacier arrived, around 23,000 years ago, to when it retreated 5,000 years later—and on into the Holocene Epoch that began 10,000 years ago and continues today.

With a modicum of exceptions, some evolutionary and others climatological but most caused by human activity, the birds we see today are pretty much the birds that existed on Nantucket when it was just another peak on the coastal plain. Significant bird evolution of the current avifauna families happened long before that, possibly as far back as the Tertiary Period, 1.6 to 66 million years ago.[5]

But ornithologists lack a chronologically complete fossil record, much less written records. They do know Nantucket's complement of birds has been relatively stable since before the glacier arrived; however, they acknowledge that every year, new species have been finding the three islands suitable to their needs; that warm climate birds fled the glacier when it advanced and returned when it retreated; and that arctic birds followed the glacial front as it pulsed southward and northward. But, in estimating what was here, ornithologists rely largely on fluctuations in climate, habitat and food source data through time.

For example, as the glacier slid down into New England and approached where Nantucket and Martha's Vineyard would be, the coastal plain climate cooled and became more arctic the closer the glacier got. Birds that currently live and breed in arctic and tundra habitats during the spring and summer but spend their winters down on and around Nantucket, such as all three species of scoters, long-tail ducks, common eider ducks, razorbills, great auks and even puffins, would likely have been living here in the spring and summer and migrating south of the area for the winter, as long as the cooler temperatures prevailed.[6]

Dr. Tom French thinks so. He is the assistant director for Natural Heritage and Endangered Species at the Massachusetts Division of Fish & Wildlife. Cognizant of the paucity of even Pleistocene mammal records, which consist of large species with big, resilient and hard-to-miss bones such as "mastodon, bison, a probable Pleistocene horse, walrus, hooded seal, and unidentified whales," French cannot find a single Pleistocene bird record from anywhere in the state. But, like Veit, he is fairly certain of what was here along with the ice, while it advanced south and north reacting to the changing climate.

In addition to the sea ducks and other marine birds I've mentioned, at glacier's edge around the Nantucket area, French believes, were most likely ptarmigan, snow buntings, water pipits, longspurs, lesser golden plovers and many other cold climate tundra birds. Birds that existed well south of the glacial ice in spruce and jack pine forests, including many species of warblers common in that type of coniferous habitat, were boreal chickadees, Canada jays, Northern shrikes, crossbills and spruce grouse. These, among many others, likely expanded their range northward, to where Nantucket is today, as the spruce and jack pine moved into the coastal plain.

Most likely missing from Nantucket's early lineup of birds were herring and black-back gulls. For one thing, these are coastal birds, and the coastline, before and during the presence of the glacier, was 75 miles south and southeast of today's Nantucket. In addition, there were no humans in the area, and thus no food: no garbage bins, no garbage dumpsters behind restaurants, no gutted fish on shores and on boat decks, no entrails from captured deer and other wild game, no roadkill, and no Siasconset Dump or Nantucket landfill. In short, there was none of today's sumptuous smorgasbord of food to entice scavengers, including gulls and crows. Says Veit, "If they were there at all, it would have been just a very small number, maybe nesting on some of the islands as they started to form, but they would have been a minor part of the avifauna."

So, except for those birds that succumbed to extinction, a constantly growing inventory of species moving into the area and those few species that shifted north or south of Nantucket, Tuckernuck and Muskeget for survival reasons, it appears that the birds that dwelled in the area during the late Pleistocene and early Holocene Epochs in Massachusetts are, with a few exceptions, the same as those currently living on our islands. Says French:

> At the time of European settlement, there were no European starlings, house sparrows, rock doves (pigeons), house finches, or ring-necked pheasants, which are common today but were all introduced later. The most abundant bird was the passenger pigeon, which was common and widespread in the summer and formed large flocks in the fall, much as starlings and red-winged blackbirds do today. Shorebirds (sandpipers, curlews, plover, etc.) were much more abundant, forming huge flocks on the shore in the spring (May-June), and most especially in the fall (July-September). In the late 1800s, Nantucket was one of the best-known spots to shoot Eskimo curlew and lesser golden plover, and it had probably always been a major concentration area. Gulls were probably not as dominant as they are today, so they would not have been so ubiquitous. Sea ducks and other marine birds were mostly the same common species we see today, but in larger numbers. These would especially include common eider, all three scoters, common and red-throated loons, Northern gannet, double-crested cormorant, common and thick-billed murre, Atlantic puffin, razorbill, and others. However, it would also include great auk and Labrador duck in the winter. We know that the heath hen was on Martha's Vineyard, so it may well have been on Nantucket, too. That probably depended on how much grassy savannah habitat there was on Nantucket. In the fall, the island would have been crawling with neotropical migratory songbirds, such as many species of warblers, vireos and buntings. Their numbers were far greater than they are today. Along with the heavy songbird migration would be a strong coastal flight of the same raptors we see today (Cooper's hawk, sharp-shinned hawk, American kestrel, merlin, peregrine falcon and Northern harriers), but in larger numbers. I think it is difficult for us to realize just how much most of our bird species have declined overall since European settlement.

One such bird, the heath hen, a game bird, the eastern cousin and subspecies of the Midwestern Greater prairie-chicken known also as the pinnated grouse, is suspected of being on Tuckernuck and possibly on Nantucket, but its presence on these islands has never been definitively proven. However, in 1893, 50 Greater prairie-chickens were released on Nantucket in the vicinity of Trot's Swamp. These pinnated grouse expanded their numbers and survived for around two years until a severe winter entirely wiped them out. Over the years, humans with hunting interests in mind also introduced the chukar partridge, the bobwhite quail and the ring-necked pheasant with annual MassWildlife help; the pheasant is the only one known to be surviving today, though in limited numbers.

In this region, the heath hen made its last stand on Martha's Vineyard aided by compassionate residents, a game warden and the state legislature. It was truly a rare bird in that its depleted stocks were coaxed, fawned over, heavily guarded and monitored right down to the very last hen, but continual and expanding human development of its habit and rampant overhunting from European settlement of mainland Massachusetts quickly shrank its numbers below the ability of the population to rebound, spelling extirpation for the heath hen from the mainland just after 1870. In his book, *Hope Is the Thing With Feathers: A Personal Chronicle of Vanished Birds*, Christopher Cokinos expends an entire chapter on the demise of the heath hen, noting:

> As early as 1792, Heath Hens had disappeared from New Hampshire. Humans had extirpated them from the Connecticut River Valley shortly after the War of 1812. By that time, Heath Hens had vanished from mainland Massachusetts. On Long Island—a favored habitat—the bird was gone by the mid-1840s. There is no evidence that the race lasted on the American mainland much beyond 1870, when Heath Hens had been exterminated from Pennsylvania and New Jersey. From then on, the Heath Hen lived only on Martha's Vineyard, where a flock had flown of its own accord at some time in the distant past.

Cognizant of that fact, Martha's Vineyard Game Warden John Howland tried a five-year closed season for the heath hen in 1890. It failed, leaving fewer than 100 heath hens in 1896. Nine years later, after Howland beseeched the state's Fisheries and Game Commission to help with enforcement lest the heath hen die out, the commission initiated another five-year closed season, but this time backed it with a $100 fine for offenders. In 1907, the state established a refuge of 1,600 acres of scrub oak plains for the heath hen on the Vineyard, in West Tisbury, kept the season closed, and began a breeding program that, by 1916, pushed heath hen numbers up to around to 2,000 and saw the birds spread off the refuge and around the island. In 1908, Massachusetts purchased an additional 600 acres for the refuge containing a house and barn that it used as refuge central and then rented 1,000 more acres.

Unfortunately, as Cokinos details in his book, a careless discarding of a match or cigarette butt in West Tisbury caused a fire on May 12, 1916. Fanned by northwest winds gusting to 32 miles per hour, the fire burned 13,000 acres of scrub oak barrens between that Vineyard community and Edgartown that heath hens required for nesting. They were decimated.

Despite continued restoration efforts that included the shooting of several hawk species, including the deadly goshawk and feral cats, plus the poisoning of rats, a practice employed throughout the life of the restoration effort, the heath hen never rebounded beyond the roughly 600 birds on Martha's Vineyard estimated by refuge superintendent Allan Keniston in 1920. The sole remaining fowl in this last bastion of heath hens in the United States, a cock nicknamed Booming Ben, was last seen on the Vineyard on March 11, 1932.

Given that Nantucket and Tuckernuck at one time shared thousands of acres of ideal heath hen habitat with the Vineyard, Veit is confident that this bird in the grouse family was on these two islands at one time. It was common and lived everywhere that there were scrub oak forest and sandplain grassland from New Jersey, up along the southern half of Long Island to Cape Cod and Martha's Vineyard and over to Tuckernuck. Says Veit:

> [When] they declined, mostly from hunting, [among] the last places they were out here . . . certainly would have been on Tuckernuck and Nantucket. I don't think they were ever actually recorded on Nantucket, but before Edith Andrews, there was basically no one there [who monitored birds]. Brewster came over a bit, but he just went out to Muskeget to look at the terns. I have a feeling that there isn't any record, no specimen, but they had to be there. They were everywhere else where that habitat was. Possibly you could argue that the Native Americans wiped them out, but they didn't wipe them out on the Vineyard, so I wouldn't think so.

One bird brought to Nantucket by humans that not only survived but prospered as a feral species is the Guinea hen, the first poultry bird introduced to the United States and one brought along by the first island settlers along with several other fowl species, including chickens, turkeys and geese. Although turkeys are just now finding their way back onto Nantucket via human intervention, with a flock or two having gone feral from their rural home yards sometime before 2010, Guinea hens—those flightless, slate-gray-and-whit pompom-shaped birds with pink, featherless heads and blackboard-scratching voices you see by the roadside sometimes near Chaos Corner on Wauwinet Road, out on Old South Road near Valero & Sons or behind the Naushop subdivision—went "wild" one or two centuries ago. But their popularity surged again during the 20th century, and many island farms mixed them in with chickens, Rhode Island Reds and Rhode Island Whites. The Guinea hens still around today are either feral deserters from modern domestic flocks on the island or domestic flocks that forage outside of their owners' properties.

Guinea hens are considered a delicacy at high-end restaurants but a nuisance on Nantucket. They're part of island heritage, because they were some of the first farm fowl to scratch in barnyard dirt for seeds and insects; however, their numbers seem to have dropped over the years.

Until Paleo-Indians arrived on the portion of the coastal plain destined to become Nantucket, Tuckernuck and Muskeget, climate; food availability; and natural, species-specific predators were all with which birds had to contend. Predators of birds in this area included other birds, such as peregrine falcons, goshawks and American kestrels, and many of the mammals coexisting with avian species at the time, including wolves, coyotes, foxes, skunks, raccoons, opossums, minks and ferrets, which all, along with opportunists such as gulls and crows, prized bird meat and eggs as an essential part of their diets. It wasn't until the Native Americans arrived in this region that birds actually experienced more of a methodical killing impact, for feathers to adorn clothing and headdresses and for food in the form of meat and eggs.

A globally extinct bird believed also to have been a victim of Nantucket's Indians and possibly, at the end, its European settlers—if any of these birds were still left in our area when they arrived—was the great auk. Although explorer Bartholomew Gosnold, who checked out Nantucket in 1602, noted that the great auk was extinct in this area, say Edith V. Folger (before she married J. Clinton Andrews) and Ludlow Griscom in their 1948 book, *The Birds of Nantucket*, the great auk's cousin, the razor-billed auk, was a "regular visitor to the Nantucket Shoals; rarely seen from land, but frequently found dead on the beaches."

New England is known to have been the southernmost edge of the great auk's range, so it is understandable that Gosnold thought them extinct, since it is unlikely that one would spot them from shore or from a ship. Both species were obviously more abundant north of New England, because it took nearly 250 more years—to 1844—for humans to hunt the great auk to extinction for food, fishing bait, and pillow feathers.

Market gunners—commercial bird hunters seeking many different species for food and certain birds for their feathers for millinery uses—did by far the most damage to bird populations living on and migrating through Nantucket. The feathers were incorporated into ladies' hats, hairpins and other fashion adornments. Sometimes, whole birds were crafted into hats.

The downy feathers from such birds as common eiders were also used for making pillows and comforters. During the 1800s, primarily 1850 through the early 1900s, market gunners nationwide shot the passenger pigeon to extinction for its meat as cheap food for slaves and lower-class citizens—almost inconceivable, given the staggering number of these birds at the time. In Cokinos's book, he notes that naturalist Alexander Wilson, author of *American Ornithology*, once saw a flock of passenger pigeons he estimated to be 2.23 million birds flying between Kentucky and Indiana. It was a mile wide and 240 miles long.

These commercial bird hunters did not travel to Nantucket for passenger pigeons because, while this bird was common on the island when it was forested with hardwood trees, Native American and European settlers needed their habitat to live and leveled it long before market gunning became an industry. Losing their hardwood forests, which they shared with the once-abundant ruffed grouse, the pigeons likely left of their own volition (along with the ruffed grouse) and so missed whatever slaughter would have occurred on Nantucket over a hundred years later.

But the lesser golden plover, long-billed curlew, Eskimo curlew (nicknamed the dough bird because when their breast meat was exposed, either by bird shot or by knives, the fat around the meat bulged outward, resembling dough), several tern species and other shorebirds, common eiders and many additional duck species didn't survive. Before the land and wildlife conservation movement gained enough momentum to have a habitat- and species-saving impact in the U.S., it was open season on whatever creature one needed to kill for food or sell for money. This meant, at a minimum, the shorebirds were harvested for meat, common eiders for down, and terns for hat materials.

Shooting birds for sport, food and clothing was nothing new. It was, in fact, an element of survival in rural areas, but this country's obsession with the wholesale harvesting of dozens of avian species peaked during the decades following the American Civil War.[7] Growing transportation infrastructure, advanced weaponry and quickly evolving means of communication reinforced this hunting boom. When all three factors collided with the vast game bird stocks nationwide, a new war erupted in America. Instead of dividing the states, this one polarized the hunting community and the recently hatched conservation movement. It brought the hunger for fashion statements and food directly to bear on what were discovered to be limited numbers of bird species. Although difficult to access at the time, Nantucket played its part in the commercial bird products industry of that era. Of some 30-odd birds preferred by the market, about half were originally found in great numbers on Nantucket during their migratory stopovers.

In its efforts to take stock of the status of game bird populations in the state during the first decades of the 1900s, the Massachusetts State Board of Agriculture produced a book in 1912 entitled, *A History of the Game Birds: Wildfowl and Shore-birds of Massachusetts and Adjacent States*. In it, authors Edward H. Forbush, Willey I. Beecroft and Herbert K. Job detailed the threats facing Massachusetts and its bordering states' bird species. It specifically discussed the condition of each market-gunner species and all the variables leading to their reduction, and then suggested conservation measures. In the table of contents, the authors list grebes, loons, mergansers, river ducks, bay and sea ducks, geese, swans, rails, crakes, gallinules, coots, phalaropes, avocets, stilts, plovers, turnstones, oystercatchers, bobwhites, grouse, pigeons and doves as those under attack, and to which several pages are dedicated in the book.

In the second section of the contents are listed birds that the authors said they believed were either extinct or driven out of Massachusetts and its bordering states: great auk, Labrador duck, Eskimo curlew, passenger pigeon, trumpeter swan, whooping crane, sandhill crane and wild turkey.

Can you identify any of the bird species listed above as those you've seen on Nantucket? George Henry Mackay could. A Boston sportsman born in 1843, Mackay became an ornithologist and wide-ranging bird hunter whose adventures frequently brought him out to Nantucket, where he eventually married Maria Mitchell Starbuck. Unique among gunners of birds, Mackay was an advocate of conservation who would have been right at home in the 21st century as a member of an organization such as Ducks Unlimited, Trout Unlimited or the Nature Conservancy. As it was, he was a member of the American Ornithologists Union and, for several years, a member of its Committee for the Protection of North American Birds. He contributed regularly to the bird journal, *The Auk*, which is still in publication. And he kept an extensive, detailed record in his shooting journal of every day he hunted birds, noting the location, weather, and birds present, whether he shot them or not.

Although Mackay was a gunner for sport, and for dinner, he was most decidedly not a market gunner, shooting only what he needed. But many Nantucketers became commercial bird gunners, especially after the death of the whaling industry and with the growing interest in Nantucket as a seasonal tourist destination. Wrote Griscom and Folger in their book, *The Birds of Nantucket*, "Wealthy sportsmen came to the island to shoot, served by boatmen and guides whose living depended on satisfying the desires of their clientele. They were a hardy and energetic lot who lived in shacks on Muskeget, hunting eiders in midwinter and brant in March. The moors were burned every August to make good feeding grounds for plover and curlew." This intentional burning of Nantucket's coastal heathlands and sandplain grasslands served market gunners and sportsmen well. When all cover was burned down to the earth, the scorched turf attracted game birds such as the lesser golden plover and the Eskimo curlew, because the flames also exposed food for these birds.[8] Although Mackay likely partook of the shooting opportunities created by these controlled burns, he abhorred the practice of market gunning and so spent much more of his island time hunting shorebirds around the ponds and on Tuckernuck and Muskeget. A game bird sportsman at an early age, he quickly evolved into sportsman-conservationist, a rare subspecies of human at that time. He lobbied for game-bird conservation bills at the State House almost entirely on his own.

Said Mackay's friend, fellow ornithologist John C. Phillips, who privately published Mackay's shooting journal in 1929:

> Even after spring shooting of shorebirds was stopped in Massachusetts vast numbers of plover were shipped from the West to eastern markets. But Mackay and a few friends working almost alone were able to accomplish wonders. Arrayed against him, when he appeared for one of his bills at the State House, were the hotel men, market men, cold storage interests, and the advocates of open season on water fowl and shore birds lasting into May. But as he has often pointed out to me, and this is where his position was a strong one, he appeared as a shooter himself, as one who knew birds from every angle—the sporting, the aesthetic, the scientific—so that his suggestions for reforms, brought to bear year after year upon a wholly unsympathetic State Committee of Conservation, finally bore fruit.

Ultimately, Mackay became known as the driving force behind several bird species protection bills signed into state laws. He had a major hand in the enactment of a state law in 1899 prohibiting hunting of birds and any other game on Sundays and was the key lobbyist behind a law enacted for Massachusetts in June 1897 that made it a crime to use Massachusetts songbirds in millinery. While Mackay was shepherding his conservation laws through the state legislative machinery, the nation was already in the mood for bird protection. Up until the early 20th century, Americans engaged in what today would be viewed as a barbaric ritual: an annual hunting event called the Side Hunt. On Christmas Day, bird hunters all over the country would fan out across their respective countrysides and shoot every bird they saw that day regardless of its rarity. Prizes were awarded for the most birds shot, and most of the dead birds were discarded.

Incredulous at what he viewed as the shocking, senseless destruction of bird species, ornithologist Frank M. Chapman, an administrator with the fledgling bird conservation group, the National Audubon Society, and assistant curator of the American Museum of Natural History, quietly fought back with a simple counting of bird species on Christmas. In 1900, Chapman organized and held the first annual of these counts, dubbing it the Christmas Bird Count. That year, 27 birders counted a total of around 18,500 birds in 25 locations around the U.S.; in 2010, the country's 111th count took place, in which 2,215 counts took place and 62,624 people counted more than 61,359,451 birds. Edith and Clinton Andrews and a friend, John Dennis, started Nantucket's in 1955.

During this era when bird conservation began to gain attention, other prominent Americans joined Chapman's cause.[9] On Nantucket, the cousins of the country's first female astronomer founded the Maria Mitchell Association in 1902 to continue Mitchell's astronomical research and generally to study and share the wonders of the island's natural world, the National and Massachusetts Audubon societies were hatched in response to killing of birds for their feathers, and several major bird conservation and protection laws were adopted.

By the time Mackay's laws got onto the books in Massachusetts, the damage to birds visiting Nantucket was already done. The numbers of the once common migratory Eskimo curlew had plummeted, and Mackay saw his last large flock of 250 on August 27, 1877. He was the last to see any of them on Nantucket when he witnessed a flock of eight flying over the west end of the island on August 26, 1897. The long-billed curlew population had met a similar fate a decade earlier when Mackay recorded the last bird shot on Nantucket in 1887. And his other favorite quarry, the golden plover, took a beating by the guns of market-gunners, mainly during the birds' midwestern spring migrations. On August 29, 1863, Mackay witnessed a flock so thick on Nantucket that it blocked out the sunlight and filled the skies. Market-gunners and game bird sportsmen shot some

7,000 to 8,000 birds that day, but the golden plover was nearly hunted to extinction in Massachusetts by 1898. Its numbers have since rebounded.

In his article, "The 1897 Migration of the Golden Plover (*Charadrius dominicus*) and the Eskimo Curlew (*Numenius borealis*) in Massachusetts," in the January 1898 issue of *The Auk*, Mackay noted that no golden plovers or Eskimo curlews had been seen on Nantucket, Tuckernuck and Muskeget through August 22.

> I made inquiries several times in the Boston markets in order to ascertain if any of the above birds had been sent in from the above localities, but could hear of none. Personally, I have not shot any. It is doubtful if over 12 plovers have been taken during the entire season on Nantucket and the adjoining islands, and not an Eskimo curlew.

On the market gunners' impact on the golden plover, Griscom and Folger (Andrews) wrote:

> The moors of Nantucket were the most famous shooting ground for golden plover in America from Audubon's time to about 1890. Its rapid decline during the next decade on the Atlantic Seaboard was principally due to the unremitting professional market gunning during its spring migration in the Great Plains. While Eastern sportsmen loudly complained of this state of affairs, they continued to shoot as many of the remaining birds on the Atlantic Seaboard as they could, until the sport died with the virtual disappearance of the species by 1898.

The sentiments of these two island authors, voiced at the turn of the 20th century, well after market-gunning was all but outlawed, echoed the growing, nationwide din of protests over wanton avian genocide. Game bird hunting on Nantucket today is reduced to just a few dozen, primarily local hunters seeking the various species of ducks, brant and Canadian geese they can shoot for food; however, Andrews and the rest of this birdfriendly island conservation and naturalist community have unfortunately also had to stand by as nearly helpless spectators of the steady, gradual shuffling of birds out of their traditional habitats on the island as developers clear land for new homes and businesses.

Granted, Nantucket is unique: from birds' perspectives in that despite sustaining several major building booms, more than 60 percent of the island's roughly 30,000 acres are preserved as open space, forever providing birds with crucial cover, feeding and nesting habitat. And although Cape Wind Associates did get the green light to build its 130-turbine wind farm in Nantucket Sound, the Massachusetts Audubon Society determined that the wind turbines' threat to birds is negligible. Likewise, habitat for nesting shorebirds remains intact on the island's barrier beaches, in its salt marshes, on its sand spits and on its two outer islands, as long as ocean sea level doesn't rise too quickly.

But unfortunately for some species, island habitat evolution is happening faster than anticipated. Just as certain birds were displaced by the harvesting of the island's original trees for home construction, pastureland and heating fuel by Native Americans and European settlers, shorebirds and beach plant community birds on Coatue are losing theirs right now. The effects of sea level rise are already being felt. Harbor waters during high tides are flowing back into previously dry areas, killing Eastern red cedars, bayberry and other barrier beach cover plants. High marsh cord grass, a typical salt marsh plant, along with sea lavender, is gaining more ground annually as salt water slowly invades the upland of Coatue.

Andrews offers other current instances of avian adaptation on Nantucket:

> Now, I think, for example, the prairie warbler nests on Nantucket. It was more the habitat that the prairie warbler likes before the trees grew up. Now, there [are] so many trees, you have a change in population of different species. Yes, we have the tree birds now; catbirds, towhees, robins. We have freshwater ducks and we have saltwater ducks, and shorebirds that go to the shore—the gulls, of course. People have studied the gulls and ended up finding out that there could be 10 or 12 different species out in 'Sconset.

Andrews also recalls the massive flocks of brant, wild geese that had been the target of market-gunners and game hunters alike for eons on Nantucket, and how a loss of eelgrass habitat in Nantucket Harbor forced the brant to seek greener shallows. Brant eat eelgrass fronds, and because eelgrass grew so abundantly around the aptly named Brant Point up until the 1930s, the brant swarmed all over the area in search of food. But when a blight wiped out that eelgrass, the brant went elsewhere in search of their favorite food.

Blessed with wings, the brant, like most birds, are amazingly adaptable out of necessity, and so they found new feeding waters around the islands. It's what any species does when faced with survival choices, and it's exactly what Ray referred to when she said the unpredictability of seasonal bird distribution on our islands is grounded in a Nantucket reality experienced by few places on earth. The island's location, combined with the uniquely high diversity of habitats for all types of birds, makes Nantucket an attractive way station for destination-driven species moving through the region—and an extraordinarily happy miracle for those blown there by accident. In fact, Nantucket is much more a truck stop than a bedroom community for avian species. It is not considered a year-round species birding hotspot, despite the variety of species that accidentally wind up there.

A brief scan of the 274 birds listed in Griscom and Folger's *The Birds of Nantucket* reveals 13 species classified as "permanent"—residing on the island year-round—while the other 261 carried descriptions such as "regular transient," "rare vagrant," "irregular visitor in the fall," "regular summer visitor," "abundant transient," "casual," "casual straggler," "casual vagrant"—you get the idea: Nantucket has great food and four-star accommodations but is obviously not the place most birds want to set down roots and raise generations of chicks.

Naturally, this wasn't always the case. Prior to the glacier's advance, many of the same birds found on the island today then populated what was a forested inland area dotted with meadows, wetlands and streams 75 miles from the ocean, lacking sea birds Nantucketers are accustomed to today. As the glacier drew closer, arctic and tundra bird species extended their range down around the interface of ice and land. Later, as the climate warmed and the ice melted and receded northward, the arctic species left the region to follow the cold climate. They were replaced by those that were fleeing the cold, and probably others that were testing the boundaries of their northern ranges. This was not a steady repopulation shift but one that ebbed and flowed with the contractions of the glacier as it, too, retreated, advanced a bit more and retreated, repeating its overall erratic melting process as it gradually pulled away. The presence of the Gulf Stream relatively close to the island—much closer during July and August when core gyres spin off the main flow, haphazardly depositing tropical fish and sea turtles into our waters—tempers Nantucket's climate, creating a confluence of northern and southern bird species that find the island more tolerable than the mainland, which doesn't benefit nearly as much from the warmth of the offshore river flowing up from the Gulf of Mexico.

Those birds living and nesting on Nantucket around 6,000 years ago, when the sea level rose high enough to make islands out of Nantucket, Tuckernuck and Muskeget, were by no means the only birds our islands got for their ark because they're . . . well, because they're birds, and as such, can relocate at a whim with greater ease than most other creatures. But island status meant the exclusion of flightless, mostly domesticated birds that wouldn't arrive until European settlers brought them out to the island in 1659. It also guaranteed the colonization, or seasonal use for nesting, of the island's shorelines with multitudes of shorebird species for the various coastal habitats that were developing, as post-glacial marine deposits were gradually building beaches, salt marshes, tidal ponds and inlets, and creeks.

When humans did arrive on the island, the word "conservation," if it was uttered at all, meant only the protection and storage of resources tapped for food, water, shelter, fuel and any other vital life-sustaining commodity. But it most certainly did not apply to preserving bird species just for the sake of their existence on the planet. Hunting them for food and millinery plumage were just normal human activity.

Although state and federal protection laws later ended such bird species decimation, and conservation movements prompted by the founders of the Christmas Bird Count, bird conservation pioneer John James Audubon, *Forest and Stream* editor George Bird Grinnell, ornithologist and bird expert Roger Tory Peterson, and others, have had an enormous beneficial impact, human development of the islands has had an adverse effect on bird populations around Nantucket. One such species is the short-eared owl. A famous resident of the sandplain grasslands, the short-eared owl, many local birders say, vacated Nantucket for Tuckernuck over the last two decades because of encroaching development on the remaining 620.8 acres of sandplain grassland and an increased human presence in this south shore habitat. Christmas Bird Counters on December 30, 2010, saw 15 of them roosting in the dunes in front of East Pond on Tuckernuck Island. They were among the 60 species counted that day on Tuckernuck and in its surrounding waters. Variables responsible for the presence of short-eared owls include proximity to Nantucket, the absence of humans for at least half of the year, and significantly fewer people there during the other half. There are abundant food sources on all three islands, but 15 short-eared owls are certainly a testament to the healthy population of field mice and voles on Tuckernuck, in addition to extremely gradual development and low human population. However, they do require relative solitude away from human activity. Despite ideal habitat existing on Nantucket in its sandplain grasslands, they obviously found Tuckernuck less congested. But many other birds aren't so uppity and can coexist with the rest of Nantucket's inhabitants just fine. The ones practiced in adaptation to their ever-changing, increasingly shrinking island habitats are the birds that tend to thrive on Nantucket, even if some of them still prefer a little bit more privacy.

THE COUNT

Lined up shoulder-to-shoulder across Folger's Marsh at sunset on January 1, 2011, 22 people walked slowly along through the soggy high marsh cord grass, eyes down, scanning the ground in the fading light. Reaching the upland edge of the marsh, they trudged back across the marsh and, not finding their quarry—the reclusive yellow rail—shifted to the western section of the marsh, clambering over a narrow creek and again walking slowly over the marsh grass.

Unfortunately, they flushed no yellow rails that day, the end of the 111th Christmas Bird Count and the 56th annual on Nantucket, but this special event on bird count day almost always rousts one or two yellow rails out of the damp marsh grass habitat where they spend their time walking, feeding and living in happy obscurity. As it was, bird counters logged 127 bird species on Nantucket that year.

They were counting during a time of year—winter—that expert birders like E. Vernon Laux, resident naturalist and property manager at the Linda Loring Nature Foundation, tell their birding friends to visit, because of the diversity of species in residence. In Laux's opinion:

> In the winter, it's fabulous birding because we're surrounded by the relatively warm ocean water, compared to inland. It's really tough for a bird to make it here in the winter, but we still have lots of lingering things that are rare inland or elsewhere, and then . . . there are the waterfowl. Nantucket is surrounded by hundreds of thousands of common eiders, all three species of scoters and then, of course, the long-tailed duck thing. I call it America's Serengeti. For ornithological interest, there is no spectacle anywhere in this country or anywhere on the continent like this. Actually, I like seeing the bats come out of the caves in Texas—there [are] 20 million bats—but I think the long-tailed ducks are more impressive. They come screaming over, there [are] just clouds of them, and they're goin' [he makes duck noises]. I'm always amazed, the people who live here who haven't seen it yet. And then people from away, once they see it. . . . I've had birders from all over the world come and look at it. You know, they're sitting there with their mouths open, going, 'whoooa,' because this doesn't happen anywhere else.

What began as a glacial-wasteland-cum-island, unappealing as an aviary for most species because of extremely cold temperatures, has grown into a multitude of ecosystems and micro-habitats that now accommodate a veritable menagerie of mostly errant birds. Radiant heating from the Gulf Stream moderates the island climate, preventing the temperature extremes of the mainland for most of the year.[10] Water temperature keeps the island, on average, 15 degrees cooler than the mainland during the warmer months and usually several degrees warmer than freezing in the winter. Water quality in the ocean and harbors remains good, but it is degraded in most island water bodies by overuse of fertilizers, road runoff and leaky septic systems. This makes it tough for ospreys to find fish in water bodies on the eastern half of the island. In fact, in the summer of 2010, of the ospreys from the three nests on Nantucket's east side, only one chick survived to fledge. Because the adult ospreys had to fly west out to Hummock and Long Ponds and Madaket Harbor for fish, expending energy to feed themselves along the way and then returning to their nests with food for their chicks, it's likely that the young ospreys didn't get enough fish to survive. By contrast, on the west side of the island, where there were nine nests, two of them failed, but the other seven produced 11 young.

For most birds, however, food sources abound on land, in the form of berries, insects, rodents and other small mammals, roadkill and the dump. There is abundant aquatic and upland vegetation, and in the harbors, ponds and the ocean there are fish, plankton, crustaceans, mollusks and plant life. There are oodles of cover options in fresh and saltwater marshes, scrub oak thickets, urban tree forests, swamps, sand dunes, cedar groves, heathlands and sandplain grasslands, and the predators, apart from other birds, are few. According to Ray:

> Birds that get here aren't inclined to leave, because we basically have a little microclimate here, and packed into this small amount of land there are so many different, sort of mini-habitats on Nantucket. We've got saltwater marshes, we've got freshwater areas, we've got salt ponds, fresh ponds, pine woods, hardwoods—you know, there [are] a lot of meadows; all sorts of different habitats crammed into a tiny little space. So, if you're a bird, almost no matter where you like to live, there's probably something here where you can refuel before you leave—or stay here. On the other hand, if you're a bird, why in the heck would you expend all that energy to fly 30 miles out here to see what's going on? Well . . . to nest or rest and refuel if the island is on the way along a bird's migration route. Many birds, such as the tufted titmouse, don't care to fly over water—that species has yet to establish itself on Nantucket for that very reason—so wind and weather systems play a big part in affecting which birds land on the island and what species establish here. Most birds prefer to fly over land or close to it, and at

night when migrating they remain near food, cover and resting spots, and out sight of predators. The chance that they'll fly out of their way to visit Nantucket for a rest stop is random at best, depending mostly on storms, the eastward movement of the Jet Stream and whether Nantucket is the bird's annual nesting destination or on its route. It is because of these uncertainties that the island has developed fame as a refuge for vagrant birds knocked off their traditional routes or out of their normal habitats.

When a storm or heavy fog forces migrating birds off course well off-shore while they follow the Atlantic Flyway, or causes them to overshoot their intended destinations while migrating down from Canada, or they are sideswiped by the Jet Stream while migrating north or south along one of the U.S.'s three other flyways, birders call this a "fall out."[11] Once these bewildered birds regain their bearings and realize they're over ocean and off-course or beyond their final landing zone, all they want is to strike land, rest and find some food. Many times, Nantucket is the first land they encounter in this region where, unfortunately, they are completely exhausted and easy prey for gulls and peregrine falcons.

Nonetheless, unimpeded, fall migration dynamics bring waxwings and many species of warblers down to Nantucket from the boreal forests of Canada: sea ducks such as the common eider; three species of scoters and long-tail ducks; brant from the arctic areas; the odd tundra swans and snow geese, which used to winter on the island in large numbers a century ago; a member of the puffin family; and razorbills. Then there are Canada geese, which are different from the resident populations, making a distinctively different call. In the spring, nesting shorebirds—including piping plovers, least terns and American oystercatchers—return to Nantucket from warm, southern winter haunts, as do ospreys and many neotropical migratory birds. These include warblers, hummingbirds, gray catbirds, cuckoos, vireos, tanagers, swallows, bobolinks, lesser yellowlegs, and nighthawks.

Although seen on Nantucket in great numbers, shorebirds, including sanderlings, lesser yellowlegs, whimbrels, willets, dunlins, least sandpipers, dowitchers, semipalmated plovers, ruddy turnstones and most other shorebirds finding their way to Nantucket, are not on the island for breeding. They stop only for extended periods during the summer and fall to fatten themselves up for their southerly travels.

Established residential birds on Nantucket include American crows, blue jays, barn owls, black ducks, mallard ducks, Northern harriers, red-tail

Northern harrier

hawks, ring-necked pheasants, woodcocks, Hudsonian curlews, rock doves, American herring and black-backed gulls, short-eared owls, Northern flickers, black-capped chickadees, mockingbirds, starlings and house sparrows. Living on the island permanently, these species actually have it tougher. That's because Nantucket's three islands, its ponds, waters and various sandbars are the only resources available to them. They're not jetting in from elsewhere to spend several weeks or months scarfing down the richest island food and refueling for the rest of their trip down to sunny, warm ports of relaxing winter repose. Like human year-round islanders, they're there for the duration.

During the winters of 2002 through 2005, Nantucket's barn owl population plummeted, leaving just one nesting pair during the winter of 2002–2003, despite roughly 40 owl-nesting boxes provided for shelter by sympathetic humans. During those cold, snowy winters when their small four-legged furry meals were hibernating, it was so cold that the unusually deep cover of snow didn't melt away several days after falling, as it typically does on Nantucket. Instead, the snow hung around, preventing these owls from surprising rodents that needed to stretch their legs and seek out food or the outhouse. Thankfully, since that time, the winters have been comparatively mild, with far less snow and ice cover. Conservation-minded property owners added even more nesting boxes to their properties, and the barn owl population has rebounded. Adults produced 40 young in 2009 and at least 50 in 2010.

The colder weather can be tough on waterfowl, including black and mallard ducks and wintering species, which need open water from which to feed and drink. Consistently cold temperatures can freeze ponds and even the island's harbors. Also, resident birds have, for some years, been forced to compete for seeds and berries with abnormally large numbers of boreal forest species, including white- and red-breasted nuthatches that unexpectedly saturate Nantucket in the late fall and winter months because of the lack of food in the Canadian forests where they live.

Still others have yet to make it out to Nantucket at all, despite the strength of winds and storms that could easily deposit them on our three islands. Two cases in point are the Carolina wren, which lives in dense brush thickets, and the tufted titmouse that likes forests of broadleaf trees. Both are common in these habitats and at feeders all over Cape Cod, Martha's Vineyard and the rest of Massachusetts. Ray says the Carolina wren was seen hopping and flying over bridges over the Cape Cod Canal to get to the Cape because they don't like to fly over the water. Today, they're all over Cape Cod, the Vineyard and Nantucket. Ray recalls the first place they were sighted on the island was near the gatehouse at the end of Wauwinet Road.

The tufted titmouse, which made it over to Cape Cod and the Vineyard, has yet to reestablish itself on the Nantucket Archipelago since the time our three coastal plain plateaus became islands because of that fear. Veit believes the tufted titmouse will most likely make the jump from Martha's Vineyard to Tuckernuck before committing to Nantucket.

Ray also cited the red-bellied woodpecker that is relatively new to Nantucket, and she recalls with excitement the elation she felt when she spotted American oystercatchers on the island. Says she, "To get out of the tweety bird areas and think about gulls, lesser black-back gulls—those numbers have just gone through the roof. I mean, to see one back in the day. . . . I can remember seeing a flock of American oystercatchers west of 40th Pole, [about] seven birds on Eel Point, and I was on the phone, 'Oh my God, I've seen seven, and they were together.' That's a bird that's expanding its range northward too, so there [have] been a lot of birding changes, a lot since I've been here year-round."

Global warming's climatological changes are affecting resident and visitor birds on the outer islands of Massachusetts. Just as the Laurentide ice sheet forced warm weather birds south of our portion of the coastal plain and ushered in arctic avian species, the current warming trend on the planet is going to shake up the bird world on many fronts. Possible examples include some unusual Cape Cod appearances: in Truro, during the week of May 15, 2011, a Cassin's sparrow normally found only in the Southwestern United States, and in Wellfleet, a Eurasian hobby, a falcon-like bird common in Europe that has been seen only once before on Cape Cod. The rise of sea levels will most certainly, over time, submerge part or all of the islands' sand spits, barrier beaches, dune systems, salt marshes and shorelines, smothering habitat used by nesting shorebirds and others stopping off for extended resting and feeding on their seasonal commutes. Unless ample amounts of sandy areas are left high enough above the tides and new shore habitat is created, this is likely to cause these birds to fly elsewhere for food, refuge and breeding terrain. Although Nantucket and Tuckernuck and Muskeget have always been about a month behind the mainland for the springtime budding, leafing and flowering of the many plant species on these islands, some of them are now starting as much as a week earlier than usual, and this trend may expand as the planet continues to heat up.

These changes are bound to shift the reproductive cycles of the insects, fish, reptiles, amphibians and mammals that birds live on by causing extinctions of some and severe population reductions in others, forcing some to depart the islands for warmer or cooler climes and causing many other impacts, including avian diseases and plant succession dynamics that can't yet be predicted. Acidification of the ocean, caused by the absorption of excessive amounts of carbon dioxide, coupled with the consequent loss of habitat beneath the waves, may decrease stocks of fish, plankton and other invertebrates on which seabirds feed.

However, changes in weather patterns, above all, are going to affect the birds we see on the Nantucket Archipelago. Indications are that there will be an overall increase in temperatures over time, with fluctuations from year to year between hot and cold, plus an increase in the number, intensity and varieties of storm systems and a gradual shifting of the seasons. Because Nantucket is one of several ocean outposts, a last filter that snags errant migratories skewed off their courses before they drop, exhausted, into the ocean, stronger, larger storms will increase the numbers of accidentals joining the island's naturals. And it's quite possible that the latter birds, those year-round stalwarts we're accustomed to seeing—crows, herring and black-back gulls, chickadees, blue jays, red-tail hawks, Northern harriers, sparrows, cardinals, Carolina wrens and many others—will begin to shift northward as the island becomes too warm for their survival.

Likewise, southern birds may find their habitats changing to such an intolerable degree that they will expand their ranges to include the outer islands of Southeastern Massachusetts. Because reforestation efforts in Latin America currently can't keep pace with unchecked logging of the rainforest ecosystem, our neotropical migratory songbirds, including the warbler chorus of birds that visits us spring and fall on their way from and to the boreal forests in Canada, may already be shrinking with their habitat.

In the end, however, global warming will not be the undoing of birds on our planet. Rather, avian species, as they've always done, will find a way to adapt and survive as the earth's climate continues to warm the planet in the current interglacial stage in the Holocene Epoch or eventually shift out into a new epoch altogether.

FERAL KINGDOM

Down in the cavernous fieldstone cellar beneath Hinchman House, the Maria Mitchell Association's space for its Natural Science Department and attendant museum, heavy cast-iron pipes snake everywhere, threatening to lobotomize anyone over six feet tall. In the northeast corner of this centuries-old basement are white Formica-faced storage cabinets, and in three wide but thin chrome-handled wooden drawers of these cabinets are the preserved remnants sampling almost all of the mammals found on Nantucket and its two neighboring islands.

An observer of these specimens, which look like shrunken, freeze-dried road kill—fur, whiskers, ears and extremities intact, eyes sealed shut—will notice that only a white-tailed deer, a feral cat, a gray seal and a harbor seal are missing—victims, no doubt, of a space squeeze. In contrast to the skins of 212 bird species reposing in neighboring drawers, there are just 21 mammal species recorded as existing on Nantucket. You can almost count the island's mammals on your fingers and toes.

I know, it's not very exciting. Just a bunch of shrews, voles, rabbits, bats, mice, rats and squirrels. But it's the selection process for these 21 species, less than a third of the roughly 69 mammal species (not counting whales, dolphins and seals) populating the mainland portion of Massachusetts, that ensnares the imagination and reveals much about how the natural world works. Unlike the case with plants and birds, the diversity of Nantucket's mammal population peaked before humans arrived to hunt the creatures, eat their flesh, make clothing out of their hides, and carve tools out of their teeth and bones. It peaked even before Nantucket, Tuckernuck and Muskeget became islands.

Able to range freely on the coastal plain, these species—and likely all the middle mammals and larger ones common in New England today—were once living on the higher parts of the plain that became today's islands. And they probably inhabited the same grounds as the megafauna of those times: mastodons, giant short-faced bears, saber-toothed tigers, ground sloths, mammoths, wild horses, caribou, moose and elk. But when the ocean waters rose, covering the land bridge between our young islands and the mainland, the barn door closed for good on our indigenous complement of animals. Anyway, they were already dodging the arrows and spears of the Native Americans living on the coastal plain. Retreating inland had been an escape option, but when the water rose, there was nowhere to hide but whichever of our three islands they were walking on. Biologists and paleontologists make the reasonable assumption that many of Nantucket's original middle and larger mammals, including white-tailed deer, raccoons, and foxes, were hunted to island extinction, and then later some species, including the deer and four species of rabbits, were reintroduced by humans.

When the islands' zoo became finite space shared with hungry Archaic Indians and, finally, Wampanoags, adaptability became one of the more vital survival credentials. That quality was crucial to making the final roster, and none of Nantucket's mammals exemplifies this more than the Muskeget vole, the only endemic species remaining in Massachusetts today. This vole, originally identified as a beach mouse, was once a simple meadow vole, of which there are likely tens of thousands on Nantucket and Tuckernuck, and millions on the mainland. Formerly part of the population of its mainland Southern New England cousin, the meadow vole, the seven-inch Muskeget vole became physically and genetically isolated from its continental relatives when the islands were formed. Since then, Muskeget's favorite rodent has adapted to its isolated surroundings, learning to eat beach grass and producing fewer progeny, but still enough to sustain a fairly level population.

It's about the size of a stunted bratwurst, covered in short, coarse pale blonde hair with a diminutive snout and a stubby tail. When it was permanently marooned on Muskeget it had one choice, really: eat beach grass or die. The short-tailed shrew and the white-footed mouse, the only other mammals known to coexist with this vole on Muskeget, have a comparatively sumptuous menu at their avail: mice, insects, snails and worms for the shrew, and seeds, berries, invertebrates such as insects and worms,

Muskeget vole

and probably tidal sea creatures, for the mouse. Dr. Thomas M. Brewer, an ornithologist, first found this vole on Muskeget in 1842, and it is for him that *Microtus breweri,* is named. Examining Dr. Brewer's discovery, S. F. Baird identified it as a separate species in 1857. Brewer and Baird determined that the stems of American beach grass alone were nourishing enough to sustain generation after generation of this former island meadow vole.

Subsisting on this Nantucket dune turf and ratcheting down its breeding capacity to no more young than the island's limited resources could sustain, four or five offspring per litter, the Muskeget vole still exists on its 292-acre namesake island. Excerpted from their paper, "Microtus breweri," published June 28, 1978, by *The American Journal of Mammalogists,* Robert H. Tamarin and Thomas H. Kunz reason that, "due to glacial buildup and erosion, Muskeget has moved eastwardly about 1.6 km (one mile) in the last 200 years. The island separated from its neighbors as recently as perhaps 2,000 to 3,000 years ago. In this time the taxonomic distinction of *Microtus breweri* has developed...."

If you should find yourself on this barren, treeless atoll of poison ivy, Rosa rugosa, bayberry and, of course, beach grass, it should be fairly easy to find signs of the vole. Look under pieces of scrap plywood near the two structures on this island and in dense beach grass for narrow tunnels through the vegetation and little piles of two-inch sections of beach grass stems. Their nests can sometime be found at the base of goldenrod plants.[1] The Muskeget vole eats the newly exposed bases of beach grass stalks to the exclusion of almost all other food. It sometimes buries caches of two-inch sections of the stalks beneath the sand to keep them fresh through the winter.

The vole's survival skills may not have proven mighty enough to deflect the onslaught of the sizable feral cat population flourishing on the island beginning around 1889.

In his paper, "The Beach Mouse of Muskeget Island," published in the *Proceedings of the Boston Society of Natural History*, 1896, Gerrit S. Miller, Jr., reported that, after the Muskeget Humane Society Lifesaving station burned down in 1889, gull and tern colony warden John Sandsbury, whose relatives began running the lifesaving station in 1883 and who had intimate knowledge of the mouse and vole populations on the island, said he could find no more evidence of the existence of this vole at the time, and that feral cats must have hunted it to extinction by 1891. However, there was a fairly healthy population of Muskeget voles on nearby Southwest Point Island and Adam's Island. Neither island had cats. In 1893, Miller, with the help of Outram Bangs and Charles Batchelder, collected 26 Muskeget voles from Southwest Point Island and reintroduced them to Muskeget. Miller believed, and some biologists agreed, that the isolation of those voles on these temporary islands, which no longer exist, significantly aided in their evolution from meadow vole to the distinct species of Muskeget vole.

Dr. Tom French, assistant director of the Massachusetts Division of Fisheries and Wildlife's Natural Heritage & Endangered Species Program, is not so sure. French thinks that a natural cycle of population boom-and-crash is the more likely explanation for Sandsbury's perceived disappearance of the vole on Muskeget.

Postulates French:

> The story, as it goes from the original naturalist [who discovered this vole] is that voles also have these population cycles like rabbits do. They get into huge numbers, then they crash. It happens about every four or five years in some areas. And so the story was that the population had crashed and that all of the voles were gone from the main island.
>
> We assume that we can take that information at face value. At least the part about them reintroducing the voles is probably correct. Whether or not they were actually gone from the island is a bit of debate because as I say, in these periods of crash, be it from natural population crashes or facilitated by cats or whatever, they could be virtually impossible to find, but if there [are] still some there, then they'll boom in three more years, and you'll say, 'Where the hell did they come from?'

Such is the current state of the Muskeget vole. It lives in just one place on the planet, and its existence is reassured as long as Muskeget remains an island. However, its very status as a distinct species could be its downfall in terms of notoriety and protection. Not every mammal biologist believes in the authenticity of Baird's designation of this vole as a separate species, or even as a subspecies of the meadow vole. In fact, the official belief of the Massachusetts Division of Fisheries and Wildlife's Natural Heritage & Endangered Species Program is that the Muskeget vole is neither. On Brewer's discovery and Baird's subsequent separate species determination, Tamarin and Kunz argue that the Muskeget vole, to which biologists refer as the beach vole or beach mouse, is bigger than the meadow vole, with a larger skull that is longer and narrower, and that it has fewer numbers of closed triangles on its rear upper molars, as well as coarser, paler fur and a blaze-like white patch of fur typically found on its forehead.[2] And while the federal government regards the Muskeget vole as a separate species—its presence was a major basis for the National Park Service's designation of Muskeget Island as a National Natural Landmark in April 1980—French and MassWildlife still officially question its heritage and do not list the Muskeget vole as its own species. Says French:

> Certainly it's true that the population of voles on Muskeget tends to be paler and some people think it has some level of uniqueness. Currently, it is recognized as a full species: the beach vole, *Microtus breweri*. A lot of people doubt that it deserves full species recognition, that it's really only a subspecies, and a lot of people don't think it deserves either one.
>
> Our agency over the years has taken the position that it might be a subspecies, [but] that it is not, from our point of view, worthy of full species recognition and probably doesn't deserve subspecies recognition, but that's an unsettled debate in science.

That the feral cat element on Muskeget had such an impact on just one species is a case study with implications for their effect on the big island. No one today can put a number on the population of feral cats on Nantucket and Tuckernuck, but conservation professionals working in the field say that signs of feral cat presence are everywhere they are working and that the cats have an untold impact on the songbird and nesting shorebird populations.

These cats are a significant island reality, and they're invisible in the wild because, as numerous as they are, stealth is their most vital skill. But they can't hide downtown. In fact, if you visit the sidewalk in front of 16 Main Street on Nantucket, you will find, laid into the bricks, a gravestone for Willie, Nantucket's most famous feral cat, who died in the late 1990s. While in Nantucket Town, keep an eye out for cats darting here and there, zipping across streets, down sidewalks and into and out of alleyways. For those intrepid homeless cats, which know where to be at the opportune times of the day, town is a great place to live, because of the amount of available food left in dumpsters behind restaurants, in trash cans along streets, and down on the wharves where fishing vessels tie up. That's not to mention the rat population downtown, nor the thousands of small birds scavenging for food scraps. The area is replete with sheltered catnap spots, and some sympathetic islanders provide specially built cathouses for shelter, much to the chagrin of Nantucket Cat Trap's feral cat neutering program efforts.

The Nantucket Conservation Foundation's Karen Beattie spends much of her spring and summer out on the Foundation's 8,848 acres, monitoring and protecting nesting piping plovers, least terns and American oystercatchers. She sees signs of feral cat activity—tracks, scat and dead birds left whole for play—everywhere she is working. But she finds them concentrated mostly in the southwest part of the island:

> We have a lot of feral cats—way more than I think people realize. I don't think anybody has any idea, but everywhere I go, on all of our properties, I see cat signs. When they're in the Middle Moors, in the middle of nowhere, you know that they're eating something that they shouldn't be eating. The [area] I see them the most is Ram Pasture in Sanford Farm and Head of the Plains, and I think it's because the dump is so close by. They have pretty big home ranges, but that's where I see the most concentrated cat scat. But they're on Coatue; they're on First Point.

Feral cats are also in the Coskata Woods and at the old 'Sconset dump, as well as all over downtown Nantucket. There are a scant few "wild" dogs, whose numbers don't even begin to approach those of the feral cats. Dogs aren't nearly as resourceful as cats are at catching and eating birds and rodents to make it on their own for very long. Feral cats are the scourge of Nantucket and Tuckernuck's songbirds and a very real threat to rare, endangered, threatened and protected species, such as piping plovers and least terns. They put a serious dent in those populations. But they are, as Beattie grudgingly admits, a necessary evil in the chain of life out in the wilds of our islands. They fill a void that coyotes, which don't so far exist on any of our three islands, would certainly crowd into if they were present.

Beattie continues:

> Cats really do serve that niche that's missing here [among middle mammals]. . . . They've been here for a while, and it's possible, if you could wave your magic wand and make them all go away, you might have a

really big rat problem. It's an interesting thing to think about . . . you have this predator that's non-native, but it's filling the role that the coyote would if it [were] here, so you can't just [remove feral cats as a factor] and expect everything to get better, because it's all connected. And rats are a big problem, too—another non-native mammal.

A coyote population on Nantucket might please many of those suffering from tick-borne diseases, because coyotes would cull the deer herd on the island, as well as the feral cats. But then this would be one non-native species eating another.

As for today's human population, Nantucket has been a challenging place for mammals to reach and remain, depending on one's survival skills. Ponder the white-tailed deer. The species was well established on coastal plain Nantucket before the ocean rose, and it remained for a time on the island after Nantucket was separated from the mainland. But it was not wily enough to elude hungry Indians and sheep farmers, and deer temporarily vanished from Nantucket and Tuckernuck until the early 1920s. When reintroduced, with moderate help from state wildlife management laws, including annual hunting seasons, they turned out to be sufficiently prolific and adept at survival—and even prospered.

Consider also the river otter: an established mainland species for sure, with strong enough swimming skills to make it over to the Elizabeth Islands and Martha's Vineyard, where moderate numbers exist today. But river otters are not found on Nantucket today, despite confirmed evidence of their temporary presence at Hummock and Sesachacha ponds and in Madequecham Valley in 2008. Or consider the New England cottontail rabbit. It is a rodent species of great procreative abilities. Yet once Nantucket became an island, despite what must have been staggering numbers of these rabbits, the population could not ultimately withstand the pressures of its adversaries and new habitat limitations. It was first hunted by humans for several thousand years and then crowded out by Eastern cottontails, a species that had been introduced to Nantucket by islanders near the end of the 19th century. The Eastern cottontail rabbit, along with the New England, the jack and the snowshoe, made the cut into those drawers in the Hinchman House basement because indigenous purity isn't the criterion of those who track the biodiversity of these outer islands. Mere existence on our shores, current or past, qualifies a creature for study as part of the larger Nantucket natural world.

If we were to use the concept of a food chain to describe the mammalian species from the beginning of the Nantucket Archipelago's time to now, at the top of this list would be two giant beasts associated with the cold weather that prevailed on the emerged Continental Shelf until around 10,000 years ago: mastodons and woolly mammoths. When the Laurentide ice sheet reached as far south as it would go around 21,000 years ago, the coastal plain south and east of the glacier's reach had a varied pecking order, at the top of which stood these two elephantine cousins. We know this because of two bits of nearly irrefutable fossil evidence found on the ocean floor and on Nantucket itself.

Part of this former coastal plain included the exposed outer lands of the once-dry Georges Bank, unbroken from its northeastern-reaching peninsula, which stretched halfway up into the Gulf of Maine, continuing to follow the edge of the continental shelf down the length of the Eastern Seaboard. And the other half of the coastal plain was an archipelago of giant coastal plain islands, now submerged, known today as Emerald Bank, Banquereau Bank, Stellwagen Bank—now a national marine sanctuary—and the Grand Banks off of Newfoundland, all created by glaciers that, before the incursion of the Laurentide ice sheet, harrowed deep channels into the coastal plain, breaking up this part of it into islands.

Commercial fishing trawlers working these fish-rich submerged portions of the coastal plain occasionally drag up fossils of mastodon and mammoth teeth, crucial bits of evidence confirming the presence of the largest of mammals roaming the coastal plain in the vicinity of Nantucket. As detailed in E. C. Pielou's *After the Ice Age: The Return of Life to Glaciated North America*, these relatives of today's elephants dined on several species of evergreen trees, which also grew in the area and for which there is fossilized pollen grain evidence in core samples taken from Tawpawshaw Bog, and Donut and No-Bottom ponds on Nantucket, as I discussed in the fourth chapter. But the teeth say it all.[3] According to Pielou, "This proves, first, that the animals were there when the bank was dry land; second, that the climate must have been suitable for them; and third, that the supply of plant food was adequate."

Paleontologists and geologists believe that mastodons and mammoths were joined by other, smaller mammals that would have lived in the region of today's offshore islands, but south of the glacial edge. These include white-tailed deer, bison, elk, caribou, moose, musk ox, wolves, coyotes and several bear species. Joining these far-ranging big mammals were most likely the middle mammals. These were more apt to stay within a few miles of their nests and burrows, which is why Nantucket seems to have more of the smaller mammals than the larger- to medium-size ones that would have been roaming a wider area at the time the waters rose and contained them on Nantucket or Muskeget or Martha's Vineyard.

About the time the first Native Americans, Paleo-Indians, are thought to have arrived in the Cape and Islands region, some 35 to 40 species of animals disappeared in one mass extinction south of the Laurentide ice sheet's glacial edge. Pielou posits that some of the mammal species that went extinct during this period were the dire wolf, five species of Pleistocene horses, the Shasta ground sloth, giant beaver, camels, llamas, two species of deer, two of pronghorn, stag-moose, shrub-oxen, woodland muskoxen, mastodons and mammoths.

Although there are several theories about what killed so many mammal species all at once, none of them has been proven. One guess is that they were hunted to extinction by prehistoric humans, possibly the Paleo-Indians of the Lithic Period who were dubbed the Clovis people, after they were identified through a site of artifacts (including the remains of mammoths) discovered in the early 1930s near Clovis, New Mexico. Species like the mammoth originated in North America and were unprepared for the incursion of humans across the land bridge of Berangia (in the area of today's Bering Strait). Those that did not adapt to these new hunters were wiped out.

Some paleontologists favor environmental causes for the mass extinctions. These mammals, including the giant beaver and the stag-moose, might have been starved out of existence as they lost first the spruce, and later pines, as their primary food sources. Another theory is that an ice-free alley between the Laurentide and Cordilleran ice sheets opened wide enough to send frigid air southward, eventually killing these mammals. Yet one more conjecture is that, at the end of the Pleistocene Epoch, summer got hotter and winter colder; more rain, snow and ice fell in different seasons and then much less precipitation, all making it tough for some mammal species to procreate and for their newborn to survive. Without a doubt, the rising sea levels that inundated the Georges Bank around 4,000 years ago aided mammalian extinctions in our part of the coastal plain.

Even after these mass extinctions, whatever their cause, Nantucket had many more mammals scurrying around its lands before it was broken up into three islands. Connection to the rest of the continent meant that mammal species moved about as it suited them, dependent on their breeding, food and cover needs. Until 8,000 to 11,000 years ago, humans weren't on the scene, so the natural top-down, survival-of-the-fittest predatory order prevailed with mammoths and mastodons until Native Americans arrived. With Nantucket's landmass just another quadrant of the coastal plain, there must have been plenty to eat, a large dating pool and lots of den development sites to choose from.

As an informed guess, Beattie believes random selection decided the mammal species for Nantucket's islands at the time the temporary land bridges, which were used by various species to move about the territory, became too deeply submerged, even on an ebb tide, to allow daily passage of mammalian commuters.

Says Beattie, "I think that all of the species that had very small home ranges that are far more numerous, like rabbits and mice, they were definitely here, but [for] some of the bigger mammals, like wolves and maybe even foxes, that have big home ranges and defend them, it could've just been a matter of chance that, as the sea level was rising, only a couple of those individuals were isolated."

Beattie's hypothesis jibes pretty closely with French's analysis of the Muskeget vole. The two biologists also agree on a nearby, present-day example: how the highly dynamic barrier beach connection between Monomoy Island and Chatham, at the elbow of Cape Cod, impacts mammal populations on Monomoy. This relationship illustrates how our islands' dwindling connectivity with Martha's Vineyard and the mainland, 3,000 to 6,000 years ago, affected mammalian behavior and distribution at that time.

When whole, South Monomoy Island connects to North Monomoy Island and, together, they merge with South Beach and connect to the mainland at Chatham. Like the submerging and reappearing connections that likely existed between Great Point and Cape Cod, and definitely between Nantucket's west end with Tuckernuck, Muskeget and Martha's Vineyard to the mainland as sea level gradually rose thousands of years ago, periodically, the ocean blows through the narrowest sections of this present-day land bridge, temporarily disconnecting Monomoy Island from the mainland. When possible, mammals of various sizes walk or swim out to the low vegetation of the southernmost end of Monomoy Island, seeking food (mainly rodents and the eggs of nesting shorebirds and the birds themselves) and refuge from the human-congested mainland; there, they join the permanent residents of Monomoy Island, including the white-footed mouse, the meadow jumping mouse and the Massachusetts shrew, as well as the larger species of white-tailed deer, muskrats and, occasionally, river otters, all of which are incredibly strong swimmers.[4] French says that, between 2006 and 2011, when this southern end of Monomoy reconnected with the barrier beach extending up to the elbow of Cape Cod, raccoons, possums and foxes immediately traveled south and joined the permanent residents of Monomoy Island. And for the first time in recorded history, coyotes—which MassWildlife documented as arriving on the Cape in the 1970s by walking over Cape Cod Canal bridges—expanded their range down onto the lower end of Monomoy Island.

Given the ease with which coyotes and other mammals have found their way to Monomoy by swimming or walking, one can extrapolate that travel among the connected, or nearly connected, islands of the Nantucket Archipelago, Martha's Vineyard and the mainland was surely a routine necessity for Nantucket's mammal species, which utilized this route until they could no longer do so.[5] This included humans: Tiffney, in his paper, "Sea Level Rise, Coastal Retreat and the Demise of Nantucket Island, Massachusetts," offers that, as recently as 3,000 years ago, with sea level approximately eight feet lower than today, the shallower waters "would have still provided a number of small islands like stepping stones for Indians commuting to and from the mainland."

With Native Americans able to move between the islands and the mainland, it's highly plausible that Nantucket's mammal population would have been able to do the same thing, at least until the swimming/wading distance became too great for their abilities and needs. Their last land-bridge travel would have been among Nantucket, Tuckernuck and Muskeget, because Smith's Point grew well westward, beyond Tuckernuck and Muskeget Islands, as recently as 1700 through 1872, and the same erosion/accretion process connecting and separating Monomoy Island alternately built and interrupted the connection between Nantucket and Tuckernuck. Once the islands' mammals lost their inter-island and mainland passage privileges, unless they opted for long-distance swimming, their fates were sealed for the time being: adapt and prosper or be eaten by humans.

With no way off of the islands now surrounded by seawater too deep and too wide to traverse, the mammals could not escape the Native American population. The Paleo-Indians had arrived probably as early as 11,000 to as late as 8,000 years ago, and certainly their descendents, the Early Archaic and Late Archaic Indians, witnessed the genesis of these three continental islands as the sea level rose around them. Now their food, in addition to what they could grow in the ground, dig from the shoreline and catch from ponds, inlets and the ocean, was set.

Nantucket's Native Americans, specifically the Wampanoags—once numbering as many as 3,400 but around 1,500 when Thomas Macy and the other original settlers arrived in 1659—cleared island forest and brush lands to build their wetus and plant crops; thus, it's likely that the island's bigger game, namely the white-tailed deer and the New England cottontail rabbit, lost much of their habitat to human development while being hunted by the Indians, and by European settlers after 1659.

As French notes:

> The islands have an incredible history of use. For some of [the mammals], the habitat may have changed and they just didn't do well, and then you get a severe winter periodically . . . and they just disappear. But there was a period after settlement when those islands were pretty well cleared of trees and there were sheep from one end to the other, and people actively didn't like predators, and so not only did they disappear from the islands, but just think of the species that completely disappeared from all of Massachusetts. They would include, first of all, the mountain lion and the wolf, but moose, bear, fisher, beaver, turkey, [and nearly] our deer, but not quite. Probably our bobcat, but we don't have good records of that. So all those things were gone from the entire state, and that was just because of habitat change, because of deforestation and persecution, so to get wiped off the island is no big surprise whatsoever for those things. There are a whole lot of things that depend on this predator-free environment.

ALL THOSE RABBITS

Nantucketers all know the island has an abundance of one mammal: the rabbit. They are seen nibbling on lawn grass, in vegetable gardens and in flower beds, and their mangled corpses are found on the island's roads, road kills that feed the island's healthy population of American crows. But few islanders know that there were once four species of rabbits hopping around the Grey Lady's underbrush, though now only three remain. One is vastly dominant, another is occasionally encountered and the other is scarcely seen by humans, if it's still present at all.

Once the prevailing species on the coastal plain hills that preceded the islands, the New England cottontail, Nantucket's only indigenous rabbit, could not be found on these islands during 2011. At that time, the Nantucket Conservation Foundation set traps on its properties across Nantucket in an attempt to determine if the New England cottontail rabbit still existed on the island.

This was the original Nantucket bunny, but once its hometown became an island, this species was handicapped by its very specialized habitat needs. It prefers dense, early, successional shrublands—low, thick and tangled shrub habitat that are the first plants to replace grasslands or to grow after damage by wildfire or hurricanes, including bayberry, black huckleberry, sweet pepper bush, arrowwood and pasture rose, and invasive species such as honeysuckle bush, autumn olive and multiflora rose—to hide among and dine on. These habitats exist at Sanford Farm; in the northern part of Ram Pasture; at the UMass Field Station; in Pocomo, Quaise, and Quidnet; and possibly in the scrub oak shrublands of the Middle Moors.

This is what's left of the once-lavish habitat for the New England cottontail after early human development, including hunters, began encroaching on it. The Nantucket rabbit became a threatened species millennia before such conservation designations existed. If the Native American and European settlers didn't displace it by habitat removal and by hunting it nearly to extinction by the early 1900s, the human introduction of a different species, the Eastern cottontail rabbit, most certainly helped thin it out significantly. Possible earlier competition from jackrabbits and snowshoe hares would have been limited, as these two species may have both been on Nantucket and Tuckernuck islands naturally prior to the separation from the mainland and the arrival of Native Americans; but by the early 1900s, only the New England cottontail rabbit and snowshoe hare remained.

From MassWildlife's records, French knows that Massachusetts introduced 16,000 Eastern cottontail rabbits all over the state between 1924 and 1941, but that it gave Nantucket its share sometime probably just before the turn of the century. When they arrived, the Eastern cottontails began crowding out the New England cottontails, likely outcompeting them because their habitat needs are not nearly as restrictive as the New England cottontails'.[6] The European rabbit, present on Martha's Vineyard and the Boston Harbor islands, has never been found on Nantucket.

As for the jackrabbit, a rabbit species generally found west of the Mississippi River, a group of Nantucketers may have been responsible for reintroducing this rabbit to the island for sporting reasons in the 1920s. In the October 20, 2004, installment of the *Nantucket Independent*'s historic structures series, "Under the Eaves," featuring Tashama Farm, Nantucket historian Bob Mooney recounted that, in 1926, a member of the Nantucket Hunt Club, William V. Justice of Philadelphia, Pennsylvania, launched jackrabbit hunting on Nantucket by introducing the species to the island, bringing hounds up from Virginia and forming a hunt club called the Nantucket Harriers. Nantucketer Robert "Pit" Grimes, whose grandfather, George E. Grimes, was the last to own and run Tashama Farm as a working dairy and vegetable farm, elaborated that the hunt club originally proposed to import foxes, but the town felt that the foxes would become a threat to the livelihood of island poultry farmers. The club then favored jackrabbits because they don't run in circles but rather run straight away from their predators—in this hunt's case, heading for the south shore beaches when released between Tom Nevers and Miacomet. Nantucketers and the state continued releasing various rabbit species on the island through 1977, including the black-tailed jackrabbit first released on the island in 1889.[7] The snowshoe hare, also reintroduced several times, survives today in very limited numbers and is only occasionally seen. Falconer Chris Bonelli's red-tailed hawk, Artemis, bagged a snowshoe hare between Tom Nevers and the airport on January 11, 2011.

DEER

Four years before the Nantucket Hunt Club brought jackrabbits to Nantucket, in 1922, another major mammal was reintroduced to Nantucket. According to an article in the August 19, 1935, edition of the *Boston Herald*, fishermen aboard the vessel *Antonia*, returning from a day's fishing southwest of Nantucket on June 3, 1922, pulled a male white-tailed deer out of Muskeget Channel ten miles from Madaket, between the island and Martha's Vineyard. The fishermen secured the large buck with rope, and when they got to Nantucket Harbor, islanders drove the deer out to Siasconset and released it. When the Nantucket Hunt Club introduced the jackrabbits in 1926, summer resident Breckenridge Long, U.S. Ambassador to Italy, bought two does in Michigan, and transported them to Nantucket in February of that year, releasing them into the island wild at the second mile marker on the Milestone Road.

Although Massachusetts initiated its statewide deer hunting season in 1910, Nantucket following with its own from 1912 through 1929, deer were presumed to be extirpated from Nantucket until the fishermen of the *Antonia* and Long reintroduced them to the island, so the need for a deer season well into the 1920s is puzzling. Even more curious is the fact that Nantucket suspended deer hunting from 1930 to 1935. Eventually though, the three deer became 280 and a nuisance to island farmers. By the mid-1930s, the town and the state were compensating Nantucket farmers for crops lost to deer browsing. In 1934, the state paid a total of $1,100 to

White-tailed deer

island farmers whose claims were more than $20 worth of damage to their crops. The town covered sums up to that amount.

To alleviate deer damage to farmers' crops, it appears from the Boston Herald story that the state's Division of Fish and Game had ordered a special one-week deer season, beginning February 11, 1935, during which 84 deer were taken. However, as happens still today during deer season, that special hunt so angered islanders that, after a day and a half of hunting, islanders' telegraphed and telephoned complaints flooded the office of then–Massachusetts Governor James Michael Curley, including a telegram from the Board of Selectmen complaining about not being notified of this hunt by the Division of Fish and Game. Curley quickly responded to this outcry over the special hunt and ordered Raymond J. Kenny, the director of the Division of Fish and Game, to end this hunt on February 12, 1935. Later that month, the town held its annual Town Meeting, at which the Nantucket Sportsmen's

Club sponsored a home rule petition proposing a three-day open season on white-tailed deer to further reduce the size of the herd and the financial damage to island farmers' crops. That action failed on the Town Meeting floor. Nevertheless, reacting to what most certainly was a high population of deer at the time, to combat browsing of their crops by the deer, island farmers raised enough of a furor for deer hunting that Nantucket rejoined the statewide, two-week season protocol in December 1936.

Today, deer-hunting season begins with archery season in mid-October, continues with shotgun season starting the Monday after Thanksgiving, and concludes at the end of December with the close of the primitive firearms season.

CAME THE SQUIRRELS

Aside from hunters crashing through the scrub oak during the fall, Nantucket's white-tailed deer pretty much have the island wilderness areas to themselves. They might see the odd feral cat darting across a path, or a mouse or a Norway rat. And looking up, they would see year-round and migratory birds and bats, but no Eastern gray, red or southern flying squirrels or Eastern chipmunks—at least according to Edith Folger (Andrews) and Ludlow Griscom's 1948 *The Birds of Nantucket*.

Say Griscom and Folger:

> Owing to their geographical location and topography, the islands of this group have an interesting but limited flora and fauna, with many southern and relict species. Heather, brought in accidentally with the Scotch pines, has established itself in various sections on Nantucket. Squirrels and chipmunks, so common on the mainland, are absent. Some of the shrews and mice, however, are endemic, owing probably to the sufficiently prolonged isolation. Many common mainland species of birds are absent, or rare vagrants.

With the all of the island's trees harvested for human use during Native American occupation and by European settlers, it's easy to see how Nantucket's Eastern chipmunks and Eastern gray squirrels, which would have been present before the ocean rose and isolated the islands, died out once their habitat disappeared. Says French, "Squirrels and chipmunks are a little interesting though. If they were here in decent population, I can't imagine even if Native Americans were targeting squirrels that they could hunt out every single squirrel to extirpation. But then, those kinds of species are more keyed in on woodlands, and the theory is that we never had a lot of woodlands. You don't tend to find squirrels roaming around out in sandplain grasslands, because they [live] in more forested areas, and we didn't have a lot of that kind of habitat."

However, this woodland rodent habitat did return and, with it, the Eastern gray squirrel. Islanders planting downtown Nantucket and Siasconset with many varieties of hardwood and coniferous trees aided the start of the restoration. The return continued gradually as the island's sheep population could no longer hold back the march of invasive plant species and other large woody plants and trees. So-called hidden forests grew up out of former kettle ponds around the moors, scrub oak smothered the once open maritime heathlands, and several Nantucketers brought Eastern pitch, Japanese black and Scotch pines to the island.

It remains a mystery how Eastern gray squirrels, unlike deer and rabbits, were reintroduced to Nantucket. Eastern chipmunks and red and Southern flying squirrels never found their way back to these islands, if they were ever here. And, according to the venerable Tuckernuck Island caretaker and boat builder, Bam LaFarge, whose family has owned houses and property on Tuckernuck for decades, none of these tree rodent species was ever on Tuckernuck Island. French theorizes that Penikese Island, one of the Elizabeth Islands, probably got its complement of white-footed mice from loads of firewood delivered by barge, with the mice living inside some of the logs, and that raccoons routinely end up in landfills around the state because of accidental transportation in garbage dumpsters in which they have been foraging. But raccoons aren't known to have been on Nantucket after 1858, the deadline by which a hired hunter was to have exterminated them all. Native foxes reportedly lasted until 1886, and prairie dogs may have been unsuccessfully introduced sometime in the late 19th century. As for the gray squirrels, the dominant legends on Nantucket are that either the trucks supplying the island's lumber yards with wood building supplies inadvertently brought squirrels with them, or the 'Sconset Woodman's hardwood log deliveries via the Steamship Authority ferries reintroduced them to Nantucket.

French is wary of both theories though he offers no alternatives:

> Fundamentally, there are only two things that could have happened: one is they got out [to the island by] hitching a ride, or they were brought out deliberately. They did not get out there on their own; they're just not physically capable of doing that. . . . Think about it. Squirrels aren't nearly as likely to ride a truck of logs, or even cut up pieces of split wood for firewood, as much as a raccoon would. A squirrel's not going

to poke around in a load of trees and stay with it, whereas a raccoon may well do that—squeeze in between the logs to spend the night and find himself riding the next morning.

Just as the squirrels lost their habitat due to man's changing needs, so, as Nantucket's farming dwindled from its heyday of more than 100 farms and Tuckernuck's down to just a handful, did the islands' year-round bat population. The likely reason: barns, the bats' primary island roosts, were torn down or converted into less open buildings. Today, bats are still found on Nantucket, but they probably do not live here year-round. During the summer, hoary, Eastern red, and silver-haired bats spend time on the island chasing insects before migrating south or choosing a cave on the mainland for winter hibernation. But as for the little brown bat, few island naturalists believe it still flies out here to dine on seasonal insects.

The silver-haired, red and hoary bats are typically found out around Squam Farm and the general Squam area, and Beattie has seen them in her South Shore Road neighborhood and every fall out around Polpis Harbor:

> Absolutely, they migrate through here to and from places. I don't think they come through here too much in the spring. I've always been told that, because our season here is so late—summer insects are hatching out two or three weeks later than everywhere else—that's why they don't breed. One of the reasons they come through here in the fall is that they're on the backside of that. You know: you get a killing frost off island and you don't get one here. They definitely move through here in the fall, for sure, but I don't think anyone has documented them as breeding here. When you think of it, with all the old buildings we have downtown, we'd have bats in all those churches if they were breeding here.

Unlike bats, which can leave the islands when insect supplies pinch off, white-tailed deer will remain on the island until their numbers increase beyond what their habitat can support or until Nantucketers decide they've really had enough of Lyme disease and take steps to reduce the herd severely. MassWildlife and the leading expert on tick-borne diseases, Dr. Sam R. Telford, III, of Tufts University, recommend that the population should go down from Nantucket's estimated 55 animals per square mile to a range from ten to 30. Although scrub oak in the maritime heathlands (moors) is their cover today, and it shows no signs of abating despite efforts of the Nantucket Heathlands Partnership to burn and brushcut it into submission, that hasn't always been the case. When Old Buck leapt free into Nantucket and the company of Michigan does in 1926, the scrub oak and pitch pine barrens were just getting started as island vegetation, but the deer still had plenty of grasses, wildflowers, and tree and shrub fruit on their menu. And the island hadn't seen deer since after the Native Americans and European settlers hunted them to island extinction. Although some scrub oak did exist on the island then, it likely failed to persist because of the sheep.

As I mentioned in the fourth chapter, humans cleared land for farming needs, in cutting down nearly the remainder of the island's trees to build houses and boats; moreover, they brought domestic livestock with them to the island. The sheep kept the scrub oak eaten down to the tiny shoots of new sprouts—or less—during their reign over the open lands, but in the 19th century, when the island's population dropped as a result of whaling drying up, the Civil War and the Gold Rush, sheep farming also faded and the scrub oak and pitch pines filled in the moors. This is where most of the island's deer find their cover today.

Development of the island to its present level did somewhat denude the heathlands of their cover of scrub oak for deer and the island's other wild creatures, at least around the periphery. But vast amounts of undeveloped interior land remains, including all of Tuckernuck Island (minus the acres occupied by roughly 35 structures) and much of the moors within the heathlands of the northern third of Nantucket, and its sandplain grasslands, upland meadows, swamps, bogs and small island forests.

In the fall of 2010, Andrew McKenna-Foster took over from Ornithologist Dr. Bob Kennedy as the Maria Mitchell Association's Director of Natural Science. He was young but well schooled in the ways the islands' habitats best suit its 21 mammal species. As he notes, it's the herbaceous mammals—those that live off of plants, including deer, the island's rodents and rabbits—that make the most of Nantucket, Tuckernuck and Muskeget.

Next to avian species, rodents, deer and rabbits fare the best on the Nantucket Archipelago, because there is so much food and year-round shelter. Large animals other than deer would likely have a tough time, except maybe scavengers, such as coyotes. In Beattie's words:

> There's a large variety of habitats here. Wetlands, uplands, grasslands, forests (not so much forest, but we do have some forested habitat); you've got that intermediate shrubland habitat, and a lot of it isn't developed. The other thing that makes Nantucket a little different from elsewhere is that there is a lot of development here. A lot of homes have been built here, but a lot of those homes are occupied for only about two months out of the year. When you think of deer, it's an ideal

place to be a [one]. You've got all these homes, and people are basically planting a deluxe smorgasbord for you. They do browse on landscape materials in the summer, but that's not when they're stressed out for food. That's during the winter, when there's nobody there to chase them away, so it's perfect for them.

Beattie thinks, what with all the feral cats, landfill garbage, ground-nesting birds, deer carcasses in the fall, rabbit road kills and dumpster food on the menu, not to mention the low brush habitat with pockets of forest, Nantucket offers a perfect habitat for coyotes—if they could get out here. To date, the only coyote to make it over to Nantucket was a dead one that washed up on Great Point in the winter of 2005–2006. As French detailed earlier, the Elizabeth Islands already have coyotes, as does Martha's Vineyard, but both agree that the swim to Nantucket is too far and too challenging for a coyote.

There's no doubt that Nantucket has thousands of acres of ideal habitat for rabbits and other smaller mammals—ideal not only in the types of plants and the terrain, but also because much of it is conservation land that can never be developed. But there's not nearly enough open land for larger mammals, such as wolves, elk, moose and bear.

Nantucket's next re-introduction of formerly extirpated resident mammal species is likely to be the New England cottontail. Because it is a heritage species on Nantucket, as well as in Massachusetts and the rest of New England, MassWildlife and the U.S. Fisheries and Wildlife Service (USFW) were devising a plan in 2001–2012 to bring this rabbit back to what they deem normal population levels by repopulating depleted areas where they used to exist. They then plan to enhance and further protect those areas where they were known to exist before they were extirpated, including Nantucket Island.[8]

In 2011 and early 2012, Beattie was in the process of setting and regularly checking traps she placed around the island to determine if New England cottontails still existed on Nantucket. As of spring 2012, she had not found a single one. Beattie's work was in cooperation with French and MassWildlife, which was then in the middle of a two-year, statewide survey of the dense, early successional shrublands habitat in which New England cottontails are known to live. French is the receiver of rabbit heads from hunters around the state, including on Nantucket, who are required to turn them over to the state for this purpose. Their failure to find New England cottontail rabbits on Nantucket suggested that MassWildlife and the USFW would likely reintroduce them on Nantucket.

OTTERS

No such reintroduction of river otters is on MassWildlife's agenda, but the organization is unflinching in its belief that river otters are a separate species, and that they are found in relative abundance on Martha's Vineyard—an estimated 35 to 150 as of early January 2011—with a few on Nomans Land, since the three-and-a-half-mile distance to this uninhabited island, southwest of Martha's Vineyard's Squibnocket Pond, is easily close enough for the otters to swim to. For his January 7, 2011, *Vineyard Gazette* story, "Oughta Know Where Otters Go, So Scientists Map Weasel Tracks," reporter Peter Brannen interviewed wildlife biologist Luanne Johnson, who lives on Martha's Vineyard and conducted a two-year study on river otters in the area, including the expansion of their range into the islands off Southeastern Massachusetts. Brannen quoted Johnson as citing the presence of river otters on Nantucket: "Otters are capable of long distance movements along coastlines, and this has been reported in studies in coastal Alaska. So it is not surprising that they have re-colonized Nantucket. They are also on the Elizabeth Islands and Nomans. I imagine they were on Nantucket historically and were, perhaps trapped out, perhaps not. The population is healthy throughout Massachusetts." However, there have been no sightings of river otters on Nantucket since 2008.

Subsisting on blue claw crabs, river otters also eat small fish, including minnows and mummichogs; medium-size fish such as white and yellow perch; and bluefish and striped bass if they're ever deft enough to catch them, all of which are available in Nantucket waters. Nocturnal roamers, river otters frequently travel between water bodies on foot. As of early 2011, Johnson was monitoring 61 areas where river otters were seen defecating and five dens on the Vineyard, but none on Nantucket.

Since the 2008 discovery of river otter tracks on the island, along with sliding marks and the whitish jelly secreted from glands near the otter's anus and used as a form of communication, river otters or evidence of them have not been seen on the Nantucket islands.[9] Signs of their presence were seen that year at Madequecham Valley, on the west shore of Hummock Pond and on the shores of Sesachacha Pond. But this is not to say that they won't be back. Their populations began surging to a certain degree across the state after 1996, largely due to a ban on trapping of river otters enacted by the Massachusetts State Legislature.

French theorizes, "I think, in the case of Nantucket . . . my guess is they're a dispersing animal, and young males, in particular, disperse enormous distances sometimes; they're the ones that explore. I suspect there [are] two options: that animal explored all over the island and it eventually died, or he left, went somewhere else because he didn't find any other otters."

A DEER PARK

Unlike the river otters, the descendents of Old Buck and his Midwestern miniharem of two does have certainly found Nantucket's varied habitats to their liking and, far from leaving the island, have proliferated. As of mid-March 2011, Sonja Christensen, Deer and Moose Project Leader for the Massachusetts Division of Fisheries and Wildlife, pegged Nantucket's herd at 2,200 deer. Christensen bases her estimate on the approximate number of deer per square mile, which she believes is 55, and she multiplies that by the 40 of Nantucket's 47.8 total square acres in which deer typically reside on the island, the other 7.8 being densely human-populated areas including Nantucket Town, 'Sconset and the mid-island area. She notes that her numbers are substantiated by the high quantities of deer harvested during Nantucket's hunting season.

The size of the herd fluctuates from year to year, due to natural senescence, vehicle-deer collisions and the deer-hunting seasons from mid-October through the end of December. Based on data from MassWildlife, Nantucket hunters harvested 600 deer in the 2010 season, 550 in 2009, 433 in both 2008 and 2007, 424 in 2006, and 361 in 2005, yielding an average of 466.8 deer taken per year on Nantucket for that six-year period.

One of the island's more experienced hunters, Doug Smith, a year-round commercial fisherman who scallops in the winter and fishes for striped bass while working on a charter fishing boat during the summer, hunts white-tailed deer with a crossbow and razor-sharp arrows. Known among islanders as "Smitty," Smith also hunts wild turkey in Western Massachusetts to help stock his larder.

Smitty has been hunting white-tailed deer on Nantucket for around 30 to 40 years. He typically takes around 20 deer per year, freezing the meat for his own consumption. This may sound like a lot, but there is no legal limit on the number of antlerless deer a hunter may take. When a dead deer is brought to the check station, the MassWildlife authorities may issue the hunter a new permit, and so the process can continue until the season ends.

Over the years, Smitty has seen dramatic changes in the deer herd and its habitat. Spending those years in Siasconset, he has witnessed wild fluctuation in the size of the island herd and in the number of hunters, but not in deer behavior, which he says has only adapted to the increases in human population and to development of their habitat. The deer continue to move in and out of populated areas as needed. A network of decades-old, well-trodden trails snakes a maze through the moors and sandplain grasslands, through dunes, populated neighborhoods, island forests and swamps, linking eating places, watering holes, sleeping areas and refuge spots. It's like the Underground Railroad of slavery times.

Smitty recalls hunting down in the former rye and potato fields by the LORAN station in 'Sconset, in and around the Siasconset Dump and on the rural outskirts of the village. Today, he says, the deer are still using their well-worn paths, albeit interrupted by new houses and yards, to move about, generally out of human sight and, they hope, out of the range of hunters. He elaborates, "Burnell Street, Plainfield, Low Beach—it's really interesting, in that the animals used to use those areas when they were wild. There was still browse [food in the form of vegetation] in the rye fields where I used to hunt them in the evenings, and now, boom, there [are] houses there. But there's still a food source there, and the animals are still in there. It's just like the houses don't bother them."

Deer hunting has been limited to certain weeks of the year, starting with Nantucket's first seasons in the late 1920s; nonetheless, because the remaining parcels of developable land around the island have shrunk to the point where only 7.8 percent of the island was left for development as of late April 2011, the deer herd is shrinking. Smitty believes development has had other impacts on the herd, as well, both good and bad: "Development gives the hunters more access to the deer. It's one reason why [I think] numbers are down. A side effect of that is this: You take an acre of wild woods and compare it with an acre of landscaped property, [and] there's more food value to the landscaped property. I read somewhere that the deer actually know and will go to a fertilized habitat rather than eating in a non-fertilized yard, because there's more protein in the plants that have been fertilized."

Smith has long since forsaken his noisy shotgun for a bow and carbon fiber arrows, later moving to a crossbow for greater stealth and hunting in close proximity to houses. Over the years, he has accumulated numerous property owners' permissions to hunt private backyards and fields from the Low Beach Road area up Morey Lane, onto Burnell Street and over to Sankaty Head Golf Club. During hunting season, he regularly sees deer bedded down in yards within the village, and throughout the year he observes deer moving through the village using their own trails. Similarly, deer are regularly seen within the Old Historic District of Nantucket Town and moving through the other denser residential areas of the island during the two-week shotgun season in early December, because they've learned where it's safest during the archery, shotgun and primitive firearms seasons that span October, November and December.

In fact, one year in the early-1990s hunting season, a deer came bounding down Main Street, leapt through the plate glass façade of what was then the Sports Locker, and crashed around inside the store before jumping out and running down Lower Main Street, out to the end of Straight Wharf, jumping into the harbor, and swimming away from the waterfront as fast as it could. Scallopers have sighted deer swimming north across the harbor over to Coatue, and the creatures have been known to move out to Coatue and the Coskata Woods on foot, as well, in hopes of escaping the slaughter. Deer stands in trees in Coskata Woods are evidence of this temporary on-island migration, and of its futility. Smith also knows of a group of hunters that spends several days living on Coatue in the hunting season because they know deer like to hide out there and that they're easier to kill there because of the low, sparse vegetation. But there really are few places they can hide on this island deer park, as the *Boston Herald* article aptly referred to it.

"Deer park" is an appropriate description for what the habitat has become. It's a term familiar to biologists and hunters alike who spend time on Nantucket. From Nantucket's foundation of sand, gravel, and rocks dumped in a pile by the glacier has come a succession of vegetation that was inadvertently manipulated into ideal conditions for deer. For our own purposes, we gradually replaced their natural habitat with croplands and otherwise leveled the island forest for lumber, heating fuel and pastures. Although we hunted the original herd to extinction, soon enough we brought more in, and they prospered, much to the delight of today's hunters. Later, we planted elaborate ornamental gardens, fancy trees and vegetable plots around large houses in the rural parts of the island, displacing the deer from their traditional habitat but providing them with more food.

It's not the kind of natural selection process one would expect, and it's certainly one that many Nantucketers afflicted with Lyme and other tick-borne diseases wish we could go back and reverse. But it is relevant to this dynamic list of 21 mammals that lie in state in the island crypt for natural things beneath the Hinchman House. That list was compiled in August 1980 by noted Nantucket fisherman and island naturalist, J. Clinton

Andrews; however, Nantucket's mammalian complement has changed over time. There are some on the list, such as the black-tailed jackrabbit, that were imported to Nantucket by overzealous humans or hunters hoping to broaden on-island game variety; these, along with the feral housecat, the little brown bat and the non-terrestrial harbor and gray seals, somehow made the cut onto Maria Mitchell's list of 21. Surely by now, though, this list is debatable, with the little brown bat most likely no longer visiting, the black-tailed jackrabbit gone and the possible loss of others we may not yet have realized. And if MassWildlife goes ahead with its re-introduction of the New England cottontail rabbit, its status on the list of 21 would go from MIA to active.

Nantucket's 21 mammals, as counted by Andrews in 1980, are:

- Masked shrew
- Short-tailed shrew
- Eastern mole
- Silver-haired bat
- Red bat
- Hoary bat
- Eastern cottontail rabbit
- New England cottontail rabbit
- Snowshoe hare
- Black-tailed jackrabbit
- Gray squirrel
- White-foot mouse
- Meadow vole
- Muskeget vole
- Norway rat
- House mouse
- Meadow jumping mouse
- House cat (feral)
- White-tailed deer
- Harbor seal
- Gray or horsehead seal

But, like the rest of our natural world on the Nantucket Archipelago, this list is subject to constant change, modification and human meddling.

WETLAND CREATURES

IN 1951, the Town of Nantucket worked in conjunction with the state's Department of Conservation to spray the entire island with DDT to kill the tussock moth. Using a C-47 Skytrain similar to the DC-3 commercial airliners flown by Providence & Boston Airlines to and from Nantucket in the 1980s, the Department of Conservation sprayed a solution of 12 percent dichlorodiphenyltrichloroethane over 31,071 acres and hired a private contractor to spray an additional 970 acres around the larger ponds with a helicopter.

A broadleaf eater that prefers shade tree leaves, first discovered on Nantucket's West End in the summer of 1949 where it had defoliated almost 100 percent of 2,500 acres, the tussock moth's presence on Nantucket prompted the town's moth control program and ten years of annual Moth Suppression Reports. In 1949's entry, Nantucket Moth Superintendent, William Voorneveld, Jr., opined, "We are hopeful that this effort will have brought the tussock moth under control. However, the results will not be definitely determined for some time. Incidental but of primary importance in rating the effectiveness of aerial DDT spraying has been the general comment by Madaket residents that the Greenhead fly, an unwelcome and annoying guest in that area, had virtually disappeared following the spraying to control the tussock moth."

Although the town had been using DDT to kill unwanted insects, including mosquitoes on Nantucket as well as on Tuckernuck and Muskeget, since the 1930s, this was the first time the state had stepped in to help with moth eradication, other than supplying funding for purchase of the chemical.[1]

Conservation was a relatively new concept in the American psyche during the mid-20th century, having gone through its fledging stages during the late 1890s into the early decades of the 1900s borne by ornithologists, amateur birders and sportsmen, including the likes of the gunner George Henry Mackay, John C. Phillips, John James Audubon and Christmas Bird Count founder Frank M. Chapman. The deadly impact of DDT spraying didn't grab national attention until the late 1960s. In the town's 1969 annual report, Nantucket's Department of Public Works Superintendent Robert M. Jones noted that he hoped to do more mosquito ditch cleaning and digging, having already dug or re-opened approximately 50 miles of ditches that year in response to the cessation of DDT use for insect control on Nantucket.

Nantucket's elimination of DDT from its insect repellent arsenal came four years before the national ban in 1972, which was largely precipitated by the 1962 publication of biologist Rachel Carson's book, *Silent Spring*, documenting the environmental havoc wreaked across the U.S. by wanton DDT spraying. While the publication of Carson's book, combined with the well-established bird conservation lobby, helped hatch environmentalism in this country, damage had already been done around the country and on Nantucket.

DDT'S EFFECTS

Those tracking the island osprey population noticed a steep decline in numbers on the island in the 1950s and 1960s; it was discovered later that DDT causes thinning of the eggshells of birds of prey, including ospreys, peregrine falcons, brown pelicans and bald eagles. Consequently, the shells break more easily, resulting in a decline in fertility. Some of the island's amphibian and reptile populations suffered similar effects, depending on how specialized their island habitat and food needs were and on the ability of their populations to sustain significant losses while still maintaining enough breeding individuals. Those species low in number or finicky about food and habitat didn't fare so well. Specifically, Fowler's toad and the Eastern spadefoot toad are believed by herpetologists to be extinct on Nantucket mainly because of the town's onetime relentless, 30-plus year use of DDT. Unlike Martha's Vineyard, with its six towns, and Cape Cod, with 15 towns and 25 villages, where each individual municipality had its own annual spraying protocol and didn't always spray every year, giving wildlife some breathing room, Nantucket is both town and county alike. And this one island town sprayed annually for more than 35 years, which spelled death for at least these two amphibians.

Here again, human meddling, not natural selection by eroding land bridges or lingering glacial ice, determined the existence of a given species on Nantucket. One of these herpetologists, James "Skip" Lazell, is quite certain that these two toads, plus at least two turtles, went belly-up because of DDT spraying on Nantucket. In the "Zoogeography" chapter of his 1976 book, *This Broken Archipelago: Cape Cod and the Islands, Amphibians and Reptiles*, Lazell details what species of amphibians and reptiles are found on the Cape and Islands, based on climate and terrain. Lazell says that three species "are definitely known to have suffered wholesale destruction by the hand of man": Fowler's toad, the red-bellied turtle and the box turtle. The box turtle survives today, but the size of its population is a mystery, and it is not known if this turtle along with another, the red-eared slider, were introduced species or found their way out to these islands on their own. The box turtle, however, is a favorite child's pet, and many have been released into the wild after their owners have lost interest, which means the box turtle, regardless of the severity of losses sustained due to Nantucket's DDT campaign, was able to rebound because of human activity. However, the Fowler's toad and the red-bellied turtle, neither sold as pets, were extirpated from Cuttyhunk, Nantucket, Muskeget and probably Tuckernuck because of relentless DDT spraying.

SEARCHING FOR SURVIVORS

Nantucket naturalist and fisherman, J. Clinton Andrews, reported to Lazell that before World War II, the Fowler's toad was abundant all over Nantucket. Lazell knew that the red-bellied turtle was a commonly found turtle on our islands during and probably well after the Native American presence on the Nantucket Archipelago, because its remains were found in middens around the island. While researching his book, prior to its publication date in 1976, Lazell did find this turtle but noted it to be quite "shy and wary" and unable to adjust to human intrusions; therefore, it's understandable that its population was already low and that it couldn't survive the DDT. And the box turtle was also abundant in widely varied habitats on the island prior to the heavy DDT spraying. Although its island populations most definitely took a major hit, this turtle still exists on Nantucket today. Three years before taking the helm of the Nantucket Land Council from outgoing executive director Linda Holland in 2004, a young Cormac Collier spent many evening hours, during and after mid- to late-spring rainstorms, driving around Nantucket and listening for the call of the spadefoot toad, hoping against hope that he could report that this native island toad species was not forever gone from Nantucket. The spadefoot toad spends years underground, surfacing from deep burrows in sandy areas near wetlands only to mate during rainstorms. Conversely, the Fowler's toad spends much of its life on or just below the surface of the ground, digging into the cooler earth on hotter days and hibernating underground during the winter months. So, it's likely that because the Fowler's toad spent much more of its time on or near the surface, even though its island population was originally much higher on Nantucket's islands than the spadefoot toad's, the Fowler's toad was much more physically exposed, and it's likely that the DDT did its species in first—although the spadefoot toad was not far behind; the last one was found in the early 1990s. It obviously had found more effective refuge deeper in the ground, which bought it more time. In addition, like the red-bellied turtle, the spadefoot toad is intolerant of the encroachment of human development, and its need for a very specialized habitat has contributed to its demise on Nantucket's islands.

Considering the way the spadefoot toad lives, its species didn't get any help from evolution in terms of population enhancement and longevity. The adult Eastern spadefoot toad, whose northern range limit extends just up to coastal southern New England, is about three inches long and sports camouflage brown-and-green markings on smooth skin. It has a specialized existence. The hard, spade-like projections on both hind feet are what it uses to dig in soft, loose soils to create the underground burrows in which it spends most of its life well underground. The toad excavates backwards as it works down through the soil, and it is drawn to the surface only during heavy spring and summer rain events, in which Lazell says it mates "in an orgy of raucous squawks and frantic courtship." Quickly—within 24 to 48 hours—the eggs left behind disgorge tadpoles that follow their parents back down deep into the ground for what could be years of subterranean living before journeying topside again for their frenzied copulation. Collier began his search for the spadefoot toad at the bottom of Madequecham Valley, in what he described as a nice wetland surrounded by sand, an ideal location for spadefoot toad breeding and winter hibernation, and also where the last known specimen had been found as road kill. Every rainy night and its following night in May and June, from 2001 through 2004, Collier visited Madequecham Valley and every other part of the island where he might find potential spadefoot toad habitat. Collier moved on to Coatue, kettle holes in the moors, the drainage basins of other former south shore ponds east of Madequecham, Toupshue and Forked Pond Valley. He also visited, briefly, Madaket, areas near Dionis Beach, and Eel Point.

At this last location, he thought he was close one night; in fact, it was the closest Collier got to finding one of these elusive toads on Nantucket. On a search prior to a rainy period, at around two in the morning, Collier had slogged half a mile through a wetland on Eel Point when he was sure he heard the classic crow-like call of a spadefoot toad emanating from somewhere nearby. Unfortunately, the call turned out to be that of a great blue heron in a rookery within the wetland.

Collier never found a spadefoot toad, and thus this species enjoys only two recorded Nantucket specimens: one found in 1965 and another identified in 1993 by former Maria Mitchell Association (MMA) Natural Science Director Bill Maple, who found one after it had been run over by a car in Madequecham Valley. Although undocumented, Lazell's last sighting on Nantucket was in 1970, in the unfinished portion of Henry Huyser's basement on New Street. Huyser invited Lazell there to explore for these toads, and in searching around on the exposed dirt portion of Huyser's basement, recently denuded of concrete for the installation of a new sump pump system, Lazell found one without much trouble.

That Lazell found this spadefoot in a basement and not out in undeveloped Madequecham Valley, where they were much more likely to exist at the time, and where Maple found a dead one 23 years later, speaks to the impact of the island's growing human population on this toad. Today, however, as Collier learned during his three-year attempt, the search may be futile, despite ample acres of suitable habitat. "I'm pretty convinced, with the number of naturalists that are on this island and the history of environmentalism and conservation," Collier concludes, "if they were here, they would have been found."

Collier and Lazell agree that the spadefoot toad is gone from Nantucket because of the town's DDT spraying program. Says Collier:

> My own opinion after nights and nights, after a few years, is that the populations that were found, both Skip's and the dead individuals, were remnant populations. . . . I think in captivity they found that they lived up to 18 years, so they're very long-lived creatures. Bill Maple found [one] in the '90s, so that could have been a breeding population in the '80s. [But] my opinion is that those [last sightings] were just outliers, that there were no breeding populations at those times, particularly the one that Bill found. [M]assive amounts of DDT [were] sprayed on this island, so it's not rocket science. With all the information we have,

in terms of pesticides with amphibians, particularly frogs and toads, it affected them. I think that it wiped [the species] out, along with the Fowler's toads.

Although he never extended his search to Tuckernuck Island, Collier wanted to search for these toads there, despite Tuckernuckers reporting to him they've never heard the spadefoot's distinctive call. He suspects that the town spared Tuckernuck somewhat from its DDT spraying sorties, and he is aware of several kettle ponds and wetland areas there that might contain spadefoot toad habitat.

Just because Collier's relentless searches turned up zero spadefoot toads doesn't mean that they're absolutely not on the islands. Like the Muskeget vole, which appeared to go extinct at the busy claws of that island's feral cat population, this toad's numbers could be so low as to make the spadefoot virtually invisible to those looking for it, especially because of its underground habitation.

Any type of creature can be rediscovered, especially the more reclusive and skittish, which most reptiles and amphibians tend to be. There are many travails involved in locating them: Nantucket has plenty of habitat for these creatures, but thanks to both the glacier, which provided the many low elevations on the island for wetlands to develop, and today's environmental protection laws, most are nearly impossible to reach and navigate.

One such success story is that of the smooth green snake. Found by Lazell in great abundance on Coatue during the 1970s, this 17-inch-long ribbon of green scales came to be considered MIA on Nantucket for the

Green snake

following 20–25 years until its seeming reappearance on Coatue in 2005, when the MMA's former director of Natural Science, Bob Kennedy, and the current director, Andrew McKenna-Foster, found two specimens. McKenna-Foster spotted them in a snake trap—essentially small sheets of plywood laid down in the underbrush that attract the snakes as hiding and cooling-off spots. Snakes being cold-blooded, meaning they're unable to regulate their body temperature themselves and must rely on the sun and other snakes for heat and on cool places to get cool, eventually slither under these plywood "traps" to hide and to cool off.

SURVIVORS: PEEPERS, TURTLES AND SALAMANDERS

Unlike this small population of smooth green snakes, Nantucket can certainly boast of spring peepers, definitely the most vocal and therefore the most readily identifiable of Nantucket's reptiles and amphibians. True, those boating on island ponds are bound to see numbers of painted turtles basking on logs, along shorelines and in among the cattails before they quickly slip into the water, and to see snapping turtles poking their heads out of the water. But there is no other representative from this group of island wildlife that mainstream people experience without mucking around in swamps and ponds. Spring peepers can be heard from late February or early March well into April, and sometimes on warm autumn nights.

By the symphony of these choral tree frogs—males and females flirting with each other—we're aware that this segment of wildlife is fairly represented on Nantucket. The same is true for those painted, spotted and snapping turtles. Although not gifted with vocal prowess, their numbers must have been sufficient enough to survive the town's DDT-spraying years, or else they all possess some kind of immunity that saved them from island extinction and allow us to see at least the snapping and painted varieties crossing island roads during the spring seeking out places to lay their eggs.

Still, like their mammalian counterparts, reptiles and amphibians also have only an incomplete regional roster on Nantucket, Tuckernuck and Muskeget, numbering somewhere around 18 or 19 species. But there is a growing list of alleged additions. Take the four-toed salamander. Never previously known to exist on Nantucket, it was found in the fall of 2009 by researchers working for herpetologist Scott Smyers, senior scientist at Oxbow Associates, Inc., of Acton, Massachusetts, a firm specializing in wetlands delineation and permitting, wildlife studies, herpetology and vernal pool ecology. The salamander was discovered beneath a snake trap. So where did it come from? Was it always on Nantucket? Or did someone bring it here? Smyers agrees anything is possible. "I think there's a good chance that it may have been there all along and went unnoticed. They may have been brought over in some logs. There's always a chance [of] somebody bringing it over with some building supplies or with some firewood or something like that. It's hard to know for sure, but it's a fun thing to contemplate and theorize on."

That's the way it goes with islands. We get what we get at the birth of our little archipelago because of climate, habitat and the natural random selection process that happened when we lost our land bridge to the mainland. But who's to say what other life forms are going to make the trip out to the island, either involuntarily with human aid, or on purpose, for reasons related to food supply, habitat loss or overdevelopment? The mystery of the four-toed salamander, the revival of the smooth green snake and the disappearance of the spadefoot toad are really one collective metaphor for all of Nantucket's reptiles and amphibians. They are at the mercy of whatever their bodies can tolerate. While they are slaves to range expansion, when enticed by optimal climate and habitat conditions or better food supplies north or south of their home ranges, our reptiles and amphibians, like other island wildlife, are on these islands mostly by chance and less by evolutionary design.

As to what was here way back when, that's even harder to determine than with birds and mammals. The people who spend their lives studying these creatures, including Smyers and Lazell, can really only conjure strong theories of what was here where and when, applying basic climatological maxims of faunal migration and range expansion based on where the ice sheet was in relation to our present-day islands at any given time. Yes, archeologists have found turtle shells in Native American middens, indicating Nantucket's Indians utilized turtles as a food source. From what we know of the legs of frogs tasting remarkably like chicken and snake meat being delicacy in some southern climes, it's entirely possible that the Archaic Indians and their successors, the Wampanoags, may have dined on snakes and frogs, although there is little evidence that they did, and there is no way of knowing for sure whether these animals became supplements to the standard regional Indian menu of deer, caribou and moose meat, along with Atlantic salmon, shad, herring, bluefish, striped bass and shellfish, and eventually maize products and other vegetable crops. On the mainland, and probably on Nantucket, the Native Americans made the most of what they could gather for food, including hunting and gathering some species to island extinction, so it's likely that some reptiles and amphibians were on this extensively varied menu.[2]

Nantucket's Native Americans were nomadic, within the constraints of the islands, both before rising seawater actually isolated the islands and thereafter by moving between inland and shoreline campsites, depending on which seasonal food was ready for eating. Because of winter hibernation, frog, turtle and snake recipes would have been reserved for the warmer months of the year, if they were used at all. However, without consistent fossil records of the late Pleistocene Epoch into the current Holocene Epoch, herpetologists must take their best guess.

MIGRATION MYSTERIES

As Lazell details in his book, the essential terrestrial zoogeography of Cape Cod and the Islands is that northern reptile and amphibian species are assumed to have been on the islands of Southeastern Massachusetts, as the unflooded coastal plain allowed them to walk or crawl to the plateaus that would eventually become islands around 6,000 years ago. And he expects that the southern species would have been on Cape Cod because of its mild climate and the fact that it was disconnected from the mainland by the Cape Cod Canal as recently as July 1914. Opines Lazell:

> I think one of the big points I tried to make in the book, *This Broken Archipelago*, is that a lot of places like Nantucket became islands before southern forms, like bullfrogs, actually were able to colonize. As the glacier retreats and sea level is much lower but coming up, southern forms are able to move north and colonize the place, and of course, you would naturally expect that if they could colonize it . . . southern forms would be more prevalent in the Cape and Islands region [than] on the mainland because it's warmer. . . .
>
> So a general prediction is that southern species should be there, but the problem with that is a lot of the islands became islands before the southern species got there and I mention that rather repeatedly in the course of the book.

Smyers agrees with Lazell. He delights in dining on the nearly infinite list of hypotheses for what was here when, what conditions existed, what plants were growing in what new-formed habitat that would support reptiles and amphibians. Because the hardier northern species, including the omnipresent spring peepers, redback salamanders and garter snakes, which are found in abundance on Nantucket and Tuckernuck (with one very large specimen actually found on Muskeget Island), are all currently so prevalent, Smyers guesses that they were likely to have been on the Nantucket Archipelago's land masses both before and after the glacier's presence. Their resiliency in colder climes most likely meant that substantial-enough populations of these three species survived to proliferate as the climate warmed. Those tardy in reaching the Nantucket islands' portion of the coastal plain—they did have plenty of time, since the glacier had left Nantucket by 18,000 years ago and New England completely by 14,000 years ago—are the species in short supply today, Smyers theorizes. These include spotted turtles, which may have had to swim short distances to Nantucket as the land bridges gradually submerged; the box turtle, which Smyers and Lazell believe was introduced with human help; and the spadefoot toad.

Lazell knew of breeding populations of the spadefoot toad existing on Martha's Vineyard until DDT spraying from the late 1940s into the 1950s there blanked them out. However, he was not aware of any such colonies on Nantucket during that time and admits to being flummoxed by their presence on these islands until the specimen was found in 1965 and he found a live one in Huyser's basement in 1970. Being a southern species with its northern range limit being southern New England, they do not fit the predicted profile for creatures that would have been present at the time the melting glacier elevated sea level enough to make the islands. Nantucket, being closest to the ocean, would have been first, followed by Martha's Vineyard, Chappaquiddick, Muskeget, Tuckernuck and the Elizabeth Islands. Lazell sheds light on this mystery:

> Thus, the zoogeographer would predict that animals best adapted to take cold weather—the situation close to the face of the retreating ice—would spread across dry land to Nantucket before the rising sea level isolated it. Following this line of thought, we would expect to find only cold-adapted species on Nantucket and both warm- and cold-adapted species on Cape Cod. Martha's Vineyard and the smaller islands might rank intermediate in species mix. The warm country species just didn't get up here in time to walk to Nantucket, and the spadefoot toad is a warm country animal indeed.

Although Lazell doesn't have a definitive answer as to how and when the Eastern spadefoot toads hopped onto Nantucket's islands, he infers that, when the distances among the young islands, the Vineyard and the mainland weren't nearly as great, possibly with remnants of land bridges still in existence, this toad may have swum or been washed over to Nantucket.

However, this is still a stretch since amphibians hydrate through their skin, so being in salt water, as Lazell describes, would subject them to osmosis in which seawater would drain out at all their fluids and kill them quickly. If the spadefoot toad had been a surface dweller in or around swamps, ponds, vernal pools and other hard-to-reach wetland areas on the islands, breeding annually instead of every few years when rainy conditions were just right, it might have had a better chance, because even though it would have been more exposed to the ravages of DDT, habitat tolerance would have been considerably broader, promoting greater surviving numbers of this unusual toad.

But then what of the wood frog? Moist woods: that's the description for wood frog habitat in Peter Alden's book, *A Field Guide to New England*. Think about Nantucket for a moment in terms of this type of habitat. The entire Squam area, the Windswept Cranberry Bog property, parts of Sanford Farm, the Coskata Woods, the Lily Pond area and any surrounding vegetative area near a kettle hole pond in the moors would qualify for ideal wood frog territory. And yet, there are no wood frogs on Nantucket. Its absence is just another example of the unique selection process that, over the millennia, has determined the menu of species on Nantucket. According to its basic characteristics, you can make a case that it "should" be here. But it's not.

In his book, Alden also lists broadleaf (hardwood) forests for spotted salamander habitat, such habitat that blankets much of Martha's Vineyard. In researching his own book, Lazell learned that no one had documented the spotted salamander on that other island, but since publication of *This Broken Archipelago*, several populations of spotted salamanders have been documented, just as the four-toed salamander was discovered on Nantucket in the fall of 2009.

Two diametrically opposing island dynamics in Nantucket's recent natural history are likely to be working the controls of the island's general animal populations, including those of reptiles and amphibians. The first undeniable truth has been the steady loss of habitat to development, both commercial and residential. As of April 2011, human development had eaten up 31.4 percent of the island; however, the other significant factor, conservation of open space, totaled 60.8 percent during the same time period and is probably serving to concentrate the island's wildlife into a sanctuary.

Wetlands were never factored in as part of the island's developable land because, ah, they're wet, and with or without the island's Conservation Commission and the Massachusetts Department of Environmental Protection to enforce the Wetlands Protection Act and the Endangered Species Act, this *terra* could never be *firma* enough for building on in any decade or century. But ringing them with development means species that live in wetlands are corralled in these areas, which become unintended refuges that, when combed through by inquisitive biologists, are more likely to yield greater numbers and even species never before known to be on our islands. Again, Smyers cites the fate of the Eastern spadefoot toad on Nantucket. The one Lazell found may have been the last of his kind on the island, or it may have been just one member of an unknown population, an antecedent of the one found in 1993. These toads could have been part of a small population living in an area surrounded by development and on their last legs (so to speak) before going extinct on the island.[3] In Smyers's view:

> I think it's one of those things where we can't necessarily say that it's a static community of amphibians and reptiles. It's more an ever-changing dynamic of populations where they're going to go up or they're going to go down, whether or not there were people on the island transporting them back and forth inadvertently or on purpose.
>
> There are all sorts of interesting phenomena when there's a big hurricane or massive rainstorm, and the mainland rivers flood and debris washes into the rivers with the trees and root balls. Any animals in them get washed out to the sea, and then [the animal] washes around for quite a while and then ends up washing up on shore. If you have a female that has eggs or babies in her, then you have a population that has nothing to do with the isolation of thousands of years ago, but something that may have happened recently.

Fortunately for whatever scaly, web-footed creatures that have found their way out to our islands through time, the last glacier did right by our reptiles and amphibians in terms of habitat. The silt flowing into Glacial Lake Sesachacha formed layers of clay and sand on its bottom 19,000 to 20,000 years ago. Today those layers underlie or surround wetlands in the northeast corner of the island where many of our creepy crawlies live, including nearly all of Wauwinet, Squam and its forests and swamps, Pocomo, Quidnet, a bit of Sankaty southeast of Sesachacha Pond and most of the Polpis area. These depressions are able to hold water year-round. As a result, several varieties of wetlands, from ponds to vernal pools to swamps to kettle holes and wet meadows, ideal for our reptiles and amphibians, were formed.

In particular, vernal pools, temporary springtime water bodies, become nurseries for the young of green frogs and spring peepers, salamanders and at one time, toads. They provide habitat for painted and spotted turtles, dragonflies, damselflies, water striders and diving beetles. Also, fairy shrimp spend their entire lives in vernal pools having sprung from eggs that hatch after rain refills the seasonally dried out pools.

For those eager to learn the wilderness locations of bullfrogs and their natural distribution as it developed over the years, disappointment is in store. Bullfrogs are, regrettably, an introduced species. They were brought out to Nantucket by rusticators who went urban but wanted a bit of the wild behind their homes in town. They built backyard ponds, festooned them with lily pads and other freshwater aquatic plants, and then yearned for the classic inhabitants of those ponds. So they imported bullfrogs to the island, probably through their pond builders. Since that time, the island's urban bullfrogs have spread to ponds and wetlands all over Nantucket and can be heard chug-a-rumming from along the edges of these wet areas.

With so few representatives from the Orders Anura (frogs), Testudinata (turtles), Squamata (snakes) and Urodela (salamanders), it's easy to place our limited ranks of reptiles and amphibians into their respective habitats around the island. As the Maria Mitchell Association's director of natural science, McKenna-Foster's expertise extends into all quadrants of the island's natural world, but for reptiles, his job is an easy one: "[W]e just look at snakes. Nantucket has lots of freshwater ponds and bogs, which are great for certain species of snakes, especially the ones that feed on amphibians and fish, so water snakes, garter snakes, ribbon snakes—it's great habitat for them. Also, all those wet areas have got a lot of salamanders and worms, which are great for ring-necked snakes. Here, they eat the redback salamanders; that's a favorite food of theirs. This is great habitat for those four species. Most of the island is great habitat for them."

Because there are freshwater sources on Tuckernuck, including the Slough on that island's eastern end and a few kettle holes, garter snakes have established a population on this island, as have ring-necked snakes.

There are other snakes on Nantucket that don't necessarily need the wetlands and instead prefer drier climes. Milk snakes are in high abundance, partly due to the wooded areas and fields on the island, but mostly because of Nantucket's prolific populations of rodents, including mice, shrews, voles and rats. Although they prefer meadows and woodland edges, smooth green snakes live nowhere else on Nantucket but Coatue for the time being, primarily because Coatue has no milk snakes, which dine on smooth green and all other island snakes. There is also on Coatue a plethora of insects on which the green snake can dine. During Lazell's research for his book in the early 1970s, he found them all over Coatue in great number, but Kennedy and McKenna-Foster's 2005 rediscovery of this snake highlighted the volatility of its island population. Although DDT is known to have impacted snakes significantly, it most certainly devastated the insect world on which the smooth green snake survives, so it's highly likely that during Nantucket's DDT spraying days between the late 1930s and late 1960s—the latter decade being when Lazell began researching his book—this snake's numbers out on Coatue were depleted before Lazell began his research on Nantucket.

Those freshwater swamps and ponds and bogs, described by McKenna-Foster as so plentiful on Nantucket: at the very edges of these wet spots is where frog-seekers and salamander voyeurs should spend their time quietly searching for slimy life. Island locales, including the network of swamps and other wet habitats in the Squam Swamp and Squam Farm area, Tom Nevers Pond, Gibbs Pond and the ponds and wet valleys along the south shore from Clark Cove east to Tom Nevers, are all excellent habitats for amphibians, such as green and pickerel frogs and salamanders. Just explore in these areas and you'll hear bullfrogs, green and pickerel frogs, and spring peepers in the wild, which seem to be everywhere at once in all of these habitats when in full voice during the spring.

Says McKenna-Foster of Nantucket's frogs and salamanders:

> Amphibian-wise, it's the bogs and swamps and ponds that make a really good habitat for them. So Squam Swamp: great habit for amphibians, frogs and salamanders—and there's a whole kind of network of swamps up in that area that's prime for amphibians.
>
> Elsewhere on the island, we have the great ponds and Gibbs Pond, and then there are the little wetlands on the south shore: Madequecham for the spadefoot toads [when they were still here], Forked Pond and Toupshue valleys and all those, and . . . those are just the common ones. [Also] Weweeder Pond. So I'm sure the frogs will utilize those areas.
>
> The bullfrogs are still in town, [but] eventually, they'll get all over the island [though] it may take a while. And spring peepers! I've seen one [at Vestal Street to the north], hopping across the road. You can hear them all over the place, but they don't live in water; they live in leaf litter and tree bark. And then the green frog. They're almost always hanging out in the water. Their refuge is the water; they camouflage well on dry land. Pickerel frogs are also living in habitats similar to the green frogs. We seem them mostly at Windswept Cranberry Bog.

But nobody is really out there looking for frogs, except maybe herpetologists and McKenna-Foster himself checking for signs of the chytrid fungus, as they were doing during the summer of 2010 when this frog-afflicting fungus was first noticed on Nantucket specimens. It is formally known as the *Batrachochytrium dendrobatidi*, Chytrid for short, and herpetologists traced the origin of this particular, fatal amphibian fungus to Africa. Little is known about how the fungus, which typically grows on the skin of frogs, actually kills its victims, but it is common knowledge among herpetologists that the fungus somehow affects the skin of frogs and other amphibians in such a way as to impede their breathing, since frogs absorb oxygen through their skin. McKenna-Foster says that the fungus spreads by contact with other frogs and by water once an infected frog enters a water body.

At the time of discovery on the island, chytrid was found to be non-lethal to Nantucket's green, pickerel and spring peeper frogs. McKenna-Foster said that, although he doesn't know how this fungus got to Nantucket, there are two likely possibilities: that it originated here and spread to the mainland or that it arrived in the Americas at several different points along the East Coast of the mainland. Either way, Nantucket's frogs, currently not the subject of any ongoing island studies, seem to be immune to this disease that is decimating frog populations around the world. Had this not been the case, given the finite habitat on the island, Nantucket's frogs wouldn't survive for long.

THE SPOTTED TURTLE

Notwithstanding Nantucket's fungus-resistant frogs, Smyers's snake and salamander research, the now mythical spadefoot toad, and resurgence of smooth green snakes on Coatue, the rock star of the reptile and amphibian world on Nantucket is the spotted turtle. This species is known to number in the hundreds on Nantucket and Tuckernuck, a high enough figure that

Spotted turtle

herpetologists aren't too worried about them surviving. In 2006, the state de-listed them from the protection of its Species of Special Concern rating—though the population is low enough that they still warranted scrutiny in 2011. Naturally, painted turtles and snapping turtles are still important, and yes, you should still stop your car to let any of these turtles cross the road, but cars will not annihilate their numbers beyond recovery. But because Nantucket is literally crawling with both of these species, the spotlight, and in this case, radio telemetry equipment, has always been trained much more on the spotted turtle. It is one of the poster children for all species of life on Nantucket, endangered or not, in company with the piping plover, the Northern harrier and, recently, the horseshoe crab. In the early years of the 21st century, the intrepid young woman charged with slogging through muddy, boggy and swampy environs, and hacking her way into jungles of poison ivy and poison sumac so she can later squint at a screen watching the movements of spotted turtles is Danielle O'Dell, a research technician and field supervisor for the Nantucket Conservation Foundation.

Among O'Dell's duties at the Foundation is to keep tabs on the whereabouts of female spotted turtles 30 to 50 years old, to which she refers as being "just the cutest." Their longevity helps to substantiate morphological evidence that purports that turtles have existed for more than 200 million years and are the oldest of all living reptiles. Their other qualities, and Nantucket habits, O'Dell describes here:

> They're not that common. They don't like the deep ponds. They like a lot of cover, a lot of sphagnum, [and] more shallow, muddy bottom area. You're not going to find them in a big wide-open pond, and if you do, it would be at the edge where there's lots of sweet pepper bush, bayberry-like stuff overhanging and good cover and sphagnum. I would guess they like the more acidic-like, boggy-type places, but open water is not their thing; you're not going to find them in a big, deep pond, which is another reason why you wouldn't see them quite as often. But if you walked in Sanford Farm in June at dusk, you'd see the females coming [out of the water] up to nest, and that's the time when most people see them: when they're coming out of the water.

O'Dell regularly traps spotted turtles to check on their health and reproductive activities, crunching the numbers on all of their data to ultimately learn more about them. In the spring of 2011, she was awaiting DNA testing results from her co-researcher at Wheaton College in Norton, Massachusetts, to determine if the Nantucket population differed from mainland spotted turtles in Milton, Massachusetts. The preliminary results from blood samples taken from both populations suggested that Nantucket's spotted turtles have a marker on their genes that is different from all other populations on the East Coast.[4]

Because of the persistent cooler climate just after the retreat of the last glacier, Lazell reasoned that spotted turtles, a southern species, would not have moved into the area where Nantucket and Tuckernuck would develop until around the end of the coastal plain's existence as dry land, as the ocean separated the islands from the mainland. The turtles must have done some swimming in the biggest, deepest body of water in the region—the Sound—in order to make it to Nantucket. They will swim in salt water if they have to. On a fairly regular basis, they swim through brackish water such as that found in a salt marsh, and Sesachacha and Hummock Ponds, so the likelihood that these turtles forded the widening gaps between the mainland and Martha's Vineyard, the Vineyard and Muskeget, Muskeget and Tuckernuck and Tuckernuck and Nantucket, over a period of decades or centuries, isn't that far-fetched—especially when one considers that Tuckernuck remained connected to Nantucket well into the 1800s. Lazell refers to them as classic examples of southern forms able to populate Nantucket—a remarkable feat at that, considering they likely had to race the rising salt water.

Tuckernucker Bam LaFarge and Collier have both confirmed that spotted turtles are also on Tuckernuck Island, and this is fairly solid evidence of the movement of these turtles between the outer islands and the mainland. But unless they walked over a sand bridge when the islands were still connected, the journey to Tuckernuck would have been quite a challenge for these high-maintenance turtles that are so particular about their surroundings, as O'Dell mentioned above.

Of all the creatures and plant life on this mini-archipelago, the reptiles and amphibians seem to have had the toughest time just getting here and then an equally arduous task of surviving, what with humans spraying the islands with DDT, destroying their habitat and squashing them with automobiles as they seek out sites to lay eggs. If they cross salt water successfully, it is an accident at best: intentionally, it's a last resort, and in many cases it's deadly. Residing in cold climate conditions isn't their cup of pond scum, either. But after the glacier receded, they either found their way back to the Nantucket Ridge before the ocean broke its low peaks up into three islands, or a combination of random distribution and human intervention took over, bringing them to their present situation.

IT'S A BUG'S ISLAND

THANKS TO THE Maria Mitchell Association, the Nantucket Land Council, and the Linda Loring Nature Foundation, some of the less innocuous members of the Nantucket insect world have gained popularity for just existing.

Each September, starting in the early 2000s, Land Council staff members began leading island students on field trips to the Smooth Hummocks section of the south shore's sandplain grasslands, where large patches of goldenrod are blooming, at that time of the year, to tag migrating monarch butterflies with micro-thin stickers.

Each sticker has a number on it and a website at which someone finding one of these large orange and black butterflies may submit the number to help entomologists build their migration and population database.

Children are set loose amongst the goldenrod and bursting milkweed pods with butterfly nets to catch the monarchs and to help stick on the tags. A happy, love-Mother-Earth mood prevails, and the students return to school buzzing about their experience and recharged for the classroom part of their insect and ecology studies.

In the summers of 2010 and 2011, Linda Loring Nature Foundation resident naturalist and property manager E. Vernon Laux led a butterfly count around the island in an attempt to inventory the island's Lepidoptera (the order name for butterfly and moth species). In addition, the Maria Mitchell Association regularly holds summer dragonfly walks and has several seasonal programs dedicated to showing people—mostly kids—the wonders of the insect world. And, in a collaboration of the Maria Mitchell Association, the U.S. Fish & Wildlife Service and the Roger Williams Zoo, American burying beetles were reintroduced to the island from 1994 through 2006 because they had been a native species on Nantucket and a useful processor of carrion.

However, all of these feel-good insect discovery, research and reintroduction programs are, unfortunately, overshadowed by the dastardly deeds of the public enemies, the most-wanted bugs, including deer ticks; mosquitoes, salt water and fresh; greenhead, deer and horse flies; biting spiders (though arachnids, not insects); tent caterpillars; several species of moths reviled by land developers because their endangered status frequently curtails or kills development projects; the many stinging wasps and bees; and fleas and brown ticks on pets. Consequently, the list of pests for which we have oodles of killing products is nearly endless.

Says Maria Mitchell Association Director of Natural Science Andrew McKenna-Foster, himself an island insect expert, "If you lined up all the species on earth, every seventh would be an insect, and every fifth of those would be a weevil, actually. If you take all the arthropods—so that would be insects, as well as spiders and millipedes—[and] weighed them, they'd weigh more than every [other living] thing on earth combined. The biomass of the invertebrates is just unbelievable."

All the creatures we perceive as insects are arthropods, which are invertebrates, animals without backbones, and they include insects, arachnids, centipedes and crustaceans. Instead of an interior skeleton, they have an exoskeleton made of chitin, a hard shell that gives functional shape to their bodies and protects their soft internal body parts and organs.[1] Their bodies are divided into segmented sections, and their arms and legs are jointed.

Monarch butterfly

In classifying arthropods, entomologists—arthropod biologists—break them up into orders. There are around 30 of these, with specific families, classes and species within. The "big four," the most diverse orders of the insect world on the planet, are the Hymenoptera (wasps and bees), Diptera (flies), Lepidoptera (moths and butterflies), and Coleoptera (beetles). Some of the other orders include Trichoptera (caddis flies), Homoptera (leaf hoppers), Anoplura (lice) and Isoptera (termites).

McKenna-Foster hints at the astounding diversity of the arthropod world, "When you start getting down into the species levels, things get a little different, but insects are so diverse that pretty much anywhere you can go, you can find interesting combinations of species. So Nantucket definitely has interesting combinations of insect species."

He estimates that there are 2,317 insect and 250 arachnid species on Nantucket—most of which we'll never see, but it's important to know that they're here, and why and how they got here.

PUBLIC ENEMIES

Much maligned are the insects and arachnids of our planet. Bad human experiences with just a relative handful of the thousands of these creepy crawlies have given all of their species a bad rap.

Yes, there are a lot of enlistees in the anti-insect movement right here on Nantucket, and there are plenty of war stories to tell. In the 1930s, islanders dug miles and miles of ditches through salt marshes to drain standing water, which is ideal egg-laying habitat for saltwater mosquitoes. We drenched the island with DDT for more than 30 years between the late 1930s and late 1960s to kill leaf-eating moths, and there's a whole cadre of Nantucketers on the island at present who want to exterminate or severely cull the whitetail deer herd in an effort to knock down incidents of deer tick–borne diseases. In the spring of 2011, the Madaket mosquito-spraying lobby was able to revive the town's mosquito control program that had been swatted by the Great Recession of 2008.

If you dare, go anywhere on Coatue, around Coskata and out on Great Point during late June through mid-August, and sit or stand in one place for more than a few seconds. Try it. Walk or drive out to Coskata Pond, or paddle a kayak up into the pond and beach it on the eastern shore, and I promise you, a greenhead fly will nail you. Their bite is like getting stuck with a knife. They're not perceived as do-gooder insects fluttering around on a light breeze, like a butterfly looking for flower nectar or like a dragonfly buzzing around a pond, hunting mosquitoes. Instead, the female greenhead flies, like female mosquitoes and the other human-hungry arthropods, want blood so they can lay their eggs. Usually they suck it from deer, horses, cattle and other large mammals, but a scantily clad human lying on a beach or exploring a shallow tidal pond will sate their blood thirst just the same.

Why we're so freaked out by getting bitten is not so much the sting of their mouthparts breaking our skin and the ensuing itchy sensation after we've squashed them dead. It's the diseases these arthropods unknowingly carry in their blood and pass on to us: Lyme disease, Babesiosis, Ehrlichiosis and tick-borne Encephalitis in deer ticks and Eastern Equine Encephalitis, Malaria and West Nile Virus in mosquitoes. And it's the ramifications of being bitten by certain Nantucket spiders, with venom strong enough to swell up a limb to a deep purple tint, and the power of bee and wasp stings sometimes to kill those allergic to them. Like ants at a picnic, collectively, they are the vacation-spoilers and fun-killers on our islands.

QUIET DO-GOODERS

Less visible and threatening, and often working behind the scenes in the leaf litter in forested and heavily vegetated areas including the moors, in swampy areas, in hidden forests and some more-visible surroundings, are other insects that do humans a kindness that most of us aren't aware we can't live without. They process the plant and animal waste of the natural world, pollinate our fruit and vegetable plants, serve as food for birds and animals, and delight children who discover their secrets.

Walk carefully in the Windswept and Milestone cranberry bogs in spring and summer, and keep your eyes open for honeybees zipping between cranberry plant flowers and their hives, along with bumblebees and other lesser-known flying insects that survive on plant nectar while unwittingly acting as plant pollinators.[2] Find a field with tall grass, a brush thicket or a garden and look for fireflies streaking their yellow-green light across the night sky, thrilling children trying to collect them in jars. As you walk out in the island wilderness, your shoes swishing through and crunching down on leaves, grasses, twigs, bark and topsoil, stop for a moment and gather up into your hands what you can of this material. Chances are an earthworm or two, millipedes, slugs, and other insects will appear within this gradually decomposing organic matter. Although the heavy-duty business of decomposing lignin, which holds trees and other wood plants upright into organic matter that is part of our soil's composition, is done by fungi, these insects are eating the spent leaves, bark, grass and other plant parts and expelling waste, which also becomes part of the soil. Without them to team with the fungi, the islands would drown in leaves and brush.

All this is to say that we need our bugs as much as they need us. Despite doing our darndest to wipe many of them from the face of this archipelago, they prove the strength of their links in our island chain of life with a fervor and resiliency that has kept them thriving for millions of years, each contributing in its own specific way while chewing, digging and scraping out a niche for itself.

ISLAND INSECT ORIGINS AND ADAPTABILITY

Laying thousands of eggs at once guarantees the survival of multitudes of insects. But adaptability to the ever-changing climate, habitat, food sources and predators is also key. And one could say that it's a good thing they do practice abundant procreation, because many, many species are food for bats, birds, snakes, frogs and some mammals. During the summer, witness swallows darting low over island ponds in pursuit of flying insects and, at dusk, bats doing the same. Dragonflies seek out mosquitoes, snakes gobble crickets and grasshoppers, and frogs go for freshwater bugs such as water striders.

As with the other creatures that reside on the Nantucket islands today and because of their versatile survival instincts, many of these arthropods, beneficial or harmful, were most likely present all over the coastal plain, including the upland portion that became the Nantucket islands. But the evolution to their physical forms happened millions of years of ago, so many of them were present before the glacier arrived and returned after it retreated. As with the birds, mammals, reptiles and amphibians of our outer islands, the arctic climate of the glacier pushed most of our arthropods southward to where they could survive and it drew cold-weather bugs to the glacial zone where they could thrive. When the ice melted, the southern species gradually returned and the northern ones migrated with the ice.

Although they did not quickly and significantly evolve to adapt to changing climates as the ice advanced and withdrew several times, the ones that couldn't survive going from hot to cold and back again—and having to move between latitudes to survive—likely went extinct. Likewise, populations of insects on our part of the coastal plain that were not mobile enough—those lacking wings—to retreat southward to survive certainly were wiped out for the time being. But the ones able to ebb and flow with the movement of the glacier, as well as with the changing climate, are the arthropods that survived to repopulate the post-glacial, pre-island landscape approximately 18,000 years ago.

In a general sense, this is what entomologist G. R. Coope asserts in his paper, "Several Million Years of Stability among Insect Species Because of, or in Spite of, Ice Age Climatic Instability?" for the January 2004 online version of the *Philosophical Transactions of the Royal Society B: Biological Sciences.* Coope says that fossil evidence shows that insects living today are here because they could survive the ups and downs of our planet's climate, the ice ages and the global warming events, or that they evolved enough to relocate temporarily or to ride out the unfavorable conditions on or near the coastal plain. Then, when things improved enough, they could repopulate the region.

As Coope puts it:

> The species that cleared the first fence of the climatic hurdle race could similarly clear all the rest. Thus the species of the fauna (and presumably also the flora) that are living today are already a selected assemblage of the geographically mobile and latitudinally independent. When the next major climatic change takes place, these species will simply adopt the same stratagem to avoid the climatic changes (unless human activities preclude such an option) that served them so well in the past.

NANTUCKET'S MOST REVILED: THE DEER TICK

One of Nantucket's clearest examples of an arthropod—in this case, an arachnid—surviving tens of thousands, and probably millions, of years of changing climate and habitats in our region, including the advance and retreat of the Laurentide ice sheet, is likely our most reviled: the infamous deer tick.

It is a common myth that the deer tick, with the four diseases it can carry in its blood, is a relatively new insect on the island scene. Since the first recognized case of Lyme disease on Nantucket was about 1977, it's easy to make the leap that these ticks somehow found their way to Nantucket just a few years before one of them first bit a human.

Instead, the deer tick is a classic paradigm of an arthropod evolving to remain in a given geographical location. That humans eventually came into contact with these arachnids—any eight-legged arthropod—is entirely our fault. There was a change, an anthropogenic change, to their habitat. The ticks merely reacted, just as they would have had to adapt to a shift in climate or a lack of food, when development brought humans within biting distance—and gave regional entomologists a renewed sense of purpose in life.

One of these entomologists and a leading expert on deer ticks and the diseases they carry is Dr. Sam R. Telford, III, a professor in the Department of Biomedical Sciences focusing on Infectious Diseases at Tufts University's Cummings School of Veterinary Medicine, who has made Nantucket his personal outdoor research lab for deer ticks. Although there is no way of knowing for sure when these tiny pests arrived in our region, Telford and the late Wes Tiffney, co-founder of the UMass Boston Nantucket Field Station, theorized that this tick and the infectious organisms inside it arrived here 15 to 20 million years ago.

They believed that their hypothesis had eight legs to stand on: the Baltic amber tick. Telford and Tiffney reasoned that the Baltic amber tick, which is morphologically indistinguishable from the deer tick, and five other ticks, all probably descended from the Russian tick, lived in a swath of the Northern Hemisphere encompassing the Cape and Islands region during the Miocene Epoch—5.3 million to 23 million years ago—within the Tertiary Period, 1.6 million to 66 million years ago. And that it's more than probable that, during this time, the Baltic amber tick had in its blood, and was transmitting, the spirochetes of the Lyme disease bacterium, Babesiosis, Ehrlichiosis and tick-borne encephalitis, Telford's four horsemen of tick-borne infectious diseases.

With the Laurentide ice sheet gradually smothering New England, covering the land 25,000 years ago, movement of all animal species away from the ice and the climate, which was cooling to arctic conditions, had already been going on for several thousand years. The life forms that were sufficiently mobile, as with plant species, relocated to refugia further east, west and south of Nantucket's part of the coastal plain.

One such place relatively nearby, which Telford and Tiffney strongly believed harbored the Baltic amber tick, its relatives and very likely the deer tick living on the coastal plain, was Georges Bank, 60 nautical miles east-southeast of Nantucket today. Eventually inundated by glacier meltwater raising the ocean to its present level and today a productive fishing ground, Georges Bank was once at the outer edge of the coastal plain as part of the mainland, but it was spared coverage by the ice. At 149 miles long and 75 miles wide, Georges Bank, likely named in the 17th century for the English patron saint, George, is between 15 and 150 feet below the surface of the ocean today.

As Telford tells it, when the glacier melted, our bugs and other creatures gradually came back from refugia such as Georges Bank:

> What we see today, or back when these things were first described in New England, back in the '70s, is a reintroduction or reinvasion from sites where they were pushed during glaciation. So, really, all of what we see in New England stems from what used to be called Georges Island (now called the Georges Bank, which, when it was an island during glaciation, was a [refugium]), and points farther south. The fauna and flora were pushed southward by the glaciers as they retreated and suitable land was formed, [and] the land got reinvaded and the ticks and their diseases came back. . . .

How all that life found its way back to the regraded coastal plain, where Nantucket, Tuckernuck and Muskeget would eventually emerge as islands, is another matter. Those with wings were able to travel great distances back to this area, certainly from Georges Island to the Nantucket area. Moth experts Dr. Paul Z. Goldstein, an entomologist specializing in Lepidoptera at the National Museum of Natural History within the Smithsonian Institution, and Mark Mello, research director at the Lloyd Center for the Environment in Dartmouth, Massachusetts, generally agree that it's an easy trip for a moth or butterfly between Nantucket and the mainland or Martha's Vineyard, so finding their way inland back to the coastal plain probably wouldn't have been that much more of a stretch. But Goldstein says that insects with wingless females and those with no wings at all would need a habitat corridor of dry land to immigrate through gradually over time to repopulate the area, a dry land area that certainly existed between the refugia of Georges Bank and the Nantucket Archipelago area of the coastal plain.

So rebuilding of insect and arachnid populations, like the replanting of the Cape and Islands, didn't happen in one great wave but in overlapping spurts, depending on the species and how each adapted first to tundra conditions, later to coniferous forests, then to hardwoods and finally to the low shrublands and grasslands of Nantucket's maritime heathlands and sandplain grasslands that dominate the island today.[3]

Mixed in with whatever arthropods, mammals, reptiles, amphibians and birds came back from the Georges Bank and other refugia were a relatively small number of southern species returning, as their temporary southern habitats heated up too much for them to tolerate, believe most entomologists, including Mello and Goldstein.

But there were also numerous Midwestern arthropod species that Goldstein says are from grassland and prairie habitats that likely found Nantucket because of the prairie peninsula, which botanists believe is responsible for seeding Nantucket's heathlands and sandplain grasslands with prairie plants, which would explain how the 27 outer Southeastern Massachusetts islands got such a good dose of arthropod species from the Midwest.

Another theory is that of Charles Willison Johnson, Curator of Insects and Mollusks for the Boston Society of Natural History and author of "A List of Insect Fauna of Nantucket, Massachusetts" for the Maria Mitchell Association. Willison believed that such an infusion of southern, or austral, and Midwestern insects could only have happened before the melting glacial ice submerged the entire coastal plain. In the introduction to his guide, Johnson postulated:

> To understand better some of the problems bearing on the distribution of insects on Nantucket there are many things to be considered. Botanists, in studying certain of the more southern plants that occur in Newfoundland, have come to the conclusion that this particular distribution could only have come about by the presence of a post-glacial land-bridge connecting New Jersey with Newfoundland, the presence of these plants so far north and on Sable Island and in favorable places in Nova Scotia representing only remnants of the flora of a large post-glacial coastal plain.

After their return, the deer ticks and their cousins and the white-tailed deer coexisted without humans for maybe 10,000 years, give or take a few thousand, depending on the hardiness of each species. This was true also of the other insects populating the emerging archipelago as they either returned from their refugia or found our coastal plain upland area for the first time.

The ticks most likely bit and infected the Native Americans after they arrived, 8,000 to 11,000 years ago. However, since they had no way of determining what bit them or how to qualify the experience, and because the science of entomology, the study of infectious diseases and science itself as a broad concept weren't even in their infancy in the human world at that time, there is no record of this early human-tick interaction. And it certainly was not documented on Nantucket, at least until well into the 20th century. Telford and Tiffney postulated that the deer tick population plummeted as the Native American population and, later, the European settlers decimated the deer habitat by leveling nearly all the island's trees for lumber, crops and fuel, and finally, to add insult to injury, unintentionally kept trees from returning by grazing 15,000 sheep while they hunted the island's deer to extinction. Deer ticks might even have been extirpated from the island.

True, deer tick larvae survive on white-footed mice, shrews, voles and birds, but the female deer tick, which has to lay the eggs from which the larvae hatch, won't drink blood from mammals smaller than a cat. While Telford admits that there were plenty of feral cats on the islands, and certainly loads of rabbits, after the deer disappeared, he says, by way of example, that he has never found more than five deer ticks on a rabbit at one time. So, deer being the dominant mammal of deer tick choice—Telford has counted up to 300 on a large buck—when they disappear, so do deer ticks.

Telford speculates that this tick may have held out in isolated pockets of the island, including hidden forests and the mature maritime oak groves of the Coskata Woods, which were never harvested and eventually protected for good by a town bylaw adopted in 1711. However, he points to a fairly thorough 1940s Maria Mitchell Association insect and arachnid survey that lists dog ticks but no blacklegged ticks (deer ticks) during the first few decades of the 20th century.

At any rate, deer ticks and their diseases didn't disappear from all of the 27 islands south of Cape Cod.[4] Specifically, Telford and Tiffney knew that a healthy deer herd and deer ticks persisted at least on Naushon Island in the Elizabeth Islands, because Naushon, the closest of this chain of islands to the mainland, has remained privately owned and its trees, a primary forest of 100-foot-plus American beech, left largely unharvested. Naushon's deer have been on that island at least since the 1600s and have never experienced a significant depletion in population due to hunting. Not surprisingly, the deer tick is quite prevalent on that island, as well. Telford and Tiffney knew this because, in the late 1920s, a team of researchers from the Harvard Medical School, led by S. Burt Wolbach, professor of comparative pathology at Harvard, was hired by a group of residents from Martha's Vineyard and Falmouth and by the Forbes family, which owns Naushon, to cull the dog tick population in their areas. To do this, experimentally raised wasps were released on the island. The wasps' reproductive method relies on them laying eggs inside the dog ticks as they feed on dog and other mammal blood. To do this, the female wasps use their ovipositor, or stinger, to puncture the tick and temporarily paralyze it with her venom so she can lay her eggs, which emerge from the base of the stinger protruding from the end of her abdomen, and go into the tick. The wasp eggs remain intact until the tick starts feeding in the next phase of its life. When they hatch inside the tick, the baby wasps eat the tick from the inside out, and new wasps crawl out of the devoured body of the tick. Before Dr. Wolbach and his team released the wasps at the three locations, they did an extensive tick survey of each, finding plenty of dog ticks and deer ticks in 1927.

It was five years earlier that fishermen on the fishing vessel, *Antonia*, rescued the white-tailed deer buck ten miles from Madaket Harbor as it swam toward Muskeget from Martha's Vineyard. When they released it in 'Sconset, it became the first of its kind to return to the island since 1922. And with this deer, and the two does that Breckenridge Long, U.S. Ambassador to Italy, imported to the island from Michigan, whitetail deer, and probably deer ticks and their diseases, were reintroduced to Nantucket. As Telford details, it wasn't just bringing back the deer that reinstated the deer tick population on Nantucket's islands.

> My guess is that as the land improved on Nantucket, or devolved, as I would say—I argue that sheep pastures are probably healthier than the scrub oak you see out there today—that birds and probably people's dogs, traveled between Naushon and Nantucket and carried the tick from Naushon back to Nantucket, and the conditions changed. As the habitat changed, and as deer density increased on Nantucket, you had the tick achieve densities that probably are way more than what would be naturally sustained, for example, in the primary forest of Naushon. That's what Wes and I came up with.

If deer, dogs and birds brought the deer tick back to Nantucket, it was humans who altered the island habitat to allow the deer and the deer tick to thrive. In the 1980s, Dr. Telford found Lyme disease spirochetes on mouse specimens in museums on Eastern Long Island from 1941 and Cape Cod from 1894, proving for him that this disease, and most likely the other three, were with us all along at non-threatening background population levels until we humans altered the ticks' habitat and began to manage—and protect—deer populations with hunting seasons, wildlife refuges and animal rights activism, allowing their numbers to grow.

The habitat necessary for deer tick survival started growing on Nantucket in approximately 1890, once the island's collective sheep herd began to diminish to the point where it no longer prevented the larger woody shrub species, including scrub oak, dwarf chestnut oak, black huckleberry and, later, pitch pine and other trees from proliferating. By the time deer were reintroduced to Nantucket in the 1920s, the island's grasslands were well on their way toward growing into dense thickets of these and other plants. In less than a decade, Breckenridge Long's two Michigan does and Old Buck from the Vineyard had spawned an island herd estimated at 280, not counting whatever existed on Tuckernuck at the time.

Reacting to what most certainly was a high population number then and attempting to combat loss of their crops to the deer, island farmers raised enough of a furor to reinstate Nantucket's deer hunting season starting in 1936. Massachusetts instituted its statewide deer-hunting season in 1910, and Nantucket followed with its own in 1912 to 1929, but for some reason, there was no deer-hunting season from 1930 through 1935 on Nantucket, except for a special hunt held in mid-February 1935.

With Nantucket's deer herd protected from hunting during those years, it was able to expand even further, as was the deer tick population. Unable to live in the comparatively arid conditions of the grasslands that the sheep created with their insatiable appetite, the ticks much prefer the wetter and humid habitat provided in the dense cover of the scrub oak and forest habitats.

Human–deer–tick contact happened as a result of these man-made conditions, Dr. Telford explains:

> We created the problem by changing the landscape and allowing deer to come back in numbers that are just unprecedented, but [the deer tick with its diseases] was around for a long time, under our nose. We did something in the early part of the 20th century by managing deer herds and controlling hunting seasons, as well as allowing the landscape to come up to this very thick vegetation, and that's the second critical aspect to this: the tick is very sensitive to drying out, and so, even though there's a lot of dew on pastures out on Nantucket, if you can find a pasture . . . that's not wet enough. It burns off too quickly. You're never going to find ticks out on the open pasture landscape. They need the thick vegetation—the poison ivy, the scrub oak, the green briar and the high-bush blueberry—to survive more than a few weeks. They require a relative humidity greater than 85 percent for most of the time.

This momentous change, occurring on Nantucket as on the mainland, escalated to the point where islanders were calling the symptoms following a strange, spider-like bite "Nantucket Fever." Identified as Babesiosis in 1969 by the Center for Disease Control, which visited the island then to investigate this "new" disease, similar symptoms, including the now-classic bull's-eye rash, were later classified as those of Lyme disease when it was first recognized in Old Lyme, Connecticut, in 1974.

Nantucket's first acknowledged case, Dr. Telford believes, was coincidentally that of 'Sconset summer resident Dr. Gustav Dammin, diagnosed in 1977. Married to Nantucketer Anita Coffin, Dr. Dammin was, in the 1950s, the chief pathologist at Peter Bent Brigham Hospital in Boston, now called Brigham & Women's Hospital. It was Dr. Dammin who first recognized organ transplant graft rejection, and he was one of three surgeons who performed the first successful kidney transplant.

Deer ticks, starting with the female's blood meal, have a two-year lifecycle. After mating on the body of white-tailed deer during a two-month period in the fall, the female falls to the ground as the male continues looking for new mates. The female overwinters and then lays her eggs—up to 2,000 if she got all the blood she needed—in the spring down in the leaf litter and dies. The larvae hatch from their eggs in early summer, get one blood meal from whatever small mammal or bird they can find on the ground, and then go into hibernation for the winter. In the following spring, they molt into nymphs, the most likely of the stage of the deer tick, the adult being second, to attach to and bite a human. At the end of that October, the nymph molts, becomes an adult and the cycle begins on white-tailed deer again.

Awareness of this newly rediscovered menace—the deer tick, its lifecycle and the diseases it carried—led many Nantucketers to report that they were experiencing or had experienced the symptoms, as well as to begin to identify for themselves what infections they might have and where they came from. But no one at this point in the history of tick-borne diseases on Nantucket was keeping tabs on numbers of cases or really examining the diseases themselves on the island. That began to change when Dr. Timothy J. Lepore, M.D., an assistant professor at Brown Medical School who ran the emergency room and the surgical side of the intensive care unit at Roger Williams Hospital in Providence, Rhode Island, spent the Augusts of 1980, 1981 and 1982 working in the emergency room at Nantucket Cottage Hospital.

Lepore, fascinated at the time by the recent discovery of Lyme disease and Babesiosis on the island and relishing the idea of being plunked down in epidemic conditions to practice medicine, leapt at the chance to join in the "fun" when the opportunity to apply for a surgeon position at Nantucket Cottage Hospital came along in the fall of 1982. Since January 1983, when he arrived at Nantucket Cottage Hospital, Dr. Lepore has been tracking incidents of Lyme disease on Nantucket with the help of Telford and others. Telford, who discovered Ehrlichiosis on Nantucket with Lepore and Pam Snow in 1995; Andy Stielman, a world-class researcher in infectious disease at Harvard School of Public Health who discovered Babesia on Nantucket in 1979; and Peter Krause, senior research scientist in epidemiology (microbial diseases) at the Yale School of Public Health, helped Lepore get up to speed.

From Telford, Lepore learned how Nantucket's deer- and tick-friendly dense habitat had evolved at the hands of its human inhabitants to become what he calls "a deer park," ideal for supplying deer ticks with ample supplies of blood for females to lay eggs. On his own, he observed how the island's development had already begun gradually to spread out onto the edges of the moors and into other island wilderness areas where deer lived. Homeowners were planting trees, shrubs and flowers that deer love to eat, thereby drawing deer closer to humans, bringing their nasty little eight-legged piggybackers along for the ride.

Not that Lepore wished any of these diseases on the members of his new island community. However, such coincidental forces of natural and man-made circumstance presented a unique opportunity for Nantucket's newest doctor and for his entomologist/pathologist researcher friends, who were similarly intrigued by how these diseases were spreading.

Lepore sums it all up with a weather-like spin on things:

> You take a look at all of the elements and you create the perfect storm: you introduce deer, you let the brush grow up and move the houses out, and you have the ticks. What more could you want? I mean, this is the perfect storm. There's nothing in between rabbits, mice and deer. No chipmunks. Squirrels are a pretty recent addition. All of a sudden, you have this enormous pressure cooker that has been created, and it's fascinating. It's fascinating to be here and see this. And Andy and Sam really put all the pieces together.

When they did, and the diseases could be identified in blood smears on slides in the hospital lab or by off-island labs, the numbers of identified cases began to expand exponentially, because public awareness of the symptoms had hit the mainstream island consciousness. In 2009, Lepore logged 411 cases of tick-borne diseases, 300 of which were Lyme disease.

In 2011, between January and August, he had 50 cases of Babesiosis. He treats around 100 cases of Lyme disease in his office alone, and he estimates that, on average, there are 200 to 400 cases of tick-borne diseases per year on Nantucket.

But these are just the infections he and other island doctors have diagnosed and treated. Many more people get bitten on island without realizing it, leave Nantucket and then develop symptoms where these diseases aren't prevalent. Lepore regularly gets calls from bewildered doctors around the world—British Columbia, England, France, Germany to name a few—trying to diagnose these short-term Nantucket visitors who accidentally met the wrong sort of local.

The disease confirmation process is equally daunting. The Centers for Disease Control and Prevention broadly directs hospitals and doctors to identify Lyme disease, Babesiosis and Ehrlichiosis by the classic red, expanding bull's-eye rash, which Lepore and many Nantucketers know could mean any one or a combination of the three diseases. Thankfully, Babesiosis can be diagnosed in the island's hospital lab from a blood smear on a slide, by looking at liver chemistry and platelets in the blood. The same goes for Ehrlichiosis, but it is more challenging because Lepore and the lab technicians must look for elevations in liver enzymes—a more difficult process, according to Lepore. However, the Massachusetts Department of Public Health won't rely on a hospital's clinical diagnosis, even the classic red bull's-eye rash, facial palsies and heart blockage. The DPH must have the serology from the patient's blood sample to confirm an incidence of Lyme disease.

Prevention of these diseases is really quite simple for Lepore, who agrees with Telford: reduction of the deer herd down from the current level of 55 per square mile to as few as ten deer per square mile, which they believe would knock down the deer tick population considerably. It's a solution that has proven unpopular on Nantucket, with the regional branch of the People for the Ethical Treatment of Animals (PETA) and even with hunters who feel that such a culling of the herd would mean fewer deer to hunt during the fall hunting seasons. Many island and visiting hunters rely on venison as part of their diet during the fall and winter months. Large-scale efforts to kill deer have proven in the past to anger island residents. Most of today's opposition weren't alive for the special hunt in 1935 but still point to human and dog injuries, destruction of property and unsightly disposal of deer carcasses.

Witness the weeklong MassWildlife-sanctioned February 2004 special deer hunt requested by Nantucket's Board of Selectmen in answer to outcry over the deer tick–borne disease epidemic. During this rare winter hunt, in which 900 deer-hunting permits were issued, hordes of off-island hunters flailed around in several feet of snow covering an unfamiliar island wilderness they knew little, if anything, about. They left deer carcasses everywhere and angered island residents, including individual hunters and the Nantucket Hunting Association, which, collectively, let fly a barrage of vitriol nearly as caustic as PETA's usual objections during the regular season.

Lepore noted, optimistically, that this hunt killed 254 deer in a week, bringing the total harvested in the 2003 season to around 800 deer. Anecdotally, he heard from landscapers and gardeners in the spring that deer browsing of residential vegetation had been much less than normal during the winter. But opposition to this special hunt was so strong that Nantucket's Board of Selectmen requested that the Massachusetts Division of Fisheries and Wildlife cancel it indefinitely, which MassWildlife did.

This left Nantucket with limited options, which it continues to ponder. A little help does come from the Damminix mousetraps named for Dr. Dammin. Their insides are coated with an insecticide called Permethrin, which is a synthetic pyrethroid grounded in a natural compound extracted from chrysanthemums. Islanders place these toilet-paper-like cardboard tubes around their yards, and the Damminix certainly kills recently hatched deer tick larvae that are getting their summer blood meal on white-footed mice that pass through the tubes. But placement of the tubes is spotty around the island at best, and entirely dependent on individual property owners' dedication to deploying them regularly.

Since outright deer extermination was proven financially and morally impossible on Nantucket, and the cost of distributing enough four-poster feeding stations—essentially troughs filled with corn at which deer must push their heads through four rolling-pin-like posts coated with insecticide to eat—around the island was deemed fiscally beyond reach, the status quo prevails.

The moving target that the Town of Nantucket and its citizens haven't been able to hit then landed, but remained unactuated, on the 2010 recommendation by the town's Tick Advisory Committee for the broadening of the existing hunting season, a plan for which there was scant political will and funding at the time. Even Lepore pooh-poohed it, reiterating what every hunter already knows, that most of the deer in a given season are shot during the first two or three days, so a longer season probably wouldn't help. Admittedly, it's been quite a political struggle, a waste of paper and an enormous expenditure of hot air, when the real—albeit drastic—solution seems already to have been tried unintentionally by hungry and cold Native Americans and European settlers, and proven effective long ago: the extermination of all of the deer on the island.

The destruction of a major component of our partially natural island world was not the course of action Nantucket pursued to combat the diseases it carries. But to think that islanders went to the extreme of even *considering* it says something about the tremendous impact of insects and arachnids on the planet, and on our island lives.

THE USEFULNESS OF BUGS

Notwithstanding designation of a CDC epidemic in reaction to the rash of deer tick-borne disease infections, deer-eradication proposals from island committees, and islanders' collective suffering of tick-borne diseases, not to mention mosquito and greenhead misery and bee and wasp venom allergies: not every arthropod deserves negative attention. They're not all out to suck your blood or sting you into paralysis, and they don't deserve to be cleansed from the face of the planet—or at least from these islands.

So, allow me to direct your attention to the soil of the island, where baby deer ticks and other children of those feared arthropods feed in the leaf litter. Alongside the hungry tick infants are a host of arthropod species, joined by other dirt-makers called detritivores, including bacteria, snails, slugs, millipedes, isopods, collembola, earthworms and even lichens, mosses and fungi that literally do the dirty work of making the island's soil by processing its organic waste. Some of them were here to help build the first layers of podzol soil from the sand and gravel medium left bare when the glacier receded. They augmented the nutrient supplies of tundra plant species that were the first vegetation to take root 18,000 to 19,000 years ago on the coastal plain upland areas.

The lichens, as I mentioned in the third chapter, do some of this work on rocks, wood shingles and tree bark, along with some mosses, but fungi alone process dead trees. All of these contribute to the production of soil. Woodlice and dung flies along with other detritivores including snails, slugs, earthworms, millipedes, fiddler crabs, isopods and collembola, munch through and absorb tiny pieces of dead and decaying plant materials and soil with organic components of many kinds, adding organic matter to the soil.

Beetles, of which there are several species on Nantucket, are another kind of waste processor, eating fecal matter and the dead bodies of mammals, birds, insects, amphibians and reptiles, and extruding organic matter that further enriches the soil, adding another source of food for plants. This part of the chain of life on Nantucket is vital to other insects on the island, such as moths, butterflies and bees that rely on plants for food and shelter.

In short, we can't live without our arthropods. As McKenna-Foster explains, "If our invertebrate population becomes unhealthy and drops down, waste is going to accumulate. We'd be up to our eyeballs in leaf litter and all this other stuff. In Nantucket, since our soils are so nutrient-poor, the detritivores, the ones that are breaking down the leaf litter, and the bacteria . . . too, are really important in terms of cycling those nutrients [and] making them available for plants to use."

Beetles were the first family of insects to be recorded on Nantucket. The first insect, discovered in 1832, was the Northeastern beach tiger beetle. A whitish-tan-colored beetle that lived on the beaches, hibernating in a burrow beneath the sand and coming out to scavenge dead animals and breed during the summer months, the Northeastern beach tiger beetle is extinct on Nantucket, likely because of heavy oversand vehicle traffic and coastal development.

Another dead-meat-eating beetle that had gone extinct on the island as of 1926 and was listed nationally as an endangered species in 1973, the American burying beetle, is a large black-and-orange beetle that lays its eggs inside of dead birds, giving its young a food source. This beetle is the focus of a restoration effort that began on Nantucket and Block Island in 1994.

What the detritivores, decomposers and scavengers do that benefits other arthropods that depend on plants for their existence is to provide a medium for island vegetation to grow. Climate change is causing all sorts of unexpected fluctuations in vegetation that carry an impact through to insect lifecycles. This is a survival dynamic that has contributed to the gradual evolution, and sometimes extinction, of all arthropod species since the beginning of their existence.

MOTHS AND BUTTERFLIES

The effects of sheep farming cessation and deer herd management have also helped cultivate our complement of moths and butterflies. Certainly, scores of moth and butterfly species already existed on the island, the breadth of their varieties ebbing and flowing with changing vegetation over the centuries and millennia, and likely joining the ticks in benefiting from the decline in sheep on the island—at least until humans decided that some moths and their respective caterpillars should suffer the same fate as deer ticks because of their appetite for the leaves of our hardwood trees. After all, humans brought some of them to the island, including gypsy moth eggs attached to cordwood shipped from the mainland, first sighted in 1917; the leopard moth, which likely arrived on Nantucket via ornamental tree saplings; and the European corn-borer that probably got to the island inside green corn husks or other larvae-favored plants.

Although the town's Moth Suppression Department originally targeted the white-marked tussock moth because of its predilection for broadleaf trees, beginning with Madaket, the spraying dealt death handily, although accidentally, to other "pests" and to untold numbers of other arthropod species. They were a land-based by-catch caught in the net of humans trying to protect their broadleaf trees and agricultural crops.

With the 30-plus-year history of DDT spraying, it's certainly possible that the tussock moth and the other species were extirpated from Nantucket by that means—or at least their numbers severely curtailed. And DDT could have pushed one butterfly, the regal fritillary, to such low population numbers that it couldn't recover. A more likely scenario, though, and one to which regional moth expert Mark J. Mello, research director at the Lloyd Center for the Environment in Dartmouth, Massachusetts, subscribes, is plant succession: new species replacing existing ones as habitat conditions change. This dynamic probably contributed to the drop in white-marked tussock moth numbers, as well.

Moths are mostly nocturnal, meaning they operate at night, and butterflies spend their waking hours during the day. Moths have short, compact bodies, comb-like antennae and colors predominantly in muted earth tones. The opposite goes for butterflies, with their brightly colored wings, slender, lollypop-shaped antennae and wings pointed vertically when they aren't flying.

The difference between the selection of moths and butterflies living on Nantucket when sheep maintained the island's grassland and those that are here now, thanks to plant succession, is staggering. This is evidenced by a comparison between Mello's island surveys and those done by Charles P. Kimball, who researched and catalogued the moths and butterflies on Nantucket for the Maria Mitchell Association from the late 1800s—when sheep numbers began to drop precipitously—through the early 1940s. Kimball published his first Lepidoptera survey in 1943 in a book co-authored by Charles Morton Jones, who also surveyed Martha's Vineyard, and followed with updates in 1944 and in 1945.

This comparison of moth and butterfly data collected at different times on the three islands is relevant also because Kimball's research was part of the fairly young and emerging field of entomological study on Nantucket. As Johnson noted in his Nantucket insect fauna book, biologists paid only "meager" attention to arthropods before 1832, when the Northeastern beach tiger beetle became the first insect to be recorded as an island resident. Johnson's insect fauna book, published by the Maria Mitchell Association in 1930, and Kimball and Jones's original lifetime Lepidoptera survey, an MMA publication in 1943, were the first comprehensive arthropod research offerings for Nantucket's three islands.

Kimball and Jones's first volume was generated by scores of Nantucketers scouring the island over a period of at least 50 years, bringing moths and butterflies that they'd found to Kimball. These specimens, along with the fruits of his own collection efforts, contributed to a list totaling 582 moth and 405 butterfly species on Nantucket alone. In surveying Nantucket for its butterflies and moths for the book, entitled *The Lepidoptera of Nantucket and Martha's Vineyard Islands, Massachusetts*, Kimball and Jones found that the two islands were not deficient in Lepidoptera species, compared with the mainland. Breadth of diversity in species, then, was not affected by each island's small acreage in relation to the mainland's or by the distance over water that these species might travel to reach either island. Rather, it was mainly vegetation that played, and still does, a major role in determining what moth and butterfly species live on the outer islands of southeastern Massachusetts. The same is true for most of the insect and arachnid world. Mello's own survey of Nantucket's moths through 2005 revealed 608 species, 152 of which Kimball didn't find and 127 more of Kimball's species that Mellow was unable to find again on Nantucket after Kimball first recorded them. That's more than a 30 percent change in the number of moth species found on Nantucket—and that's not counting butterflies. Mello believes the reduction was the result of vegetation changes since Kimball was counting on Nantucket.

Mello notes that the largest category of moth species (and by extrapolation probably butterfly species as well), no longer found on Nantucket and Tuckernuck, encompasses those species that depend on grassland plant habitat. Although these two islands still have large areas of sandplain grasslands, the only explanation with which he is comfortable is that of plant succession over time. As Mello tells it, "The single biggest reason is probably habitat succession. I mean, there was hardly a tree on the island when [Kimball] was collecting. I think sheep grazing had just ended, so it was a very different landscape than it is today. Part of the evidence is that the largest category of species I found that he didn't are a species that feeds on oaks and other trees—tree oaks rather than the scrub oaks—so those two things are pretty good evidence. And they're things that are common, and they're things that are common on the Vineyard; they're not obscure species that he's likely to have overlooked."

An additional explanation is that prescribed burning by the Nantucket Heathlands Partnership, during the spring and fall since 1993, may have had an impact on the species diversity. Also, well before the NHP employed fire for their invasive species control and enhancement of sandplain grassland habitat, the island's Native Americans used it, and game hunters of various shorebird species in the late 1800s into the early 1900s would burn the moors from Milestone Road to Tom Nevers every August to level their cover and make good feeding grounds for golden plovers and Eskimo curlews.

But Mello has no explanation for the disappearance of the regal fritillary, a butterfly that was abundant on Nantucket before 1889. The larvae of the regal fritillary, a nearly two-inch-long orange-and-black butterfly with white spots on its wings, feeds on violets that still exist on Nantucket's grasslands.[5] The adult butterflies dine on milkweed, thistle, goldenrod, clover, ironweed, blazing star, bergamot and cornflowers, most of which still grow on Nantucket and Tuckernuck. And yet, today, only one holdout regal fritillary population exists in the East: at Fort Dix, New Jersey.

The regal fritillary's inability to make it on Nantucket, despite an abundance of its favorite foods and ample habitat, is a cautionary tale that underscores the survival traits one must have to exist and prosper on this trio of islands. There is an entrance fee, a slate of prerequisites that are leveled on all life forms in this archipelago, including humans in present day. Like those islanders who tough it out year-round, really earning their places on Nantucket by exerting more effort than is required on the mainland and during Nantucket's summer season, the arthropods, reptiles, amphibians, birds, mammals, marine life and vegetation have to want it, really *want* to be on the island, because the habitat is sparse and disagreeable. The soil is poor and shallow, food and cover resources are limited and the winters can be harsh, with howling salt-drenched winds, snow, ice, rain and a spring that is about a month behind the mainland and growing. And although more than 60 percent of the islands are preserved as open space, encroaching development remains a factor in cramping the survival style of many species. But then, this has always been the status quo on the outer islands of Massachusetts.

SURVIVOR: NANTUCKET, THE INSECT EDITION

Certain biologic credentials—essential body parts or abilities—cover the price of admission to these islands, guaranteeing at least on-island existence. An individual species's prolonged prosperity is dependent on a host of factors, including adaptability to habitats, food sources, predators, climate conditions and reproductive prowess. Grasshoppers and crickets can hop and fly. Ants can burrow into the ground, as can some wasps, while others of this family can make paper nests in trees and under eaves. Spiders can spin webs to catch and eat other arthropods from the islands' unlimited supply. There are honeybees, *Apis mellifera,* a species introduced in Europe in the 1600s and probably shortly thereafter by European settlers to Nantucket, and bumblebees, which Goldstein said certainly were able to fly long distances over water, and 48 other species of bees. All found a way to make it on the islands . . . for now.

Habitat evolution, as Goldstein, Mello and McKenna-Foster said, is the biggest determining factor of island arthropod diversity. Goldstein explains, "The island insect faunas undergo regular turnover, with species disappearing and being replaced by others at rates that depend on the island's size, its proximity to the mainland, and how quickly its landscape is undergoing change, vegetational and otherwise."[6]

DRAGONFLIES AND DAMSELFLIES

One order of insects that entomologists are pretty clear was in existence, going back through time to when the three islands were upland areas on the coastal plain, is *Odonata*: dragonflies and damselflies. As conspicuous an insect on Nantucket as mosquitoes, but much more graceful in flight and certainly no threat to your blood, these helicopters of the arthropod world have most likely been present since the beginning of island time, and millions of years before that. Go out to Miacomet Pond, Hummock Pond, Clark Cove, the little marsh at the northwest corner of Sesachacha Pond, the Slough on Tuckernuck and its small ponds, and possibly the tiny ponds and wetland areas on Muskeget, or any of the other ponds surrounded by cattails and common reeds during July and August, and you'll see these mosquito-eating insects darting everywhere. But know what you're looking at. If you see something with a long, skinny abdomen, flying tentatively, eyes wide apart in a hammerhead configuration and delicate-looking wings held together up over its body at rest, you're seeing a damselfly. A similar looking insect that flies aggressively and with great agility, because each of its four wings is powered by its own muscle group, the dragonfly has a thicker, beefier abdomen, its eyes draping almost all over its head (surely the inspiration for the term "bug eyes"), and its wings—each set a different size and form—jutting out straight from its body when at rest.

Where there's fresh water, there have always been dragonflies and damselflies. Both families of this order likely inhabited our portion of the coastal plain during the late Pleistocene Epoch before the glacier arrived. They gradually flew to refugia on Georges Island or south or west of where Nantucket would be someday, and then returned over time.

Only a few of these insects, such as the giant green darner, a blue-green dragonfly, migrate between Nantucket and points south, possibly as far as the Caribbean. And obviously, their migrations are successful, as these large dragonflies are buzzing all over the island during the summer and even into the fall.

Dragonfly

Like birds, insects with wings and the strength to travel distances came and went from Nantucket as they needed, depending on the location of the glacier. Yes, some species arrived on the islands for the first time via ships from the mainland and from ports around the world, but a majority would have found the island on their own wings, on the bodies of birds and mammals, on the wind.

Unlike mammal biologists, botanists and reptile/amphibian biologists, but similar to ornithologists working on the outer islands of New England, the potential for entomologists to discover new arthropod species is huge out on the Nantucket Archipelago. The temperature of the planet is gradually rising, and though it's easy to think that the warmer it gets the more southern species will find Nantucket, fluctuations in temperature also affect the rate of their arrival and storm intensity. These factors can randomly bring new species of insects and birds to the islands at varying speeds. And, due to their size, some arthropods may not have been discovered. It's highly likely that entomologists will continue to discover either species new to the island or those that have remained undetected.

ARACHNIDS

Such discoveries occurred during the first decade of the 21st century. Arachnid and arthropod experts McKenna-Foster and Cheryl Beaton, both at the time in the employ of the Maria Mitchell Association, found two spiders never before documented on Nantucket. The first, the Northern black widow spider, likely arrived on Nantucket and Tuckernuck a couple thousand years after the glacier melted back up into Canada, but before the ocean crept into the lowlands to make our islands. These black widows are members of the cob weaver family, *Theridiidae*, alongside the Southern black widows, which were introduced into the Northern black widow's range and are found in and around houses. The Northern black widows are the country cousins to their residential southern and more notorious—and deadly—relatives, preferring less contact with humans. These spiders most likely arrived on our part of the coastal plain by air. The baby spiders produce a balloon of silk at birth, which in most cases allows the wind to carry them several feet away from their mother, but sometimes the right wind can carry them for miles. As McKenna-Foster describes, "Northern Black Widows probably dispersed in this way to all the islands when they were still just inland hills. The ocean level rose and isolated the populations. For whatever reason, the widows flourish on Tuckernuck. There may be too much development on Nantucket for them, or there could be too many other species that they have to compete with."

Although Tom Chase, director of special projects at the Nature Conservancy on Martha's Vineyard, discovered Northern black widows in Nantucket's Ram Pasture in the 1980s, McKenna-Foster and Beaton have been unable to find them there or anywhere else on Nantucket.

What this pair of arachnid hunters have also found on Nantucket, and also on Tuckernuck in exceedingly high numbers, is a member of the tarantula family, the purseweb spider. McKenna-Foster and Beaton discovered the purseweb spider on Tuckernuck in June 2006, publishing their findings along with Professor Michael J. Draney of the Natural and Applied Science Department at the University of Wisconsin-Green Bay.[7] At the time, it was thrilling for them, because they knew that the northernmost boundary of its range, extending north from Florida, was Block Island.

After this initial discovery, McKenna-Foster and Beaton set up transects within two study areas—one each on the eastern and western sides of Tuckernuck—to walk along to count spider purse tubes. They also picked three parts of the island randomly to walk around and see what they found. They found that the purseweb spiders on Tuckernuck tend to group their webs together in clusters of two or more in open areas where Pennsylvania sedge, huckleberry and bayberry are growing. The numbers of webs they found were astounding: around 100 webs on the western side of the island and about 343 on the eastern side, where webs were distributed so densely that they continued out of the study area.

Both of these discoveries are testament to the biodiversity of these islands and examples of species range expansion during the current interglacial stage, more of which are sure to occur as the earth's climate continues to warm.

At different times in island natural history thousands of years apart, these spiders appear to have found new habitat on Nantucket and Tuckernuck through their own devices, by way of strong winds, or a little of both. In any case, their arrivals were more or less random occurrences in nature.

REUNION TOUR: BEETLES

Unlike the spiders, the reintroduction of the North American burying beetle to Nantucket, 1994 through 2006, required an effort led by the U.S. Fish & Wildlife Service.

This carrion beetle's return to Nantucket was crucial to the survival of its species. In addition to there being few scavenger/carrion beetle species on the islands, Block Island, Rhode Island, was the site of the only naturally occurring population of the North American burying beetles east of the Mississippi River. If Block Island's population went extinct, Nantucket's could be there as backup. The species was listed as a rare and endangered species in 1973, and the U.S. Fish & Wildlife Service had already tried a reintroduction on Penikese Island in the Elizabeth Islands west of Martha's Vineyard, but the population died out after seven years. Nantucket was the second choice.

Once common in 35 states in the eastern temperate part of North America, the North American burying beetle now only exists sparsely in Arkansas, Massachusetts, Nebraska, Ohio, Oklahoma, Rhode Island, South Dakota, Kansas, and Texas, according to the USFWS.

So, in the summer of 1994, the Fish & Wildlife Service worked in conjunction with the Maria Mitchell Association, Mass Audubon, the University of Massachusetts at Boston and the Nantucket Conservation Foundation to release into Nantucket's eastern moors 22 pairs of these beetles and four individuals grown by the Roger Williams Park Zoo in Providence, Rhode Island. Prior to this reintroduction, the North American burying beetle was last recorded on Nantucket in 1926, and before that in 1898.

During the 12-year period, beetle researchers, including McKenna-Foster, placed mating pairs of beetles in dead quails (any dead animal 2.8 to 3.5 ounces or larger will do). With one male and one female beetle in each quail, they buried the birds and beetles in the ground, and the beetles laid their eggs inside the quails, which they used as a food source for themselves and their young.[8] Each spring and summer since the reintroduction began on Nantucket, researchers—McKenna-Foster since 2004—have set out traps in the ground baited with rancid chicken meat, which the beetles detect with their antennae. The researchers have followed up with population assessments. In 2010, they caught 191 beetles, the most ever since the reintroduction began and the best proof yet that the effort was worth it.

Says McKenna-Foster of this project, "We're trying to figure out where beetles work, at least in the eastern moors and in Sanford Farm. Sanford Farm is terrible. The eastern moors are super-successful. We trap north and south, and then to the east of that six or seven square miles, and Windswept [Cranberry Bog] is one more site. They're definitely there. They move all over the place. It's a really exciting project."

PAPARAZZI: MONITORING MIGRATION

Other efforts to understand insects and spread the knowledge into the island community, mostly via students in local schools, include the Land Council's participation in a nationwide effort, called Monarch Watch, to monitor monarch butterfly migration. Founded in 1992 by Dr. Orley R. Taylor, professor of entomology at the University of Kansas, Monarch Watch is not only an educational outreach program but also an ongoing monarch butterfly migration and population research project that works in tune with the monarch butterfly migration, depending on the season.

Monarch butterflies are unique in the butterfly world in that they not only migrate much farther than any other butterfly—up to 3,000 miles one-way—but they do it in stages by new generations of butterflies. Monarchs that hatch in the summer up in the northern zones live only two to six weeks, with sometimes three generations being produced, if the growing season is long enough in a given zone. But the late summer to early fall generation of monarch butterflies lives up to eight months. Passing through or staging before leaving Nantucket, monarch butterflies in this generation are caught by curious island students who, with the help of their teachers and Nantucket Land Council staff, affix ID stickers to their wings. And then these butterflies fly down to Mexico, where they spend the winter clinging together in massive roosts in trees up in the mountains.

In the springtime, this same generation of monarchs begins to fly north to find milkweed plants on which they can lay their eggs. Unable to make it the entire way, this late-summer-to-early-fall generation monarchs stops mid-migration and, after laying its eggs, dies. Their offspring continue the migration northward to produce the summer monarchs, and the cycle begins again.

On Nantucket's islands, monarchs and other butterflies flutter around on prettily colored wings, harming no one as they drink the nectar of beautiful flowers. They are a part of our mosaic of island rural living that we accept as a bucolic essential, like rows of sweet corn in the fields of Moors End and Bartlett's Ocean View Farms; tall grass along Polpis, Hummock Pond and Wauwinet Roads; the scent of wild grapes on late September breezes; and the late summer symphony of chirping crickets.

They, like other human-friendly arthropods such as fireflies, dragonflies and praying mantises, for some of us circadian and season-watching types, are insects whose annual arrival is recorded in calendars. During its summer natural world educational programming, the Maria Mitchell

Association takes humans with a love for insects deeper into their island world with its arthropod discovery classes.

Twice a summer, Maria Mitchell details the physiology of dragonflies and damselflies, their lifecycles, diet and habitats in the classroom on one day and, on the next, instructor and students travel out to the edges of ponds to catch and observe both species from these families in the *Odonata* order. Albeit a little scratched up and bug-bitten, participants walk out of the reeds with a new-found appreciation for another insect species, especially after hearing how part of their diet includes both saltwater and freshwater mosquitoes.

But did you ever hear about a mosquito talk and field trip? How about the ones for deer ticks? No? Well, maybe you know of countless deer tick and Lyme disease public forums over many years, in which local and regional experts, Dr. Lepore, Dr. Telford and the town's Tick Advisory Committee urge Nantucket citizens to approve various deer and tick eradication plans, including one aimed at culling the deer herd down to approximately ten to 30 deer per square mile. Their standing proposal is a modification of the 2004 MassWildlife-sanctioned February deer hunt, in which the current three deer seasons during the fall would be expanded so more deer could be harvested. The one-time hunt in 2004 was deemed successful by the state, but a disaster by islanders, and reimplementation remains on paper. The most recent attack on arthropods began toward the end of the first decade of the 21st century. During the town budget crisis precipitated by the Great Recession of 2008, the late Department of Public Works superintendent Jeff Willett did not fill the lone mosquito control position in his department when that person retired, which meant that distribution of Altocid larval-killing donuts in publicly accessible bodies of inland water and salt marshes ceased, and the already limited mosquito ditch cleaning efforts were further curtailed. Although this environmentally safe larvicide had helped significantly to reduce mosquito numbers in island problem areas including Madaket, it was part of a two-part program that included regular winter maintenance of the island's scores of miles of mosquito ditches.

During the Great Depression in the mid-1930s, out-of-work people could find jobs through the Works Projects Administration. On Nantucket, the WPA put jobless islanders to work digging ditches in virtually all of the island's salt marshes, on the premise that the eggs of saltwater mosquitoes wouldn't get the chance to hatch if these marshes emptied and filled rapidly with the tidal ebb and flow. Additionally, fish could swim further into the salt marshes and dine on what mosquito eggs they could find laid just beneath the surface.

Without regular cleaning and maintenance by the town, the ditches fill in with vegetation, mud and decomposing plants and animals, and these essential organic marsh-building ingredients fuel a natural process that never ceases. As the marsh ditches rise in elevation, the channels that once drained well are gradually cut off from tidal currents, and standing pools of water, ideal for mosquitoes to lay their eggs in, develop.

Although the Town of Nantucket cleaned some of its mosquito ditches in Madaket between October 2007 and the spring of 2009, even developing a salt marsh restoration plan for certain sections of Madaket's salt marshes, many of the island's salt marsh ditches are no longer open enough to function, and continue to clog. Not waiting for the work to get done, a contingent of Madaket residents, some of whom had hired private mosquito control contractors to spray their properties with insecticides since the cessation of the town's program, organized to include a question, Question Three, on the special town election ballot on June 14, 2011. Prompted by the approval of Article 39 at the annual Town Meeting in April 2011, which called for the town to raise $100,000 to hatch an island-wide mosquito program by fiscal year 2013, Nantucket voters, 776-586, supported the "Proposition 2½" override to reignite the town's mosquito control program with $100,000. At the September 28, 2011, Board of Selectmen meeting, the board appointed a committee to develop this mosquito program and the committee continued to form its recommendations.

When this plan comes to fruition, eventually, at least some of the flying bloodsuckers are going to be vanquished, the coast cleared, for the moment, for barbequing and all other outdoor activities, faith in the town's jurisprudence restored and its property owners' spirits rekindled. But these pests, these arthropods we feel obligated to annihilate, were all here before humans arrived, and they will most surely outlive us. They will expand their varieties and numbers, making human efforts to pause their survival into a mere blip on the dial of the island's natural history.

WATER: SALT AND FRESH

You may have seen yellow bumper stickers adorning island vehicles with the word "Eelgrass" or white ones with "No Eelgrass, No Scallops" in black letters. The first is the name of a now-defunct island bluegrass band, which gives you a hint of what's on Nantucketers' minds with respect to the environment and how it relates to their livelihoods, and their pastimes.

But the second one is a seemingly simple phrase that speaks volumes: the loss of eelgrass in Nantucket's harbors equals the demise of Nantucket bay scallops. In fact, eelgrass is the life-giver, directly or indirectly, for pretty much everything that grows, swims, crawls, burrows and lives in the harbors and estuaries of this three-island archipelago.

Salinity and oxygen levels play equally vital roles, as do tidal circulation, food and nutrient content, but anyone who has ever pushraked for scallops, dragged quahog rake tines across the bottom of the harbor or gone snorkeling in these warm waters has seen the multitude of near-shore marine life living among the emerald-colored fronds swaying to the pulse of the tides.

Marine animals that don't take refuge among the blades of this underwater linguini, or lay their eggs on it or in it, use it for cover, hunt for food around it and in it and/or live beneath it. And at least one species of bird, the Atlantic brant, has a specialized gland allowing it to drink salt water and thus is able to eat primarily eelgrass. Members of the goose family and the namesake for Brant Point, thousands of these birds fed on the massive eelgrass beds that once covered the bottom around Brant Point and the inland tidal areas before the town filled them in.

For biologists, high diversity of species is a clear indicator of a healthy harbor ecosystem. Although the Massachusetts Estuaries Project deemed Nantucket, Polpis and Madaket Harbors to be in various stages of impairment by nutrient loading from a variety of sources, by and large the island's harbors are fairly clean and getting better. Nantucket's waters are known among shellfish biologists, fishmongers and seafood connoisseurs as harboring the last remaining viable bay scallop population on the East Coast of the United States. Marine Superintendent Dave Fronzuto has said regularly that Nantucket's commercial bay scallop fishery is sustainable at around 15,000 bushels annually. Among other limiting factors, including the numbers of licensed commercial fishermen and possible fishing days, product demand and fishing boat and equipment costs, this is because it is Nantucket's good fortune that its harbors are located 26 miles from the mainland and mostly unaffected by the water quality ills of "America."

Fronzuto sees it this way:

> I think that it's such an important part of the fabric of Nantucket. I don't think the fishery will ever go away—at least, I certainly hope not. As far as what [our shellfish biologist is] doing, if we can take the highs and the lows out of it—you know, not have a 10,000-bushel year and then a 40,000-bushel year and then an 8,000-bushel year and then a 15,000-bushel year—if we can take those highs and lows out of it . . . I'm not saying it's always going to be a minimum or a flat line, but I'd like that flat line to be between 15,000 and 25,000 bushels. That's a sustainable fishery with the economy, with the price, with the number of people going, the relatively short season; that's where I'd like to see the line hover around.

Although Nantucket is its own worst enemy when it comes to polluting its waters, and the pristine label many island tourist promoters affix to Nantucket is not entirely accurate, the community can still claim clean enough harbors for the harvesting of scallops to sustain 60 to 75 fishermen, their families, their openers, several fishmongers, and many restaurants and marine supply stores. Fronzuto sees this status quo lasting at least until 2022. Nantucket's harbor soils and sediments and its microscopic saltwater food sources remain healthy enough for year-round digging of quahogs, seasonal collecting of soft-shell clams and the activities of several private aquaculture farms.

High water quality translates into many things, but for the purposes of Nantucket's harbors, it's a guarantor of vigorous eelgrass growth and a high diversification of species, altogether painting a portrait of relatively healthy harbors. Tracy Curley, a former town biologist for Nantucket, agrees that eelgrass is a key gauge of harbor health:

> As the eelgrass disappears, there will be a shift in species inhabiting Nantucket Harbor. It starts with water quality, which dictates light conditions, then whether the plankton community shifts, for example from diatoms to dinoflagellates, and just as important is the growth of the opportunistic epiphytes [plants that attach to the eelgrass blades]. The more epiphytes, the less surface area that is available for scallop attachment—although I think that point is controversial, for the reason that the blades grow from the bottom and new eelgrass growth should allow for some attachment. However, the bottom line is that there is less surface area for attachment, so fewer juvenile scallops will survive. It is a pretty complex ecosystem, and it is all interdependent.

As Curley noted, bay scallops need eelgrass to live. Scallop larvae attach to eelgrass blades after two weeks of hanging out in the water following a spawning event. Once they grow shells and detach, they live within the eelgrass beds. These beds concentrate plankton and algae, which scallops eat by filtering the salt water into and out of their gills, which also absorb dissolved oxygen. Shellfish species in general, including quahogs, softshell clams and others, rely on eelgrass in similar ways.

This amazing sea grass is the harbors' multitasking organism on which so much near-shore marine life depends. It is the equivalent of salt marsh cord grass in the intertidal zone or the grasses of the sandplain grasslands along Nantucket and Tuckernuck's south shores.[1] In addition to the shellfish, winter flounder and finfish species spend their adolescence utilizing eelgrass groves, as do young shrimp, several snail species and geese species along with the brant.

In addition to serving as a marine animal nursery and a safe zone, eelgrass acts as a baffle in the water, concentrating plankton and other microscopic foods for shellfish and other marine animals in these areas. It also traps sediments, preventing them from washing around in the harbors, which enhances water clarity and decreases turbidity. Although it can tolerate only low levels of nutrient input into the harbors, it, like salt marsh vegetation, removes and uses various nutrients entering the harbor from the shore sediments, inland sources and the atmosphere.

And to a certain extent, eelgrass engages in nitrogen fixation through the movement of oxygen from its fronds down into its roots and rhizomes and into the harbor bottom, where it is converted into nitrogen

Eelgrass

that is taken up by the eelgrass roots from the rhizosphere, the harbor soil in immediate proximity to eelgrass roots where most chemical reactions and conversions take place. As Dr. David Burdick, eelgrass consultant to the Nantucket Land Council, explains, it is this underworld movement of energy through the harbor food web, via eelgrass, that is a vital component of these marine ecosystems. Burdick, an associate research professor at the Jackson Estuarine Laboratory in the Department of Natural Resources and the Environment at the University of New Hampshire, says that energy on this level passes through a detrital food web.

Microbes in the sediment do the dirty work of processing the castoffs from the world above, the harbor bottom, the water, its surface and the shorelines, turning spent organic material back into energy that the eelgrass and other salt water plants and creatures depend on for food. The unseen transport of this invisible energy within the detrital food web forms a key argument for the protection of eelgrass. That Nantucket has so much eelgrass in its harbors, compared to coastal towns in the rest of Southeastern Massachusetts, should be cause for both local pride and copious, widely varied protection efforts beyond what's currently in Nantucket's arsenal of marine habitat defense policies.

As Burdick tells it:

> This is an organism, which creates habitat. So its physical structure is creating habitat, which attracts many organisms. They hide there; they try to get away from their predators there. If you're a predator, you've got to go there and hunt there because that's where everybody's hiding from you. It makes a very active thing with predator-prey relationships going on in there. And the other very valuable part of sea grass is that when those blades die, they get decomposed by bacteria and microbes, and those little bits, they break down, and there's a whole host of organisms that will eat those little bits. Not scallops (that I know of) but oysters and mussels. Part of [the way] they're getting energy is they'll [eat] those little bits of what we call detritus, which is sea grass and marsh grass and all kind of different plants that didn't get eaten when they were alive. And it goes through their guts and they strip off the energy from the microbes and they poop out the detritus because it's not very digestible, and that's ready to be re-colonized by microbes and bacteria.

These microbes may not be popularized in seasonal island restaurant menu items, interior decorating elements or embroidered motifs on preppy trousers, as other, more edible sea creatures are, but these contributors to the eelgrass lifecycle—and, by extension, those of the marine animals dependent on this sea grass—are invaluable players in this ecosystem.

It is likely that the first eelgrass seeds either washed into Nantucket's waters or arrived stuck to shorebird legs and feathers; however, before they could grow, and before inshore marine creatures could establish themselves, the harbor had to form. During this process, probably as soon as Coskata Pond formed between 2,000 and 3,000 years ago, eelgrass and other marine vegetation likely took root, fish swam in and the larvae of mollusks, crustaceans and other marine life collected in the growing cove, populating the sand spit corral as it inched toward Brant Point well before Nantucket Harbor finished growing. But the natural aquarium most certainly didn't jell entirely until its Coatue boundary grew westward enough to enclose the open water of Nantucket Sound.

Eventually, Nantucket Harbor grew to be some five and a half miles long from the Haulover in Wauwinet west to Nantucket Town, where European settlers would relocate after their original harbor at Sherburne Town on Capaum Pond was closed up by a storm in 1722, thereby expediting shoaling over of its entrance that had been going on for years. The gradually intensifying tidal current of this new harbor eventually prevented Coatue from growing longer. Eelgrass probably sprouted first in Nantucket Harbor's two major inlets and upper harbor zone: first Coskata Pond and shortly thereafter the Head of the Harbor and Polpis Harbor, where the inland saltwater environs were stable and protected enough to support harbor plant growth, even before the main harbor was completely formed.

Geologists, including Oldale and Shaler, think that Coskata Pond originated as marine deposits of sand and gravel that were carried south down the west side of Great Point—originally dubbed Great Head—and the Galls over several thousand years. Shaler also believed that the sand to build Coatue came from the bottom of Nantucket Sound, moved by the wave action and currents washing southeast toward Nantucket. Once Coatue grew to about the modern-day Bass Point (the northeastern most of the six cuspate spits on Coatue's inner shore), it protected an area of the young harbor—known as Coatue Bay in Shaler's day and now called Head of the Harbor—and it offered, with the help of the Haulover, enough protection for Coskata Pond's salt marsh and eelgrass to thrive.

Polpis Harbor, Oldale believes, was once a large kettle hole filled with fresh water, both from the ice chunk that formed it and from meltwater cascading off the retreating glacier that left the chunk behind. When the surrounding ocean water rose high enough to gnaw at Nantucket's north shore, the kettle hole's northwest edge probably collapsed onto the beach. Once the seawater entered this coastal pond, it probably scoured out what material it could and then, gradually, sediments and marine deposits brought its bottom up high enough for salt marsh habitat to grow. Tidal flow certainly carried sand into this smaller harbor while forming Quaise Neck, which hooks southeast into the harbor, protecting it from heavy wave action.

Other, smaller inlets currently ingrown with salt marsh species, including Folger's Marsh, Shimmo Pond and the marshy areas of Shimmo Creek immediately east of Abram's Point, and possibly the Creeks, were likely slow to start evolving into the habitat they are today until Coatue grew to its fullest, protective extent.

At the island's west end during roughly the same time frame, development of Madaket Harbor was a much less complicated affair. Marine deposits that gradually formed Eel Point and Smith's Point created this harbor with littoral drift carrying sand west down the south and north sides of the island. In the process, Shaler believes, a series of "creeks" that had formed of the remnant bottoms of outwash valleys on the north side of Smith's Point—including, running west, Hither Creek, Broad Creek, Narrow Creek and Further Creek, facing Madaket Harbor—became short inlets.[2]

Today, Hither Creek, the largest of the four, remains intact. Arguably, vestiges of Further Creek, the westernmost of these "creeks," on the north side of Esther Island, indicate that it is still holding its rough position, as, possibly, is Narrow Creek on the southeast side of Esther Island. However, Narrow Creek is likely combined with the remains of Broad Creek where Hurricane Esther separated most of Smith's Point from Nantucket on September 20 and 21, 1961, when it blew into the barrier beach a 1,200-foot-wide, 20-foot-deep channel that remained open water before it was completely closed over by Hurricane Gloria on September 27, 1985. The Patriots' Day nor'easter again made Esther Island a true island in April 2007. Coastal geologist Peter Rosen maintains that, because these were originally deep cuts in the sandy outwash plain before the ocean rose up, Broad Creek and possibly Narrow Creek made it easy for the hurricane's ocean waves to cleave the beach at this point and create Esther Island. And once tidal currents widened and deepened the channel, even though the new island reattached, the water had established an easier entryway should conditions exist again for such a blowout in the beach. On the other side of Madaket Harbor, on the south side of Eel and North points, salt marsh developed as this northwestern extremity grew, and when both this peninsula and Smith's Point had developed fully, the latter at one time extended down past the south side of Tuckernuck Island and just west of Muskeget Island.

As longshore currents, wind and waves sculpted Nantucket's harbors and inlets, the marine flora and fauna that inhabit them today didn't wait until each protected bay or estuary was completely finished. As they could, fish, mollusks, crustaceans and other inshore marine organisms expanded. Fish swam in and out as they pleased, probably with increasing frequency because of growing amounts of smaller fish, such as sand lance, Atlantic silversides, Northern pipefish, striped killifish, mummichog, sheepshead minnow, the odd seahorse and zooplankton. These were probably joined on the menu by the larvae and eggs of shellfish, including bay scallops, quahogs, soft-shell clams, razor clams, oysters, moon snails, whelk snails and myriad other hard-shelled organisms, along with horseshoe, blue claw, lady, spider and green crabs and possibly lobster, in addition to many other salt water creatures that had found this new harbor an ideal place to live.[3] Algae, including the green, stringy enteromorpha; sea lettuce; brown algae, including rockweed; possibly Irish moss; and, of course, eelgrass germinated and sank their roots into the sandy harbor and estuarine bottoms.

Says Tom French:

> That [process] is possible even now. These sorts of marine organisms, be they eelgrass or estuarine fish or marine fish, they're able to disperse fairly freely up and down the coast at different places. Even if you had a new island, a volcanic island out in the Gulf Stream, a lot of these things would find their way there.
>
> All those things have larvae that are generally zooplanktonic when they're very small, so they move around and settle down into places. So I don't think having a new harbor form and having razor clams find their way there is any big surprise.

THE PONDS

What is perplexing for zoologists, ichthyologists and biologists, including French, is how fish found their way into Nantucket's bodies of fresh water—its kettle hole and outwash valley ponds. Whatever was in freshwater ponds and waterways before the glacier arrived either fled the cold climate ahead of the glacier's advance, seeking refugia on Georges Bank and along the coast well south of New England, or perished in the arctic conditions bearing down on the Coastal Plain, the glacier wiping out all freshwater fish species that existed before it blanketed New England.

In their book, *Inland Fishes of Massachusetts*, David B. Halliwell, Karsten E. Hartel and Alan E. Launer assert that, as with the other fauna able to escape the cold climate and ride it out until the glacier withdrew northward around 18,000 years later, the freshwater fish capable of swimming away from the steadily chilling water ahead of the glacier, or those fortunate enough to be living already in these biological safe zones south or east of the terminal moraine, were the species that would become the native species in Massachusetts from around 14,000 years ago through the present. How these fish found their way back to this area is a matter of some speculation, depending on the species, but this trio of ichthyic-minded researchers believe that some or all of the island's ponds were somehow connected to rivers and streams flowing onto the Atlantic Coastal Plain after the glacier retreated. This might have allowed some of the fish from Northern New England that are related to Great Lakes species, which survived the Wisconsinan glaciation in the Mississippi Valley, to swim from that part of the country through glacial streams, bogs and lakes into the early Upper Hudson and Saint Lawrence basins, into the Connecticut River Drainage, into Massachusetts drainage basins and then down onto the coastal plain where Nantucket's islands would eventually form. But French doesn't quite agree.

He acknowledges that it's a little harder to explain how freshwater fish reinvaded the Atlantic coastal watersheds if they could not find waterway routes from the Mississippi Drainage into the Great Lakes and Lake Champlain. This explains why Massachusetts has so few native freshwater species: it's because many fish just couldn't swim back into this region. As a result, a high percentage of the state's current population of freshwater fish is non-native species that found the Massachusetts habitat to their liking. The authors of Inland Fishes of Massachusetts estimate that 48 percent of freshwater fish in the state are non-native species brought in by humans.

All agree that most of the freshwater fish species swimming their way into Cape and Islands ponds and other freshwater bodies came from refugia to the south and from Georges Bank.[4] Still, French admits that the specifics of freshwater fish distribution from refugia south and east of Nantucket are murky at best. Apart from the fish known to have been introduced by humans, Nantucket's fish either made their way into bodies of fresh water before the islands formed, or they, French believes, had a difficult task ahead: "[I]f they didn't do that, there's a whole barrier of salt water to get across, and that doesn't happen very often for freshwater fish. So you've got eight or ten freshwater species on the island that had to get there somehow, and there's a much, much bigger barrier for them than we're talking about for the harbor marine fish."

These fish experts can say, with a high degree of certainty, which species are now in Nantucket's great salt ponds, namely Sesachacha, Miacomet, Hummock and Long Ponds. They are all either saltwater fish or species requiring both fresh and salt water for their lifecycles. The certainty is because Native Americans and European settlers learned to open these and other ponds to the ocean by digging a trench in the beach between pond and ocean in the spring and again in the fall, in order to trap and harvest blueback herring (sometimes confused with alewives), white perch, American eels and probably other species no longer in great abundance. The European farmers learned this practice from the Wampanoags, and it enabled them also to drain meadows and to attract game birds to mudflats for hunting. The herring are anadromous fish, meaning that they migrate up into rivers, streams and freshwater ponds to spawn. Their young, called fry, swim out of these waterways in the fall and reside in the ocean until they reach sexual maturity and can migrate inland to spawn. Catadromous fish, including eels, spend most of their lives in these freshwater to brackish places, leaving only in the fall as adults to swim out to spawn in the Sargasso Sea, west of Bermuda in the middle of the North Atlantic Ocean.

In the spring, adult blueback herring, alewives and shad run up into mainland rivers from the ocean to spawn from late March through mid-May. Alternately, the herring also swim into Nantucket's salt ponds when they're opened in April to spawn as the yellow-flowering forsythia blooms on island. Juvenile eels swim into the pond to begin their freshwater lives. And when the ponds are opened in the fall, juvenile herring on their way out to the ocean join adult eels swimming to the Sargasso Sea to spawn. Additionally, white perch, another anadromous fish species, also find their way into the island's great ponds, commuting for sex, along with the herring. Depending on how long a pond remains open to the ocean—up to two weeks, but usually less than a week—other fish species, namely saltwater fish like striped bass, bluefish and tomcod, have been documented in these ponds after ocean currents have sealed them shut with sand. Sesachacha Pond stayed open for five months during the summer twice in the past, but as usual, longshore currents eventually closed it over with sand.

For the last three-plus centuries, pond openings have been the most plausible method of natural distribution of fish into Nantucket's coastal great ponds, sometimes called great salt ponds. Fish often swim into and out of Sesachacha, Hummock and Miacomet Ponds through these temporary channels between pond and ocean. Wampanoags and the early European settlers also probably opened Squam, Tom Nevers and Capaum Ponds to the ocean, with Capaum remaining open long enough for Nantucket's original town of Sherburne to use it as a harbor until a storm closed it over. These three ponds are no longer opened to the ocean, and neither is Miacomet Pond, because it became largely a freshwater system. But the channel leading from Squam Pond to the ocean remains very much intact and is visible from the beach in front of this pond, accessed by a public way between 51 and 49 Squam Road.

It took a coordinated effort to glean fish and oysters from Sesachacha, Hummock, Miacomet and the other smaller ponds the settlers and Indians opened. Through 1933, the process was at the whim of fishermen going after their intended fish for personal consumption and for wholesale.

Just as the town's Marine Coastal Resources Department does today, they timed their opening schedule for when the wind was blowing down from the inland end of the pond toward the ocean, the tide was falling and the pond was full enough to produce a head strong enough to push the water out. Using a team of horses or oxen pulling a plow, fishermen worked together to gouge a trench between ocean and pond. As the water rushed out, it eroded the sandbanks of the temporary channel wide enough so that the pond dropped to the level of the ocean. Realizing the benefit to these ponds and to island fishermen, the town funded pond openings using mechanical earth-moving equipment from 1933 through 1981.

Although the settlers and the Wampanoags were known to have opened Long Pond from its southern ocean end, that didn't last. In 1665, a cooperative arrangement between the two was struck to dig the Madaket Ditch and connect the pond with Madaket Harbor and the ocean via Hither Creek. Since then, saltwater species, including striped bass, bluefish and white perch, have found their way into this west-end pond. Additionally, fishermen angling for striped bass know that the spring and fall openings of Hummock and Sesachacha ponds mean there's a good chance of hooking fish off the beaches where the pond water is flowing into the ocean, because their quarry seem to know when a pond is open and that there is new food entering their habitat.

However, it is nearly impossible for anyone to say specifically which freshwater fish species first found their way into Nantucket's inland ponds, because Nantucket and the Vineyard have far fewer of the main native species than the larger drainage basins found in the rest of the state. Ichthyologists, for the most part, rely on anecdotal information and inferences to theorize what species might have been where and then found their way into Nantucket's ponds.

The reality, the information derived from those anecdotes and inferences, is more cryptic than enlightening. It remains challenging to determine how and why specific species ended up in various drainages and/or ponds. The task for those concerned with the study of freshwater fish on the island is to decode the existing, incomplete distribution data that is partially influenced by anthropogenic activity over the last 400 years, which includes extirpations during the 1700s, humans' moving of fish between various bodies of water to suit their needs, and the ability or the inability of fish to find their way through canals between drainages. Further muddying the research waters is the fact that ichthyologists didn't conduct comprehensive surveys of freshwater fish in Massachusetts until the 1940s, which makes the baseline information, from which distribution patterns might be built, difficult to set because the data is too recent.

Surveyor, author and agriculturalist J. Hector St. John de Crèvecoeur noted in his famous 1782 book, *Letters from an American Farmer*, that there were abundant fish in the ponds of Nantucket. And archeologists have found white perch and yellow perch bones in Indian middens. Unfortunately for the few native species that are in Nantucket ponds—long-time pond fishermen Bill Pew and David Goodman say white perch, yellow perch, chain pickerel and pumpkin seed, a species of sunfish, are Nantucket's original freshwater species—self-serving pond fishermen have introduced many non-native species to Nantucket's ponds in hopes of expanding the variety of game fish.[5]

This included the state's stocking of Nantucket's ponds with native species until 1921; the Nantucket Anglers Club stocking Washing Pond in 1998 with 550 brown, brook and rainbow trout; and an unknown fisherman putting catfish into Washing Pond as well. Goodman put large-mouth bass in the North Head of Hummock Pond around 1991. Crappie were introduced in the mid- to late 1980s to Hummock and Miacomet ponds. And this otherwise mainland freshwater fish found a way to move about the island. As Goodman remembers it, "The crappie have been taken from all these ponds. A lot of people have a bucket and . . . when they're fishing, they throw the fish in there and they take them and they'll put them in other ponds, so there are crappie in Water Company [Pond], there are crappie in Tom Nevers and they're definitely in Miacomet, because that was one of the first places. That and the North Head of Hummock."

Into Gibbs Pond, the large kettle hole just northwest of the Milestone Cranberry Bogs, islanders have added white perch, small-mouth bass and Northern pike. Goodman believes the latter were introduced by the former operators of these bogs, Northland Cranberry of Wisconsin, where Northern pike are plentiful. As a result, Goodman discovered a hybrid of the non-native pike and the native pickerel, which he describes as having the tail of muskellunge, a large freshwater fish in the pickerel family found in the Great Lakes region, plus strange, dotted markings on its sides reminiscent of the chain markings on the pickerel.

The official list from MassWildlife detailing freshwater fish inhabiting Nantucket's ponds—native or not—includes yellow perch, white perch, pumpkin seed, brook trout, chain pickerel, crappie, swamp darters and golden shiners. But Goodman and Pew know that what's really in Nantucket's ponds can't ever be nailed down precisely. Rarely, believes Goodman, have species introduced from the mainland done well enough to become part of the ecosystem within the ponds to which they've been introduced. Mainly, they've served only to provide temporary diversions from the species typically caught in island ponds.

French says of this relaxed attitude on stocking island ponds, "People, especially from 1900 through the 1950s, put everything imaginable in the ponds. It was basically a grocery store kind of mentality, and that is: 'What would you like to catch? Let us know.'" How these foreign fish have survived in island ponds depends a great deal on the depth of the pond and its acreage, both of which determine the amount of food, cover and habitat for freshwater fish. Many of the kettle hole ponds out in the moors are small in area and only a few feet deep, while Sesachacha is believed to be 43 feet at its deepest, and Hummock maybe six or seven feet. Those like Hummock and Tom Nevers Ponds make up for their shallowness with large acreages, including most of those along the south shore.

In his book, *Fishing Around Nantucket*, fisherman and self-taught Nantucket naturalist J. Clinton Andrews confirms what Goodman and Pew knew of the natural and not-so-natural stocking of Nantucket Island ponds:

> Many of the ponds are remains of glacial meltwater river valleys. When the land and therefore the watershed of these valleys was larger, the natural opening of these ponds to salt water probably happened more often than at present, and the outflow of water may have lasted longer. During flood periods, the water probably extended along the inner face of the foredune and connected adjacent ponds. An aerial photo of Martha's Vineyard some years ago shows this clearly. Such temporary connections provided a natural pathway for freshwater fish to spread into our ponds from the larger river systems. During the late 1800s, fish were transported indiscriminately from one pond to another whenever people thought natural shortages had occurred.

EARLY ISLAND FISHING PRACTICES

Stocking was not a problem for the harbors, because they were all open to the ocean, from the time of their formation up through present day. The limits on species were, and are, depth of water, water quality, habitat, available food and, eventually, hungry islanders. Unhampered by the ills of human development that Nantucket is trying to correct in its harbors today, food for marine fauna itself was so abundant in the past that fishermen from the mainland spent considerable time fishing island waters, both inside

Nantucket Harbor and out in Nantucket Sound, because of the rich fishing grounds offshore and the thickly settled shellfish beds in the harbors.

Inside of Coatue's six cuspate spits are the bends from which sand is eroded and onto which it is re-deposited, as part of the dynamic equilibrium of wind and tidal currents that maintains the shape of that inner northern shore of the harbor. The first five bends, running west to east, are known as First, Second, Third, Fourth and Fifth bends by islanders, but over time, they've all been given different names for various people. At one time, First Bend was also called Asey Small's Bend, for Captain Asa William Nathaniel Small who, along with Captain Reuben Charles Kenney—both from Harwichport, Massachusetts—bought land near the Haulover and built the first version of the Wauwinet House in 1876. Second Bend had been called Sid's Bend, for Sid Fisher, who had built a house along this bend. Third Bend too, had a different name: Burdett's Bend, for Captain Burdett who built boats on the island at one time. And Fourth Bend was jointly named Haulover Bend because it was the narrowest and therefore easiest section of Coatue for fishermen to haul their dories over into and back from the Chord of the Bay. While I can't find an alternate name for Fifth Bend, Fourth Bend got its third name from the mainland coastal town from which fishermen came to harvest bay scallops in Nantucket Harbor. As Andrews recalls in the "Scallops" chapter of his book, the Chatham fishermen set up camp at what today is called Chatham Bend, building shacks in the early 1900s. At the time, they were able to pass through the Haulover cut at Wauwinet to go cod fishing, since it remained opened until 1908. In Nantucket Harbor, they gathered bay scallops to use as bait for their cod fishing expeditions and to sell back in Chatham. Because of the rift between Nantucket's scallopers and the Chatham fishermen, based on the visitors' non-Nantucket fishing practices, the town began regulation of the bay scallop fishery in 1903, requiring all bay scallopers to reside on Nantucket year-round. Not wanting to miss out on what was becoming a lucrative catch, some of these Chatham fishermen actually moved to Nantucket so they could keep fishing in its harbors for bay scallops.

When the Paleo-Indians arrived on the coastal plain around 8,000 to 11,000 years ago, the ocean was several days' walk from where Nantucket's three islands exist now. The Indians living in the neighborhood dined, as they always did, on plants, berries, nuts and roots, meat from mammals, birds and freshwater fish. Those living on the edge of the continental shelf probably added ocean fish to their diet. Five centuries from the fateful

6,000-years-ago mark, when sea level rise made islands out of the Nantucket Ridge, the Early Archaic Indians moved into the Cape and Islands region. Although the spear remained their best hunting implement, this new wave of Native Americans eventually enjoyed a surf-and-turf diet as the ocean crept higher and higher, finally severing Nantucket's uplands from the mainland and other islands, and bringing ocean fish close enough to harvest without a lengthy hike to the eastern edge of the coastal plain.

The ocean and the islands' ponds were major sources of sustenance for the Late Archaic Indians, who came to Nantucket by canoe about 5,000 years ago, bringing with them their archery hunting equipment and skills. While there is no evidence of a blending of cultures between the Paleo, Early and Late Archaic Indians, the latter two groups of Native Americans appear to have adapted to their changing environment by using what was on hand. The same goes for the Wampanoag Indians, who were living here in the mid-17th century when the white man arrived to stay.

Shellfish and fish bones in Indian middens prove that the islands' first humans made good use of the local food found in the harbors and ponds, and it is well documented that Nantucket's Native Americans were temporarily relocating to the edges of the harbors during the warmer part of the year to make use of available food after Nantucket became an island.

Humans have been altering these ecosystems to suit their needs, from the time when Nantucket's Early and Late Archaic Indians gathered food in the young harbor and collected fish from the great salt ponds and freshwater ponds—actually building a rock jetty out into Sesachacha Pond off its north and south sides to serve as a spear fishing platform—to the discovery by the Wampanoag Indians and the European settlers of the bounty of shellfish and finfish in the island's harbors. At its core, fishing was a basic survival skill unrestricted by environmental protection laws until the mid-20th century, so it was a free-for-all to put food on tables and into storage for later use. The aforementioned cooperative arrangement between the early settlers and the Wampanoags for the digging of the Madaket Ditch, originally called Alewife Ditch, between Hither Creek and Long Pond was done to encourage spawning alewives and herring to swim into this west end pond so they could be caught in weirs and seine nets. The Indians were to receive half of the fish caught as long as they diligently worked the weirs.[6] In addition to the Madaket Ditch, another was dug between Hummock Pond and Head of Hummock, possibly for the same purpose, but not until sometime after 1932.

By the time Nantucket, Polpis and Madaket Harbors came into being, the Late Archaics and Wampanoags, having become proficient fishermen, had learned that most of the fish in which they were interested swam close enough to shore to be diverted into fish weirs they had built of small trees, saplings and branches, to be seined in their nets or to be speared. And they had learned to open the great salt ponds to the ocean to trap spawning herring, alewives and other anadromous fish, along with American eels, a practice they later taught the European settlers. In addition to edible mammals, birds and plants on land, these Indians found good sources of food in tautog, bluefish, cod, haddock, halibut, hake, flounder, mackerel, pickerel, white perch and yellow perch.

Of their expertise in catching cod, Andrews noted in his 1986 *Bulletin of the Massachusetts Archeological Society* article, "Indian Fish and Fishing Off Coastal Massachusetts":

> The records of Nantucket's early settlers indicate that the Indians became very good codfishermen, but by that time they were fishing for trade, not for subsistence. The fact that large cod often stranded on the outer beaches in the fall complicates relating their remains in middens to prehistoric deep-sea fishing. A few vertebrae used as ornaments could have come from stranded fish. However, many early accounts tell that the Indians did use their canoes in the ocean, and we know that they went back and forth between Nantucket and the mainland on a regular basis.

To wit, for the many fish species including mollusks, their refuge from the developing subsistence and commercial fisheries out in Nantucket Sound and the ocean around Nantucket, and in Polpis and Madaket Harbors, had been shrinking at the hands of hungry Native Americans several thousand years before Nantucket settlers and their descendents entered the cod, whale and bay scallop fisheries.

But Andrews admits that nearly all of this historical fisheries information is speculative at best, because all there really is to go on is a combination of fish bones discovered in middens, vertebrae used as ornaments and the knowledge that local Native Americans had seasonal fishing encampments.

EVOLVING HARBORS

Although the islands' settlers engaged in open ocean fishing for cod and other saltwater fish for food and for profit from the earliest days of settlement, by far the two biggest events in the natural world of the harbors in terms of fisheries were the organic growth of the waterfront into the whaling capital of the world and the growth of the bay scallop, quahog, eel and white perch fisheries. Other than the Native Americans' pond openings to trap fish for food, two actions were the island inhabitants' first significant modifications to their marine environment for commerce and sustenance: the altering of the waterfront in preparation for fishing operations and later whaling, and the stunting of the growth of Coatue through the construction of the jetties.

Where Water Tower Beach is today, off of Washing Pond Road, Capaum Pond was open to the ocean on the north shore until a storm closed it in 1722. The settlers also maintained landings in Madaket and where the current town waterfront is now, calling it Wesko (now spelled Wesco) Landing, at the eastern side of where the Wesko Hills gradually lead down to Great Harbor (the original name of Nantucket Harbor).

During the last five or six years of the shoaling of the mouth of the first harbor, ending with the storm that eventually closed it, the early Nantucketers were already transitioning to the new urban area of the island around Wesko Landing on the slopes of the Wesko Hills. Retaining its original name, Sherburne, until 1795 when it was renamed Nantucket, this new municipal area lay in between Quanaty Bank, the high east-facing coastal bank immediately behind today's Union Street with Orange Street running along its upper edge from Main Street south down to where it joins Union Street, and the Cliff, the coastal bank stretching from the intersection of Easton Street and Cliff Road out to the private beaches in front of Washing Pond.

Although Sherburne's town center was moved to Wesko in 1673, development of the young waterfront on Great Harbor began around the time that Joseph Coffin purchased the 40-foot-wide Wesko Landing in 1716. Lot purchases in this area spiked in 1717, the year that the original wooden Straight Wharf pier was built. This meant that much of this part of the island's natural habitats, and the creatures using them, were elbowed aside by the growing village.

In the building of the town, some of the streets laid out and developed between a once-much-larger Lily Pond, with visible open water, and the vicinity of Children's Beach smothered an island tributary of Lily Pond that ran down to the harbor and was called Barzillai's Creek. According to the Land Bank, as this part of town was filling in with new streets and buildings in 1723, a girl named Love Paddock, digging with a clamshell on the eastern bank of this pond, cut a trench deep enough into this shore for the pond's water to break through and wash in a torrent down to the harbor, demolishing her father's mill, uprooting fences and swamping a few boats in the harbor. What remains today of Barzillai's Creek is an outflow pipe in front of the Nantucket Yacht Club that drains the entire area into the harbor, including what's left of the Lily Pond, now overgrown with cattails and lacking any open water. And construction of India Street, originally dubbed Pearl Street, erased another creek or stream that ran from the countryside west of Wesko Landing, between old and new Sherburne, and likely entered the harbor near where the Dreamland Theater is today. Evidence of this erstwhile stream comes in two forms. A subdivision of what were to be small commercial lots known collectively as Bocochico, were laid out roughly where the Dreamland property is today. Corroborating this reference are the results from test bores conducted in 2006 by Cape Cod Test Boring of Orleans at the edge of the South Water Street sidewalk in front of the Dreamland property. Found in the recovered bores were sand and pebbles believed to have come from the stream that once flowed down Pearl Street.

By 1720, Nantucket whale oil was being exported from Boston to London, and several years later, probably around 1723, whale oil was being shipped directly from Nantucket to major European ports. As the whaling port of Nantucket grew, so did this town on Great Harbor, and that growth demanded that the waterfront expand to include new streets and building lots. Years before Bocochico was laid out in 1744, Richard Macy augmented the wood pier of Straight Wharf with a solid fill pier in 1723 to create an extension of Main Street. The divvying up of Sherburne's waterfront land and its ensuing development necessitated a great deal of filling in of tidal areas known as tidelands. Dominated by salt marsh cord grasses, eelgrass and other typical salt marsh and tidal area vegetation, tidelands exist in places all around the harbor today. Today they are known as the Creeks, Shimmo Creek, Folger's Marsh, Pocomo Meadows, Medouie Creek and the salt marshes around Haulover and Coskata ponds.

When Coatue stretched out to its fullest extent westward 2,000 to 3,000 years ago, the heavy ocean waves and strong tidal currents in the harbor gradually subsided, and the harbor became more sheltered, with regular but subdued tides. Sediments began to build up, and tidal lands were able to develop, with salt marsh vegetation growing where Nantucket's waterfront is today. Essentially, the Creeks habitat, interspersed with sandy areas just south of the Great Harbor Yacht Club on Washington Street Extension, originally ran along the shore from that southern end of the harbor and probably right along the edge of Quanaty Bank, all the way to Brant Point and, to a limited extent, along portions of the Cliff to somewhere south of where the Cliffside Beach Club is today. Quanaty Bank, like the Cliff, is part of Nantucket's younger outwash formed by meltwater from the retreating Cape Cod Bay Lobe of the glacier, and it likely endured the ocean breaking against it at high tides before the Haulover and Coatue grew and created Great Harbor.

When Sherburne became busy with the construction of Union Street in 1730, which was part of these major alterations to Great Harbor's natural world, it was necessary to cut into Quanaty Bank, as tall as 100 feet in some places, to get away from the soggy tidal ground. The town used some of the excavated material to build the foundation of Union Street, and it used the rest of it to fill in several acres of salt marsh areas between this new street and the harbor along which Washington Street was eventually built. The infill of natural tidelands included much of the Brant Point area right up to the Cliff, from near the location of today's U.S. Coast Guard Station Brant Point, where there was a tidal opening to the harbor at the time, to a salt marsh area mixed with sandy areas and dunes that encompassed much of the land between the beaches and dunes along Hulbert Avenue westward to the Cliff. You can see the remainder of these wet areas, on Easton Street looking north just past the White Elephant Hotel, behind the Point Breeze Hotel and in the backyards of many of the houses between North Beach Street and the Cliff. Anyone who has been around the intersection of Easton and North and South Beach Streets during an astronomical high tide, particularly during a storm surge, has witnessed how low this area is in elevation.

Continuing on from the 18th century, Nantucketers carried on filling the tidelands, followed close behind with street and structure construction, until the waterfront we have today along the west end of Great Harbor was completed. Nantucket Harbor's builders also used clean fill, in the form of harbor sand and mud from various harbor-dredging projects over the years, including one in 1924, which pumped its slurry on land between the Nantucket Yacht Club and Harbor View Way to make Children's Beach, and another in 1929 that blanketed the marsh and mudflats behind South Beach, making it into a proper beach of white sand.

Over the years, human intrusion pushed out over the sandy, muddy saltwater environment of the harbors into harbor life, continuing with the construction of the wharves along Great Harbor, including Steamship, Old North, Straight, South and Commercial Wharves and eventually the town pier; two piers on the Monomoy shore; another out in Wauwinet; several that have come and gone on Coatue; the Nantucket Yacht Club's wharf and piers; the South Beach Boatyard; and the Jackson Point Pier, F Street Pier, and Hither Creek Boatyard in Madaket, as well as the various piers and docks on Tuckernuck. They displaced shellfish, smothered eelgrass and fouled the water with various forms of pollution from the growing human population on the island. Then as today, piers, docks and floats shade the sunlight from eelgrass beds, and the piers' once creosote-covered pilings further polluted the harbors. Gradually, man shoved his world out into the natural one of the harbor, filling wetlands and the harbor itself for more streets, buildings and infrastructure, constructing wharves and docks, and eventually building ships that would fill the harbor during the whaling days.

Well after Coatue had stopped growing westward, the same tidal currents that had formed a natural channel between harbor and sound conspired to close the Great Harbor as well, first causing problems in the first three decades of 1732, with a sandbar that probably grew in time with Coatue. The influx of sand from shoals just outside the harbor and the gradual choking off of its entrance by these ever-expanding and shifting sandbars became a major detriment to marine life and to the whaling commerce of the island. The culprit was the Nantucket Bar, a shoal extending from North Point, on the west end of the island, east almost to the Coskata end of Coatue. Much of the bar still exists today. The next time you're on one of the slow boats coming into or out of the harbor around low tide on a calm day when the water is fairly clear, look down into the water as you're passing out of the jetties or approaching them and look east or west, and you should see this sandbar. If you happen to be flying to or from the island during similar conditions, the bar will be plainly visible.

Now imagine it continuing across the mouth of the harbor and being less than eight feet below the surface at high tide, and then picture a massive schooner or whaling vessel—without the modern aids of radar or a global positioning system—trying to enter or exit the harbor during any tide other than high. For a visual representation of this problem, go down to Steamboat Wharf during the summer when the Steamship Authority's M/V *Eagle* has docked but hasn't been unloaded, and look at the numbers painted below its bow and stern, descending into the water. Each number represents one foot, and the closest one to the surface shows how much water the ferry draws (sits down in the water). Fully loaded, the *Eagle* draws about ten feet, six inches, so were the Nantucket Bar still in place, the *Eagle* wouldn't be able to get into or out of the harbor at high tide when full of vehicles and passengers.

This was the forces-of-nature reality of their new harbor that Nantucketers grappled with for nearly a century prior to the installation of the Jetties, after the sandbar had grown to the point of preventing whaleships and other large ships from entering the harbor. In fact, the island's original settlers likely chose the open Capaum Pond as their harbor for this very reason, speculated Nantucket historian Edouard A. Stackpole in his April 1940 *Historic Nantucket* article, "Nantucket Bar." Stackpole guessed that Nantucket's first settlers, as sheep farmers, were much more focused on establishing pasturelands for their livestock than worrying about a good, protective anchorage and safe, reliable access to and from boats and ships. The need for the jetties became evident as the island's whale economy swelled. Whalers, when heavily laden with whale oil, drafted more than eight feet and were shut out. Eight feet was the water displaced by a 118-ton ship built in Nantucket in 1732—without cargo. Incoming ships that couldn't get over the Nantucket Bar had to anchor in the Chord of the Bay and be offloaded by lighters, smaller vessels that could easily traverse the infamous shoal in order to ferry a ship's cargo into the harbor or, conversely, load outgoing ships with their voyage provisions. An alternative to the lighters came along in 1842: Peter Ewer's camels. These floating, wooden dry docks were partially flooded and sunk low enough to allow ships to position above them, and then the camels were pumped out, lifting the ship high enough to be towed safely into or out of the harbor.

Discussions and the ensuing machinations for building rock jetties to increase harbor circulation by using tidal currents to blow out and maintain a hole in the Nantucket Bar began in the early 1800s, but fell on deaf ears at the congressional level until 1874. A January 8, 1803, proposal made at a Town Meeting to petition Congress for funds to survey the Bar and dredge a channel through it ultimately foundered. Government engineers and two town committees recommended east and west wooden piers be installed on either side of the channel to increase the velocity of the tides in order to cut a channel through the Bar, when Town Meeting voters sank this idea in fear of its navigational hazards. Up until construction of the Jetties was approved by Congress and the U.S. Bureau of Engineers some

80 years later, numerous surveys were funded by Congress after being petitioned by various committees of concerned citizens, town officials and whaling business owners and lobbyists. Dredging of a channel through the Bar by steam dredge, after a Congressional appropriation of $44,265.56 was secured, failed in June 1829 because the dredged channel filled in as fast as it was dredged.

Although the concept of building a breakwater of rocks or wooden piers on the west side of the channel arose in 1803, it wouldn't be until 1874 that Nantucket could agree on a solution and Congress, finally hearing a unified cry for help from the island, recognized that commerce through Nantucket Sound, which had increased to almost 30,000 ships annually, was worth its protection—and that these vessels required a harbor of refuge with no obstructions preventing their passage in and out when needed.[7]

The process of building the modern jetties began that year. Stackpole described their plan best:

> The engineers' plan was the construction of a western jetty in the northerly direction from the beach, with a view of concentrating the ebb tide and scouring a channel through the Bar, which, at that time, was a half mile in width, with a ruling depth of about six feet at low water. By building the jetty out about a mile, it was thought the current would scour a channel to the required depth. If the deep water of Nantucket Sound could not be reached in this manner, it was thought that a jetty would have to be built from Coatue. This was ultimately done, becoming the present eastern jetty.

Workers for the jetty-building contractor F. K. Ballou of Boston, Massachusetts, dropped the first boulder of the west jetty on April 26, 1881, and completed the work in August 1884. During this three-year construction period, Nantucketers contributed by hauling glacial erratics from Quaise Pasture, Saul's Hills and other parts of the island and ferrying them to the growing jetty on barges. Nantucket scalloper Carl Sjolund's grandfather from Norway worked on the construction of this jetty after quitting the ship he worked once it arrived in New York City Harbor from Norway. According to Sjolund, his grandfather, Karl Sjolund, joined a crew that hauled much of this jetty's stone from Connecticut. Work on the east jetty began in the 1890s, shortly after Nantucket and the government's engineers realized that, although the west jetty did create some scouring action, a second jetty, extending out from Coatue, was essential to harnessing the natural dredging action of the tides to cut a deep channel through the bar. Building it in sections as the west jetty had been, Belding & Company of New Haven, Connecticut, completed the 4,885-foot eastern jetty in 1910.

While these currents did blast a channel through the bar, albeit more than a century too late, the Nantucket Harbor channel has required regular dredging to keep it 15 feet deep at mean low tide.

Ideas on how to enhance circulation in the harbors, other than building jetties and dredging out channels, included busting through the various barrier beaches and sand spits protecting the harbors. During the decades that Nantucket languished without its jetties, some Nantucketers floated the idea of opening the Head of the Harbor to the ocean through the Haulover, because they felt such an opening would fire up the velocity of the harbor tidal currents, causing it to plow more aggressively through the bar and gouge out the much-coveted deep-draft channel. Other islanders countered—and Peter Rosen agrees with this theory—that it would cause the harbor to fill in with shoals, with the six points of Coatue gradually extending southeast across the harbor and eventually forming six coastal ponds.

As I described in the first chapter of this book, the Haulover opened on its own in December 1896 during a winter storm. It remained open for 12 years, during which time fishing vessels used the opening as a shortcut to the fishing grounds east of the island.

In 1949, Nantucket, working with the U.S. Geological Survey, proffered the notion of digging a 300-foot-wide, six-foot-deep channel between the Head of the Harbor and Nantucket Sound, across Coatue northwest from Chatham Bend, to help clean out the shoals within the harbor, improve circulation and, they hoped, enhance bay scallop populations in the harbor. The USGS concluded that that the channel would significantly improve tidal circulation in the harbor but might do irreparable damage to bay scallops because it could suck out crucial nutrients and food required by the scallops to live. (The study also noted that scallops found in the Head of the Harbor have large shells but small abductor muscles and that the best scallops were found on the hard bottom near Wyer's Point.) The town never opened this channel between the Sound and the Head of the Harbor.

With the jetties in place, it was thought, shipping and boat channels would always remain open, because the force of the tides would only inhale fresh oxygenated salt water and marine animal food in the form of plankton and small fish, and exhale excess sand, toxic runoff, dead plants, dissolved carbon dioxide and unneeded nutrients. Instead, maintaining the depth of Nantucket Harbor's channels, safe for navigation and the circulation at an optimal rate—currently, it takes 70 days to cycle the water out of the Head of the Harbor and replace it with fresh seawater—meant numerous dredging projects in the main channel, between Pocomo Point and Fifth Point, and in the Polpis Harbor channel in 1993. The town hopes to dredge a section of this channel's east side, currently filling in with silt, during the winter of 2012–2013. And the 1930s installation of a wide, V-shaped heavy timber bulkhead, or whaler, at the isthmus of Polpis Harbor's east and west lobes prevented the flood-tide-borne sand coming into that harbor from shoaling up the channel leading to the western part of Polpis Harbor. The Marine & Coastal Resources Department replaced that bulkhead in December 2006 because the original had fallen apart in the 70-odd years of its life.

And out in Madaket in 1977, the town considered the opposite of opening a channel through the barrier beach that connected the island to Esther Island in Madaket, which was opened by Hurricane Esther in September 1961, and recreating the namesake island. In their paper, "Nantucket's Broad Creek Opening," Wes N. Tiffney and Robert Benchley, III, detailed various ideas on closing this opening. Hurricane Gloria did the work for Nantucket on September 27, 1985, reattaching Nantucket with Esther Island, a.k.a. Smith's Point.

HARVESTING THE WATERS

From the time the first settlers arrived on the island through the travails building the harbor waterfront, developing the town, plowing out a navigable shipping channel and generally taming the island to their liking, they fed themselves from the surrounding waters. Starting in the 1870s, they began to deliver local seafood to mainland markets. They dug steamers, harvested oysters from the harbors and salt ponds, and likely found pockets of blue mussels to utilize as food. They also found an abundance of American eels, white perch and herring in Madaket Harbor, Long Pond and the other great salt ponds, which they almost certainly ate and sold locally. The harbors held quahogs, bay scallops, young winter flounder, striped bass, bluefish, crabs and lobsters.

Quahogs were plentiful in the new-formed Nantucket and Madaket Harbors, in sheltered water between Smith's Point and the south side of Tuckernuck in 1890, on the north side of this island and between it and Muskeget north of the Gravelly Islands, and in massive beds in Nantucket

Sound. They were a staple of the Native Americans' diet and also that of the European settlers, along with eels and possibly bay scallops, and they became another source of income for Nantucketers. Large concentrations of quahogs appeared in the lee of barrier beaches after they were opened to the ocean, either intentionally or by a storm, and then closed again. Such locations included Smith's Point in its once-elongated form stretching past Muskeget, the beach connecting Nantucket to Esther Island, the Haulover and some of the great salt ponds.

In the early 1900s, Dr. David L. Belding, M.D., the state's shellfish biologist, was tapped by the Massachusetts Commissioners of Fisheries and Game to study the state's shellfisheries. To this day, Dr. Belding is regarded by many Nantucket shellfishermen as the preeminent expert on bay scallops, quahogs and the other shellfish in local waters. In assessing quahog stocks during the period he conducted his studies, 1905 through 1910, Dr. Belding reported that Nantucket Harbor had 2,290 acres of quahog beds; Madaket, 300 acres; the eastern end of Tuckernuck, 200 acres; and from the western end of Tuckernuck to Muskeget Island, 2,500 acres, the latter population comprising mostly littlenecks.

There is scant specific historical information on the digging and use of quahogs by early humans on Nantucket's islands, other than that they were found in Indian middens and were known to be used as currency by the Native Americans and as food for all people living on these islands. Andrews found that records began in 1870. In 1890, when Smith's Point extended between the west end of Tuckernuck and Muskeget, as Andrews tells it, the ocean water flowing through breaks in this end of the point created eelgrass beds so dense that quahoggers built 15 to 20 shacks on the Gravelly Islands and Muskeget so they could harvest the quahogs, row them back to Nantucket and ship them to fishmongers in New York City.

By far the largest number of quahogs existed in Madaket Harbor and around Tuckernuck during this time, although Andrews acknowledged a fair amount in Nantucket Harbor, including a thick bed that formed after the Haulover cut closed in 1908. As of June 1913, Nantucket's quahog fleet was 90 strong. Many boats were outfitted with dredges for dragging the beds in Nantucket Sound that were too deep to be dug by hand or raked, and catches were hauled from in-shore flats to the island in Swampscott dories. It was around this time that the town began regulating the commercial quahog fishery. Andrews recalled, "The business was important enough to call for some conservation regulations. The sale of seed to off-island companies was prohibited, and the minimum-size regulations of two inches in length were enforced. The requirements had already been enforced against the Chatham fishermen, who were not eligible for licenses."

With steam-powered fishing vessels overtaking those relying on the wind, and with newer, longer-range quahogging boats, fishing grounds opened up as far away as Vineyard Haven and New Bedford. Expanded fishing grounds meant greater supply, and greater supply eventually glutted the quahog market, forcing mainland dealers buying them by contract to supply only clam chowder makers. The beginning of the end came in 1940, when the soup companies started mixing sea clams in with quahogs because commercial fishermen by then had hydraulic dredges that used a hose to blast a stream of water onto the bottom in front of their dredges. This action exposed more clams and allowed the fishermen to dredge for them in Nantucket Sound and south of the island, where they were significantly more abundant than quahogs. Luckily, Nantucket's Board of Selectmen prohibited the use of these destructive hydraulic dredges in March 1924, because, as Andrews notes, they would have emptied Nantucket's waters of quahogs well before the state ended the commercial harvest of quahogs in 1957.[8]

Relegated to using box rakes and bull rakes, quahoggers did a fair job getting after these shellfish in the harbors and near-shore waters under normal conditions, until a resurgence of the population occurred during the eelgrass blight of 1931 and 1932. While this blight, which biologists later determined to be eelgrass wasting disease, crushed bay scallop populations, it was a boon for quahogs, because when the blight cleared out the grass, they had much more room to grow. As a result, they provided a steady source of income for the many islanders laid low by the Great Depression.

EELS

Likewise, fishing for eels in island waters supplied a source of food for early settlers and Native Americans alike. Shipping of what were then called black eels but are now known as American eels began in 1874. But, like the quahog fishery, commercial eeling eventually reduced eel populations down to recreational fishing numbers.

The Wampanoags called them "eeshaws" and probably harvested the eels by getting them at the ocean end of the island's great salt ponds in the fall and spring, prior to openings, by spearing them through holes cut in the ice during the winter while the eels hibernated in the mud of island ponds and harbors or by spearing them when the water was cold enough to force them into shallower, warmer water amongst weeds. Andrews explained that eels mature over several years, males after three years old and females after four to seven years of age, and they go through three stages of metamorphosis before they can spawn; therefore, pressure put on their island populations by commercial eelers, and by recreational fishermen looking for food, meant the quick decline of this snake-like fish.[9]

Although spearing the eels through the ice during the winter months was the predominant method of capture, commercial eelers eventually adopted the eel pot. This method of capture really took off starting in 1920, when eelers set out scores of pots during the late summer and early fall, a practice that Andrews recalls as lasting only seven or eight more years before eel populations were depleted. Chances for a rebound of American eel stocks on Nantucket were stymied further by the digging of mosquito ditches throughout the island's salt marshes in the 1930s. Though they still exist in Nantucket's great salt ponds, American eels never returned to their once plentiful numbers.

SCALLOPS

The fisheries based in Nantucket's harbors and its inshore waters collectively became somewhat of a salve for the deep wounds cut into the island economy by the loss of the whaling industry. Fishing for clappers, which scallops were called until about 1900, became a way of life for those fishermen not tempted off island by the California Gold Rush or those affected by the general lack of work on Nantucket. Starting in 1872, three years after the last whaling vessel left Great Harbor, demand for scallops grew enough in mainland urban areas to nourish markets in the Northeast, according to Andrews. Prior to that time, scallops, in addition to being used as bait for cod fishing and other groundfish species, were used as fertilizer because they were so plentiful.

The 1870s were also a time of renewed prosperity in Nantucket's history, when new forms of industrial production, along with mechanized farming, replaced the economic engine of whaling. Providing further proof of economic improvement, the mainland steamer began making two round trips to the island a day in 1874. One of the newest forms of commerce on Nantucket was ice harvesting from island ponds, an already lucrative industry in New England that became possible on Nantucket with the advent of the icebox in mid-19th-century America. Ice could be cut from almost any of the ponds on Nantucket and Tuckernuck when they froze solid and thick enough for ice harvesters to venture out with handsaws and sleds to cut out chunks to haul back to ice houses, insulated with straw, for storage. The Head of Hummock Pond and Maxey Pond were said to be the best because the water was the clearest.

As Andrews noted, though, the freshwater ice industry on Nantucket was barely productive enough to meet islanders' needs:

> In January 1877, fourteen hundred tons of eight-inch-thick ice was harvested. Nantucket is not cold enough to do very well in this trade, and eight-inch ice was all that could be counted on, although occasionally, as in 1893, thirteen-inch ice developed. The winter of 1897–98 was so mild that no ice was cut. Some ice was usually imported. Ice used to preserve fish is chopped in small pieces and placed on the bottom and top of containers, and occasionally in the middle of a barrel as well. There was great competition to get the skim ice, which could easily be chopped this way. It was harvested with scoop nets for immediate use, and every pond and puddle was visited.

As production of ice expanded on the island to keep iceboxes supplied with pond ice, and before Captain John Killen built Nantucket's first large-scale artificial ice plant in 1902 and William T. Swain followed with his in 1910, fishermen had the ideal method of transporting their catches fresh to mainland markets in Boston and New York City. Although the drying and salting method was continued, seafood packed in ice in tight wooden boxes, kegs and barrels, and insulated by eelgrass, was sent fresh to mainland markets in large enough volumes to make these fisheries into legitimate industries.

This practice of harvesting island ice continued from the early 1870s, when fish from the harbors, Nantucket Sound, the ocean and—seasonally—the ponds were first packed in ice to ship to mainland markets, until 1960, when transportation costs made shipment unprofitable.

Oddly enough, commercial scalloping began from shore. Fishermen raked for them through eelgrass beds in the shallows of the harbor and gathered them in dip nets, then heaved them into nearby skiffs or horse teams pulling wagons on the beach. The next progression was to dories, in which one person rowed while the other tended to ropes towing two dredges outfitted with twine nets instead of the chain-ring bags used today to harvest the larger scallops in deeper water. According to Belding, Nantucket's use of chain-ring bag dredges didn't happen until sometime after

Bay scallop

the first decade of the 20th century. Although mainland markets developed a hunger for bay scallops by 1872, Nantucket's serious commercial scalloping effort began in 1883, around the time when scalloping by catboats came into its own, in which the boats towed dredges roughly two-and-a-half-feet square with twine bags dangling from them.

    Unlike today's fleet of mavericks, who work their outboard motor power boats singly or in pairs, the catboat crews, in dredging by sail, had to work together. They lined their craft up in a staggered row when the wind cooperated, sailing up and down with their dredges behind them, and then all tacking one after the other to beat back. This continued into the early 1900s, when a few fishermen began adding the new-fangled outboard motors as auxiliary power to their catboats' sails. Invented in 1903 by Yale engineering student Cameron Waterman, the first outboard was a four-stroke gasoline engine, the type of engine preferred today because of its high fuel efficiency, low pollution and quieter operation. Waterman made 12 of his outboard engines in 1907, two years after securing his patent, and then several thousand through 1912. It wasn't until after 1909 that scallopers figured out how to fish using the engine, hanging off the transom of the catboat, as their primary source of power. The trick then, as it is today, was to find the happy medium between operating the engine at a high speed, which would keep the dredges off the bottom, and too slowly, which caused the dredges to fill up with all the muck, shells and rocks on the bottom, mixed in with some scallops. Boats moving at the right speed scoop up mostly scallops, mixed with eelgrass, other marine species and some bottom debris.

Although some scallopers eventually added four-cycle car engines to their catboats sometime after 1935 and found their equilibrium for dredging under power, and some industrious islanders paired outboard motors with dories in 1932, it was probably too late for them to take much advantage of the new technology, because of the eelgrass blight that hit the East Coast in the early 1930s.

This wasting disease, caused by the slime mold *Labryrinthula zosterae*, kills the eelgrass plant by covering its fronds with black-brown spots that eventually spread to smother all the blades, thereby denying the plant its energy from the sun. Because the disease spreads on contact and through the water, it easily leveled Nantucket's eelgrass beds in all of its harbors and estuaries. Altogether, 90 percent of eelgrass forests along the East Coast were gone by 1933, actually causing a species of limpet to go extinct because this shelled invertebrate lived entirely off eelgrass. Closer to home, death of the island's eelgrass beds meant also the loss of one of the island's game birds: the brant, which numbered in the thousands when eelgrass beds were thick, especially in the vicinity of Brant Point. Upon returning to the island during the fall and winter months, they wandered onto the land in search of food and were easy prey for hunters.

The only places small eelgrass populations survived during this blight were up coastal streams. Burdick says that the wasting-disease slime mold doesn't like fresh water, so pockets of eelgrass were able to survive. Nantucket's harbors may have been re-seeded when seeds of eelgrass washed into the harbors on tidal currents, but bird distribution is the most likely repopulation scenario, considering that eelgrass spreads at a rate of just 25 to 35 inches per year from the main plant, sending its stems out laterally, injecting rhizomes into the sandy bottom and sending up new leaves as it goes. It also flowers, with male pollen moving through the water to fertilize the female's ova, creating seeds that scatter along the harbor bottom. When the eelgrass was destroyed, naturally the harbor creatures that are dependent on eelgrass for food, cover, spawning areas and general habitat took a big hit. And while bay scallops didn't go away entirely, their larvae, while somewhat able to attach to various forms of algae in the harbor, suffered seriously. The scallop seasons during the blight period barely lasted through November. One scalloper still fishing in the second decade of the

21st century, the 67-year-old Sjolund, remembers scalloping with his uncle in the late 1940s and 1950s when the eelgrass was returning to the harbors:

> When I was just a kid, it was coming back. The grass was coming back and it seemed like it was coming back into Madaket and Tuckernuck [first]. When it started to come in the harbor, it came into Hulbert Avenue, the Horse Shed, Hussey Shoal, the lower part of the harbor, and then it started to spread up harbor. So, as the eelgrass started to spread up-harbor, you got more and more areas to fish. You can't catch 'em on sandy bottom. They can't settle on sandy bottom; they need the eelgrass to attach to when they're just in the larval stage.
>
> And then I got my license, I guess I was 12, 13. You could get your license [easily] in those days; nobody would care. It was $5. And then, when I was in junior high school, I'd go on Saturdays—or any kind of a vacation—on a boat, by hand, four dredges. Charlie Sayles and I did it, you know. And we could see the eelgrass spreading further and further up harbor, and there were some pretty lucrative years. I don't mean financially, but we had some pretty good crops. But you only hear about the good times. They weren't all good seasons.

The eelgrass blight of the early 1930s was not the first of its kind on the East Coast to affect Nantucket. Former town biologist Ken Kelley cites eelgrass thinnings in 1894 and 1913 along the East Coat, which Burdick said were probably attributable to eelgrass wasting disease. They may well have affected Nantucket's scallop harvests. But as Sjolund noted, while he was fishing with his uncle and later with Sayles, the eelgrass was gradually growing back in the harbors, and by the 1960s, Nantucket's eelgrass beds had all but recovered.

The eelgrass first returned with thick coverage to the Horse Shed, the part of Nantucket Harbor just west of the end of Coatue, then to the harbor bottom in front of Jetties Beach inside the West Jetty and around Tuckernuck—all areas adjacent to strong tidal currents, noted Andrews. In his 1981 report, *The Nantucket Bay Scallop Fishery: The Resource and its Management*, Kelley commented, "During the 1960s, however, eelgrass has made such a remarkable recovery that many persons now regard it as a nuisance because of the fouling of motorboat propellers, and unsightly accumulations washed up on bathing beaches."

It goes without saying that Nantucket scallopers welcomed the return of thick beds of eelgrass in all of the harbors and around Tuckernuck and Muskeget, but around the same time, another marine scourge of limited impact found its way to Nantucket the way the wasting disease virus invaded our eelgrass. *Codium fragile*, called Codium on Nantucket and also known as Japanese moss, looks like thick, green dreadlocks. It attaches to rocks and the shells of shellfish and often has a smothering effect. Andrews first noticed Codium in Nantucket waters in 1966, and by 1968, he found it washing up on the harbors' shores in large quantities. Kelley reported that it is known to impede circulation and sedimentation movements, attaching to scallops and limiting their mobility, causing scallop strandings because the plant produces a gas on warm sunny days that allows it to float, bringing with it whatever it's attached to. He found in 1981 that the upper reaches of Nantucket Harbor had the most Codium, with fewer occurrences the closer one got to the stronger harbor currents. Overall, 6 percent of scallops in Madaket Harbor had Codium, while 16 percent were covered in Nantucket Harbor at that time. In that year, Andrews noted that Codium had stopped expanding in some parts of the harbors, and Kelley reported that, because eelgrass was still gaining in the harbors, it could have been slowly crowding out the Codium.

Other scallop enemies include green crabs, an invasive species from European and African coasts first seen in Massachusetts coastal waters in 1817; whelk snails, for which the town paid Works Project Administration workers $1 a pound for adults and 5¢ a foot for strings of egg cases between the Depression and into the early 1950s; and ultimately, humans, with their dredges and modified commercial fishing and recreational boats. But Nantucket's bay scallop fishing technology has only evolved so far. The wrought iron frame dredges, first draped with twine netting bags, may have changed a bit in size, but the chain bags used today are the biggest change.

Fishermen transitioned from using outboard motors as auxiliary power for their catboats to relying on them and inboard converted car engines exclusively around 1935. Then they fitted them to dories, and eventually to larger boats, as outboard motors became the norm. Only the addition of powered winches for hauling dredges—their prohibition lifted in 1930 after the town had banned them because mainland quahoggers would use them to get Nantucket scallops during the day and their main catch at night—as well as culling boards and the styles, shapes and sizes of the scallop boats used for hauling have changed the fishery over the years. Since the 1950s, many fishermen have converted recreational boats into bay scalloping vessels.

The bay scallop is a finicky mollusk that can't tolerate poor water quality, and the fluctuation of scallop harvests has become a metaphor for the health of the whole harbor, particularly since the transformation of Nantucket into a summer resort and tourist destination. Annual harvest data collected by the town's Marine & Coastal Resources Department from 1978 through the 2011–2012 season reveals a somewhat steady decline in total bushel counts, with a few strong years beginning with 1980–1981's record harvest of 117,000 bushels and running down through the abysmal low of 3,800 bushels taken in the 2006–2007 season.[10]

Many scallopers and environmentalists make the connection between the decline in harvests, accompanied by the drop in the number of commercial scallop licenses purchased over this period, and the largely residential development within the watersheds surrounding Nantucket, Polpis and Madaket Harbors over the last 20 to 25 years. Nantucket's resort and tourism identity began with its transformation into a summer artists' colony and with actors retreating from mainland cities to 'Sconset near the end of the 19th century and into the early 20th, but the degradation of Nantucket's harbors began later and continued through to the present, with developers buying up large tracts of land to develop into residential subdivisions, and people building summer homes around the harbors. Yes, much of town and some outlying areas were sewered, but exponential growth of large "second homes" on the harbors and inland at first generated the use of now-outlawed cesspools, essentially open pits for collecting sewage that then leached, untreated, into the ground and flowed into the harbors. Even after they graduated to septic systems, many of those would fail over time. Property owners well off enough to afford such opulent summer cottages generally desired large lawns and ornamental gardens, requiring copious amounts of fertilizer to satisfy the need for "perfect" summer properties.

Always a factor in the decline of good water quality in the harbors, atmospheric deposition of pollutants—up to 70 percent of total harbor pollution—including nitrates and phosphates when joined with the remaining portion of pollutants from humans, including fecal coliform bacteria seeping out of leaching fields and antiquated cesspools into the harbors, along with excess nitrogen from fertilizers used on these properties, eventually took their toll on the overall health of Nantucket's harbors and ponds. And as the harbors' scenic real estate disappeared under giant houses crowding onto the edges of the inner harbor shores, along with their pools, tennis courts, guest houses and garages, use of the harbors by mainland ferry companies, charter fishing boats, mega-yachts and all manner of other recreational boats grew. The late Walter Beinecke's re-jiggering of the waterfront, from its whaling/fishing past into wharves packed with art galleries, shops, bars and restaurants, and the construction of the Nantucket Boat Basin, to accommodate fleets of pleasure craft sweeping into the harbors with growing frequency each successive summer, added to the morass.

If a Nantucket working its waters for seafood and whales, unbridled by modern-day environmental laws, let flow into the harbor all manner of contaminants, in the form of paints, hull sealants, creosoted pilings, whale parts, sewage, general runoff and the waste of 15,000 grazing sheep (among many other unchecked nasties), it is no wonder that, as Sjolund said, you never heard about the bad years of scalloping in the "good ol' days," when scallops were so plentiful they were rated only slightly more valuable as food than as fertilizer. Many an older scalloper, when asked, will say that harvests from year to year are a cyclical, Mother-Nature type of thing, and that the same is true of the density of eelgrass beds. But as Sjolund admits, since humans inhabited these islands, it has always been a combination of factors altering the habitat of the harbors, contributing to their overall downturn in health.

Having grown up when the island was maturing into what she is today, Sjolund hints that a sea change of the island's economy and human populations increased all of these inputs that had been innocuous at lower levels during the harbor's early years. Sjolund opines:

> Years ago, you put on some horse or cow manure [as fertilizer], and that was it, and the harbor wasn't anywhere near built up as it is today, with the fancy houses and all that. And I'm not saying that's the only thing. A lot of things contribute, but one [good] thing is that people are much more aware of it today, about runoff and oils and fertilizers and detergents, and you could just go on and on. I think I read someplace that the scallop is one of the most sensitive shellfish to pollution. They will go first.

Commercial harvesting of quahogs and oysters in the harbors never really took off on the scale of other fisheries. The bay scallop remains, along with whelk snails, locally called conchs, for which a few islanders set out pots. The practice of gleaning fish and shellfish out of the ponds for anything other than a home-cooked meal faded away, as islanders turned to occupations in the tourist industry, construction and other employment opportunities, gravitating to the ponds only for recreational fishing and boating. Although the practice of opening the great salt ponds to the ocean has continued, and blueback herring and eels still swap environments for spawning purposes, the thinking behind management of the salt pond ecosystem and their fisheries has changed with the times.

THE SALT PONDS

Until achieving environmental equilibrium supplanted the hunger of islanders to feed themselves and draw a seasonal living from the ponds, opening them was considered a necessity.

Everything changed in 1981, however, when the Massachusetts Department of Environmental Protection decided that it could no longer allow Nantucket to open its great salt ponds on its own, without a state permitting review, and declared the activity now required substantial oversight beyond the abilities of island citizens.

That year, empowered by the Massachusetts Environmental Protection Act, the Nantucket Conservation Commission told the town that, before it could open any of the ponds again, it had to complete an environmental impact statement that examined all the possible negative effects of pond openings, and it must prove to the Conservation Commission and the Massachusetts Department of Environmental Protection that the impacts would be negligible. At the time, the Pond Management Committee, a selectmen-appointed committee of Nantucketers supporting pond openings, argued that opening the great salt ponds would continue to allow eels and herring to complete their lifecycles, would biannually cleanse the ponds and was, moreover, a natural way to subdue mosquitoes. Other benefits included the restarting of an oyster fishery within Sesachacha Pond and dropping the level of ground water that seeped into houses within the ponds' watersheds during the spring and fall. The overwhelming sentiment among islanders was that Big Brother from America, incarnate in the form of DEP officials, was attacking the Nantucket Way.

Opponents countered that the erosive action of the openings shifted beach sand offshore, were an ineffective method of mosquito control and siphoned off precious fresh water from the island's sole source aquifer while weakening the fresh-salt water interface and inviting more seawater into the island's aquifer. Regardless of Nantucketers' reasons for or against pond openings, however, the crux of this issue trickled down to who owned the ponds and therefore held jurisdiction over them: the town or the state. Originally, New York claimed ownership of all the islands in the waters off southeastern Massachusetts, along with Nantucket, until relinquishing them.

In Nantucket's case, the 27 original settlers of the island, the Proprietors of the Common and Undivided Lands of Nantucket, took possession of all rights to the island from the government of the Province of New York in 1691, including rights to the ponds. A special act of the Massachusetts Bay General Court confirmed this transfer of jurisdiction over Nantucket from New York in 1693. Since the adoption of that act through present day, ownership of the island's ponds has held up in all court challenges and was reaffirmed in 1993.[11]

Unable to produce the environmental impact statement needed to satisfy the Conservation Commission, the Pond Management Committee and its supporters succumbed to the will of the opposition, whose voices joined with those of the Conservation Commission to carry the farthest, and no great salt pond was opened by the town between 1981 and 1993. However, Hummock, Sesachacha and Miacomet ponds were opened illegally by several pond-opening proponents, including scalloper Steve Scannell, who would actually phone former Nantucket Environmental Police Officer Don LaHaye, a.k.a. "Clambo," to report that he would be out at a certain pond to dig a trench between it and the ocean. Scannell always gave Clambo the date and time he'd be digging because he hoped the officer would arrest him and Scannell could get a court hearing, forcing a test case so that Nantucket could re-establish total local autonomy over the island's great salt ponds. Several times, digging with only a shovel, Scannell was able to open Sesachacha and Hummock ponds before Clambo caught him in the act.

Eventually, the state paid attention to Scannell's antics and the growing number of Nantucketers calling for the state to recognize the island's sovereignty over its ponds. On Nantucket's first stab at this, Governor William Weld vetoed a bill embodying this effort that originated as a 1992 Town Meeting article containing a home rule petition. The bill sought legislative adoption of an act restoring Nantucket's rights to manage its ponds without state intervention; Weld vetoed it because it named only the Board of Selectmen as the managing body. In 1993, however, a revised home rule petition included provisions for oversight by both the selectmen and the Conservation Commission, with former Pond Management Committee member Shamus Hayes advising the town on when to open the great salt ponds, and the new version had better luck. It cleared Town Meeting and the Massachusetts Senate and House of Representatives. Governor Weld signed the bill into law on October 22, 1993.

Despite the obvious victory for Nantucket, Scannell disliked what he perceived as the state's inability to reaffirm Nantucket's *absolute* control of its ponds. He shared his thoughts in the October 27, 1993, issue of *The Nantucket Beacon*: "I have mixed feelings. On the one hand, I'm glad to see the ponds able to be opened. I'm just kind of bitter the way things happened and what we ended up with." Scannell continued, "We should have had this out in court. I don't think this will last. It's just an appeasement—we'll be brought into line with the rest of the state sooner or later. It's a minority that can't live with Nantucket independence."

Today, the town opens Sesachacha and Hummock ponds at will, operating only under a recurring permit from the Army Corps of Engineers. While Nantucketers were bickering amongst themselves and with the state, the inhabitants of Sesachacha and Hummock ponds were feeling the strain of the ponds not being opened. It's highly probable that the health of these ponds degraded during that time. Having been opened consistently for centuries with few interruptions, these ponds and their inhabitants counted on regular infusions of salt water. The oysters and soft-shell clams and eels, white perch and herring needed both ocean and pond environments to complete their lifecycles.

Goodman recalls catching very few white perch in Hummock Pond during the 13-year pond-opening hiatus. Between 2001 and 2011, he caught no chain pickerel, yellow perch and pumpkin seed in that pond because, he theorizes, the salt content, promoted by regular openings after 1993, reached a level intolerable to these species. However, he did catch a bluefish in this pond a month after it was opened and then closed by itself. And after the Blizzard of 1978 plowed sand between Hummock Pond and its western half, Clark Cove, separating the two, Goodman noticed that the salinity of this pond increased, and so did the number of white perch.

Nowadays, prudent fishermen find out when pond openings are scheduled and make a point of being on the ocean beaches when the ponds are opened, in hopes of catching striped bass, which can sense the pond water emptying into the ocean and know there will be herring or eels in the water. While there are usually just a handful of anglers going after stripers at pond openings, within these first two decades of the 21st century, the island's relatively new residents from countries in Central and South America are the latest Nantucketers to harvest fish from the great salt ponds. Whereas Goodman, and Pew before he moved off island, and the other islanders fishing mostly for sport were traditionally the only people ever fishing these ponds, today, during the spring, summer and fall, Latinos outnumber recreational fishers working Sesachacha, Miacomet, Hummock and Long Ponds from their shorelines, hauling in and keeping any and all fish regardless of size. Because Nantucket is the only town in the state where freshwater fishing licenses aren't required and where enforcement of bag limits is extremely lax, depletion of fish stocks, almost certainly more severe than one can discern, goes unchecked.

Generally, during this time period, however, pond openings have become more and more about flood control and cleansing their respective watersheds of excess nutrients and toxic runoff than about maintaining the various fishery stocks. Both Sesachacha and Hummock, along with both halves of Long Pond and Miacomet Pond, have been declared impaired bodies of water by the Massachusetts Estuaries Project. In the Estuaries Report on Sesachacha Pond, released in 2006 for the town and the state by the School of Marine Science and Technology at UMass Dartmouth, guided by Dr. Brian Howes, SMAST classified Sesachacha Pond as "showing signs of eutrophication in 2006."[12]

Despite their description of the ecosystem of this pond as highly overloaded, Professor Howes and SMAST listed Sesachacha as probably the least threatened by overloading of nutrients of all Nantucket's great salt ponds, as well as the least dirty, noting that nearly half of its perimeter was surrounded by conservation land, opining that fertilizer use on the cranberry bogs is not a factor in its degradation and stressing that the potential for increasing development was "slight." As for remediation, their prescription was for opening Sesachacha Pond at least three times a year and keeping it open longer to ensure a good flushing out of nutrient buildup and a healthy influx of salt water, oxygen and fish food.

Each of the island's ponds and harbors is undergoing eutrophication at some level. As of late 2011, SMAST had done estuary analysis and reports for Sesachacha Pond, Nantucket Harbor (including Polpis Harbor) and Madaket Harbor, with plans to get going on Hummock Pond. For Nantucket Harbor, SMAST's report said that this harbor is "at risk of eutrophication," noting its relatively high water quality despite being beset from every angle with pollutants.

The report recommended a reduction of fertilizer use within its watershed, installation of sewer collection system extensions within unsewered areas of the harbor shoreline and rebuilding the jetties as full breakwaters not inundated during even astronomical high tides.

To Nantucketers gathered at a meeting in September 2007, Howes said that Nantucket needs to care for and rebuild its wetlands, which remove nutrients from the harbor; to step up educational efforts on the dangers of excessive fertilization; to explore the use of centralized and decentralized septic systems; and to maintain and improve harbor circulation through dredging. Four years later, he attached an addendum to his previous recommendations, telling a group of mostly summer residents at a water quality forum that rebuilding the jetties to full jetty height, out of the water even during astronomical high tides, would achieve most of what his original prescription was designed for. In fact, three rounds of harbor circulation computer modeling done by SMAST for the town in 2011, showed that raising the jetties alone, in addition to improving circulation significantly within the harbor, would substantially flush it out daily.

Madaket Harbor is so much smaller than Nantucket Harbor and so open to the ocean and Nantucket Sound, and Howes and SMAST have told Nantucketers that this harbor is fairly clean and is well flushed by the strong tidal currents flowing between the west end of the island and Tuckernuck. But for Hither Creek, the Madaket Ditch and Long Pond, the early report is pretty grim. "Severely impaired" is the phrase Howes used at several public forums, pointing out that input from the Nantucket Landfill, septic systems, water bird guano, and nitrogen and phosphorus from fertilizers, along with atmospheric deposition and the fact that the Madaket Ditch doesn't drain and refill adequately, all contribute to its poor health.

Hither Creek's contamination is such that the town regularly closes Madaket Harbor to the taking of shellfish, except scallops from July 1 to December 31, because of high fecal coliform counts in that harbor. Though some blame this on seabird droppings, all of Madaket is unsewered, which means failing septic systems can leak their contents into Hither Creek. However, on April 19, 2007, the cut was opened between Nantucket and Esther Island by a strong nor'easter, and it remained open long enough for the Marine Department to come within one clean sample of harbor water to reducing that half-year ban to just July, August and September—but the last sample came back dirty. The state's Department of Public Health requires at least three clean water samples in a row for bodies of water containing shellfish beds to remain open, and that won't happen for Hummock Pond in the foreseeable future. SMAST plans to tackle this former outwash valley next but has no date set for completion of its assessment.

No matter. Oktay and Dr. Jim Sutherland, a limnologist, released the findings of their 2010 study of this pond, sponsored by the Land Council and the UMass Boston Nantucket Field Station, and it wasn't pretty, declaring Hummock and its head eutrophic to hyper-eutrophic. Already, in early October 2009, the town's health inspector, Richard Ray, had closed this pond and the Head of Hummock to swimmers and pets because of high concentrations of toxic cyanobacteria (blue-green algae). He closed it again in 2011. Oktay and Sutherland shared what no one wanted to hear in the conclusion of their report: "Hummock Pond and Head of Hummock Pond are highly productive bodies of water plagued with excessive concentrations of phosphorus and nitrogen. It appears that both ponds are close to, or have reached, their assimilative capacity with regards to these nutrients and require the implementation of specific management practices to reverse the present trends." What they mean is that Hummock Pond is so overloaded with nitrogen, phosphorus—the primary polluter of fresh water—and other pollutants that if it and Head of Hummock Pond absorb nutrients beyond what is currently flowing into them, blue-green algae and invasive aquatic plant species will eventually take over these ponds more quickly than the natural process would.

Miacomet Pond has evolved into an almost entirely freshwater ecosystem. Infusions of salt water twice a year would kill its inhabitants. Though SMAST may do an analysis of it, Oktay and Sutherland have already examined it in a study done for the Nantucket Land Council in 2009 and released in 2010. They found that it, too, is eutrophic, with cyanobacteria in its waters. Much of its inland end is heavily grown-in with aquatic vegetation such as cattails, common reeds, duckweed and purple loosestrife, an ongoing process that all ponds on Nantucket are undergoing. The report's verdict is:

> The aquatic plants identified in Miacomet Pond are all native forms, which, under normal conditions, would comprise a healthy component of the aquatic ecosystem. The circumstances in Miacomet Pond, however, are not normal and the aquatic plant community has become overproductive and a source of internal nutrients to the system. Allowed to continue, the plant community soon will reach 'nuisance' proportions throughout the Pond and greatly accelerate the process of eutrophication toward hyper-eutrophication.

Nantucket's focus on its harbors and ponds is evolving into a self-arrest of sorts, with ever-growing numbers of concerned Nantucketers taking pride in trying to stem the pollution entering its waters, to protect the plants and animals living in them and to educate the island's population, and its visitors, on the vital importance of these precious bodies of water.

In the ponds, it's clean-up, plus a part of a gradual shift away from Nantucketers' reliance on the island wilderness as life-sustaining, economically viable ecosystems toward being recreational outlets for humans, refuges for wildlife and conservatories for plants. In the harbors, it's a race to choke off land-based and water-borne pollution inputs and to preserve existing fisheries sustainably while divining a tolerable level of human use.

As Nantucket rushes to fix the problems that most attribute to overdevelopment of the island, the fallout of overuse of the harbors and ponds is happening all around us. The current poor condition of the island's great ponds is one tragedy. It's sad that the island's land-use planning strategies, recent and present efforts excluded, couldn't prevent excess septic and lawn nutrients from entering these ponds.

The other tragedy is the thinning, fragmenting and total loss of eelgrass beds in certain parts of the harbors, due largely to the same failure. While eelgrass wasting disease lost its virulence sometime after arriving in local waters in the 1930s, it remains present and on the leaves of eelgrass, just waiting for the right conditions—probably poorer water quality than exists today—to begin exponential, devastating growth. Like the scallops that depend on it for their survival, eelgrass is sensitive to fluctuations in water quality, especially when excess nutrients push harbors toward eutrophication. Surveys of Nantucket's eelgrass beds began during former town biologist Ken Kelley's tenure. Before that, anecdotal accounts, such as those from Sjolund and Andrews, were all the town and eelgrass experts, including Burdick, had to go on. In 1995, DEP scientist Charlie Costello mapped 46 embayments in the state, including Madaket Harbor, from the air, on the water and using digital imagery. Costello found eelgrass declining statewide, due largely to an overload of nitrogen from septic systems. And in Nantucket's case, nitrogen from lawn and garden fertilizers surely aids in eelgrass losses in the harbors.

While Costello surveyed only Madaket Harbor, it's well known that the Head of the Harbor, Polpis Harbor and Quaise have always been severely devoid of eelgrass. Most biologists, scallopers and environmentalists agree that eelgrass loss is directly linked to degraded water quality resulting from overdevelopment within the harbor watersheds.

If this point isn't clear enough, think of it when you're flying over Nantucket Harbor in February. Notice how bright green many of the lawns are

Eelgrass dead on Pocomo Beach

along Nantucket Harbor, even in winter. If you own property within either of the harbor watersheds or spend time in the Head of the Harbor, recall this passage when boating or swimming up there. Burdick feels this way: "I think it's clear that eelgrass is in decline in Nantucket Harbor. There used to be a lot up in the Wauwinet area, and it's almost all gone now. If you look at the maps, I think you'll find that the deeper areas of eelgrass are disappearing and when we see that, the lower edge moving shoreward, we think of water quality decline."

Howes, who contributed to a study done by the Woods Hole Oceanographic Institution and its resulting report in March 1997, supports this premise, identifying the stimulation of phytoplankton growth, light transmission decline, the growth of the epiphytes on eelgrass leaves and the creation of low oxygen conditions from the decomposition of increased amounts of organic matter as the effects of nutrient overloading in Nantucket Harbor that kill eelgrass.

In addition, the chains of boat moorings resting on the bottom of the harbor, especially during the low tides and with a decent wind blowing, cause what look like underwater crop circles, as winds from various directions move the boats around, dragging their chains and scraping off the eelgrass in that area. Equally damaging are the boat-washing detergents that boat owners continue to use. These contain surfactants, which, in addition to breaking up dirt as intended, also break up whatever petroleum products rest on the surface of the harbor, carrying them down to the bottom where their hydrocarbons have been shown to kill scallop larvae and other marine life. Unfortunately, the town's public awareness and education campaign is the only available weapon against their use. Luckily, the outmoded practice of dumping sewage from boat holding tanks, despite pump-out stations in the Nantucket Boat Basin and at the town pier, ended when Fronzuto had Nantucket's waters, in a measured area surrounding the islands three miles out to the Sound and sea from their shores, designated a federal no-discharge zone in 1993. This made the dumping of boat sewage and gray water, and washing machine, dishwasher, shower and sink water a federally punishable offense. Since then, the town has purchased a pump-out boat able to motor out to boats anchored or moored in the harbor and pump their holding tanks into its own tank, which, when full, is connected to sewer collection lines running beneath the town pier and pumped into that system. There is also a fixed pumping station at the harbor end of the town pier. Sewer collection pipes also run beneath the piers of the boat basin. Nantucket Boat Basin staff use mobile pumping units, located all around their piers, to tie into these pipes and pump out holding tanks. They also maintain a fixed pump-out station near the end of Commercial Wharf.

THE GREAT NUB CONTROVERSY

Biologists blame all this pollution, combined with gradually warming ocean water due to climate change, for one of the more obvious impacts on scallops, one that has befuddled their human predators. It all surfaced at a Harbor & Shellfish Advisory Board meeting on October 7, 1997, when divers Pete Kaizer and Phil Osley told the board that a lot of scallopers were harvesting seed. What other scallopers, Fronzuto and the state, along with Kaizer and Osley, perceived as seed, many other scallopers, including then HSAB member Ken Kelley, saw as sexually mature "nub" scallops. At that meeting, HSAB voted to recommend to the selectmen to change the definition of an adult scallop from having a raised, well-defined growth ring to one having such a growth ring about the size of a penny, about ten millimeters up the shell from the hinge, a vote Kelley objected to because of his knowledge that most Madaket scallops' growth rings were smaller than a penny, meaning to him that if the selectmen made this change, most Madaket scallops would have been off limits.

The nickname "nub" stands for what the latter group saw as the raised, well-defined growth ring required for harvest by the state's Division of Marine Fisheries and by the town. The group took it to indicate that a scallop had spawned after its first year in the water and was growing its second year of shell. When the ring was smaller than a penny, it was thought to indicate the scallop's first year of growth. The second year of its shell growth was much larger and aided in its adult appearance.

Nub scallops, so-called because the growth ring can be as tiny as a pencil point, up to ten millimeters, are the outcome of adult scallops spawning in the fall when the water temp is fairly warm, from September 1 on. They go into winter dormancy having grown only that large. When the water warms up in the spring and they start feeding, their shells begin to grow out from under their original growth, continuing through the spring, summer and fall, with some of these scallops able to spawn in their first late summer. As they go into dormancy for their second winter, they have the controversial full-grown appearance but with a tiny nub for a growth line, in many cases a half to three quarters of an inch up their shells from their hinge. These nub scallops continue growing the following spring and can spawn during the early summer and possibly late summer.

Biologists, including Curley, believe that warmer water temperatures in the harbors have pushed the fall spawn closer to when harbor water temperatures start to cool off, causing the nub-scallops-to-be to stop feeding and growing for the winter. Scallops spawn during two periods of the year: during the late spring and early summer, when the water reaches about 68 degrees Fahrenheit, and in early fall, when it approaches that same temperature range as the harbors cool off. Curley thinks poor water quality affects the quality and quantity of food in the harbors, adding to minimal scallop growth after spawning and causing the nub as their first growth ring.

Two years after the nub scallop brouhaha, Fronzuto noted in a March 3, 1999, letter to Division of Marine Fisheries Director Philip G. Coates that, after much scrutiny by biologists, scallopers and town officials, all evidence pointed toward the nub scallops being biologically adults, but under state law, seed. In that letter, Fronzuto told Coates it was proving impossible to examine every single scallop harvested, so, in his words, his interpretation of adult scallops would not include use of a magnifying glass to see the growth ring, scratching the surface of the shell with either fingernail or knife, inspection of the gonad, overall size of the shell, epiphytic growth or indication of a nub or shock-line.

Instead, despite objections from some scallopers and others who believed the nubs were in fact seed and hadn't spawned yet, Fronzuto's interpretation was that adult scallops had to have a raised, well-defined growth ring, regardless of its size. Period. This meant nubs were included, because Fronzuto felt that their brief, first period of growth after they were spawned in the fall counted as a growth ring.

This nub issue arose again at the start of the 2008–2009 commercial scallop season when Fronzuto, upon direction from DMF Chief Biologist Michael J. Hickey, announced two weeks before the season started that he would began enforcing the 10mm rule recommended by HSAB to the selectmen in 1997. Hickey's letter of October 21, 2008, came shortly before the start of a season in which much of the scallop population in the harbors was already known to be scallops with nub growth lines shorter than 10mm.

The first two or three days of that season saw hardly any scallopers bringing in their limits. Most did not even bother to fish. One after another, four emergency HSAB meetings were called. From those meetings came a compromise that stands today: scallops are accepted as adults if their nub growth ring is 10mm or more up their shell from the hinge or if the scallop itself is 2.5 inches in height, or both. This ruling, now enforced by the town and DMF, remains because the DMF wants to collect more data on the nub scallops before making a definitive regulation change encompassing this nub phenomenon.

RUST TIDE

Recently, in the first few years of the 21st century, one of the more visible manifestations of nutrient overload has developed in Nantucket Harbor—specifically, in the water of the Head of the Harbor. It is *Cochlodinium polykrikoibes,* a.k.a. the rust tide, believed by many, including town shellfish biologist Tara Anne Riley, to be negatively affecting bay scallops and quite possibly other shellfish. Most commercial scallopers, the Nantucket Shellfish Association, HSAB and Fronzuto are sure that this algae was responsible for lower scallop meat weight per bushel during the 2009–2010 season, after the summer of 2009's rust tide bloom was especially thick. This algae, when it blooms late July into August, clogs the gills of scallops, denying them both oxygen and nourishment, because their gills filter out much smaller, digestible algae from the harbor water as food. If you happen to be flying over the harbor around this time, look for reddish swaths between Pocomo Point and Wauwinet, and between those shores and Coskata Pond. It's quite dramatic when you see it—but would be even more so were you to try to eat it, which is what scallops and other filter feeders do without realizing it's in their water. All scallopers and their openers from the 2009–2010 season recall how much smaller the scallops' abductor muscles were, as a result, they believe, of the presence of this rust tide. In fact, this algae is blamed for decreasing the average number of pounds per bushel that scallopers get, from eight pounds down to about 5.5 pounds because, it's believed, the scallops' feeding and breathing ability was impaired by the algae.

And it's highly probable that this rust tide, along with the poor circulation in the upper reaches of Nantucket Harbor, may determine the fate of ospreys living on the eastern half of the island. Starting in 2009, Bob Kennedy, former director of natural science for the Maria Mitchell Association, in his ongoing research of ospreys on the island, found that nesting osprey pairs on the east side of Nantucket were having a difficult time catching enough fish to feed their chicks. To track this developing trend, in a collaboration with the Trustees of Reservations and Maria Mitchell, he fitted a male osprey from one of the nests in the Glades, just northwest of Coskata Pond, with a satellite transmitter and discovered that this osprey, which he named Mr. Hannah, flew as far west as Hummock Pond and Long Pond in search of fish.

Kennedy could not definitively attribute the lack of fish in the Head of the Harbor, Coskata, Polpis Harbor and Sesachacha Pond (all of the bodies of water in Mr. Hannah's neighborhood) to their overall declining water quality, but he does believe that poor circulation in the Head of the Harbor and Polpis Harbor leads to high turbidity, exacerbated by nutrient loading. Turbidity is a measure of the clarity of water. Low turbidity means less junk in the water to cloud it up, making it easier for ospreys to see down into it from heights reaching 100 feet above the water before they dive down to as much as two feet under the surface for fish that they spy from above. But higher turbidity, such as found in the poorly circulated waters of the Head of the Harbor and in Sesachacha Pond, means ospreys can see only several inches, maybe up to a foot, into the water.

The rust tide has been appearing in upper parts of the harbor since around 2005. In the 2010 nesting season, ospreys were having to fly ten miles to find food to sustain themselves. Once the osprey did catch a fish such a long way from the nest, it needed energy and ended up eating much of the catch on the way back. Whatever remained went to the oldest, strongest chicks, while the youngest chicks got little or no food. That year, out of three nests on the east side of the island, only one chick survived. The number of nesting pairs decreased over time on that side of the island, whereas on the west side, out of nine nests, two of them failed entirely, but the other seven produced 11 young that fledged.

THE NANTUCKET LAND COUNCIL

These harmful anthropogenic liberties taken with the fresh and salt water environs, which have caused declining harbor and pond health and have negatively impacted their respective organisms, do not necessarily equal a lost cause. Luckily, a lot of people were paying close enough attention in time to start correcting the trajectory toward total collapse of these ecosystems.

In this light, Nantucket's harbors and ponds have a friend in the Nantucket Land Council, for their high quality of water and the survival of their plant and animal species was always championed by the venerable, tenacious Linda Holland, the Land Council's first executive director, and today by her successor, the determined Cormac Collier. Before Collier's time, Holland lobbied for and successfully created harbor watershed protection districts for Nantucket and Polpis Harbors, Hummock Pond, and for Madaket Harbor. She and the Land Council also pushed hard to get the town and the voters to map out a wellhead protection district, as well to protect Nantucket's sole source aquifer.

Founded in 1974, two years after the year the federal Clean Water and Clean Air acts were put into action, the Land Council's birth was part of a nationwide awakening of environmental consciousness just starting to gain traction among Nantucket's residents who had, for centuries, looked to their harbors and ponds as their own personal pantry and nothing more. Although tourism came to mean something in the minds of those making a living in this new industry on the water, stewardship of natural resources and recognition of the rarities 26 miles at sea took a while to catch on.

For all the time Nantucketers lost in getting at the problems plaguing water ecosystems, they have certainly made up for it with the giant steps taken in the following years. One example is Nantucket's decision to ban the use of DDT four years prior to the national ban.

Water quality testing of the harbors and ponds dates to a collaboration in 1989 between the Marine Department and Dr. Howes, and it was this early and more or less continuous effort that pushed Nantucket to the top of the Massachusetts Estuaries Project priority list. The results of Estuaries Reports on Nantucket Harbor, including Polpis Harbor, and on Sesachacha Pond are already leading to remediation efforts in these respective bodies of water. Whether the town decides to open Sesachacha more than twice a year remains to be seen, but in early November 2011, Riley talked enthusiastically to HSAB about her water quality testing of Sesachacha Pond to determine if it could be used for aquaculture. Currently, oysters still grow in this pond, but not nearly to the size for harvesting. The next time the pond is opened, take a walk around its perimeter, especially on its southern sides, and you'll see small oysters, the size and color of regular flavor Cape Cod Potato Chips, encrusted on rocks and the temporarily exposed bottom. Oysters thrive in somewhat poor water quality conditions and could potentially help cleanse Sesachacha Pond.

No such hard-shelled bivalve filters will be working on Hummock Pond. Its Estuaries Report is pending, but time is not being lost. Acting on the dire recommendations in the Land Council/Field Station study, the Hummock Pond Homeowners Association got together with the Nantucket Conservation Foundation and the Land Council in 2011 to install a solar-powered floating aerator in Head of Hummock Pond that adds dissolved oxygen to the water in an effort to prevent phosphorus mobilization and to curtail the effects of cyanobacteria (blue-green algae) blooms. Although monitoring of invasive species and ground water, creation of a management plan and use of an aquatic plant harvester are recommended for bringing Miacomet Pond back to life, none of these strategies was in place by early June 2012.

By far the most vigorous water world restoration is what's going on in Nantucket's harbors. In the last ten years, the town has gotten busy cleaning up. It began an ambitious project to replace all 32 outflow pipes that drain the downtown area and beyond into the harbor with new ones that pass through special storm drain catch basins, called storm-ceptors, designed to create a whirlpool of runoff that spins out debris and forces it through filters that catch trash, toxic sediments and even petroleum products. The filters and the storm-ceptors are cleaned regularly, and while installation of these catch basins was the right move in a series of necessary steps to keep the harbor clean, an effort to stem the dirtiest flow of bad stuff into the waters where we're trying to grow scallops and thicken eelgrass hasn't yet been completed.

This project is a multi-year cleanup aimed at cleaning up the flow of runoff into Consue Springs (also known as Goose Pond), the pond partially surrounded by cattails and common reeds and almost always packed with ducks on the east side of Union Street at the sharp bend near its intersection with Orange Street. This collaboration of the town and the Land Council, using state and federal grants, involves several infiltrator systems, essentially buried gravel pits within the pond's watershed that allow large amounts of runoff to leach gradually into the soil, trapping pollutants before the water flows down to the harbor via the pond. Consue Springs' watershed runs southwest and uphill from the pond bounded by part of the Boys & Girls Club field, Sparks Avenue, and alternating parts of Prospect Street and Orange Street. Water running from this area and draining into Goose Pond contains nitrogen, phosphorous, arsenic, cadmium, lead, selenium, barium, and fecal coliform bacteria. Down in the pond itself, the large waterfowl population contributes a significant amount of fecal coliform bacteria and nitrogen to its waters. The collaboration has put infiltrator systems up next to the Sparks Avenue entrance of the high school and underneath the Silver Street parking lot off Pleasant Street, with the intent of locating others closer to the pond, but the biggest part of the project is cleaning out the pond itself and reestablishing tidal flow between it and the Creeks. During heavy rain events and astronomically high tides, the bottom of the pond gets churned up, at the same time that large quantities of the polluted pond's water are flowing into the Creeks and out into Nantucket Harbor.

Consue Springs used to function as part of the larger salt marsh of the Creeks. It was a filter that cleaned out pollutants from the environment by breaking them down into usable nutrients for growth. But this dynamic worked only when there was a good flow of tidal seawater coming in and out of the wetland. The two concrete culvert pipes between the pond and the Creeks are not large enough to flush the pond properly; worse, they have become clogged, and so much polluted sediment has built up over the years that the level of the pond has been raised higher than the tide reaches.

In the first half of 2012, the town and the Land Council were in the final phase of this clean-up project with the Department of Public Works, working with an engineering firm to design how to dredge out the pond's polluted, sludgy sediment bottom, lower it to the level of the harbor, install two 18-inch culverts side by side beneath the old rail bed for the former

Nantucket Railroad and clean the ditch to the harbor to get the tidal currents working to keep the pond and its watershed clean and refreshed.

Areas feeding into Nantucket and Madaket Harbor watersheds have undergone a similar cleaning through septic system inspections mandated by Nantucket's Septic Management Plan, one of the recommendations in the town's Comprehensive Wastewater Management Plan.

Under this program, all property owners with septic systems within these harbor watersheds were required by the town to get their systems inspected. Those within certain town-delineated zones closest to the water who failed their inspections had 18 months to get them replaced. Those further inland, outside this zone, had 24 months. The Estuaries Report for Nantucket Harbor recommended extending sewer collection lines into Monomoy and Shimmo to cancel out some of the septic systems in this watershed. Although the town would like to build a sewage treatment plant out in Madaket, it's more likely that it will run a sewer line out there from the Surfside plant.

With Nantucket Harbor rated as the cleanest out of 20 embayments in the first round of harbor studies by the Estuaries Project and given the "acceptable" classification, Howes still had some strong words for islanders and their municipal leaders when the report went public in the fall of 2007. He felt that Nantucket Harbor could easily be pulled back from the brink of becoming significantly polluted through several measures that would be relatively easy to accomplish because the island's harbors and ponds are all under one town government. If Nantucket would just throw itself into this effort, he said, it could completely restore the health of Nantucket and Polpis Harbors. He commended the town for the septic regulations requiring inspections of all harbor watershed septic systems and repairs of faulty ones, and for having much of the populated areas of the island already sewered.

In the fall of 2011, after Howes made his suggestion that Nantucket's jetties be raised to full height—high and dry during full and new moon high tides—members of the U.S. Army Corps of Engineers inspected them and noted to Fronzuto that they were the most poorly constructed jetties they'd ever seen, with many gaps between rocks that appeared to have been merely laid down in the water to form the elongated piles of the jetties. The corps noted that larger rocks were used to build the west jetty and smaller ones for the east jetty, many of which were falling down off this jetty because of battering from constant wave action. Fronzuto, for his part, had begun several years earlier to push for rebuilding them. In late January 2012, the Army Corps returned to the island to do bottom surveys of the main channel and around the foundations of the jetties themselves. They informed Fronzuto that they might have a source for rocks near Boston and that this project would cost $10–15 million.

Whatever the outcome of Nantucket's harbor and pond reparations in the works and those yet to come, the no-eelgrass-no-scallops mantra emblazoned on island car bumpers forms a subconscious chant in the minds of Nantucket's scalloping and environmentally enlightened communities. As shrill a call to action as its creator originally hoped it would be, though vehicles bearing this bumper sticker are dwindling on Nantucket, its message continues to be relevant today.

It is embodied in the Land Council's pilot eelgrass restoration project that began in 2010, and also in nearly all of the 122 recommendations of the town's 2009 Nantucket and Madaket Harbors Action Plan. Also figuring into the movement are the horseshoe crab surveys in Nantucket and Madaket Harbors, the eelgrass mapping done by the state, a joint Maria Mitchell and Environmental Protection Agency study of the harbor, the founding of the Nantucket Shellfish Association, the hatching of a Shellfish Management Plan and a scallop seed-stranding rescue team formed by scalloper Matt Herr.

Should you find yourself stuck in traffic somewhere on the island staring at the prophetic bumper sticker, you should divert your route over to the east end of Easton Street, where you can check out what's happening in the red-roofed marine lab just behind Brant Point Light. In this space, Riley, who is really deserving of many more paragraphs in this book, accomplished in her first two years what several shellfish biologists and a private organization had been unable to do before her: grow enough scallops to augment natural populations in the harbor substantially. In 2011, she raised and released 70 million bay scallop larvae, inspiring her to plan for 140 million more in 2012. In addition to raising scallops, Riley also nurses oyster and quahog seed, oversees the town's water quality testing program for the harbors and ponds, mentors a handful of private aquaculture operations in the harbor and supervises multiple ongoing harbor- and pond-related research projects. She accomplishes this with the help of several interns, including one scalloper-intern each season. She operates on a scant budget from the town's propagation fund of commercial and recreational shellfish license fees, an annual flow of revenue directed appropriately, just as portions of mooring and slip fees pay for the maintenance of navigational buoys, public landings and town pier amenities. Some individual and private nonprofit contributors lend a hand from time to time, though levels fluctuate from year to year. Moved by what they see on a tour of the boathouse lab, their hearts and minds tugged by memories of a Nantucket they recall or wish they could see in the future, they give to help keep the harbors and ponds healthy and productive.

The treasures that are Nantucket's harbors and ponds were surely not lost on the first humans to live here, but only in the most primal, survivalist sense did they realize how precious and limited their resources had become. Today's islanders and visitors now know that what once were plundered out of necessity and left to recover on their own are coveted ecosystems that everyone wants to save and revel in.

A BACKYARD OCEAN

BEING ON GREAT POINT, that most fragile yet defiant of Nantucket extremities, is the zenith of many a fishermen's existence.

Striped bass and bluefish are drawn to the waters off the point where the North Atlantic and Nantucket Sound waters converge, mid-spring through early fall. False albacore and bonito join them during the autumnal equinox.

Clad in waders or barefooted, standing ankle- to thigh-deep on its gravelly, sandy tip, the anglers are buffeted by the boiling maelstrom of tidal and ocean currents and the wind as they inch as far out into the waves as they dare and cast sharp, shiny lures of hope into the oblivion of the Great Point Rip. It is a singular joy, to be had at just one place on earth. This nirvana draws saltwater anglers from up and down the East Coast and from Nantucket itself, because this fishing experience immerses mainland-weary and summer-crowd-harried humans in the marine/beach wilderness.

Unfortunately for these fishermen, while the convergence of ocean avenues carries all the swimming food these fish could ever eat, it also attracts herds of gray seals. Seals have always been in our coastal waters. They have traditionally been a rare treat for fishermen and beachgoers alike, who are startled to see a big, dark seal head poke up out of the water, quickly survey the oversea world and then slip back under the surface. Gray seals, along with a smattering of smaller harbor seals, have been, from the 1980s through the early part of the 21st century, just regional threads in the fabric of sea life living in our waters, not whole bolts of cloth smothering their environment.

That a political action group, composed mostly of recreational fishermen and calling itself the Seal Abatement Coalition (SAC), coalesced in the fall of 2011 is an indication that some Nantucketers no longer see these seals fitting into the summer vacation Kodak Moment category. A significant swell has occurred in the gray seal population in the North Atlantic Ocean along the Eastern Seaboard. As a result of the Marine Mammal Protection Act of 1972 and other lesser factors, hundreds of thousands of gray seals are now roaming these ocean waters, from Atlantic Canada down to Long Island. The exponential expansion of their numbers turned Muskeget Island into the home of the third largest breeding colony of gray seals in the North Atlantic, behind ice floes in the Gulf of St. Lawrence and remote Sable Island off the coast of Nova Scotia.

With their breeding locations now including Green and Seal Islands in Maine in addition to those three locations, these seals are less likely to migrate north to breed, because there is more food per seal in our area than is available to the Canadian colonies. Upwards of 2,500 pups, one per female, are born annually on Muskeget from January into early February. Gray seal researchers, including Stephanie Wood, a contract biologist for Integrated Statistics in Woods Hole, and Solange Brault, an associate professor in the UMass Boston biology department, count seals by the number of females and their pups, so 2,500 females giving birth on Muskeget means at least 5,000 seals in our waters. That's not counting males, which Wood and Brault admit are much tougher to track because they can have up to six mates.[1]

What these population statistics mean to fishermen is that the hundreds of gray seals occupying Great Point during much of the year has forced the Trustees of Reservations, which owns and manages the 1,117-acre Coskata-Coatue Wildlife Refuge, and the U.S. Fish & Wildlife Service, owners of the 21-acre tip of Great Point, to close off the Point to vehicle and foot traffic for most of each year since 2008. That perfect fishing experience at the end of Nantucket's index finger no longer exists.

Already frustrated with seasonal beach closures instituted by the Trustees to enforce federal and state laws protecting nesting piping plovers and least and roseate terns since the mid-1990s, three surf fishermen and year-round island residents—Peter Krogh, Guy Snowden and Peter Howell—driven by memories of the heady experience of fishing from the tip of Great Point sans seals, hatched the Seal Abatement Coalition during the fall of 2011. The purpose: to diffuse the impact of gray seals on recreational saltwater fishing in Nantucket waters. SAC's stated mission is to amend the Marine Mammal Protection Act (MMPA) so that the National Oceanic and Atmospheric Administration (NOAA), which protects marine life and also regulates ocean fishing in federal waters through its National Marine Fisheries Service (NMFS), removes gray seals from its "rare status" listing, thereby loosening up enforcement of the act as applied to gray seals and allowing fishermen back onto Great Point's terminus regardless of the seals. This would allow people to fish within much closer proximity to the seals without incurring fines and jail sentences, and it would at least partially restore that magical fishing experience. The fishermen are also trying to persuade NOAA to allow the use of sonic seal dispersing equipment, called seal scrammers, which have been successfully deployed in Oregon and Scotland for repelling seals from commercial fishing areas.

They characterize their approach as a passive, humane one, dealing not only with an impediment to their cherished sport, but also with the potential economic impact should fishermen choose Montauk Point on Long Island, Block Island or some other premium saltwater fishing destination over Nantucket. If you know of the brevity of Nantucket's pulse in the summer, you know it needs every single bit of its shoulder season action.

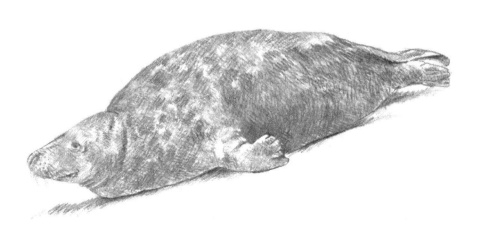

Gray seal

Adamant about SAC's purpose, Krogh described how their motivation originated in October 2010:

> It came principally out of our experience in the Cranny Cranston Fall Classic Bluefish Tournament last year, when we were, all of us, getting stripped of our fish by the seals—not only our fish, but our gear. So this put a big damper on the tournament, reduced the results, and really drove people away from this island. Those who had come out [before] for the Cranny Cranston, which is over Columbus Day Weekend, said they're just not coming back, they just lost too many fish to the seals, they'll take their four-wheel-drive vehicles and their cash someplace else.

GREAT WHITE SHARKS

Whether or not the Seal Abatement Coalition's efforts succeed, it's highly likely that Poseidon will oblige anyway, in the form of great white sharks. Gray seals may be an annoyance to fishermen who must follow proper legal channels, taking years to remove them—or fail to—from Great Point and other beaches. But the sharks, which have been showing up in greater numbers in the waters of Southeastern Massachusetts since 2005, can dispatch seals instantly. They have only to attack, eat and move to the next victim without waiting for federal and state permission. And they have been doing so in the waters off Chatham and within Chatham Harbor on Cape Cod with increasing frequency. Sharks 12 to 18 feet in length have been seen there, as have gray seals bitten in half or severely wounded and exhibiting giant bite marks.

From 1987 through 2004, the Division of Marine Fisheries (DMF) logged one confirmed white shark sighting every couple of years. The DMF's shark biologist, Greg Skomal, pretty much the expert on sharks in Massachusetts, noted that during that time period, the DMF could go years without a white shark sighting. Rarely would he get more than one in any given year.

In 2004, during an extremely high tide, a 14-foot, 1,700-pound great white shark swam into a salt lagoon called Northwest Gutter, a popular swimming hole near Hadley Harbor at the northeast end of Naushon Island, the largest of the Elizabeth Islands. It caused a regional media frenzy. The female white shark eventually found her way out of the pond, but it's highly probable that she was the beginning of a gradual increase in white shark sightings in Cape and Islands waters that continues today.

Since 2005, Skomal has annually logged incrementally higher numbers of these perfect killing machines, going from two per year to three to five and up to eight. In 2009, he had more than 20 confirmed sightings. Being a scientist and ever a skeptic, Skomal wondered if more boaters on the water and more people catching sharks during these years were the reason for the bump up in sightings. But when he factored in the burgeoning gray seal population, it made sense that the numbers of great white sharks were increasing in Massachusetts waters.

White sharks, part of whose normal habitat includes Massachusetts up into Canadian waters, are in the vicinity of Nantucket May through November, expanding their range well north of coastal New England during the summer and shrinking it southward as the water cools off. They then work their way down into water off the southern coastal states. It is not unusual to see white sharks close to shore, feeding on gray seals. The smell of the seals in the waters washes out to the open ocean, where these sharks typically roam, and tempts them into coastal waters.

Skomal puts it this way: "I think what we're seeing with the gray seals now is that [they're] starting to concentrate, or aggregate, white sharks in specific areas, namely off Chatham, off the east coast of Cape Cod, perhaps off Nantucket as well. We're not necessarily seeing an increase in the population, but we're seeing possibly a population shift from offshore waters to near-shore waters to take advantage of this rebounding food resource."

In 1936, 16-year-old Joseph Troy, Jr., of Dorchester, Massachusetts, swimming 150 yards offshore of Mattapoisett, died after a six-foot shark took a five-pound piece out of his left leg. Although no humans have been fatally attacked in Massachusetts since then, Chatham has taken no chances, closing both South Beach and beaches within the harbor several times after sharks were seen. Skomal even anchored an acoustic sensor buoy at the mouth of Chatham Harbor so that he could track the movement patterns of seven great whites in the area that had been tagged with special transmitters. The first time he uploaded the data from that buoy, that same summer, it had recorded more than 400 visits by one of the tagged sharks.

Skomal tagged five great white sharks in 2009; six great whites, including one with an acoustic transmitter, in 2010; and eight in 2011 during the filming of the second episode of the Discovery Channel's "Shark Week," which focused on great whites frequenting the near-shore waters of Chatham. The segment alluded to their expanding presence in the area but only hinted at the possibility that they might add Nantucket gray seal hangouts to their range.

With the gray seal population continuing to grow in our waters and around the rest of the islands and Cape Cod during the first two decades of the 21st century, the great white sharks' larder is well stocked. Add to this cornucopia of marine mammal meat a protection act for sharks, which was adopted in 1997–1998 and is enforced by National Marine Fisheries Service, the federal fisheries regulatory agency responsible for federal waters. The law prohibits commercial and recreational fishermen from keeping great white sharks, basking sharks, tiger and dusky sharks, and other species added since the law went into effect. They must be released alive when caught. Protection measures exist also at the federal and state levels, including size and bag limits, quotas and quota monitoring, all enforced to maintain the various shark species populations at sustainable numbers. These laws must be working, judging by the number of white sharks showing up in Nantucket's waters, and by the fact that Chatham's attractiveness to white sharks caught the notice of the Discovery Channel.

The sharks could certainly save the SAC a lot of time and money when they discover the seal haul-out spots on Nantucket, including Great Point, Low Beach in Siasconset, Smith's Point and Muskeget Island. That expansion of hunting range for the great whites was at least in the reconnaissance stage by the summer of 2011. While leading a charter fishing trip in early July, Marc Genthner, captain of the Nantucket fishing charter vessel *Just Do It Too*, spotted a 16-foot great white shark in three feet of water in the Great Point Rip about a quarter of a mile east of Great Point.

Sharks have survived more than 400 million years of evolution, so they had to have been dining on seals of all kinds, probably on small whales and, always, on larger dead ones. They were almost certainly in Nantucket waters when sea level rise created our islands about 6,000 years ago, bringing with it many of the fish and marine mammals that swim in the Atlantic Ocean and Nantucket Sound today. And the early 21st-century domination of Great Point is definitely not the first by gray seals. It just happens that this particular seal Occupy Great Point movement involves disgruntled fishermen and duty-bound governmental agencies.

This eons-old predator-prey relationship shouldn't shock anyone, at least not until it breaks on our shores with seal halves littering the beaches and Nantucket's Marine Mammal Stranding Team responding to calls about severely wounded seals with some degree of frequency. What should give Nantucketers cause for wonder is that, like the case of the white-tailed deer and many of Nantucket's other species, humans, directly or indirectly, helped create this situation. Not that gray seals won't continue to expand their numbers and haul out on Nantucket's beaches on their own, and not that great white sharks will be crossing seals off of their grocery lists anytime soon, but SAC's formation to drive the seals away from their precious fishing spots is only going to push the problem onto someone else's beach, if it succeeds at all.

The foraging instincts that are hardwired into our DNA for survival had humans, indigenous people and colonists alike, killing gray seals for meat, clothing and probably the manufacturing of crude tools. Gray seal bones have been found in Native American middens in this region. When people no longer needed to harvest them, seals eventually became a nuisance to fishermen, so, to protect groundfish stocks, we put a $5 bounty out for every seal nose hacked off of their dead bodies. Only in 1962 did that practice cease in Massachusetts and Maine. And Native Americans may have hunted sharks for food, but depletion of their numbers happened mostly because of sport and, to a certain extent, a strong market in Asia for their fins to use in soup stock and as aphrodisiacs.

We invited these two species back into our waters in exercise of our collective planet-saving conscience and with our conservation laws, so when we see them in greater abundance in our waters and on our beaches and in national television programs, there should be no surprise. The balance of ocean life will eventually right itself and shift the seals elsewhere, because the sharks will multiply and really begin to thin them out. They're only part of an anthropogenic resurgence that resulted after humans figured out that their presence in the web of ocean life was a necessity and adopted laws to protect them.

Just as we have done on the dry land of our islands, we've meddled with the species in our waters to meet our needs.

LAYING CLAIM TO NANTUCKET'S OWN

The maxim of interconnectivity, that chain of life, was the case well before humans presumed to call the uplands of our coastal plain by name: Nantucket, Tuckernuck, Muskeget. And we subsequently laid claim to the seawater that rose up from beyond the edge of the Continental Shelf, and to all the creatures within it, for whatever uses we required for our own survival. Laws governing fishing and ocean development were nonexistent; early island humans took what they needed, paying little if any attention to the consequences.

When we talk of sea life and the marine environment of Nantucket Sound, that's a span of only around 7,500 years when the fish, marine mammals, invertebrates and plant life associated with Nantucket existed, because that many years ago is around the time when sea level got high enough to begin running into the lowlands of this portion of the coastal plain. Tracking the chronology of the marine life in Nantucket's part of the ocean, which includes Nantucket Sound and the open ocean east and south of the island, is fairly simple, because we know roughly when the ocean came up and created the three islands; therefore, from fossil records, recorded history and anecdotal accounts, we have a pretty good idea of what was in Nantucket Sound and in the ocean surrounding the island. We also know that, by 7,500 years ago, fish and marine mammals were pretty much finished evolving and were in their current physiological forms. What is challenging to quantify is which species are Nantucket's.

Technically, Nantucket's waters extend three miles beyond shore; that is the limit of a state's jurisdiction over its seawater and everything living within it, and every use in and on it. Recognizing that this boundary is human-established, though, there is no way to convey this rule of human law to the species that live here and migrate into and out of "our" waters. Well beyond the three-mile limit south of Nantucket Island—actually, about 80 to 100 miles out—is the 1,000-fathom contour line, the delineation between the shallow coastal waters and the deep ocean. Deep-water species that are heading north or west rarely swim closer to land than this line, and coastal water species heading east and south into the deep ocean, out toward and beyond the edge of the Continental Shelf, generally do not venture past this line.

Naturally, there are the iconic beasties we all associate with the ocean around our islands, including certain species of whales, porpoises, seals, sharks, groundfish and sport fish. Just having them here, however, doesn't make them Nantucket's, in the sense that the Muskeget vole is native to Muskeget, the Nantucket bay scallop is unique in taste from other bay scallops in the region, or the Nantucket shadbush is found primarily on Nantucket. But because they are identified with Nantucket, it's worthwhile to learn their history in relation to Nantucket, from when they arrived in our waters through today.

When the water began filling Vineyard and Nantucket Sounds 7,500 years ago, it brought with it most of the species we know today: sandbar, dusky, blue, dogfish and great white sharks, seals, whales, bluefish, striped bass (during the summer and fall), shellfish larvae, herring, cod, mackerel, pollock, flounder, haddock, halibut, lobster and all the other fish and marine mammal species we have in New England. But there were probably other species no longer here because conditions, such as water temperature, food availability and predators, drove them away.

Ichthyologists know there were white sharks and various species of other sharks in the area at that time, because local collectors have found their teeth in the bluffs on the southern end of Martha's Vineyard. But the early millennia of the Holocene Epoch were definitely too late for the monstrous dinosaur-era shark, megalodon, the 50- to 60-foot prehistoric ancestor of today's sharks. Joining those early sharks were the whales for which Nantucket is well known, including the same varieties as today: right, humpback, finback and minke whales. And, at one time, the Atlantic walrus was a resident of our waters, which were likely a good bit colder than they are now, due to lingering glacial effects.

WALRUSES

Walruses are known to have been in Massachusetts waters as recently as the 1930s, and walrus teeth and tusks have been found as far south as Florida. During colonial times, two Atlantic walrus rookeries existed relatively close to New England: the Macklin Islands, in the mouth of the Gulf of St. Lawrence, and Sable Island, Nova Scotia. Tom French believes there was another rookery on Stellwagen Bank at the opening of Massachusetts Bay, which today is roughly 100 feet beneath the surface of the ocean. This could explain why the Atlantic walrus was as far south as Cape Cod during European settlement of New England.

The colonists, who would eventually perfect their marine mammal harvesting skills by hunting and processing whales, warmed up those skills by hunting the Atlantic walrus. These colonists, surely including Nantucketers among a majority of people from the Boston Bay Colony, traveled up to the Macklin Islands and Sable Island to kill these walruses for their oil and their tusks, severely depleting their populations. French knows of two records substantiating the existence of Atlantic walrus in Boston waters. One was killed on Thatcher Island, off Cape Ann, in the 1930s and the other sometime in the 1700s in the vicinity of Boston Harbor.

But they are no longer there. The Canadian Species at Risk Act ranked the Northwest Atlantic walrus population found in Quebec, New Brunswick, Nova Scotia, Newfoundland and Labrador as extirpated in April 2006. The Department of Fisheries and Oceans Canada, the Canadian counterpart to NOAA in the U.S., reports that there are probably a few thousand Atlantic walruses in Canadian waters, but definitely not in the Northwest Atlantic region. It currently has no restoration plans for this species, whose females produce young only every three years, depending on available mates.

THE WATERS OF NANTUCKET

The whales, the walruses, and the rest of the sea life found this part of the planet agreeable to their needs because of the collision of the Labrador Current and Gulf Stream. The Gulf Stream is a 60-mile-wide, 2,000-foot-deep current flowing from the Gulf of Mexico. It carries warm water northward and absorbs warmth on its eastern side from the Sargasso Sea, which reaches some 3,500 feet down into the Central Atlantic Ocean and is kept in place by the clockwise motion of the North Atlantic Ocean.

After taking a jog to the northeast just north of Cape Hatteras, the Gulf Stream fans out a bit. In doing so, it spins off gyres of warm water toward Nantucket and the rest of coastal New England, bumping up water temperatures around 15 degrees Fahrenheit or more, warmer than the ocean north of Cape Cod, and warming air temperatures as well.

Moderating this influx of warm water is the chilly Labrador Current of Arctic Ocean water that flows down from the Davis Strait in Baffin Bay between Baffin Island and Greenland in the Canadian Arctic and along the Nova Scotia coast, hitting the Gulf Stream where part of the Arctic water turns east. Being cold water, it contains much more oxygen than the warm water of the Gulf Stream, as well as a great deal of plankton, zooplankton and small fish, including sand lance, shrimp (usually farther north), capelin and krill.[2]

Because the warmer water of the Gulf Stream has a higher salinity than the cold water of the Labrador Current, when that cold water, moving deep in the water column, runs into the Gulf Stream out through the Great South Channel and at Nantucket Shoal, it's like an air current hitting a mountain range and getting forced upwards. This upwelling underwater brings all of the food from the Labrador Current's colder water up to within about 150 feet of the surface, where air-breathing marine mammals—including seals, common and white-sided dolphins, and whales, which have evolved filtering mouth parts—are searching for food. As a result, these species generally call this region their ocean habitat from April through November.

Nantucketer Blair Perkins, a whale watch trip guide and a long-time island-ocean naturalist, is able to find great numbers of whales east of the island for his tours. He knows just where he'll find the four local cetaceans (right, humpback, finback and minke) nearly every time, out past Orion and McBlair Shoals, because of the amount of food in the water.

Perkins tells it like this:

> It's oxygen-rich, it's nutrient-rich, and the Gulf Stream's different salinity acts like a wall and shunts stuff to the surface. That's what it's all about. It's getting that nutrient-rich water, because then you're getting into the layers where sunlight can hit it, so you've got photosynthesis going on, forming zooplankton and phytoplankton. It's phytoplankton first, and then you have zooplankton feeding on that. You've got the whole food chain stacked right there.

THAR BE WHALES

Twenty years after the Pilgrims' 1620 arrival on the mainland, armed with whaling knowledge of their own, they got busy going after whales in their waters and previously venturing up into Atlantic Coastal Canada in search of walruses for blubber oil and tusks. Nantucketers didn't get around to whaling until about 1670, when a sick Atlantic gray whale that the settlers called a "scrag," a rarity in our waters in any century, swam into Great Harbor, remaining there for three days until a settler, armed with a harpoon specially fabricated just for this purpose, killed it. The Wampanoags then showed the newbie whalers how to filet it and use it for lamp oil, food and tools. From this time until 1760, the whales hunted at sea or scavenged on the beach were only right whales, aptly named because they swam slowly and floated when killed, making them easy to kill and process.

The island's Late Archaic Indians had, in their canoes and brandishing wooden harpoons fitted with carved deer antler tips, already been going after whales that swam close to shore. The Indians also gleaned what they needed from the bodies of dead whales that washed ashore, thousands of years before the Wampanoag Indians and before the Starbucks, Macys, Mayhews and Gardners and the other original settlers arrived on island. The Native Americans claimed exclusive rights for their sachems to all whales and seals that washed ashore, dead or alive. This eons-old cultural tradition, along with active hunting of live marine mammals from their canoes, yielded oil to Nantucket's first humans, who stored the oil, along with fish they used as food, in jars and gourds in the ground. While early Nantucketers parleyed a deal with the Wampanoags to share in their delicious beachcombing finds shortly after they killed the scrag whale in the harbor, most of the settlers organized a formal effort to go into the whaling business, since sheep farming could offer barely more than subsistence living. This new industry could not have come along at a better time, because within the first 30 years of the European settlement of Nantucket, according to records kept by the town, the new Nantucketers were already close to exhausting what little timber, poor growing soil, and pasturelands they had. They quickly found they couldn't make a go as islanders without diversifying and bolstering the Nantucket economy in some substantial, sustainable way. Whaling would turn out to be that crucial missing element needed to keep the island alive.

Nantucket historian Nat Philbrick, in his book, *Away Offshore: Nantucket Island and its People, 1602–1890*, encapsulated it this way:

> The Nantucketers also desperately needed whaling in not only an economic but also in an ecological sense. The town records through the 1680s and 1690s are filled with measures to conserve and protect grass and farmlands as well as trees. With an ever-expanding population, the pressure was mounting on Nantucket as the English and the Indians vied for an ever-diminishing supply of natural resources. In this respect, whaling was for Nantucket what the frontier would be for the nation, providing the island with an escape valve through which to vent the increasing pressures of a growing population. Here at last was a way for the islanders to make a living that did not depend on the productivity of Nantucket's not-so fertile land.

So, to learn the practice of along-shore whaling, the precursor to multi-year whaling voyages, the islanders, in true Nantucket fashion, brought in some consultants, asking for the help of two men who had been alongshore whaling since the 1640s in the Southampton settlement on the eastern end of Long Island. In 1672, the town of Sherburne hired John Savage, a cooper, most likely to craft harpoons, and James Lopar, a whaleman, to instruct Nantucket's inhabitants in the whaling arts. In exchange, the town offered Lopar ten acres of land, 20 sheep, three horses and one cow. They made the same offer to Savage, and although Philbrick showed that only Savage took Nantucket up on its offer, Macy indicated that it wasn't known for sure whether either of the Long Island whalemen moved to

Nantucket and actually taught whaling here. Either way, both Macy and Philbrick agree that the town did successfully hire, from Yarmouth on Cape Cod, a fisherman and whaleman named Ichabod Paddock to come out to the island and instruct the islanders on whaling.

When they did get it together, Nantucket's first foray into along-shore whaling was in vessels no more than 20 feet in length that took several pairs of men to row. In some cases they could be sailed, in the pursuit of whales. These along-shore whaling boats were eventually adapted to be carried by the whaling ships around the world to be used by whaling crews to head out to harpoon whales once a pod had been spotted from the ships.

The along-shore whaling by Native Americans, and with European settlers joining in later, didn't make much of a dent in the populations of right whales that were plentiful in our part of the ocean and close enough to Nantucket's east and south shores for one-day sorties. Macy observed:

> There was no perceptible decrease of the number of whales during the period of the first thirty or forty years from the commencement of the fishery. It appears that in 1726 they were very numerous, for eighty-six were taken in that year, a greater number than were obtained in any one year, either before or since that date. The greatest number ever killed and brought to the shore in one day was eleven. This mode of whaling continued until about the year 1760, when the whales became scarce, and it was by degrees discontinued. Since that date, whales have only occasionally been obtained by boats from the shore.

Eventually, as the near-shore populations of these species shrank, with minke and finbacks, even then, not being as abundant as rights and humpbacks, Nantucket whaler design was economically conscripted by the

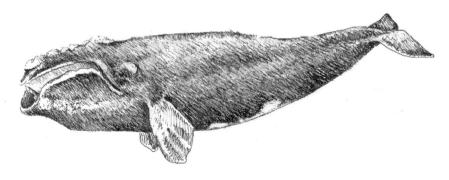

Right whale

necessities of whaling vessel evolution, essentially skipping many steps in the progression from narrow rowboats to massive, multi-masted ships built specifically to hunt whales far from Nantucket. The result was a whaling ship with the ability to deconstruct whales systematically, boiling their blubber to render it in onboard tryworks into lamp oil and sealing the oil in barrels for what could be whaling trips lasting up to six years at sea. At the height of Nantucket's whaling prominence, 85 whaling ships were based in Great Harbor. Many of them were venturing around the world on whaling voyages in search of the ultimate catch: sperm whales, which were larger and contained the highly sought head-case oil, spermaceti, which was found in their skulls and believed to aid somehow in the whales' ability to dive deep in search of giant squid. The spermaceti, a thick, wax-like substance, is the best lubricant known to man, even today, and it also burns with incredible brightness.

Today, as when the island's Wampanoags and the Late Archaic peoples went a-whalin', the only whales most Nantucketers witness in person are those that wash up dead on the island's shores. A 55-foot finback whale washed up on the north shore in 1969; its skeleton hangs intact in the main lobby of Nantucket High School. On New Year's Eve day, 1997, a 47-foot male sperm whale was spotted in the surf just off of Low Beach in Siasconset. Sperm whales are never seen close to land unless ailing or dead, and this one died and washed ashore the next day. Nantucket Whaling Museum personnel extracted scores of five-gallon bucketfuls of sperm oil, and when they ran out of buckets, with the spermaceti still gushing from the forehead of the whale, a large nearby dinghy was used to catch the rest. The entire skeleton of this whale hangs in the Nantucket Whaling Museum. Another sperm whale, a 46-foot male reduced to skin and bone, washed up dead on the east side of the Galls section of Great Point June 8, 2002, and on July 16, 2011, a 36-foot adult humpback whale washed up dead on Smith's Point. Further confounding Nantucket's Environmental Police officer and NOAA authorities, an unknown individual nearly hacked off this whale's tail, preventing its towing off of the beach.

Common and white-sided dolphins regularly get into Nantucket Harbor, and sometimes Madaket Harbor, by accident. Gray seals haul out on beaches around the three islands, either in large groups or alone, as their needs require. The odd whale bone turns up in fishing gear or on a beach now and again and often winds up adorning island houses, but the once vital economic relationship between marine mammals and Nantucket now persists only in tourism dollars flowing into the Nantucket Whaling Museum and local ocean wildlife tours.

NANTUCKET'S UNDERWATER NEIGHBORS

Our connection with the seawater around us—Nantucket Sound and the North Atlantic Ocean—is a fraying thread stretching back to when commercial fishing, for more than a century, sustained islanders after whaling ended. Today, other than ferry passenger and freight services, and recreational boating and fishing, these are little more than perfunctory trimmings around an otherwise service- and hospitality-driven economy.

The Nantucket Archipelago marks the northernmost boundary of many southern species and the southernmost of quite a few northern species; at the same time, it is the last dry land before the open ocean. This positioning, combined with the local climate—specifically, temperature and wind—has meant that the Nantucket aviary is well stocked with a wide variety of birds from up and down the East Coast, both migrating to and from the island and residing there year-round. Underwater, the fish and marine mammal populations make the same choices: water temperature, food availability, and tidal and ocean currents play a central role in determining what is swimming around in Nantucket Sound and Nantucket's portion of the Atlantic Ocean. The interplay of the Labrador Current and the Gulf Stream remains the conduit through which these conditions once made the waters of New England, including Nantucket, some of most productive fishing grounds on the planet, in places like Georges and Stellwagen Banks, and the Grand Banks off Nova Scotia. Untold millions of pounds of groundfish, including cod, haddock and halibut, and—eventually—flounder, fluke and pollock, were hauled in by the colonists.

COD

Nantucketers were among the New England fishermen catching cod, the fish known for elevating the early Massachusetts colony from the Puritan pattern of foraging ineptly for food to a wealthy major commercial center in the New World. But because Nantucket is near the southern end of the cod's North Atlantic Ocean range, the peak of the island's season was always very short. Andrews noted that, when earthworm castings showed up on the surface of island fields and meadows in April, cod were said to be plentiful in nearby waters, but they stuck around only until June when the bluefish came and drove them out. When cod returned in October, the fishing lasted until it became too cold and stormy to go out in dories to fish.

To get a sense of the volume of fish available to early Nantucketers and to those who, after the whaling industry petered out, became part of the island's commercial fishing industry that survived well into the 1960s, an account from Nantucket's sole remaining commercial dragger fisherman operating out of Nantucket Harbor is quite telling. Bill Blount, captain of the *Ruthie B.*, recalled the late Charlie Sayle, Sr. (father of Charlie Sayle, Jr., of Sayle's Seafood), telling him that, in the early 1900s, they caught one million pounds of haddock in dories off of Surfside in one week, and shipped them off the island.

Cod and haddock were the predominant catch Nantucketers went after in the late 17th century. Haddock was merely a bycatch of cod. It was certainly in great abundance and tasted good enough to be used and sold as food. The settlers did go after groundfish during their shore whaling period and the industry's salad days. Commercial fishing began rather unceremoniously on April 15, 1673, when John and Richard Gardner got a license from the town to buy an acre of land near Sesachacha Pond from the Wampanoags, next to a plot owned by John Swain, who was also setting up a fishing operation. Ten years later, the Dongan Patent authorized Nantucketers to hunt and fish her lands and waters.[3]

Codfishing seemed like the thing to do at the time, as an alternative to sheep farming, but when whaling began, its financial benefits were obvious to the settlers, so the codfish/haddock fishery became a service industry supplying food for whaling vessels. The Nantucket Shoals, a group of shoals extending from just off 'Sconset to around 80 miles to the island's south and southeast, are one example of local fishing grounds; Nantucket codfishermen first ventured out to such fishing grounds in the original whaleboats or in yawl boats—short, open sailing craft with a large mainsail in the bow and smaller mast and sail in the stern. Nantucket codfishermen adopted the dory when it arrived in Nantucket waters in 1857, several years after it had been invented in Gloucester. A smaller craft that could be rowed by one or two people, the dory had a flat bottom, sloping sides and turned-up ends, making it ideal for getting through Nantucket's choppy waters and out to the shoals where the fish were. The fishermen used hand lines baited with mollusk meat.

On land, fish-processing shacks sprouted along the island's east shore, including the Quidnet area and the Bank in Siasconset. Codfish Park got its name sometime after 1883, by which time fishing shacks were being moved down onto the beach below the Bank, where the ocean had been breaking just 30 years prior. This part of the island widened eastward enough to support a small village of fishing shacks that, today, have all been converted into or replaced by residential structures.

Codfishing, geared primarily toward supplying whaling ships with food for their long journeys, declined in step with the foundering whaling industry on Nantucket. Whaling lost most of its steam by the 1850s, but large-scale island ice production, intended in part for shipping fish fresh to mainland markets in urban areas, began in the early 1870s, and this was just the boost Nantucket's commercial fishery needed. The fishermen's catch could be shipped fresh, packed in pond ice, to Boston, New Bedford and New York City markets on the steamboats that were running between the mainland and the island because the growing island tourist economy demanded regular service.

Remarked Andrews on this mutually beneficial arrangement:

> At various times, the steamers were fully loaded with fishery products when returning to the mainland. In addition, some bluefish were taken to market by fishing smacks, which stopped at Nantucket for provisions, or to finish up a load when fishing was poor. It was an uncertain way to market fish; not only was the market price variable, but the erratic winds made a voyage to Boston or New York unpredictable. Sometimes, there were more bluefish than they could carry. They took all the fish they could and sold them, then paid the skipper when they came in on the next trip.

MACKEREL

For a period, island fishermen went after mackerel and flounder, both also in abundance before overfishing really got cranked up. A member of a family of ten oily fishes that also includes king mackerel, Spanish mackerel and blue mackerel, Atlantic mackerel was never as heavily fished as cod by early Nantucketers. A pelagic fish, Atlantic mackerel are accessible in large numbers only when they move into coastal waters after spending the winter months in the depths of the open North Atlantic Ocean. If the bluefish didn't drive them out when they arrived in the late spring and into the summer, Nantucketers would troll for the mackerel while dumping a chum paste of crushed menhaden or herring and water behind the boat. Andrews said the trolling lines had to be equal length or else the mackerel wouldn't go for the hooks baited with mackerel bellies or other fish parts. An additional tactic was to throw out salt along with the chum, which fishermen at that time believed would keep the mackerel close to the boat.

Before long, two large-quantity mackerel-harvesting methods quickly crowded out smaller-scale fishermen from the waters surrounding Nantucket and well beyond her shores. In the mid-1800s, purse seiners—fishing boats under sail used most effectively in late summer into the fall, when the mackerel were schooling before moving out into the deeper ocean—set a net in a circle around a school of mackerel and then drew in the net, like the strings of a purse, to haul the fish on board. And two of Nantucket's steam-powered fishing vessels, the *Petrel* and the *Wauquoit*, set out gill nets at the peak in the spring and summer, when these fish were most abundant, and often caught mackerel and bluefish and sold both. Gill nets catch fish by ensnaring them by their gills when they try to swim through the nets. Shortly after 1900, according to Andrews, the Nantucket mackerel fishery had peaked.

FLOUNDER

Islanders also went after winter flounder (sometimes called black-backed flounder), which hatch and spend their juvenile period in eelgrass beds in the harbors and in the rock cobble just off the eastern shore, as well as summer flounder in Nantucket Sound. Eventually, they pursued yellowtail flounder on the shoals east of the island from catboats and other sailing boats used for fishing, using the otter trawl to catch these species living on the relatively sandy bottom. Steam-powered fishing boats like the *Petrel* and the *Wauquoit* followed sail-driven fishing boats, and then trawlers with gasoline and diesel engines became the norm.

When the flounder populations began to pinch off in the Sound between 1915 and around 1919–1920, fishermen added floats to the nets to raise them up so they could simultaneously catch cod, which swim at shallower depths. During this period of declining flounder, in March 1917, fishermen caught the first yellowtail flounder on Rose and Crown Shoal. This offshore fishing trend progressed after 1930, when larger boats were built to fish for flounder on the three nearby banks.

CAUSE AND EFFECT: THE EVOLUTION OF FISHING AND THE DECLINE OF CODFISH

The infamous and inevitable decline of the codfish affected Nantucket less on the commercial front than it did mainland Massachusetts. It began with the 1713 introduction of the faster, sail-powered schooners out of Gloucester, Massachusetts, and Lunenberg, Nova Scotia. Such vessels were used to reach the three major offshore banks well into the 20th century, before they were replaced by coal-fired fishing vessels with steam engines and steel hulls, including the *Petrel* and *Wauquoit*.

These advancements in fishing vessels, combined with fishing gear improvements, left dory fishing behind. Gear improvements had begun with purse seining and moved on to the long-lining technique, gill nets and then the otter trawl just before 1900. The otter trawl is a cone-shaped net with two wooden "doors" on either side at its mouth that channel fish into the back of the net. By the time diesel engine–powered fishing boats came on the scene and were supplemented by onboard sonar and other electronic onboard fish-finding equipment, the cod and many other groundfish species didn't stand a chance.

Blount, who has been fishing since he was seven years old, first with his father and eventually on his own, has witnessed firsthand, in his own backyard, both the bounty of the North Atlantic and its steady decline. Starting out in a dory when he was eight, he spent most of his childhood fishing days swordfishing with his father. At 13, he graduated to a 19-foot dory built in Lunenburg, Nova Scotia, homeport of the Grand Bankers, schooners that fished the Grand Banks. He then fished in high school during vacations and the summer. Fishing on his father's boat, the *Narragansett*, followed. The *Narragansett* was the first automated stern trawler in the U.S.; it featured a net drum and an automatic winch, both of which his father invented.

Excitedly, Blount recalls working on this innovative trawler:

> There were fish everywhere. I can remember my father built the *Narragansett*, I worked on it, so my first summer out of high school [in 1963], in one day, seven men—I was one of the seven crewmen—we put down 100,000 pounds of haddock in 24 hours. Another time, later on, when I was out of the service, I was with Jack Jacobson and I'd bought the *Narragansett* after he let me fish with him for a while, and we weighed out 150,000 pounds [in 1970]. I remember I took out 200,000 once in New Bedford. . . .

THE FISHING INDUSTRY ON NANTUCKET

Despite the limits of their relatively crude vessels and fishing gear, Nantucket fishermen at the start of the whaling era were already seeing fewer fish in the waters around the island, due to the natural ebb and flow of population cycles and mounting human pressure on these fish stocks. As the human population increased on the islands and on the mainland, fishermen, with their ever-expanding ability to find the fish, didn't take long to clean out Nantucket Sound. Then they figured out that vast quantities of groundfish were to be found well offshore.

From 1935 into the 1950s, while never becoming a significant commercial fishing port as the other Massachusetts harbor towns of New Bedford, Boston and Gloucester did, Nantucket enjoyed plenteous years of commercial fishing.

A handful of small draggers in the 40- to 50-foot range operated out of Nantucket. Blount recalls four to six between 1945 and 1950. The size of the boats had little impact on their ability to bring in huge amounts of fish, namely yellowtail flounder, cod, haddock and some pollock. These draggers could sprint out to the Nantucket Shoals and catch 30,000 to 50,000 pounds of fish in one night, fill right up to the gunwales and then be back to Nantucket Harbor in time to ship it all off island on the morning steamer. They effectively pulled off a fishing trip in a quarter of the time it would take a dragger from Gloucester, Boston or New Bedford. During this period, in which the waters around the islands supported Nantucket-based commercial fishermen, the islanders really had a goldmine of fish just offshore, not only because of its proximity to the island, but because the island fishermen knew so well the Nantucket Shoals fishing grounds east and south of the island.

This changed several years after a fisherman named Jerry McCarthy moved to the island from Woods Hole with his wife and seven children. McCarthy was a day scalloper, meaning he went out on one-day sea scalloping trips and, in his case, according to Blount, brought his wife and children along to help shuck the scallops at sea as they were caught. Because the Nantucketers "took a shine" to McCarthy, the island fishermen began to show this Woods Hole fisherman how to pilot his dragger among the shoals. Fairly soon, McCarthy was going out on his own and doing "crazy good."

Before complications from diabetes eventually ended the Nantucket portion of his commercial fishing career, McCarthy trained some of his fishermen friends from Woods Hole how to navigate through and fish the Nantucket Shoals, and gradually, these fishermen, along with some Norwegians out of New Bedford, supplanted the Nantucket fishermen, many of whom moved to New Bedford as Nantucket-based commercial fishing gradually dried up. Among the contributing factors pushing Nantucket deeper into the realm of recreational fishing were heavy competition from mainland fishermen, and the rise of tourism and seasonal residents on the island, with all the associated shore work they generated.

Blount, however, had chosen commercial fishing as a career and had no intention of taking up any of the resort trades growing rapidly on the island. When he brought his dragger to Nantucket to fish, no one had commercially harvested groundfish out of Nantucket Harbor for ten years. He remembers how thrilled the islanders were that he had chosen the island as the base for his commercial fishing.

Of this time, Blount says:

> When I started with the *Ruthie B.*, codfish made a resurgence. My first year with the *Ruthie B.*, I caught a million pounds of fish (1979–1980). The big decline started by 1985 ... and I'm not sure why it started going down. I guess a lot of things could be the problem. I don't know why the fish declined. However, the fish have gone through cycles. There was a time on Nantucket when they had five fish hatcherie here to grow flounders and codfish, about the turn of the century. They were so worried that codfish and flounders were going to go extinct. So the cycles are not an uncommon thing and you know, fish will totally disappear and then come back again.

A study done by the National Marine Fisheries Service of the National Oceanographic & Atmospheric Administration found a variety of reasons for the low populations of cod on Georges Bank and in the Gulf of Maine: commercial fishing within coastal spawning areas; pollution of the cod's habitat; depletion of their food, including haddock, whiting, sand eels, squid, crabs, and mackerel, and mollusks such as mussels, lobsters and sea worms; and dam building, along with destruction and disturbance of the gravelly, sandy benthic habitat where cod lay their eggs in the winter at depths between three and 350 feet, and where juvenile cod grow. The NMFS also feels that, in addition to the pressures of fishing, the number of cod killed during the fishing process also impacts the chance of bringing codfish stocks back to life.

Today, commercial fishermen from the mainland frequently tie their boats up at the end of Straight Wharf and the town pier during hurricanes, nor'easters and other strong ocean storms, outnumbering the blue-and-white *Ruthie B.* but, in joining her, offering a glimpse of what the harbor's waterfront may have looked like more than 50 years ago. Throughout the summer, mainland day-fishing boats hunting fluke tie up their boats at the end of the town pier, selling their catch to buyer boats that come over from the mainland, as well as to island fishmongers.

Several Nantucketers are also engaged in fishing for whelk snails (which they call conch), setting conch pots out in the harbor, out in the Chord of the

Bay, west of Nantucket and in Nantucket Sound. Conch meat is highly prized by the Japanese and the Chinese, especially the Japanese since the magnitude 9.0 Tōhoku earthquake on March 11, 2011, that originated in the Pacific Ocean near the northeast coast of Honshu, Japan. Because the earthquake severely damaged the Fukushima I Daiichi Nuclear Power Plant in Okuma and Futaba, Japan, crippling the reactor's cooling systems, which leaked radioactive liquids into the ground and the Pacific Ocean, the Japanese are understandably cautious about eating any seafood from their own waters.

There are a handful of islanders fishing commercially for striped bass; however, proposed new striped bass regulations, driven by the recreational striped bass lobby, were working their way through the Massachusetts Legislature prior to the 2012 season. These could further protect striped bass but put commercial fishermen out of business. Three sought to require testing for contaminated fish, and two requested consideration of the economic impact on the recreational fishery when commercial limits are set. However, four others hoped to prohibit commercial fishing and the sale of striped bass, slot-limit the recreational keeper size to 20 to 26 inches and 40 inches or more, and restrict the bag limit to one fish per person per day. This marked the second time such striped bass legislation was attempted in Massachusetts.

Nantucket also has several lobstermen and one or two who harvest blue mussels sometimes in Madaket Harbor or in the waters on the north side of Tuckernuck Island whenever there is a good set of them in either location. And a few islanders actually make year-round, full-time livings as commercial fishermen, scalloping during the fall and winter and fishing for stripers and or conchs and other fish in the spring and summer. Blount, the anomaly with his dragger, is one of them, as the only fisherman currently operating such a vessel out of Nantucket Harbor, going out for groundfish and sea scallops, and bay scallops during the winter in a smaller boat.

FISHING REGULATIONS AND THE COMMERCIAL FISHERMAN

In early 2012, however, Blount was barely making it, thanks to the National Marine Fisheries' steady ratcheting down of smaller commercial fishermen's abilities to make a living at sea. With two unforgiving federal fishing regulatory systems, days-at-sea quotas and sector fishing, controlling fishing outside of the state three-mile limit, monitored and enforced by the National Marine Fisheries Service, Blount feels he and other small fishing boat captains are being purposely squeezed out of commercial fishing by the NMFS in an effort to relax the pressure on rapidly disappearing fish stocks.

The first option is the days-at-sea system in which fishermen are awarded, by the NMFS, a certain number of days a year to go fishing for each species of fish that they choose to go after. They receive permits with limits on the poundage of these species that may be fished, based on the number of pounds they landed in one of the years between 2000 and 2004.

In 2008, Blount struggled to hold on to his 400-pounds-and-under sea-scalloping permit because, during the prescribed four-year period, he was unable to do better than 680 pounds to meet the minimum landing weight for sea scallops of 1,000 pounds in any of those years. He had planned to use this permit to augment his groundfishing permit that the NMFS said was valid for just over six weeks a year. But as of early October that year, he had yet to use any of his groundfishing days, relying solely on his sea scallop permit. The Fisheries Service ended up revoking Blount's sea scallop permit in September 2008 because he couldn't show that he'd caught the minimum 1,000-pound requirement for sea scallops. A tragic fire had all but destroyed the *Ruthie B.* in January 2004 and landed Blount in dry dock, draining him of more than $1 million in repairs, but this carried no weight with the New England Fisheries Management Council, which reviews and rules on all NMFS violations, appeals and other commercial fishing enforcement matters in New England federal fishing territory. There is no consideration for hardship, and Blount was not alone: this restriction eventually removed 500 of the 800 sea scalloping boats from that fishery alone.

The newer system, called sector fishing, went into effect on May 1, 2010, and has fishermen forming cooperative groups, or sectors. The sectors are awarded dedicated percentages of the allowable annual catch for all species of fish open for commercial fishing. Fishermen in each sector can fish without limits on days at sea or numbers of trips. Each fisherman's share of the total allowable catch of each species within his or her sector is based on his or her individual landing history over time on a sliding scale, which the NMFS tracks. The lower or higher one's landings, the lower or higher the poundages that fisherman can catch of that species.

The NMFS views sector fishing as another way to stave off the collapse of groundfish stocks in U.S. waters, including Nantucket Sound and east and south of the island. It hopes this solution will end the financially devastating overfishing penalty battles between NOAA/NMFS and fishermen, and will spawn a rebound in fish populations. In New England, there are

19 sectors, three for Cape Cod, in which groups of fishermen and their vessels in a region are dealt these annual catch percentages for all fish open to harvest.

Although sector fishing encourages the fishermen in each sector to manage their group's annual catch percentages for different species, so each fishermen should, theoretically, get a share of the catch worth his or her time fishing for it, it also penalizes fishermen who catch more than their prescribed pounds for each species. Any overage—fishermen are forbidden from throwing back the amount of fish over their limits—and the offending fisherman faces fines of $130,000 per violation along with an end to fishing for that year.

If it doesn't appear to a fisherman that he can catch enough fish to make a given year's total sector allocation worth the time and money to land it, he can lease part or all of his allocation to other fishermen. Blount's 2010 Section Allocation was 94,633 pounds; that included cod, haddock, yellowtail, pollock, redfish, white hake, plaice, winter flounder and witch flounder, running from as little as nine pounds of yellowtail in the Gulf of Maine up to 6,000 pounds of plaice to 71,142 pounds of haddock on the Grand Banks.

Leasing means another fisherman pays a certain amount per pound for a portion or all of a colleague's annual sector allocation, betting that he'll be able to land all of that fish and somehow make back his lease money, or at least come close, when he sells his fish. In 2010, another fishermen offered to lease all of Blount's sector allocation for $4,000 at a rate of 23.6¢ per pound. This wasn't enough to cover his expenses, so Blount declined.

Since 2004, commercial fishermen have been required to have on board a vessel monitoring system unit so the NMFS may track all fishing vessels from dock to fishing grounds and back. Monitored by computers via satellite global positioning systems, each VMS box enables the NMFS to keep tabs on commercial fishing vessels to ensure that they do not stray into restricted fishing zones or fish more days than allowed for a given species permit. Such infractions, logged by the system as individual violations, carry a stiff fine of $130,000 per violation, a cost that could cripple the smaller commercial fishing operations. The cost of this black box alone—$1,200 to $3,000—proved too much for 3,000 sea scallop fishermen, who consequently got out of commercial fishing. Then there there's the $5,000 to $10,000 in annual membership and management costs that Cape Cod sector fishermen pay on top of the black box cost.

Blount, who believes sector fishing in New England could cull 50 to 75 percent of the boats off the water, didn't know how he'd keep going. He has toyed with options, including donating his boat to a nonprofit as a tax write-off, getting a government boat buyout, using his swordfish hand-gear permit and fishing in the less restrictive state waters within the three-mile limit for lobsters, fluke—whatever he can catch that is in demand. Unfortunately, the bad news isn't going to stop. The tenuous bond between Nantucket's fishing past and its present is continuing to disintegrate. More restrictions on codfishing are almost certainly in the offing. In November 2011, NOAA/NMFS released a preliminary cod stock assessment estimate for the Gulf of Maine that essentially expressed doubt that shutting down the cod fishery would restore their stocks by 2018 to biomass levels required for production of a sustainable harvest. NOAA had originally predicted the Gulf of Maine cod population would rebound with healthy numbers by 2014, but this latest assessment hints at a frightening disparity between the 2008 and 2011 predictions: the recent report suggests that the 2008 estimate of the stock was almost 300 percent over what actually exists in these waters today.

This doesn't bode well for Blount, but then he doesn't rely on cod nearly as much he does on haddock, flounder, other groundfish and sea scallops. It's the multi-vessel fishing operations, heavily dependent on cod, that will get hurt the most. None of them operates out of Nantucket, but they are fishing in the same waters.

CAPE CODLESS

As a solid economic engine for Nantucket, the New England cod fishery was almost always out of the islanders' reach anyway, during most of the 400 years it took humans to push their stocks to near collapse. Whaling not only sated the Nantucketers' thirst for a stronger community-building industry more than sheep ever could, but it also offered a salve for the island's disadvantageous position at the cod's extreme southern boundary. Luckily, Nantucket was close enough to be able to catch enough of this fish to stock whale hunt larders, to feed ourselves and briefly to augment the island's economy during the codfish's fading abundance. Luckier still, there were other, more plentiful groundfish within our reach in the Sound and offshore.

Human hunger for cod overshadows the ecological effects that, although tracked by NOAA, probably aren't reported as widely as is the tragedy of this fishery's impending collapse. Cod, like haddock and the other larger groundfish, sit atop the ocean food chain, behind only seals, whales and humans. They play an integral role in their marine ecosystem of consuming the lesser sea creatures. Without the cod to keep their populations in check, it's believed that their smaller prey are aiding in the cod's demise by eating their eggs and fry.

Another scapegoat is the gray seal, which many commercial as well as recreational fishermen have long blamed for paring down cod stocks. In a paper done by Canadian scientists Robert O'Boyle and Michael Sinclair, formerly of the Bedford Institute of Oceanography of Dartmouth, Nova Scotia, and published in the March 2012 issue of the journal, *Fisheries Research*, called "Seal–cod Interactions on the Eastern Scotian Shelf: Reconsideration of Modeling Assumptions," this pair contends that gray seals have had a much greater impact on cod stocks than previously thought. The seals, the Canadian commercial fishing community believes, are as much to blame for the destruction of the fishery as is overfishing.

After the collapse of Canadian cod stocks in the 1980s, Canada's Department of Fisheries & Oceans (DFO) issued a moratorium in 1992 on the landing of northern cod in Newfoundland and Labrador. The DFO partially lifted the moratorium in 1997, then clamped it down indefinitely in 2003 when northern cod was declared an endangered species in Atlantic Canada.

THE FINALS: GRAY SEALS V. WHITE SHARKS

Given how we've ground down our natural marine resources to such a niggled, tightly regulated industry in which fishermen are being forcibly expelled from their trade by economies of scale, in which these mom-and-pop fishing operations are sunk by depleted fish stocks and federal regulations favoring larger fishing fleets, it's hard to believe that, at one time, there were enough fish in the ocean around Nantucket to feed everyone on the island, in the region and around the world, and that humans hunted gray seals for food. Now, we focus on saving what fish we have in our waters, but we're still going after the seals.

Naturally, the results of O'Boyle and Sinclair's study emboldened the Seal Abatement Coalition. But SAC's troubles stem from only recreational concerns, supplemented by a touch of localized economic woes. Those concerns can't compare with the Canadian cod situation, in which tens of thousands of jobs were lost and an entire fishery closed down. Instead of an electronic seal deterrent and a federal act amendment, the DFO proposed in 2011 to reduce the Nova Scotia gray seal population by 70 percent over five years in an effort to help restore cod stocks.

The Nantucket solution to the seal problem most certainly is going to be the great white shark. In the second week of August 2011, Fronzuto helped Skomal install a shark tag sensor buoy just off of Great Point. It was something of an answer to Genthner's encounter with the great white in early July, but it also amounted to an admission of the very real potential that the gray seals holding ground on Great Point these days are going to become the next blubber-and-guts buffet for the great white sharks showing up every summer in greater numbers in the waters around the Cape and Islands.

But during the last week of 2011, Skomal said the Great Point white shark detection buoy hadn't registered any of the seven white sharks tagged with special transmitter devices during that summer and fall. That none of the seven great whites tagged with transmitters were logged near Nantucket doesn't mean that these sharks aren't in the area during the season; it just means that the sharks aren't close enough to be detected by the buoy. And Skomal doesn't know the bathymetry around Great Point well enough to say whether or not great white sharks could get within striking distance to pick off seals near the shore, or if they'd be relegated to hunting in deeper water well off of the Point.

But Skomal believes their presence in Nantucket waters, at some distance off Great Point, means it is only a matter time before the number of great white sharks off Chatham outgrows the local supply of seals and moves to other seal haulouts, such as those on Nantucket. Already well documented off of Nantucket, great whites reach local waters in May or June, swimming up over the edge of the Continental Shelf and hanging out south of the islands before swimming northward as the water warms.

Generally, great white sharks, especially the sizable ones now frequenting Monomoy Island and Chatham beaches, probably won't be visiting Muskeget Island for seal flipper pie or seal short ribs, at least not within sight of its beaches. The highly variable water depth adjacent to a given seal haulout or rookery plays a major role in whether any sharks at all will go after seals in certain areas. Skomal believes Muskeget is not going to be one of those locations in Nantucket waters, because of the shallowness of the water around it and because of the many nearby shoals and sandbars, which are constantly shifting around. Because great white sharks can't maneuver well in six feet of water or less, they most likely won't be seen near Muskeget Island in large numbers, if at all.

But Great Point is another can of sardines, as Skomal suggests:

> I'd have to take a little closer look at the bathymetry around Great Point, but there are areas that are accessible, and I would expect that white sharks, if they're not already, will be taking advantage of that area. And it may be a function of numbers of white sharks. Right now, if a white shark can go to Monomoy [Island] where it can approach very, very close to shore, and there's not a tremendous amount of competition from other white sharks, it'll go to Monomoy. But as soon as large numbers of white sharks—if that occurs, and certainly it can, on the order of, say, dozens of animals—start to hunt an area, it gets a little tight, and they tend to expand to other areas.

If the gray seal presence in our waters continues to expand, Nantucketers should prepare for an increase in white shark encounters like Genthner's July 2011 brush with one off of Great Point, and other sightings over the years by Nantucket charter boat captains off the eastern shore of the island. Whether shark attacks on humans will be part of this scenario is anyone's guess, but given the numbers of people swimming off island beaches, even from Great Point, the Galls and south down to Codfish Park, and along the south shore, plus the surfers riding waves (to sharks, they resemble seals in distress), there could be a repeat of the 1916 Jersey Shore shark attacks. There, over the course of 12 days, four people were attacked and killed. The incident is believed to be part of the late Peter Benchley's inspiration, along with the life of Montauk, New York, shark fisherman Frank Mundus, for *Jaws*, his fictional account of a monstrous great white shark preying on humans in the waters around the fictional Martha's Vineyard town of Amity.

Thanks to the Marine Mammal Protection Act, the gray seal population is only going to get larger around Nantucket, which means, given Skomal's thoughts on the matter, that great white sharks probably aren't going dine solely on Monomoy Island and Chatham seals. The Gulf of St. Lawrence population of gray seals, last surveyed in 2008, produced 13,000 pups. Sable Island produced 55,400. To calculate the full seal population, each number of pups should be at least doubled to account for the pups' mothers and the totals further boosted to account for the unknown number of adult males. O'Boyle and Sinclair believe the numbers are much higher, putting the total population at possibly 350,000 in Nova Scotia's coastal waters.

With only so much food in the water, breeding space and competition for mates, that many gray seals in Canadian waters has meant an expansion of range southward as far as Long Island, and the inevitable establishment of their southernmost East Coast breeding colony on Muskeget.

Wood believes many factors contributed to the steady increase of gray seals in these waters. There is the 1972 adoption of the MMPA in the U.S., which came, in a dramatic reversal, after many years of bounties paid for seal noses. Gradually, the human presence on Muskeget faded out to just ornithologists and the two property owners. There had been a greater human presence on Muskeget previously: the game bird hunting camps, a Humane Society Lifesaving Station and many cottages, which kept the seals from claiming Muskeget as theirs. Add to these variables the overcrowding in the huge breeding colonies in Canada, plus the fact that humans no longer hunted seals for food, and Muskeget eventually became a seal colony.

In 1988, NOAA documented five gray seal pups born on Muskeget. Gray seal researcher Valerie Rough, says Wood, then logged an untold number of gray seal births in the 1990s, and Crocker Snow, Jr., who owns roughly 173 of Muskeget's 292 acres, recalls 19 gray seal pups born on Muskeget in 1994. Since then, NOAA documented 1,023 in 2002 and 1,982 in 2005. Wood's last survey in 2008 logged around 2,000 pups, which made Muskeget's seal population more than 4,000. Combine this number with the gigantic Canadian breeding colonies, and it is obvious that gray seals are no longer rare.

Clarifies Brault, "They were, right up until the beginning of the Muskeget colony in the mid-'80s. They were actually extirpated from the area, but now they have increased to the point where the population isn't at any risk. Part of the [new] risk is whether the population is able to increase and this population is [obviously] in an exponential mode of growth."

The Seal Abatement Coalition's concerns about the gray seal's enormous population numbers in the North Atlantic, including on and around Nantucket's three islands, is not lost on Wood, Brault and NOAA. In the fall of 2011, NOAA began reexamining the status of the gray seal, with the possibility of removing it from the rare status listing. The species is not listed as threatened or endangered under the Endangered Species Act. Whether this will have any impact on the number of seals hauling out on Great Point and swarming in the waters around Nantucket's three islands remains to be seen, but it doesn't seem likely that NOAA is going to remove the gray seal from the protection of the MMPA, regardless of its population numbers. Whether it allows SAC to disperse them humanely, with the sort of electronic scramming equipment used in Scotland and Oregon, has not yet been determined. One thing that does seem certain is that the populations of striped bass, which NOAA in early 2012 believed healthy and well above its female spawning stock biomass target of 37,500 metric tons for species sustainability, in addition to bluefish, bonito, false albacore and Spanish mackerel, should get somewhat of a boost, because fewer Nantucket fishermen are standing on the tip of Great Point fishing.

But then, there are always the seals.

EROSION, THE REAPER

IT IS LITERALLY the foundation on which our lives on these islands are built—along with generous amounts of gravel, clay, glacial erratics and a thin layer of soil.

You can't go anywhere on Nantucket and not find beach sand. It washes down cobblestoned Main Street as if over a rocky riverbed; we track it into our houses, vacuum it out of our vehicles and wash it off of our suntanned bodies during the summer. Crack open a street sweeper and don't be surprised if more than half its contents is sand. We've even coined celebratory colloquialisms, such as "you've got sand in your shoes," referring to one's inability to move off of Nantucket, and "dead sand," meaning the difficulty of driving through it on certain beaches.

Sand is the post-glacial deposit that made the Haulover, Coatue, Great Point, Smith's Point, Eel Point and the extremities at either end of Tuckernuck. Without sand, Muskeget wouldn't even exist.

It is also, unfortunately, a siren call to those with the wherewithal to build a dream summer house within sight of the ocean and barefoot walking distance to the beach, who are allegedly cognizant of the hazards of doing so but are nearly always, it seems, blinded by the mystique of living just steps from salt water. Defiantly, these houses go up several hundred feet or less from the pounding surf. Did the brokers, while showing eventual buyers around these properties, spend far less time warning of erosion rate statistics than sharing amenity details? Did the prospective owners see the historic photographs of early Nantucketers repeatedly moving their houses back from the edge into lots purposely laid out as elongated narrow rectangles protruding inland? Probably yes and probably not, respectively. But it can't be that they believe *their* sand would somehow defy the ocean's hunger, and the sea would wash away only from their neighbors' land.

"Erosion" is the next key word you need for this chapter's lexicon. Think about it. It's what makes this place so special: that these three flash-in-the-pan, inimitable islands aren't going to be around for very long, certainly not nearly as long as the nearby continent. Because of this reality, all of us Nantucketphiles should enjoy this place as often as we can.

Local estimates for the remaining lifespan of Nantucket and its two smaller islands are between 400 and 1,600 years, given the ever-changing rate of erosion, which averages ten to 15 linear feet a year on sections of the south shore and more than 50 feet at certain spots along this side of the island. Measurements of the annual rate of erosion, as recorded on charts between 1846 and 1955 by the United States Coast and Geodetic Survey and later compiled by the U.S. Army Corps of Engineers Beach Erosion Board, in addition to aerial surveys done between 1938 and 1970 and real-time beach surveys, were all used to create the 1979 *Nantucket Shoreline Survey: An Analysis of Nantucket Shoreline Erosion and Accretion Trends Since 1846*. This survey showed that the portion of south shore between Ames Avenue and Miacomet Pond was moving inland at three to 30 feet a year. Massachusetts Coastal Zone Management found in 1999 that Nantucket's south shore was eroding 2.2 to 12 feet a year.

TOM NEVERS AND SIASCONSET

From Tom Nevers Head, former home of the Tom Nevers Hotel overlooking Tom Nevers Pond, up to Sankaty Head Lighthouse, a different erosion dynamic played out through this survey's study period. Erosion reduced the beach from Tom Nevers Head to immediately south of Siasconset village from 1846 to 1887, while—believe it or not—from Siasconset up to the lighthouse during this period, accretion was the norm. From 1887 to 1955, the accretion continued. It affected an additional 2,000 feet of beach extending south of the village, with an annual average of eight feet of beach building seaward and a total growth eastward of 300 to 450 feet. The sand dune area beneath the bank that Front Street sits on in Siasconset grew more or less in step with this beach, enough by 1883 for fishermen to move their fish-processing shacks down into this area, eventually inspiring its name, Codfish Park. In 1853, that area had been underwater.

Things got ugly for this section of Nantucket's shoreline starting in the 1950s and 1960s and continuing on through the present day. The survey authors, in 1979, noted the potential for significant property loss in this area:

> The implications of this data is [sic] particularly serious near Siasconset. Residential development along this section of shoreline in the past was limited to the area landward of the cliffs and bluffs. However, the rapidly accretional shoreline here provided a new beach for development. The deposition of sand building up the beach led to a false sense of security and eventually the construction of seasonal homes on this low lying accretional beach. Unfortunately, the sea has played this same trick over and over again. A seemingly stable and building beach can rapidly become unstable and erosional due to changes in wind, wave and offshore bar conditions. This is what happened at Siasconset and many of the homes built here are now endangered by an encroaching sea. Unless the pattern reverses, these homes will either have to be removed, or they will be carried off to sea. What the sea gives, it can very easily take back.

As predicted, the pattern did not reverse, and there were significant losses. During the first half of the 1990s, unusually strong ocean storms hit, including several nor'easters, at least one of which was deemed a 100-year storm, plus the so-called Perfect Storm, or no-name storm, of October 1991. Together, they almost systematically destroyed or forced the moving of all the houses on the ocean side of Codfish Park Road. During my time as the environmental reporter for the island newspaper, *The Nantucket Beacon,* now shuttered, after helping to hurriedly remove as much of its contents as possible, I witnessed the destruction of a beach cottage owned by the family of another Beacon reporter, DeWitt Smith, during a nor'easter in early 1993. Shortly after the water got too close and it became too dangerous to continue rescuing treasured, irreplaceable possessions, 15- to 20-foot waves first undermined the house and then wrestled it off of its foundation to just off the beach, where several massive waves pulverized it.

Last to go from Codfish Park Road was Donald Hollings's house, which had been built to the flood plain code of a foundation of pilings driven into the sand keeping the house a certain number of feet above the predicted reach of storm surge. Before Hollings moved his house to a lot up on Sleetwing Circle, off Low Beach Road, around 1995, the ocean completely undermined the house, leaving it tilting severely toward the crashing waves, with all of its pilings exposed. A surviving reminder of those terrible storms, including the one during the winter of 1993, is the

Codfish Park swing set, which was moved across the street and is still there today.

It was around this time that Siasconset Beach Preservation Fund (SBPF) was organized, with the hope of collectively solving its members' own erosion issues. When this group of property owners, mostly representing Baxter Road, did coalesce, they mined beach scarp and cliff-top coastal erosion data from aerial photographs and field surveys done in December 1957, November 1977, April 1990, and April 2005, in order to paint an accurate picture of the erosion trend for this part of the island and to make their case for a multi-property erosion abatement project.

Adding to the existing body of shoreline change data for Nantucket's east shore, SBPF calculated erosion rates that were logged at 15 sites on the beach, between the south end of Sesachacha Pond to about 1,800 feet south of Codfish Park, and showed that erosion between 1957 and 2005 averaged 235.5 feet among the 15 sites. The highest single figure was 379 total feet for a site south of the lighthouse in a high-erosion area along Baxter Road. The lowest was 105 feet near the southern end of Sesachacha Pond.

All efforts of Baxter Road residents trying to protect their property aside, you can see how sand worship applies on a level that matters little in the bigger picture of the island washing away. But it comes down to where every inch of land matters to individual property owners, who each winter

Erosion soil detail

watch what is, in some cases, generations of summer memories tumbling down the bluff to the gnawing waves below.

THE NORTH SHORE

The north shore, eroding southward, doesn't tend to lose such large amounts of sand and other soils, because Nantucket Sound is relatively shallow and the distance that the waves travel before breaking on Nantucket is less than 30 miles. In contrast, waves breaking on the east and south shores, although subdued somewhat by shoals between the beach and deep water, have nearly an unlimited fetch over which they can build up their height and energy. During ocean storms, the shoals do little to dilute their waves' impact on the south and east shores.

The zone from Great Point down to the east jetty, where just offshore lies about half of the Nantucket Bar, has generally experienced more accretion than erosion. Geologists believe that longshore currents flowing down from Great Point and to the west formed Coatue through littoral drift of sand. During the 32-year period from 1938 to 1970, Dr. John Fisher of the University of Rhode Island documented by aerial photographs the evolving shores of Nantucket, including the outside of Coatue, which Fisher showed grew by an average of two feet each year, with the west side of Great Point and Galls accreting as much as 15 feet a year. Although certain stretches of this portion of the island eroded between 1951 and 1970, the Nantucket Shoreline Survey, which relied on Dr. Fisher's photos as part of its information in producing the survey, found that the prevailing dynamic was accretion.

Those with houses along the coastal bluffs of the north shore would probably disagree, but this side of Nantucket, historically, has not been as active as the south shore. From the west jetty down to Eel Point, during the same period, 1938 to 1970, while net erosion was around one foot a year, accretion was, again, the name of the game. Anyone frequenting the area near the west jetty or owning property there knows that this part of the north shore hardly erodes at all. In fact, during Dr. Fisher's study, it gained one foot per year. The other growth along this shoreline was the peninsula of Eel Point, which gained six to 12 feet per year, and the tall dunes and bluffs between these two points on the north shore saw increases between one and three feet. However, this may no longer be the case for this segment of the shoreline. Based on the satellite photography of Google Earth, as of February 2011, 24 properties showed erosion control installations, including rock walls, heavy-duty snow fencing, American beach grass plantings, rock and wooden groins, bulkheads and riprap walls at the toes of the bluff.

THE WEST END

The Nantucket Shoreline Survey paid little attention to the west end of Nantucket, noting only that the north side of Smith's Point (generally called that when Esther Island is attached to it) saw around five feet of erosion per year at its west end and 1.5 at its eastern portion. However, the south side of Smith's Point is akin to the highly active east side of Great Point, generating some fairly incredible numbers during the study period. The south side of Esther Island grew 19 feet a year between 1846 and 1887. In the 1900s, accretion was 11 feet per year, but the most dramatic change was the growth of Smith's Point/Esther Island. From 1887 to 1955, this southwestern extremity of Nantucket grew 1,100 feet toward Tuckernuck. If a time-lapse film could be shot from the beginning of the islands' life, 6,000 years ago, to now, it would show Nantucket, Tuckernuck and Muskeget gradually moving in a northerly direction while steadily shrinking in size as they are eaten by the ocean. And with the unpredictability of global warming—for example, the mild winter the island experienced in 2011–2012—the Grey Lady and her two sisters could disappear even faster. Fascinated by these vanishing islands and always with an humorous twang in his words, the late Wes Tiffney shared his vision of Nantucket's future in the mid-1990s:

> The island averages about 18,000 feet wide. At the historical erosion rate of about 15 feet each year, Nantucket has a comfortable 1,200-year life expectancy before it suffers the fate of Nantucket Shoals and slips beneath the water to form the basis for another Atlantis legend. But if rising sea level rise predictions are correct, and sea level rises three times more rapidly in the future than it had in the past, the erosion rate will triple to 45 feet each year, and Nantucket will be gone in about 400 years.

You, the intrepid, well-read Nantucket addicts, and you, the island storm chasers religiously making the circuit from one island erosion hot spot to the next, after each fall hurricane remnant tears up the south shore and every winter nor'easter batters the east end of the island, know of this coastal volatility. And many of you are aware of the tragic financial dichotomy between erosion-embattled homeowners residing on Baxter Road, and on Smith's Point and Sheep Pond Road in Madaket, all of whom live each storm, starting with a twitch in the pit of their stomachs while watching weather forecasts and ending with the inevitable good-news-bad-news call from their caretakers afterwards. By and large, Baxter Road property owners are maligned, and unjustifiably so, for having the means not only to temporarily repel the unwanted advances of the ocean through costly beach and bluff stabilization structures and protocols, but also to move their houses if need be.

Any skeptics out there should walk a summer in their flip-flops before casting aspersions on their motives. During the summer of 2007, *The Nantucket Independent* published a series called "Voices from the Bluff" in a Q&A format to help readers understand SBPF's thought process behind their proposed beach nourishment project and to explain what appeared to most non-members as a waste of time and money battling the elements, and the paper then followed with a counter-series called "Voices Away from the Bluff" seeking opposing views. In his interview during the former series, Kermit Roosevelt, whose house at 101 Sankaty has been in his family for seven generations, but is not threatened by erosion, succinctly represented SBPF's feelings. In answer to the statement, "Respond to the following statement in whatever way you feel is appropriate: You're wasting your money—Mother Nature is going to take your property no matter what," Roosevelt's response was:

> There is no intrinsic virtue in being passive in the face of threats from Mother Nature. But we are not trying to fight her. That would be foolish. Rather, we are trying to modify her effects. This is common sense and common practice. To take a mundane example, each of us does this in a small way when we change our clothes in response to changes in the weather. It is the same thing when we install a lightening rod on the roof of our house. Larger groups do it when they construct storm sewers or build dams. Closer to home, Nantucket did it 150 years ago when the harbor was being choked by sand. There were those then who said you can't fight Mother Nature. Fortunately, there were others who chose to pursue a then controversial plan to dredge the harbor rather than let Mother Nature follow her course. Beach nourishment is not experimental. It has been successfully employed throughout the world since the early part of the last century. It is, today, widely and actively used in hundreds of shoreline communities in the U.S.

As all of the original 88 lots along Baxter Road, originally dubbed Atlantic Avenue, were laid out by William Flagg in a development called Sankaty Heights in 1883, re-drawn in 1892, the developer of this affluent island neighborhood was one of the few islanders with forethought enough to realize that the inescapable reality of beach erosion could someday compromise the integrity of Bluff soils and structures. Putting this vision to work, he drew his lots long enough to allow inland retreat of houses. Unfortunately, many property owners, with plenty of lawn and bluff between their porches and beach, didn't share Flagg's clairvoyance when they first bought their properties. They subdivided their lots, cashing in on the inland portions and thereby eliminating any and all second chances for generations of familial summer memories when the Atlantic Ocean came a-knockin'.

Most Smith's Point and Sheep Pond Road dwellers, however, do not have the resources to generate formidable group erosion combat tactics and can only hope to be able to move their little slices of heaven when the time comes. One by one, the ocean has swept their sand away, redistributing it further west down the shore or out onto shoals just off the island. It has either claimed their sunny homes—strewing them down the beach, with septic systems, utility wires and water pipes exposed for all to see—or forced them to pick up and move deeper into what remains of their lots or elsewhere on the island. The lucky ones get to take this step.

The unhappy fact is that they join the former owners of the houses along the section of Hummock Pond Road that used to do a dogleg at its beach end to the west and run toward the pond, in addition to residents of odd-numbered Baxter Road homes and, to a certain extent, owners along the north shore of the harbor, as the summer "cottage" owners along the north shore who were once seemingly immune to the ravages of the opposite coast but are now fighting for the lives of their own shingled museums. All are fighting a battle that cannot be won.

PREDICTIONS

When the glacier was melting, the Nantucket Ridge, as Shaler called the coastal plain area encompassing the three islands, was around 75 miles north and roughly 50 miles west of the ocean. As the glacier melted and the sea rose from its approximate starting level beyond the edge of the now-submerged Continental Shelf, it is believed to have risen at its fastest rate of 50 feet every thousand years to around 7,500 to 6,000 years ago and 11 feet every thousand years between 6,000 and 4,000 years ago.

What the erosion rate was between 2,000 years ago, well after the islands were formed, through to 1846, when the USCGS began recording annual erosion data on Nantucket, is unknown. However, in the 166 years between 1846 and 2012, given the annual average erosion rate of six to ten feet a year with the average occasionally higher at 12 to 15 feet, conservatively, Nantucket on its south shore alone eroded at least 996 to 1,660 feet, or, in the extreme, 1,992 to 2,490 feet.

My calculations are based on the available data and personal knowledge of the high-energy erosion of the south shore over 20 years of island living. The shifting of wave-breaking shoals and the frequency of ocean storms, plus global warming–induced sea level rise, must be factored in. Certain sections of the south shore seem to have eroded up to more than a half-mile during the period studied by Nantucket Shoreline Survey, leading to a prediction that, with the continuation of these conditions and the current trend of an average of ten to 15 feet of erosion annually, even if the sea level rise doesn't increase—which it surely can—in the next 166 years, 996 to 2,490 more feet of the south shore are likely to erode inland. Smith's Point and Esther Island, along with all of the houses in their part of the island, would be washed away. Hither Creek would be opened to the ocean, with Jackson Point at least starting to disappear altogether, and a portion of Little Neck whittled down. Many of the houses south of South Cambridge Street would eventually disappear; Long Pond would be opened to the ocean, and say goodbye to the remaining houses on Sheep Pond Road. Further east, the ocean could push well into both Clark Cove and Hummock Pond, changing these ponds to a mostly saltwater environment, and much of Ram Pasture in Sanford Farm would be underwater. All of the houses in Cisco Estates will eventually go into the drink, as will those on Mothball Way. The ocean could push well up into Miacomet Pond, take the Shack behind the dunes on the east side of this pond, claim the Surfside Wastewater Treatment Plant, a good portion of Surfside and its near-shore structures, the southwestern half of Nantucket Memorial Airport's Runway Six and portions of the southeast ends of Runway 33 and Taxiway 30. It most certainly could take the remains of the old Navy base, immerse all the houses south of the intersection where Old Tom Nevers Road splits off from Tom Nevers Road, and completely wipe out Tom Nevers Pond.

The wind- and wave-driven dynamic of longshore or littoral drift involves the movement of sediments, including sand and smaller gravel, along a shoreline. Depending on the velocity of shore currents in the water along a shoreline (also called the littoral zone), and their angle to the shoreline, they remove sand from one section of a beach and distribute it to another section or to the constantly moving shoals offshore. It's impossible to say whether the ocean will advance in this way or not. But even the most conservative estimate is still going to be pretty grim for Nantucket, and a lot sooner than many of us realize.

This puts any attempted erosion control measures in stark relief. For property owners trying to get a few more summers out of an island house, or maybe another decade or two, their desires, not their logic, are understandable. It doesn't matter what's in their wallets.

Tiffney's thoughts on the matter were clear:

> Most engineering solutions to coastal erosion, often called 'beach armoring,' are costly failures. High energies implicit in storm waves simply smash the structures or waves overtop seawalls and remove sand from behind them, causing failure, water washes out their foundations, causing collapse, or rising sea level simply submerges them to the point where they become ineffective. Groins built perpendicular to the beach may trap sand moving in longshore currents, but at the expense of landowners downstream. Offshore breakwaters designed to attenuate wave energies, and more innovative applications such as artificial seaweed and beach dewatering may succeed for a while, and cost vast sums for construction and maintenance, but all must ultimately fail in the face of rising sea level.

EROSION CONTROL INNOVATION

With Tiffney's foreboding words fresh in your mind, consider some of the attempts during the late 20th and early 21st centuries, large and small, engineered to stop time, as it were, for certain sections of the island.

Other than several small groins along the north shore and the old standby, wood-slat-and-wire sand-trapping snow fencing planted in front of dunes, and retired Christmas trees that islanders have tossed over the edges of coastal banks and bluffs for ages in vain, desperate attempts to trap sand and build up the dunes, there really weren't any large-scale coastal property protection projects until the Siasconset Beach Preservation Fund was formed in 1994. SBPF proposed a beach dewatering system called Sta-Beach. Studied and researched since 1940, the process of "dewatering" a beach to expand its width first broke on the scene when the Danish North Sea Research Center, on the shore at Hirtshals in Torsminde, on the northern coast of Denmark, had the Danish Geotechnical Institute install a water filtration system to pump seawater into its aquarium. Perforated pipes extended 650 feet out under the beach into the ocean to draw water into the facility, but after six months of operation, the inflow had decreased significantly and the beach in front of this research center had grown 65 to 100 feet in width, forcing the extension of perforated pipes farther out into the water.

One of the first practical applications of this process, which the Danish Geotechnical Institute patented, was at Sailfish Point in Stuart, Florida, where Coastal Stabilization, Inc., of Rockaway, New Jersey, installed a 580-foot Sta-Beach system in 1988. It was later proven to have grown the beach and protected it from erosion. The Sta-Beach dewatering system is a network of perforated PVC pipes buried beneath the beach and connected to a well with an inline pump. As waves break on the shore, with the pump running constantly, the seawater is sucked into the beach and into the perforated pipes. It is then pumped back out into the ocean through an outflow pipe. The sand is left on the beach and gradually builds the beach seaward.

The Siasconset Beach Preservation Fund got Conservation Commission (ConCom) approval for the installation of this beach dewatering system in 1994 for three sections of the east shore, including the beach in front of Sankaty Head Lighthouse, Baxter Road and Codfish Park, but SBPF's first erosion control attempt was deemed ineffective. The system was eventually decommissioned, wrapping up in 2010. Over the years since, this nonprofit beach protection group installed plastic sand fencing called DuneGuard along certain parts of the base of the Bluff. It also got ConCom permission in February 2004 to do terracing of high-energy sections of the Bluff. A bluff face stabilization method, terracing employs thick coconut fiber net-like mats anchored at the toe of the bluff and then folded over, accordion-style, up the Bluff, with sand sandwiched in between each layer and four-inch-by-four-inch posts holding the mats in place. Long planks run between the posts across the bluff face to strengthen this installation further.

Additionally, during this period, some SBPF members drilled wells on lots and sank perforated pipes down through the layers of clay that run through to the bluff face in this part of Siasconset. On some lots, where the clay runs down toward the bluff face, whenever it rained moderately hard, rainwater would percolate down through the organic soil and through the sand and, upon hitting the impermeable clay layer, run out and down the bluff face, eroding it from the top down. More than 90 wells were drilled and their perforated pipes installed to carry the rainwater through the problem clay layer and down to the sandy soils beneath, where it was able to percolate down into the ground. However, strong multi-day nor'easters during the first decade of the 21st century washed much of the terracing down the Bluff, scattering the mats, posts and planks up and down the beach. Several times, SBPF replaced and expanded the terracing.

SBPF realized it needed a more substantial method of holding member properties in place. Several property owners, from 85 Baxter Road north toward the lighthouse, moved their houses back from the edge—some of them twice during this period. In 2005, SBPF began the permitting process for beach nourishment of three miles of beach, from just north of Sankaty Head to just south of Codfish Park, with 2.6 million cubic yards of sand, later scaled back to 1.9 million cubic yards. The sand was to be dredged from the western slope of the Bass Rip shoals, a 345-acre area in 25 feet of water just three miles east of this beach. The sand was to be barged close to shore and pumped in slurry form to the beach through pipes from the barge. Once this new sand was on the beach, SBPF would have filled giant geo-textile tube bags to be buried beneath the permanent beach at key spots along the toe of the Bluff and covered them with sacrificial sand, put in place for storms to take. Ultimately, a beach 200 feet wide and 16 feet high was to be built. The plan called for re-nourishment of the beach every five to seven years, depending on the severity of the storms.

Island residents, including many charter and commercial fishermen who rely on striped bass and other fish for their livelihood, decried the project because the dredging of sand and the building out of the beach would have smothered fish-rich cobble rock areas just offshore. Though SBPF proposed to compensate these fishermen by building artificial reefs and rock piles to mitigate the loss of this natural habitat, which serves as a nursery and feeding ground for many game and bait fish, the groundswell of opposition forced SBPF to scrap its beach nourishment project in 2008 and withdraw it from the Conservation Commission's public hearing process.

The beach nourishment near-miss spawned two long-term preventive measures. Nantucket's Town Clerk, Catherine Flanagan Stover, successfully pushed through Nantucket's annual Town Meeting in 2008 two articles requiring the town to develop a coastal erosion structure policy for town land, because much of SBPF's beach nourishment would happen on public property beneath the private land up above on the Bluff. Stover also proposed a moratorium on such structures until December 31, 2010, or activation of the policy; however, the expiration date was extended to 2013.

While SBPF was being handed its hat and shown the door, the 'Sconset Trust, with the lighthouse-moving expertise of International Chimney of Buffalo, New York, in the fall of 2007 successfully moved the 450-ton, 164-year-old Sankaty Head Lighthouse approximately 250 feet west and 400 feet north of its imperiled previous location of 76 feet from the edge of the bluff. Obviously not believing that erosion control measures would be reliable in the long-term, the 'Sconset Trust had opted for the safer protection of the historic lighthouse. Its move was not a problem for ships, because with the advent of global positioning systems, Sankaty is no longer relied on by most vessels for navigation.

Not giving up on its members whose houses and yards were facing extinction, and wanting to be ready for when the coastal management principles were written and adopted at Town Meeting, SBPF filed a notice of intent (an application) with the Conservation Commission in May 2011, gambling that the principles would be written and the moratorium lifted when they got their ConCom approval, to armor the toe of the Bluff in certain places with plastic geogrid containers filled with large rocks covered with sand. Seeking approval for 20 properties along the fastest eroding section of the Baxter Road Bluff, if it got the green light to do so, SBPF planned to lay on the bluff face so-called marine mattresses made of the geogrid material filled with angular rocks, followed by rock-filled geogrid gabions, baskets filled with rocks in two sizes laid in front of the marine mattresses, and cover it all with sand. They hoped to apply this latest salve against erosion on town beach property beneath two sets of three adjacent properties within a 2,000-foot section of the Bluff between 99 and 55 Baxter Road.

In early February 2012, Nantucket's Board of Selectmen rejected the latest incarnation of the coastal management principles written by town beach manager Jeff Carlson, and then the ConCom closed SBPF's public hearing on February 1, meaning it would take no more comments and submissions. A favorable ConCom vote would mean SBPF need only wait until Carlson and the selectmen agreed on coastal management principles, and Town Meeting voters adopted them, to begin installation of their latest erosion control measures. However, the commission voted down this project on February 15, 2012, 5–2.

Another multi-property ocean-tamer that never got wet was the Nantucket Beach Foundation's WhisprWave wave attenuation installation that Sheep Pond Road beach property owner Jonathan Betts took before the Conservation Commission in the summer and fall of 2003. WhisprWave erosion control technology, invented by Wave Dispersion Technologies, Inc., of

Mountainside, New Jersey, consists of polygonal high-density plastic modules lashed together with synthetic rubber. The modules were to be stacked in three tiers, two submerged and one floating on the surface, creating a break that Betts and WDT predicted would effectively take the energy out of the waves, knocking them down before they hit the beach and caused erosion.

WDT planned to anchor the WhisprWave array with helix moorings, which screw into the ocean floor, in 20 to 30 feet of water. The WhisprWave was to be installed in 1,000-foot sections, with chain or steel cables attaching WhisprWave modules to the anchors at ten-foot intervals. The resulting WhisprWave breakwater would be articulated to flex with the wave action; moreover, the WhisprWave's modules are designed and built to also disperse a wave through channels in between the hundreds of modules in a section of breakwater. Because WDT estimated that Nantucket's waves average seven seconds apart, this proposal involved custom-built WhisprWave breaks 15 to 18 feet wide to handle Nantucket's waves.

But WhisprWave never made it out of the ConCom public hearing stage. In the winter of 2011–2012, Betts's Sheep Pond Road house sat on cribbing waiting to be moved farther inland on his lot, away from the rapidly eroding beach.

THE WESTERN END

After weakened hurricane waves in August 2003 washed out a section of Sheep Pond Road, disconnecting the eastern end of this road from residences at its western terminus, the town partnered with the Nantucket Conservation Foundation to remake this road for the isolated residents. But the ocean was not finished with Sheep Pond Road. In 2007, the April 19 nor'easter, dubbed the Patriot's Day Storm, took Charlie Warner's house at 25 Sheep Pond Road and, two months later, his second, tilting house had to be removed before it, too, went over the edge. Several years previously, Warner had secured Conservation Commission permission to armor the beach in front of his houses with giant geotextile bags filled with sand, but the ocean got the better of these houses by going around the bags, splitting some of them open, washing away their sand and scattering the bags all around Nantucket's beaches.

In December 2009, Betts's neighbors at 3 Sheep Pond Road, Jim and Donna Wyland, lost their house when wind-driven waves undercut its bluff and it slid down onto the beach. And one of the longer-lasting properties on Nantucket's south shore, 19 Sheep Pond Road, owned by the notorious

Gene Ratner, who had protected his house, like Warner, with giant sand bags but had also fought the ConCom and the state's Department of Environmental Protection (DEP) for more than 20 years to be able to protect his house, agreed to dismantle it in late September 2010 when ocean waves, including those from Tropical Storm Earl, finally cut around both sides of this house, almost making an island of it on the beach.

The carnage gets worse the farther west one explores in Madaket. A passage from the Nantucket Shoreline Survey regarding erosion of the Smith's Point neighborhood holds true today:

> Madaket: The area just east of the breach into Madaket Harbor has been eroding at an average rate of about 13 feet/year. This is a particularly critical erosion problem because this area, especially to the west of the Ames Street bridge [Millie's Bridge], is low-lying and subject to flooding and overwash during severe hurricanes and northeasters. Although the data indicates that the area is not stable and is therefore unsuitable for development, this is one of the rapidly developing areas of Nantucket.

Anyone tracking what would seem to be systematic reclamation of sand by the ocean from the southwest end of Madaket Road and westward knows that one by one, and sometimes in twos and threes every year for many decades, beach cottages and small houses in this part of Madaket have been dropping into the ocean or retreating inland deeper into their lots, or even relocating to new spots well away from the shoreline. In March 2008, I reported in The Nantucket Independent that 15 out of the 57 houses on Smith's Point had been under constant attack by the ocean for the preceding five years. During that time, Tom Erichsen, a former resident of 34 Rhode Island Avenue, estimated that Smith's Point eroded 250 feet inland, due to the loss, he believes, of a shoal 500 feet off Smith's Point during a winter storm in 2002.

Wes Tiffney found that Smith's Point eroded an average of ten feet a year from 1900 to 1950, and five feet annually from 1950 to 2000. Nantucket Conservation Foundation Executive Director Jim Lentowski estimates that, from 1998 to 2007, Smith's Point lost 117 feet, an average erosion rate of 13 feet per year.

This western end of the island has even less protection than Baxter Road. The Bluff at Baxter Road contains a lot of clay, which probably formed the bottom of Glacial Lake Sesachacha, whereas Smith's Point is really all outwash sand deposits held in place by American beach grass and some snow fencing. There are significant losses out on the Bluff during the winter, depending on the severity of the storms, but it could be argued that the Smith's Point neighborhood where the streets are named for U.S. states is washing away faster because it's much lower in elevation, nearly level with its beach.

The breach mentioned by the Nantucket Shoreline Survey, above, refers to the narrow beach section between the ocean and Madaket Harbor that, during the survey's research period, was still open from a December 1962 storm that further severed the end of Smith's Point from Nantucket. The ocean, especially during ocean storms, has had a predilection for blasting through this area because of Broad and Narrow creeks, through which geologists believe glacial meltwater ran from the glacier out to the edge of the Continental Shelf down through the bottoms of two former outwash valleys that were on this approximate part of the coastal plain where Nantucket's west end would eventually exist. With this ancient underwater trench to follow, the ocean has blown through that spot several times with ease, including in the 1950s, in 1961 and again in April 2007. It's possible that openings will occur with greater frequency in the future because of continuing sea level rise.

The Massachusetts Department of Environmental Protection takes a tough line on hard erosion control structures such as rock walls, groins, timber structures and seawalls made of riprap, because of the impacts these structures have on the beaches, beach and near-shore habitat, marine life and shorebirds. Longshore drift moves sand down a beach, constantly removing it from one part of the beach and depositing it on another, so when such a structure is placed on the beach, it blocks the flow of sand down-current, which can cause severe erosion of beach, dunes and near-shore inland areas. The erosion-accretion dynamic is a natural process that many, including the state's DEP and Nantucket's Conservation Commission, do not want to interrupt, not only because of the destruction of the beach, but also the loss of habitat for nesting shorebirds, loss of beach vegetation and the deprivation of beach soils that would otherwise remain for natural protection of the shoreline.

All of this is what Joe Farrell, Jr., who owns property in the Smith's Point neighborhood of Madaket, said he could keep intact with yet another proposed solution to Nantucket's perceived erosion woes. (I say "perceived" because it depends on how one looks at erosion. Beach property owners' attitudes are going to favor defenses against losing their houses, while the average inland citizen may view erosion as just one more fact of weather-related processes, the way the world works.) Mr. Farrell, although his Madaket land is not in harm's way, wanted to help out. Owner of Resolve Marine, one of the three largest salvagers of ships, oil rigs and other gigantic marine structures in the world, Farrell is a rescuer of stranded ships from sandbars and other perilous situations at sea, handling, in addition, hazardous material clean-ups from oil spills. He is also responsible for safeguarding 45 percent of all oil tankers entering U.S. waters as an emergency first-responder. Thirty-plus years of experiencing the effects of ocean currents on shoals and sand piqued Farrell's interest in the how and the why of sand transport in seawater, and how he could apply that knowledge to helping preserve the integrity of his Smith's Point neighborhood and maybe help protect other spots around the island threatened by erosion.

Melding his curiosity with the technical know-how of engineers Sandy Williams and Todd Morrison of Nobska Engineering, who invented an ocean current–measuring meter called the MAVS-3, and coastal scientist Steve Elgar of the Woods Hole Oceanographic Institute in Woods Hole, Massachusetts, Farrell began watching sand move in the water in the fall of 2008 from a small shed just off the beach in Madaket.

The current meters use light beams to measure the speed, direction and sand content of the water at the molecular level. Data was collected using two MAVS-3's planted off the South Shore at intervals of 290 and 490 feet offshore, at 11 and 13 feet deep, respectively. They were wired to Farrell's computer in the shed by low-voltage cables. Farrell found that the sand moved at about two miles per hour and went whichever direction the currents just offshore were going.

After measuring the movement of sand in the water in front of his neighborhood using these sand meters, Farrell offered to install 60' by 20' steel containers he called "shoal modules" just offshore that he believed would act like shoals breaking large waves. These containers could be filled with water, sunk to the bottom and anchored in place, and then pumped out and moved whenever they needed to be.

Convinced that he could help with the erosion along the Madaket Beach, Sheep Pond Road and Smith's Point sections of the south shore, Farrell hoped to be able to replace the shoal obliterated during that 2002 storm. He sought to do this first installation in front of the Smith's Point area and then to get the town to support installation of shoal modules in front of other erosion hot spots, such as the sewer beds at the end of South Shore Road and in the water in front of Baxter Road.

Farrell's shoal modules are about as close as Smith Point property owners are likely to get to achieving something approaching unified erosion control on the magnitude of SBPF's bluff terracing, beach dewatering, beach nourishment and now rock-filled cages, and the modules are something that might really help their situation. However, Smith Pointers, though well represented by their homeowners group, the Smith's Point Association, have not shown they have the means to pursue anything beyond Farrell's offer of testing his idea *pro bono* off of their shores. As of the winter of 2011–2012, Farrell hadn't filed a plan with the Conservation Commission.

THE FINAL WORD

I have all due respect for beach and bluff property owners grappling with steady erosion of their land and the reality of either losing their houses to storms or—if they can afford it—having to move inland, away from where they'd much rather enjoy their summers. However, here near the end of the final chapter in this book is where this writer's natural world leanings show through a bit (if they haven't already over the years). Given all of the information presented herein about the natural history of Nantucket, from the erosion of Smith's Point back to the very formation of these islands, one thing should be clear by now. The ocean is coming. Man cannot stop it. It can only be held back for a spell. The next glacial stage within the Holocene Epoch (if global warming allows such a thing to happen) is the only mechanism that can cause the ocean to abate. No matter how much money there is, and no matter the kinds of new technology that owners of threatened properties may apply to the problem, it won't work forever, and maybe not even long enough to be worth the expense. It is not a permanent solution.

As a journalist writing on Nantucket for most of his career to date, I have witnessed the proposals for and permitting processes of the Siasconset Beach Preservation Fund's controversial beach dewatering, terracing installations, beach nourishment, and rock-filled geogrid mattresses and gabions projects—and lived to see their ultimate failure. With dogged fortitude, I have endured hundreds of hours of spirit-crushing, posterior-disintegrating Conservation Commission meetings for the consideration of erosion control measures, documented and written about scores of island storms and houses lost to them, and watched the severing of Esther Island from Smith's Point—and, gradually, its reconnection. Coastal property owners, when faced with either moving a house, losing it to erosion, annually contributing to a group erosion control effort or employing an independent erosion abatement strategy, must also contend with a significant financial outlay, no matter the solution and regardless of where along Nantucket's 82 miles of shoreline they reside. Although many of us inland dwellers find it easy to pass judgment on what's on the surface, we should respect that these property owners didn't confront their dilemmas half-heartedly, and they spent their money based on considerable weighing of bleak options.

Moving to a new lot—and there are currently plenty of them available in the many nearly empty subdivisions developed before the Great Recession in late 2008—is the sensible preservation choice, from this writer's perspective. The cost of buying a new lot and moving one's house, not to mention the extreme emotional downshifting involved in leaving one's treasured island spot, is deeply painful. But this choice involves the least hassle for all concerned. With little land left between you and the flood, and if the house is hemmed in by an unforgiving front yard setback beyond which there is no relief from the Zoning Board of Appeals, then follow the wisdom of early Nantucketers and move off of your lot instead of pursuing the futility of holding back the ocean from what little of your property remains. Sand may be your friend in July and August, but she is your unwavering enemy September through spring.

The Conservation Commission is not unsympathetic to the erosion woes of beach, bluff and coastal bank property owners and will generally work with applicants to find the best solution for both sides, but the ConCom is always going to be biased toward protecting the natural resources within its jurisdiction. Those who find themselves before the ConCom shouldn't hear any member of this town wetland regulatory board chide, "You should've known better than to have purchased or built where steady or severe erosion was inevitable" (egregious violations notwithstanding). But there can be an almost palpable vibe in the public hearings, at times—an unspoken admonishment. No grudges fester here, just devotion to the mission, but then the Conservation Commission is, in addition to its wetlands defender duties, Nantucket's sand police. The sand is all going to wash away eventually, and the ConCom strives to see that happen through natural processes unaffected by man-made structures.

So, considering the loss of Smith's Pointers' and Hummock Pond Road's houses over the last few decades and the likely fate of those remaining, and the relative inability, so far, of Baxter Road residents to slow the erosion of the Bluff enough to keep all of SBPF members' houses in place, the best bet would seem to be to move a house, rather than to armor a beach, bluff or bank, or to play chicken with Neptune. Nantucketer Tom Erichsen, the former resident of Smith's Point at 34 Rhode Island Avenue who was able to move his year-round house to a new lot on Ticcoma Way in May 2008, feels lucky to have been able to do so. Erichsen had already moved his house deeper into his lot several times, including a 46-foot retreat in 2007, but he moved inland for good the following year after Hurricane Noel grazed Nantucket on November 3 of that year. Many Smith's Pointers were scrambling around to move further into their lots, and Erichsen felt lucky to get out of the way of the ocean. He shared his reaction in a story in the March 18, 2008, issue of *The Nantucket Independent* on the neighborhood-wide shock of the sea's ferocity after that winter's storms:

> We've spent 23 years on Smith's Point in the neighborhood and I'm familiar with the neighborhood and with knowing people and the kids growing up there; it's devastating. This is something you don't prepare for. This is something you have to deal with. I can't speak for the other neighbors, but again they feel basically the same way. We were all aware that the south shore did erode, but the rate of erosion in the last five years has been more than we could ever imagine.

Whether or not the specter of global warming entered Erichsen's and his neighbors' minds during this period of rapid erosion, what they know, for having lived through it, is that the ocean is coming, and probably a lot faster than the National Oceanographic & Atmospheric Administration's records and research reveal. Through 1992 from 1900, the data shows continual sea level rise at a rate of 1 to 2.5 millimeters, 0.04 to 0.1 inches a year. Now, NOAA admits that the sea could be coming up faster. Since 1992, the rate has been 3 millimeters, 0.12 inches a year, which is pretty close to NOAA's annual ocean rise for Nantucket of 2.95 millimeters per year.

As the water continues to come up, Nantucket's sand just won't sit still. The western tip of Tuckernuck, Bigelow Point, is growing closer and closer to Muskeget now, as evidenced by a series of three aerial photos and several others shot by island pilot and aerial photographer George Reithof in June 2007, July 2009 and February 2012. To see these photos chronicle the nubbin that was Bigelow Point in 2007, moving to 2009 when it looked like a fat fang dangling toward its tiny sister island to the west and, finally, just three years later, a long, thin sand spit jabbing out nearly a third of the way over to Muskeget, in the vicinity of the former location of the Gravelly Islands, is just an amazing representation of how much sand is moved up and down the south shores of Nantucket and Tuckernuck. And it's certainly a cautionary tale for anyone with coastal property.

Those older Madaket residents and Tuckernuckers who have seen this latest incarnation of Bigelow Point are likely to have reminisced about the days when Smith's Point ran all the way past the south side of Tuckernuck and just beyond Muskeget. Conversely, at the other end of Tuckernuck, Whale Island, the disputed sand spit jutting off its eastern end, has shrunk way back toward the larger island, its dogleg that once fronted Smith's Point worn down considerably. Could it be that all the sand from east of and in front of Sheep Pond Road, westward along the rest of Nantucket and over to Whale Island, has moved down the south side of Tuckernuck to grow Bigelow Point out into this magnificent sandy finger since Ratner's sand bags are no longer there to stop it? Sure seems like it.

We can't even imagine the configurations that the waves, currents and wind will bend out of our sand before the ocean reclaims these three islands that the glacier brought here 21,000 years ago.

Those who can spend time watching these three islands not-so-gradually succumb to the implacable will of nature are fortunate. Nantucketers, brave year-rounders gutting it out through long winters to revel in the glowing golden days from late spring to early fall, along with their seasonal islanders, are witnessing the wildly beautiful and the unruly sides of the Atlantic Ocean imposing its will on the Grey Lady and her two sisters.

EPILOGUE

Have I used the word "unique" enough in this book? And have I beaten to death my perception of how extraordinary the Nantucket Archipelago is on this planet?

I think so.

Yet I think these superlatives can't be overstated, particularly in light of the radical changes in the earth's climate headed our way. Global warming—human-induced or part of a natural glacial-interglacial cycle, whichever belief system lets you sleep at night—is upon us. All indications are that low-lying coastal areas, and yes, that includes islands, especially islands perched on sand, are going to be the frontlines of catastrophic natural disasters. They are going to experience intensified ocean storms, tsunamis and simple inundation by sea level rise.

Your favorite beaches are going to disappear, and the islands, probably starting with Muskeget, are going to return to the ocean that made them. In the meantime, new species of flora and fauna will find these islands suitable for their survival, while some of those currently living and growing here will depart for warmer or colder habitats. The human population, although growing now, will begin to dwindle as the size of Nantucket shrinks and its natural resources become depleted.

Big changes are a-comin'. So, what else is new?

OK, it probably won't happen in our lifetimes, and if we're lucky, not within our children's. But it's likely that life on Nantucket's three islands, along with the rest of the islands off the East Coast, will be indicators, the proverbial eelgrass and bay scallops, for the rest of the U.S. The mainland will be watching to see what sea level rise and warming temperatures do, so that it may gauge how it might prepare for its own turn.

This brings me to a drum I've been beating as an environmental writer and in writing *Walking Nantucket,* and it's one I don't think I will ever stop beating. We should all get out and explore these islands. Experience how privileged we are to be able to spend at least some of our lives here, because of the place they hold in the grand scheme of the life of our planet. My point in making these end-of-the-island predictions is this: learn about, and teach your children, where you live, because—unlike the mainland—Nantucket isn't going to last. Explore these islands on foot, by bike and in a kayak, if you're able. Get to know this unique island natural world. Take a Maria Mitchell Association class and enroll your children, too. Go on the Great Point Natural History Tour, join the Christmas Bird Count at least once, paddle Coskata Pond in a kayak, hike the moors in the winter and help out with the annual horseshoe crab survey. If you can, place a conservation restriction on your land.

Regularly visit the UMass Field Station, the town's Brant Point marine lab and all three of the island's libraries to read about the creatures and plants sharing these islands with us. And give your money to the conservation organizations that protect wild Nantucket.

In short, with reverence and respect, engage Nantucket, Tuckernuck and Muskeget as if you had just one year to live here. See it all and do it all.

ENDNOTES

A LAURENTIDE JUNK HEAP

1 Oldale believes that marine water flooding of the deeper lowland areas of Vineyard Sound and Nantucket Sound began around 7,500 to 8,000 years ago for Vineyard Sound and about 6,000 years ago for Nantucket Sound, which is roughly when our three islands began detaching from the mainland. However, seawater didn't begin creating the shape of Nantucket's three islands until between 2,000 and 5,000 years ago.

2 Although it is not definitively known what specific climate change dynamic initiated global warming and caused the Laurentide ice sheet to melt and recede from Nantucket and New England altogether, there are several strong theories. One popular theory credits the Dansgaard-Oeschger Cycles. Based on Greenland ice core samples dated back to the Sangomonian Interglacial Stage (which preceded the Wisconsinan Glacial Stage), some climatologists believe that 25 times during the Wisconsinan Glacial Stage, about every 1,470 years, the earth experienced rapid warming periods. As the theory goes, these warming trends may be the result of interruptions in the circulation of ocean waters in the North Atlantic that could be sparked by relatively sudden infusions of fresh water—such as those occurring in the six Heinrich events discovered by Marine Geologist Hartmut Heinrich. Heinrich found that, during the Wisconsinan Glacial Stage, large chunks of ice would break off glaciers of the Laurentide ice sheet, floating free into the North Atlantic and lowering the salinity of the seawater as they melted. This impacted the thermohaline circulation of ocean currents, which is regulated by the density of the water. Also called the ocean conveyor belt, thermohaline circulation is partially driven by winds blowing warmer water—the Gulf Stream—into the North Atlantic, where some of this saltier, denser, now-cooler water sinks to the bottom, a large portion of it having already spun off toward the U.K. and Europe. From the North Atlantic, it then runs down into ocean basins and comes up in the Southern Ocean and the North Pacific Ocean. This highway of water current carries heat all around the earth to be transferred into the atmosphere, so substantial introductions of fresh water, in the form of massive glacial ice chunks, to the denser, warm salt water of the Gulf Stream may have caused this lighter, less dense fresh water to float on top, preventing the salt water below from reaching the surface and thereby stalling thermohaline circulation. With the influx of fresh water temporarily affecting the circulation of water around the globe, heat from the warmer water normally released into the atmosphere in one place could have been released in another. Climatologists postulate that the Heinrich events caused the Dansgaard-Oeschger Cycles, which began the melting of the Laurentide

ice sheet during the Wisconsinan Glacial Stage. Another theory posits that the amount of heat produced by the sun may have increased as oscillations in the rotation of the earth moved it temporarily closer to the sun.

3   Trott's Hills run perpendicular to Primrose Lane, westward to the wetlands on the east side of the North Head of Long Pond. Although roughly in line with Nantucket's terminal moraine, they are not part of the moraine but instead of the younger outwash plain deposits from the Cape Cod Lobe, according to Oldale. He also states that the hill on which Orange and Fair Streets run, Academy Hill, and Sunset Hill are also part of this younger outwash plain, rather than part of the island's terminal moraine.

4   At least two people—Edward Wayman Coffin, author of *Tuckernuck Island* and *Nantucket's Forgotten Island: Muskeget*, and frequent Tuckernuck visitor, geologist Dr. John England, Professor at the University of Alberta (Edmonton) and a Natural Sciences and Engineering Research Council of Canada's Northern Chair of Earth & Atmospheric Sciences—say that the boulders present on Tuckernuck's northwestern side and just off its east end, most notably Great Rock, and soils on its eastern end show that these parts of Tuckernuck contain moraine deposits. "[T]he till is much thicker on the east side of the island which is essentially a moraine from top to bottom (i.e., from the Walker House right down to the modern beach where huge glacial boulders—erratics from the mainland—are widespread)," says England.

5   "It didn't come out of the water," says Oldale. "As the sea was rising, [the glacial deposits] acted as a foundation for the marine deposits. [His map shows this foundation just ten feet beneath the surface with marine deposits on top, just barely making Muskeget an island.] The whole process that brings material to the shore by waves was the source of all the material there. You didn't get some kind of rise in the glacial deposits to keep pace with sea level rise, so it must have been very close and it might have been much larger when sea level was lower. You can think of Muskeget as nothing different than Nantucket except that there are no occurrences of glacial deposits on the island and they must be somewhat below sea level."

6   There is, it turns out, a great deal more to Great Point than just post-glacial marine deposits of sand and gravel topped with beach grass and a lighthouse, as hydrogeologist Eugene H. Walker learned while producing, for the U.S. Geological Survey, his two-sheet map entitled "Water Resources of Nantucket Island, Massachusetts." Down beneath the dunes, Walker found that "a hole 301 feet deep at Great Point penetrated glacial outwash composed of sand and gravel to a depth of 150 feet below which beds of fine sand, silt and clay of pre-glacial (Tertiary) age extended to a depth of 301 feet, the bottom of the hole."

7   Former UMass Boston Field Station director and co-founder, the late Wes Tiffney, used to say that, because Nantucket is sitting on a pile of mostly sand and gravel, the island had about 600 years before it eroded back into the ocean. Here, according to Walker, is what Tiffney said will get washed away: "A test hole drilled to a depth of 1,686 feet near the center of the island penetrated Pleistocene outwash of sand and gravel from zero to 250 feet, Tertiary sand and greensand from 250 to 350 feet, Cretaceous varicolored silty clay with some sand and several thin layers of lignite 330 to 1,145 feet, and Cretaceous white to gray clayey sand three beds of clay between 1,145 and 1,500 feet deep. From 1,500 to 1,540 feet, a red-brown layer of weathered rock overlies hard igneous basalt of probable Triassic era, which extended to the bottom of the hole at 1,686 feet."

8   Because groundwater is the only source of drinking water on the island, the U.S. Environmental Protection Agency declared Nantucket's groundwater as a sole source aquifer. The Nantucket Land Council, Oldale and Walker describe groundwater as water in pore spaces

between soil particles, with the upper portion of groundwater nearest to the surface classified as the water table. The water table is found bubbling at the surface out of the ground at several island springs or in the form of ponds and swamps. It is also as deep as 100 feet below the land around Altar Rock and Folger Hill, according to the Land Council.

9 According to Walker, salt water is one-fortieth more dense than fresh water.
10 "When you see a diagram of the freshwater water table salt water, it usually involves great vertical exaggeration and it looks like a bowl with steep sides; well, that's as far from the truth that you can get. The water looks like a saucer. The freshwater reaches the altitude of the sea level at the shoreline . . . can't push it any higher, that's as high as that interface is at the shoreline. That's the top of the freshwater lens as it meets the sea . . . it tapers to zero right there at the shoreline. It can go beyond that if it's got a head, but the head is usually zero under ideal conditions."
11 As Oldale describes in his book, there are pockets of fresh water trapped in clay deposits beneath Nantucket's aquifer. "Two zones of freshwater occur with the groundwater. One zone occurs from 730 to 820 feet [below the surface], and a second zone occurs from 900 to 930 feet. The water in these zones is trapped between impermeable clay layers and may be a remnant of a freshwater recharge that occurred during glacial stages when the continental shelf was subaerially exposed."
12 Allen Reinhard, Middle Moors Ranger for the Nantucket Conservation Foundation, said that in the early 1980s, the Foundation hired a team of geologists from Harvard University to identify the glacial erratics at and around Altar Rock, as well as those lining the south side of Barnard Valley Road. The team determined that some of these boulders came from New Hampshire in general, some specifically from the White Mountains and some from the Connecticut River Valley.
13 This scenario, Oldale details in his book, is more likely than that these materials flowed out from a gap in the moraine west of Sankaty, called an ice-contact head, a collapsing of glacial till in front of the ice that is spilled out onto the landscape by melting water.
14 Oldale calls the woods section of Sanford Farm a "drumlin" and describes its composition as "unexposed, composition not well known. Two auger holes reached only shallow depths because of saturated drift and indicate that uppermost sediments are composed of muddy gravelly sand, possibly till. Shallow water table, encountered in auger holes at about four feet, is probably perched and indicates that unit may be composed of impermeable silty or clayey till." This woods drift, which likely forms the drumlin that Oldale believes lies beneath the hill, is convincing evidence of a sub lobe of the Cape Cod Bay Lobe. "The unexposed Woods drift forms a drumlin-like hill probably underlain by till. Because it is probably composed of till, the Woods drift might be part of the Nantucket moraine. However, the moraine in this part of Nantucket is composed of stratified drift and the position of the Woods drift well south of the trend of the moraine makes it likely to be a separate unit. Its shape and probably composition suggest that it is a drumlin. If so, it was formed subglacially and is evidence for a sublobe of the Cape Cod Bay lobe that advanced some distance south of Nantucket. Kettles within the younger Nantucket outwash plain also support the presence of the sublobe."
15 Rosen posits that—in addition to south-to-north long shore drift carrying sand from Nantucket's east shore up toward Wauwinet, building the barrier beach that would become the Haulover toward the island of Coskata—the waves hitting Coskata on its west, east and south sides broke on its shores and, reverberating backwards and to either side as new waves, carried sand southward, extending a peninsula that eventually met the one growing from Wauwinet.

16 Oldale believes that sand, carried by littoral drift north to south and by wind down the west side of newly formed Great Point, eventually began to build up against the hard soils of Coskata, forming its tidal pond. Later, as the beach northwest of the pond widened, growing toward Nantucket Sound, dunes formed, the remains of which are the low ridges on the Glades. An east-to-west longshore drift then likely developed, building to the west the sand spit that would become Coatue.

17 While the Haulover cut remained open for 12 years between December 1896 and 1908, the tide in the harbor aligned with the tide of the ocean on the east side of the Haulover. Had the cut remained open, Rosen believes it would have spelled the end of the elongated shape of Nantucket Harbor, because while the cut was open, the tidal flow in and out of the harbor slowed down. This meant that the tidal currents didn't erode the ends of the spits with the same intensity, allowing them to continue growing toward the harbor's inner shore. Eventually, the spits would have connected with the inner harbor shore and segmented the harbor off into a series of brackish ponds, says Rosen. Nantucket Harbor might have been limited to a much smaller body of water, cut off from the rest of the original harbor by a sand spit extending from First Point over to Monomoy's shores. But with the Haulover intact, tides at the Head of the Harbor are around an hour to an hour and half later than the tide times back in town. There is enough of a current flowing in and out of the harbor to flush it out completely every 72 days, according to Nantucket Marine Superintendent Dave Fronzuto. "As you may know, there is a history to the origin of the Coatue Cuspate Spits, from the Native American interpretation of the paw print of the Great Bear, to the work of Jones [whose grandson recently died on Wauwinet] in the early 20th century. He interpreted the spits as relicts of swirling tidal currents," said Rosen.

18 According to *Names of the Land: Cape Cod, Nantucket, Martha's Vineyard, and the Elizabeth Islands: A Compendium of Cape Area Proper Names with Derivations*, by Eugene Green and William Sachse, Smith's Point is named for one of two early Smiths who lived on Nantucket shortly after it was colonized in 1659: either John Smith, one of Thomas Mayhew's partners, or artisan Richard Smith, who arrived on island in 1661. The Wampanoag Indians of Nantucket had their name for Smith's Point: Nopque, possibly translating to "dry land," or "middle of the waters."

19 As Coffin noted in his Muskeget book, an August 1894 issue of *The Inquirer & Mirror* carried a report by Polpis school teacher, George M. Carey, of his walk to the very westernmost end of Great Neck, where he was able to see around the northwest corner of Muskeget.

20 Prior to Whale Island's attachment to the eastern end of Tuckernuck Island, landings on the island were at this end of the island. In recent history, the late Walter Barrett and the late Franklin Bartlett both built piers off Sheep End Point. As of the printing of this book, Whale Island remains attached to Tuckernuck, forming a lagoon where boats can be moored, tied up to several piers, or beached or anchored for the day.

INSTANT ISLAND: JUST ADD LIFE

1 In the "Quaternary History of the Cape and Islands" section of his book, Oldale seems to say that, during the transition from the barren, recent post-glacial appearance of Nantucket to heavily vegetated habitats, Nantucket truly was just a huge pile of sand, gravel and boulders. "The age of the oldest organic deposits on the glacial drift surface indicates that the glacial landscape may have remained essentially unvegetated for several thousand years. Throughout the Wisconsinan, the coastal plain south of the glacial limit had a cold, periglacial climate, and vegetation was tundra-like with low bushes, grasses, and stands of arctic trees. Nevertheless, this arduous environment was a place of refuge for plants and

ENDNOTES

animals that would first colonize the island made available by the retreat of the Laurentide ice sheet. The plants and animals that currently characterize Southern New England retreated far to the south during the Wisconsinan stage and returned very slowly following the glacial retreat. Many tree species did not arrive in southern New England until the early Holocene, and some varieties of trees common to the present forests of southern New England, including the Cape and Islands, arrived during the middle Holocene."

2   The Younger Dryas Cold Episode between 10,000 and 12,900 years ago interrupted the warming trend that began with Tioga ice maxima of the Wisconsinan Glacial Stage approximately 21,000 years ago, causing existing icecaps and glaciers to expand and forested areas to revert back to tundra vegetation. This period of rapid cooling in the Northern Hemisphere, believe scientists at the Bjerknes Centre for Climate Research, the University of Bergen in Norway and colleagues at ETH (Eidgenössische Technische Hochschule), Zürich, was "driven by large-scale reorganizations of patterns of atmospheric and oceanic circulation."

3   Luanne Johnson, a wildlife biologist with a PhD in environmental studies from Antioch University, Keene, N.H. who, living on the Vineyard did a two-year river otter study in this area, including the expansion of their range into the islands off of southeastern Massachusetts. Said Johnson in mid-October 2010: "Otters are capable of long distance movements along coastlines, and this has been reported in studies in coastal Alaska. So it is not surprising that they have re-colonized Nantucket. They are also on the Elizabeth Islands and Nomans [Land]. I imagine they were on Nantucket historically and were, perhaps, trapped out."

4   Biologists use the term "endemic" to describe a species found in only one part of the planet.

5   The Nantucket Biodiversity Initiative is the collective effort of the island's conservation organizations to identify, catalog and understand all of Nantucket's species for the purposes of education and conservation, and for the protection of rare and endangered species. During its first year, NBI divided the island up into 25 plots, each 25 acres, for scientists and biologists to explore. The following year, many of these researchers presented their findings at the Nantucket Biodiversity Conference. Every two years, the researchers lead public field trips to their study sites around the island, and in the intervening years, NBI holds conferences for the biologists to present their latest findings. Learn more about the Nantucket Biodiversity Initiative at http://www.nantucketbiodiversityinitiative.org/.

6   Continues Pochman, "Anytime you walk out your door and down a trail, when you open your eyes and you are looking at what's there, you realize that oh, there are a lot of different plants, and you start to see the insects and see the different ones, and you look for the birds. . . . [My husband] Tom and I just keep a list of birds that we see in our yard over the course of a year, and we probably have about 100 birds, 100 species of birds that come through our yard, and that's just one little tiny place."

7   "In the dead of winter, one can find at least ten species of gulls," says island bird expert Ken Blackshaw. "Observers from inland are excited to see scores of Iceland and lesser black-backed gulls off the island's east end. At the west end, there is an incredible flight of long-tailed ducks back and forth each day, as perhaps a million of them commute from the western part of Nantucket Sound south to shoals, 30 to 40 miles south of the island, and back. The fact that our climate is tempered by ocean waters that seldom freeze makes Nantucket a place where birds appear that can't be found elsewhere during the New England winter. In the spring, Nantucket is often the recipient of birds seldom seen in New England. We call these birds 'overshoots.' These are birds, perhaps on their first flight north, that are picked up by strong, usually southwesterly, wind currents and deposited hundreds or even thousands of miles from others like them. Birds like blue grosbeaks and summer tanagers are

not unusual on the island at this season. Swallow-tailed kites, whose summer range cuts off along the Carolina coast, have been seen here several times. Even more spectacular are the records of fork-tailed flycatchers, birds from the northern coast of South America."

8. "Nantucket's heathlands are unique in eastern North America, including 25 plant and five animal species considered rare, endangered, or of special concern," says Oktay. "This special habitat is dominated by lichens, grasses, and dwarf shrubs. It evolved as a result of Native American timber use and fire followed by over 200 years of intense grazing activities promoted by European settlers. Today, these heaths are preserved by conservation ownership and managed by brush cutting and controlled burns."

9. "Black widow spiderlings can balloon ('fly' using a silk line like a kite)," says McKenna. "This means they can disperse fairly rapidly. Most only go a couple meters, but in rare instances, a spiderling can be carried miles. Northern black widows probably dispersed in this way to all the islands when they were still just inland hills. The ocean level rose and isolated the populations. For whatever reason, the widows flourish on Tuckernuck. There may be too much development on Nantucket for them, or there could be too many other species that they have to compete with."

10. In his book, *The Sibley Guide to Birdlife & Behavior*, David Sibley describes this habitat: "The boreal forest extends north across the continent from Alaska to the Canadian Maritime Provinces. It consists mostly of firs, spruces, pines and larches, with intermittent pockets of such cold tolerant deciduous trees as poplars and birches. The boreal forest receives moderate amounts of precipitation and experiences long, cold winters, with snow for up to two-thirds of the year."

11. With straighter backs and less arched tusks than elephants and woolly mammoths, mastodons shared the mammoths' thick hair for survival in the mostly spruce forests with cold climates near and on glaciers. Scientists believe that the mastodons, which lived from 10,000 to 4.9 million years ago, were leaf-eaters because of their teeth, which had blunt, conical projections on the crowns of their molars, which were more suited to chewing leaves than the high-crowned teeth mammoths used for grazing.

12. Glyptodons, about the size of a large bull, were mammalian relatives of the armadillo that lived during the Pleistocene Epoch. The glyptodons were armored with bony scales on their backs, the ends of their tails and on their heads. The glyptodon was probably a herbivore, finding its diet of wetland edge vegetation, including grasses, near streams and small ponds and lakes.

13. Oldale says, "The animal community would have included mammals, birds, reptiles and fish. Large animals probably included deer, bear, wolves, moose, caribou, bison and musk ox. Elephant teeth, frequently dredged from the sea floor of the continental shelf, show that during the Laurentide glaciation, and perhaps as recently as 10,000 years ago, mastodons and mammoths roamed the region of the emerged continental shelf. As the Laurentide ice sheet retreated and the climate warmed, plant and animal life slowly migrated northward to occupy the Cape and Islands, and the rest of New England.

14. In *After the Ice Age: The Return of Life to Glaciated North America*, author E. C. Pielou describes the extinctions as abrupt. "Over 50 species went extinct during the whole course of the Wisconsinan Glaciation, but most of the extinctions happened in one short burst at the end, in the interval 12k to 10k B.P. (assuming that each species disappeared soon after the date of its most recent known fossil). According to some researchers, the wave of extinctions ended at 10k B.P., and no mammals have gone extinct on this continent since. This certainly makes 10k B.P. the end of an epoch in the colloquial sense, the epoch being that of the great ice age mammals."

ENDNOTES

AN UNLIKELY GARDEN AT SEA

1 Dunwiddie said that this boreal assemblage of trees and plants is typical of many other New England areas developed shortly after the glacier began melting northward. "Because sea levels were lower at this time, Nantucket was attached to the mainland, and species were able to migrate readily into the area," says Dunwiddie in his paper.

2 "Soils begin to form on glacial and windblown deposits soon after deposition ceases and the surface becomes stabilized," Oldale says. "The upper part of the deposits begins to weather, disintegrating because of physical and chemical processes caused by exposure to air and water. Plants slowly begin to colonize the glacial landscape, and plant litter starts to accumulate on the ground surface."

3 Radiocarbon, or radioactive, dating employs sensitive instruments to measure the amount of radioactive carbon-14 isotopes in organic material. All living things absorb carbon-14 from cosmic rays in the atmosphere while alive: plants absorb it in the form of carbon dioxide and animals through the food chain. Because this absorption stops when they die, and because all organic material will always have the same ratio of radioactive carbon to ordinary carbon, scientists can determine an object's age by comparing it to the amount in living creatures. The level of carbon-14 in a plant or animal's tissues decays to nitrogen-14, a more stable isotope, at a constant rate after death; therefore, the time since death can be determined by measuring the amount of carbon-14 in the organism.

4 Like carbon-14 isotopes, beryllium-10 is a radioactive isotope of beryllium, but which reaches the earth via cosmogenic rays in the atmosphere through rain. Geologists can calculate the age of rocks by measuring how much beryllium-10 a rock absorbs over time.

5 O'Keefe and Foster said that "The huge quantities of water trapped on land as glacial ice had once been seawater; consequently, sea level was several hundred feet lower than at present, leaving vast areas of continental shelf off the present-day East Coast exposed as refugia as well. The forests in these various refugia contained species mixtures unlike any we are familiar with today. As the climate warmed and the glaciers melted, the trees began their migration north at rates determined by the method of seed dispersal and the climatic tolerance of each species."

6 Oldale says that "Marine waters entered the deeper parts of Vineyard Sound approximately 7,500 years ago and flooded Nantucket Sound about 6,000 years ago. About that time, the Islands separated from each other and from Cape Cod, and sea level continued to rise. Thus, about 2,000 years ago, the Cape and Islands began to physically resemble how they look today, even though the shoreline was probably one-half to several miles farther seaward."

7 Dunwiddie admits that both Muskeget and Tuckernuck's plant species are much fewer than Nantucket's 1,265 vascular and 207 non-vascular plants, and he hinted that historical data for Muskeget is less complete than that available for Nantucket's plant species: "The vascular floras of Muskeget (160 species) and Tuckernuck (353) are significantly smaller corresponding to their lesser area and lower density of habitats than Nantucket. The lower proportion of introduced species as well on these islands (27 and 23 percent, respectively) also may reflect the lower level of human activity on these islands. Only two species, *Galax maritime* and *Ribes uva-crispa* from Tuckernuck, have not been reported from Nantucket. The Muskeget flora is a dynamic one, with frequent additions and deletions. Easily seen and identified species like red cedar (*Juniperus virginiana*) appear to be recent arrivals, not having been mentioned by McAtee in 1916. Others, such as cranberry (*Vaccinium macrocarpon*) and rosa pogonia (*Pogonia ophioglossoides*), which were noted by McAtee, are missing today and suggest that disappearance of bog habitat from the island.

A total of 12 species have not been recorded since 1920, and many of these may be extirpated from Muskeget."

8   Wesley N. Tiffney, Jr., the founding director of the UMass Boston Nantucket Field Station, who spent the final years of his botany career managing the field station right on Folger's Marsh, wrote in his paper, "Sea Level Rise, Coastal Retreat, and the Demise of Nantucket Island, Massachusetts," that core samples from this marsh prove when this salt marsh began. "As little as 3,000 years before present, Spartina (chordgrass) grasses first colonized the present Folger's Marsh on the University of Massachusetts Nantucket Field Station property. We know this because the salt marsh Spartina grows at the mid-tide level, and the late Alfred C. Redfield used cores taken from the marsh to radiocarbon date Spartina peat eight feet deep as 3,000 years old."

9   Oldale says that "prior to that time, the submergence of the region may have been too rapid for extensive marsh deposits to form" and that "the salt marshes on the Cape and Islands form in sheltered bays and estuaries where accumulations of sand and mud have shoaled the sea floor to intertidal depths. As the area of shoal water increases, the marsh advances toward deeper parts of the embayment. With a rising sea level, the marsh also advances over the upland."

10 William A. Niering and R. Scott Warren, in their article, "Vegetation Patterns and Processes in New England Salt Marshes," in the May 1980 issue of *Bioscience of the American Institute of Biological Sciences*, estimate "that between 3,000 and 4,000 years ago, the rapid post-glacial sea level rise of 2.3 millimeters per year began to slow to about one millimeter per year. During this time, marsh sedimentation rates approximated those of sea level rise by expanding seaward on to newly formed mud flats and landward towards the increasingly flooded upland and freshwater marshes."

11 In their salt marsh book, the Teals detail a probable scenario of the initial beginnings of a salt marsh with the arrival of birds to a suitable area searching for food and nesting grounds. "A flock of birds settled on the protected shore in their northward search for tundra on which to nest. On the previous day, they had rested on wet mud miles to the south. When they settled to rest the following day, the mud, which had dried on their feet, flaked off. In the mud were seeds of marsh plants. Perhaps, some seeds germinated and survived the first time they were deposited on the barren shore, or perhaps there were many arrivals and reseedings before the first plants took hold successfully, but successful they eventually were. Grass began to grow at the edge of the water where the tides covered the ground less than half of the time. *Spartina Alterniflora*, a tall coarse grass, grew above the mid-tide level while *Spartina patens*, a finely textured relative, grew above the *S. Alterniflora* at high water level."

12 "At low tide, the salt marsh is a vast field of grasses with slightly higher grasses sticking up along the creeks and uniformly tall grass elsewhere," say the Teals in the introduction to their salt marsh book. "The effect is like that of a great flat meadow. At high tide, the look is the same, a wide, flat sea of grass but with a great deal of water showing. The marsh is still marsh, but spears of grass are sticking up through water, a world of water where land was before, each blade of grass a little island, each island a refuge for the marsh animals, which do not like or cannot stand submersion in salt water."

13 "It was during the xerothermic period that elements of the prairie flora most likely extended eastward into New England," says Leslie J. Mehrhoff in her research essay, "Thoughts on the Biogeography of Grassland Plants in New England," published as part of "Grasslands of Northeastern North America: Ecology and Conservation of Native and Agricultural

Landscapes," by Peter D. Dunwiddie and Peter D. Vickery. "A possible route for some of these plant migrations may have been through the lowlands of Central New York."

14 Dunwiddie describes vascular plants as those well-evolved species, including seed-producing plants and fern species, that carry plant nutrients outward from the leaves through tissues called phloem, in which perforated sieve tube cells do most of distribution of food from the top half of the plant and xylem tissue, which moves water and nutrients upward into the plant from its roots.

15 According to Eveleigh and Tiffney's *Nantucket's Endangered Maritime Heaths*, preparation of Nantucket's northeastern section for heathland came in the form of human and natural processes: "An extensive maritime heath developed on Nantucket as the result of five years of burning, firewood collection, and subsistence agriculture by Indian people; and nearly 300 years of periodic burning, continued firewood collecting, increased agriculture, and intensive sheep pasturage by European settlers and their descendents. Heath development was encouraged by a cool maritime climate, characterized by strong winds and wind-vectored salt spray that inhibited tree and shrub growth. The heaths reached the peak of their development about 1850, concurrent with Nantucket's highest population, greatest use of natural resources, and heaviest grazing pressure. Decrease in heath dominance and succession to the present day shrub and tree dominance began with the fall in human population after the Civil War and resulting diminution of pressures tending to create and maintain heaths."

16 Nitrogen falling to the ground as particulate matter and in precipitation leaches into the soil, where symbiotic nitrogen-fixing bacteria swarm root hairs of bayberry, sweet fern and other nitrogen-fixing plants, according to Tiffney and Eveleigh. Expanding exponentially, the bacteria kindle root nodules, bulges comprising the bacteria and the plant's cells inside of which the bacteria convert nitrogen into ammonium nitrate and nitrite on which these types of plants rely as food. With this built-in plant food source, essential to plants in poor soils like Nantucket's, these scrappy plants may well have crowded out less competitive heath plants with their superior survival skills and thus helped scrub oak to proliferate. "We suggest that the nitrogen-fixing nodular associations on bayberry roots provide significant amounts of nitrogen to the plant, contributing to its success in competition on nutrient-impoverished soils. We conclude that successful invasion of heaths and dunes by bayberry leads to diverse shrub cover in these areas."

17 Dunwiddie believes the Eastern pitch pine species was a pine that grew on Nantucket's land mass after a warmer climate escorted tundra vegetation northward, not a human-introduced species: "Although the pollen record indicates that pitch pine occurred naturally on the island in the early Holocene, it appears to have been scarce or absent by the time of European settlement. It was finally reintroduced in 1847, when Josias Sturgis planted pitch pine seeds on Nantucket Island; his example was followed by others in the following decade. This planting resulted in the gradual increase of pine pollen, as evidenced in the uppermost 20 centimeters of both cores. The percentage of pine pollen in the cores increased still further in the 20th Century as the pines spread and additional planting was carried out in the State Forest in the early 1900s."

18 In the Nantucket Conservation Foundation's research of Nantucket's heathlands, reported in *Natural Habitats of Nantucket*, to get a sense of how these scrub oak/pitch pine barrens would evolve through time, the NCF compared Nantucket's moors (omitting the variables of prescribed burns and mowing) with the former barrens of Cape Cod: "On Cape Cod, many former barrens communities have already reverted to upland forests because of the

lack of periodic fire or other disturbances. Because of Nantucket's recent history of sheep grazing, mature forests are still relatively rare on the island. However, given time and the absence of fire, many scrub oak barren communities here will eventually become similar to the forests on Cape Cod today."

19. Coastal Plain Pond Shores, those edges of kettle hole ponds, Dunwiddie and Sorrie say, alternate between drought-year and wet-year species, "in which water levels fluctuate widely both seasonally and annually. The substrate is often sandy, but may be mucky as well. Species composition varies widely between years depending on water levels. In wet years, vegetation may be sparse, with only a few emergent and floating-leaved aquatics present. In dry years, a dense growth of small herbaceous species appears. Characteristic species include several species of St. Johnswort (*Hypericum boreale, H. canadense, H. adpressum*), spatulate-leaved sundew (*Drosera intermedia*), golden hedge-hyssop (*Gratiola aurea*), yellow-eyed grass (*Xyris torta*), Northern meadow beauty (*Rhexia virginica*), lance-leaved violet (*Viola lanceolata*), brown beaksedge (*Rhynchospora capitellata*), and tinklegrass (*Agrostis hyemalis*, var. *scabra*). Several rushes (*Juncus militaris, J. Effusus, J. Canadensis, J. pelocarpus*) are common as emergents. Some of Nantucket's rarest plants are pondshore specialists: Annual umbrella-sedge (*Fuirena pumila*), slender marsh-pink (*Sabitia campanulata*), pondshore nutsedge (*Sceleria reticularis*), and three-angled spikesedge (*Eleocharis tricostata*)."

20. A general description from ecologist E. C. Pielou of how pre-glacial vegetation reacted to the advance of the ice sheet is that the ice first decimated and covered vegetated areas and, after retreating, left conditions suitable only for tundra plant species: "The responses of vegetation to growing ice sheets on the one hand, and to shrinking ice sheets on the other, were entirely different. When an ice sheet expanded, one of two things happened, depending on the cause of the expansion. If the ice spread because of climatic cooling, then the cooling would also have affected the vegetation ahead of the ice front. The less hardy plants gradually died off, and permafrost [perennially frozen ground] formed, seriously inhibiting the growth of trees. In other words, a strip of tundra would have developed or, if one was already there, it would have widened ahead of the ice. But if the surging ice lobes caused the expansion [see the first chapter], full-grown forests would have been overrun by ice, which crushed and buried them."

21. According to Dunwiddie and Sorrie, other species include pondshore flatshed, softstem bullsedge, saltmarsh threesquare, mudwort, shore pygmyweed, saltpond flatsedge, saltpond grass, saltpond pennywort, saltpond dock and low cudweed.

22. Although some botanists knowledgeable about Nantucket wetland vegetation have said that Nantucket contains no true swamps, Dunwiddie and Sorrie detail at least two in their island vascular plants book, and Dunwiddie says the term "swamp" can be applied across a wide spectrum of wetland habitats: "The bigger swamps are probably too large to have been formed by melting ice blocks (the typical origin of kettles), and were probably formed, again, by topographical features and substrate materials in the moraine and outwash plains that impeded drainage. Generally, where there is some through-flow of water, they tend not to become so acid, and hence don't develop into a classic bog."

23. The Nantucket Conservation Foundation, through its research on the island's wetlands and the plant species on NCF properties, details another picture of plant succession in the Habitats section on their Web site: "Immediately after a pond is formed, nature begins to reclaim the land at its shallow edges. Emergent wetland plants that colonize this area form a thick mat of root stalks and vegetation just below the water's surface. This becomes covered with plant debris that settles and decays, gradually replacing the shallow water with damp, organic soil. Wetland shrubs, such as sweet pepperbush and high bush blueberry,

are then able to colonize these areas, crowding out aquatic plants and thereby reducing the size of the pond."

24 According to the Nantucket Conservation Foundation's Ponds and Bogs section of its online Habitats page, "As the top portions of these plants grow, the underlying layers become deprived of sunlight and die. Thick mats of dead Sphagnum gradually accumulate and become compressed by the weight of the waterlogged plants above them. Highly acidic conditions prevent this material from completely decaying, and it builds up and forms extensive layers of organic material called peat. At this point, natural succession has transformed the pond into a bog, and most of the visible areas of open water are gone. Other plants, such as cotton grass and swamp azalea, are then able to colonize the bog's peaty surface."

25 In addition to acidifying the waterlogged soil in which it lives by the decaying of its dead plants, sphagnum moss also absorbs cations (positively charged ions), including magnesium and calcium, from the soil and releases hydrogen ions, the very essence of acidity, into the soil, further contributing to the poor soil conditions in which only a select cadre of specialized plants can exist.

26 Cranberry cultivation may be best explained by Nantucket's modern bog owner and operator, the Nantucket Conservation Foundation. "Cranberry vines are planted by gently pushing vine trimmings into a prepared bog that has been leveled and covered with a layer of sand. New plantings must grow for about three years before they will bear harvestable fruit. If properly cared for, the 6-to-8-inch-tall plant will produce berries indefinitely. Modern management practices include weeding in the spring, fertilizing in the summer, pruning in the fall to keep the vines at their optimum length, and periodic re-sanding in the winter. A complex water distribution system must irrigate the bogs in dry weather. This same system is also used to protect flower buds and the ripe berries from spring and fall frosts. Also, flooding is required during the fall harvest and throughout the winter months to minimize the effects of cold and wind damage." Read the complete cranberry story at www.nantucketconservation.com/page.php?section=1&page=cranberry_bogs.

BIRDS—NATURALS AND ACCIDENTALS

1 Commonly referred to as krill, the primary diet of baleen and blue whales, the crustaceans that long-tail ducks eat are similar in their shrimp appearance but are not krill. Generally described as amphipod crustaceans, *Gammarus anulatus* also appear in staggering numbers off Nantucket in the winter and, packed with protein, are what draw long-tail ducks to this part of the Atlantic Ocean each winter.

2 Living or spending large blocks of time on Nantucket tends to spoil birders, especially when it comes to raptors, which appear in such abundance on Nantucket. E. Vernon Laux, property manager and resident naturalist at the Linda Loring Nature Foundation off Eel Point Road on the North Head of Long Pond, notes, "The thing about Nantucket is it's really good because it's so open. It's a fantastic place to see raptors. The density of red-tailed hawks [is high], and we have the highest breeding density of Northern harriers of anywhere in the world. Two years ago, there were 56 nesting pairs discovered on Nantucket. They're a threatened species elsewhere in the state, so it's fantastic to come to a place where they're common. I see them every day. I mean, that stuff doesn't really happen anywhere else."

3 The Atlantic Flyway works well for migrating birds, because they have no mountains or hills to fly over and because the necessities of air travel—food, water and cover—are abundant along its length; however, there are three other flyways running north to south across North America. The migration route of the Mississippi Flyway tracks a swath of the continent from

Canada along the Mackenzie River to the Mississippi River down to the Gulf of Mexico. The Central Flyway fans out from Central Canada down into the Great Plains of the United States and ends along the western and northwestern coasts of the Gulf of Mexico. And following the Pacific Flyway, birds travel between Alaska and Patagonia, South America.

4 From the Georges Bank and other locations off of Massachusetts, commercial fishermen have been dredging up the teeth and bones of large mammals that once roamed the coastal plain, because these fossilized remains were tough enough to survive thousands of years in the ground beneath the ocean. Archeology Consultant Tonya Largy, laboratory assistant and preparator at the Peabody Museum of Harvard University, notes that fossils from any living thing do not always appear in great numbers in most places. Avian fossils, delicate as they would be, might not survive being unearthed and brought to the surface by fishing gear. A case in point, says Largy: "Teeth of extinct sharks were recovered from the soils of the Lucy Vincent Beach site on Martha's Vineyard. There probably is a geological explanation for their presence in the dry sands of the site, which is actually located on a bluff above the beach. Preservation means that organic remains, including bones, must survive degradation. There must be certain conditions for preservation to occur. Bones that are found in excavations are only a sample of what was once discarded on a site. Recovery means that proper systematic methods must be used to actually separate the bones from the soils. In the old days, archaeologists never screened for artifacts and materials such as bones or plant remains and so large amounts of data were lost."

5 At Cornell University's Lab of Ornithology, where they seemingly know everything there is to know about birds, Irby Lovette, director of the Fuller Evolutionary Biology Program, can say with fair certainty that Nantucket has some very old birds. Lovette says, "Very few (if any) birds have split into separate species in your time frame (late Pleistocene/early Holocene). Most existing forms that we classify as separate species split hundreds of thousands of years ago, or longer. So what was present on Nantucket in the late Pleistocene/early Holocene would be species we know today, plus any that have gone extinct (maybe Labrador Duck, Great Auk, Heath Hen?). Sea mink too."

6 As the Grateful Dead say, "I'm goin' where the climate suits my clothes" (from "Goin' Down the Road Feelin' Bad"). This is an apt description of how present-day avian species moved in and out of our area, depending on climate as regulated by the advance-retreat-advance-retreat movement of the glacier. To put it in Dick Veit's words, "Depending on how far away the ice edge was, presumably when the ice first left, that must have been tundra habitat. So there could have been nesting shorebirds and waterfowl that are restricted to tundra. I don't think there's any evidence of that in terms of bones or birds, but I . . . think it would be likely that the tundra nesting [species] could have been there for a while as the glaciers receded, and then, presumably, there would have been a shift through boreal birds as the climate got warmer as habitats went through that spruce stage, pine and then eventually oak."

7 Although market gunners and the companies they shot for knew well enough where their targets were from season to season, no single group knew the destructive cumulative effects of market gunning on American's bird species better than conservationists. In 1912, the State of Massachusetts published a then-recent history of the overall decline in bird species in the Commonwealth, blaming, among other devastating dynamics, the market gunning industry for the decimation of scores of species and the extinction of several others, including the passenger pigeon and the great auk: "The chief causes of the decrease of game are market hunters, spring shooting, the sale and export of game, overshooting generally, and the destruction of breeding places of birds by settlement, agriculture and lumbering. All these

destructive influences have been augmented by the great improvements in firearms, and their cheapness. The improvement and extension of means of transportation have widened considerably the activities of the gunner. Steamboat lines, railroads, electric cars and automobiles are tremendous factors in the destruction of game. The extension of the rail service and of the telephone and telegraph, combined with sportsmen's journals as a medium of advertising, have opened up the whole country, so that the gunner can get information from all parts of it and follow the game wherever it appears. Most settlers, many lumbermen and some farmers live more or less upon game."

8 Ginger Andrews, daughter of Edith Andrews and the late Clinton Andrews—Edith being Nantucket's preeminent bird expert and Clinton an extremely knowledgeable, self-taught island naturalist in his time—helped in the interview of her mother for this book. At many times during the interview, she contributed bits of historical information on the island's birds. From her father, she knew the reason for burning the land for game birds and imparted this information here: "That was the original purpose of the prescribed burning. Dad told me they would wait for a northwest wind, and they'd go up to Head of the Valleys by Milestone Road and let 'em fire off and burn to shore. And in those days, the island was very grassland. There were very few shrubs and trees. Their version of the fire safety patrol was a team of horses and a plow, so that tells you that the flame heights were so low that you could control it by plowing a furrow down and furrow back, and just the bare ground was enough to stop it. The shorebirds would be attracted to that burned area, as they are today, finding [food], and then [gunners] could shoot them, of course—no convenient grass to hide in [and] abundant food."

9 As millinery reached a decade-long crescendo in the 1890s, not only plumage but whole birds were being used to decorate hats. Public outrage over the mass killing of birds for these purposes began to grow, as well. Frank M. Chapman's answer to the Christmas Day Side Hunts was only part of the beginning. Fourteen years earlier, George Bird Grinnell, owner and editor of *Forest and Stream*, started the first version of the Audubon Society in 1886 to promote and expand the work of ornithologist, explorer, and wildlife artist John James Audubon. Although this early iteration of the National Audubon Society failed in 1888 because Grinnell lacked the time to manage it, several high society Boston women founded the Massachusetts Audubon Society in 1896. This provided the impetus for 14 other states to follow suit during the following three years. While the Audubon societies drew attention to the plight of imperiled bird species and lobbied for their protection, state and federal acts adopted over the next two decades made laws out of these grassroots efforts. In the same year as Chapman's inaugural bird count, Congress adopted the Lacy Act of 1900, which banned the shipping of birds and mammals between states when their shippers violated state laws. The National Audubon Society figured heavily in the adoption of the Audubon Act of 1911, which prohibited feathers of native wild birds from being sold in New York, and the federal Migratory Bird Treaty Act of 1918, which banned the capturing or killing of many non-game bird species. Because of the National Audubon Society's efforts, gulls, terns, American and snowy egrets, waterfowl and several species of insect-eating birds were saved from possible extinction. And in many respects, broader-scope federal environmental acts that followed, including the Clean Air, Clean Water, Wild and Scenic Rivers and the Endangered Species Acts, went a long way toward increasing protection for all bird species in the U.S.

10 Nantucket's most knowledgeable bird expert, Edith Andrews, with Ludlow Griscom, published the book, *The Birds of Nantucket*, in 1948. Key to knowing island birds is understanding the weather. As Andrews and Griscom detailed, "The climate of Nantucket is profoundly

modified by its insularity, the chief tendency being a greater evenness, with less difference between extremes of heat and cold, as compared with Boston. In a heat wave the temperature will be 15 degrees cooler at Nantucket than at Boston. The spring and early summer are cold, raw and foggy, the fogs sometimes lasting through July. But late summer and early fall are superb, the climate progressively milder than Boston as the season advances. Severe killing frost will sometimes be a month later. The winter is usually mild and open. While snow is frequent each year, it is rare for it to remain on the ground more than a week. In really mild winters, the ponds never freeze over."

11 Birds that have lost their bearings make up a significant percentage of those that can be found on the island at any given time, but, says Laux, many of them intended to end their journey on the mainland. "For land birds, because of Nantucket's geographic location, all the incectarious birds that breed in Northern Canada in spruce forests or inland are nocturnal migrants. . . . The predominant wind direction in the fall [on Nantucket] and the ideal night wind for migrating is a northwest wind, and if you think of where Nantucket is, [and that] northwest means the wind is coming from the northwest . . . if a bird is on that wind, it is traveling to the southeast, so Nantucket is the furthest thing southeast anywhere off the New England Coastline. A lot of birds, it's their first migration, they screw up, they get blown too far to sea, and there are days here in September, October when just anywhere along the south or east side and all day long, you'll see little exhausted birds flying in from [the ocean] . . . they went 200 miles too far. I've often seen groups of herring gulls, laughing gulls out on the beach on nights when there are a lot of white-throated sparrows and small sparrows, exhausted birds, coming in, and they're sort of knocking them in the water and eating them."

FERAL KINGDOM

1   Other than the discovery of the Muskeget vole by Miller and the identification of it by Baird, there exists scant research on this former meadow vole and hardly any on its breeding abilities and its current population status. In a paper they wrote in 1974, Thomas H. Kunz and Robert H. Tamarin detail some of Miller's observations of the Muskeget vole's adaptation to its new environment: "In habits, the beach vole closely resembles the meadow vole, *Microtus pennsylvanicus*. Runways are constructed above ground through the beach grass. In open areas, runways are less distinct. The runways often contain grass cuttings. The nests are constructed both above and below ground. Tunnels seem more common in winter. Nests containing young resemble those of *Microtus pennsylvanicus*, and may be constructed at the base of golden rod (Solidago) or beneath fragments of wreckage. If no such shelter is available, these voles construct short burrows (from 30 to 60 cm long) at a steep slope of 45 degrees, presumably to reach more rapidly the moist, compact sand below. The end of the tunnel is filled with a bulky nest. Apparently the beach vole prefers the lower, wetter, grassy areas and during periods of low abundance they are restricted to this habitat."

2. Although Tamarin and Kunz stand by their belief that the Muskeget vole is its own breed, at the end of their 1974 paper in their Remarks section, they list some of their colleagues' challenges: "M. breweri has gone through several taxonomic revisions, and its species status today is still questioned by some. The specific name breweri is commemorative, proposed to honor Dr. T. M. Brewer, its discoverer. Allen (1869) reduced A. breweri to a race of the meadow vole, A. riperius [=pennsylvanicus], because some beach voles were of the ordinary color, and some meadow voles, living on the sand dunes of Ipswich, Massachusetts, had a light color similar to that of the beach vole. Merriam again in 1888,

elevated the beach vole to species status. Starrett (1958), on the basis of pelage color and cranial characteristics supported a specific status for M. breweri. Wetherbee et al. (1972), however, reported that they have cross bred beach and meadow voles in the laboratory. They give no further details, and it is doubtful this fact will change the species status of this insular taxon."

3 E. C. Pielou found in the research for his book that mastodons might have been more abundant during the Pleistocene Epoch than the woolly mammoths around region of the Cape and Islands because: "Mastodon teeth have been found in much greater number than mammoth teeth. This may imply that mastodons were more numerous than mammoths, or it may merely result from the greater strength of mastodon teeth, which are less likely to disintegrate than those of mammoths. In any case, the presence of mastodons almost certainly implies a supply of coniferous trees for them to browse on. It is harder to deduce conditions from the mammoth finds because they do not completely match any known collections from other regions. They are comparatively small and may represent a dwarf variety of the woolly mammoth. If so, it seems reasonable to conclude that the vegetation consisted of a mixture of tundra (for the mammoths) and coniferous parkland and black spruce (for the mastodons)."

4 Beattie experienced a great example of the skill and speed of white-tailed deer in the water while walking her dogs in Ram Pasture: "My dogs one time chased a deer that was bedded down in Ram Pasture. It jumped up and ran into west Hummock Pond, and they were right on its tail. The deer was outrunning them, but when it went into the water . . . I thought, 'Oh, God, I've got couple retrievers, they're good swimmers, they're going to catch up to it and they're going to get a hoof in the head or something.' That deer outswam my Chesapeake and my Labrador. I couldn't believe how fast—once it got going, it was like a motorboat. . . . It would have to have some serious stamina to make it from Monomoy [Island] to Great Point, but I've seen them swimming in the harbor from Coatue. I've heard other people say they've seen it, too."

5 Like Monomoy Island's temporary natural bridge between the mainland and its southern end, Nantucket and its other two islands experienced the same mammal range and distribution. According to Dr. Tom French, "The same thing was happening with Nantucket. As long as there was even a low tide connection, things were making those crossings. You'll see foxes even today out on salt marshes and even mudflats, foraging, so they have no qualms about going out over open space, and coyotes and deer still swim great distances, and even raccoons will do it. I found a raccoon washed up dead on Nomans Land Island. Who knows where that animal came from? And you know, not all of them make it. We had coyotes wash up dead on the Vineyard several times before we finally had a live one out there, and now we have at least one, if not more coyotes, on the Vineyard. (We have, we think, just one for the time being.) So yes, it's dynamic. But as long as there's an opportunity [for] these midsize carnivores, they're quite mobile, they're middle-size animals, they're not like mice; they can cover some ground in a day."

6 Eastern cottontail rabbit distribution in Massachusetts happened not because this species hopped northward from its northern range limit in New York state, but with human help. French explains, "First of all, the Eastern cottontail is not native to Massachusetts, so probably the only rabbit native to Nantucket in recent [history] is the New England cottontail. Now, I have no doubt that there were native populations, at some time during the geologic history, of the snowshoe hare as well. . . . The native range [of the Eastern cottontail] went as far south as extreme southeastern New York. That was the northern range of the Eastern cottontail. They were liberated in many states. Two hundred forty Kansas

cottontails were liberated in Massachusetts in 1924. Sixteen thousand were imported from the Midwest to the state between 1924 and 1941. At least 4,600 were transplanted to mainland Massachusetts from a rearing colony on Penikese Island in Dukes County, so Penikese Island was a rabbit-rearing facility that our agency set up for a time, the concept being that you get these fluctuations in rabbit populations, which are quite dramatic: you can have rabbits everywhere and then virtually no rabbits. And the belief was that you could raise them in a different place. Penikese, being offshore, wouldn't be susceptible to that same cycle, and then when that cycle was down on the mainland, you could bring rabbits from the islands and repopulate the mainland, so that happened."

7   For whatever reasons, island residents, the town and the state thought it prudent to introduce several rabbit species on the island from 1889 through 1977. French details more of the introductions here: "Black-tail jackrabbit: 25 pair were released on Nantucket Island in 1889. . . . Additional releases from an unknown source were made by the Nantucket Harriers Hunt Club from 1925 through the early 1940s. . . . Six confiscated jackrabbits from the Middleboro greyhound track were released on Nantucket in May 1975. Small numbers continued to persist. Fourteen were seen at the Nantucket airport by Jim Cardoza [MassWildlife's director in 2011] in 1977 and one at Coatue in the mid-1980s. A shipment of 50 jackrabbits was received from Kansas in 1920. Twenty survived and were liberated on Martha's Vineyard but did not become established. Best I can tell . . . it appears that jackrabbits are no longer out there, but who knows? One could pop up."

8   MassWildlife is well aware of the places around Massachusetts where New England cottontail rabbits are doing just fine; French said that half of their efforts are to protect these healthy pockets: "Our motherload of New England cottontails that we're aware of is the upper part of the Cape around Barnstable, Sandwich, Mashpee, Falmouth—that part of the Cape. And so we're spending a substantial amount of money, with grants from the U.S. Fish & Wildlife Service, to improve that habitat for New England cottontails, which means making it very dense and thick with vegetation. We're also toying with the idea of putting them on Nomans Land south of the Vineyard. We're a little concerned about what impacts they'll have on vegetation, but the idea there is that it's a substantially large island, it's a square mile that has no potential competition from Eastern cottontails. And so if we get to the point where we're worried about losing New Englands completely as a species, we're thinking about little reservoirs like that—refugia, as it would be—to hold New England cottontails, but that's a long way off before we make that final decision. We did that on two of the small Boston Harbor islands. They persisted for at least a decade, decade and a half, but they appear now to have disappeared and it's the same problem. It's this normal population fluctuation they go through being in really enormous numbers and then totally crashing. Most of those times, they survive it, but every now and then those crashes are terminal for the whole population."

9   French, in agreement with Johnson, is perplexed by the absence of river otters on Nantucket. "First of all, it's a mystery to me why you don't have a lot of them there now. As I said earlier, there are a lot of otters on the Vineyard. Otters are perfectly capable of swimming from the mainland to Nantucket; they don't have any problem swimming from the Vineyard to Nantucket. . . . That doesn't mean they won't be downstream a little bit, but they are extraordinarily good swimmers and they have endurance. If they get tired, they can rest. . . . I found an otter den in an embankment on Nomans Land one year. That's [three] miles off the Vineyard, and that's a hike. It's also a gamble. It's not a very big target in a very big ocean heading south of the Vineyard, especially when I can't believe for a minute that an otter can see it. But that was a one-year phenomenon."

ENDNOTES

WETLAND CREATURES

1. Nantucket's Moth Suppression Reports later came under the successive report headings of "Insect Control Report," then "Tree Commission" and, finally, "Pest Control within the Department of Public Works Report." Scary as it seems, given what we now know of the harmful effects of DDT on wildlife, in 1966, when this town department was formed, the state considered DDT use to make good land conservation sense. The following entry in Voorneveld's 1949 report was, "The State made no charge for the use of the helicopter or the 70 barrels of DDT of 500 pounds each shipped here via air freight. The cost of the insecticide and helicopter service to the state was between $6,000 and $7,000. The complete area of 2,500 acres was sprayed."

2. Although there is no hard evidence of significant reptile and amphibian consumption in the diet of Native Americans living on Nantucket, a passage from the "Native Americans and the Environment" section of *The Encyclopedia of New England* is descriptive of the lengths to which our island natives went for food. "New England Indians no doubt possessed extensive knowledge of the natural world. They collectively defined as edible an extraordinary variety of terrestrial, riverine and marine resources, including seals, white-tailed deer, moose, beavers, rabbits, turkeys, passenger pigeons, migratory waterfowl, and various crustacea, shellfish, and fish, as well as nuts, seeds, and berries. Many resources varied seasonally and geographically, and Indians developed diverse strategies to exploit them. During the 17th century, people often moved according to the season from coastal sites near crops and maritime food supplies to inland sites near deer and other terrestrial and riverine resources. . . ."

3. The search for the spadefoot toad on Nantucket by those who haven't given up on its existence here will likely drive those still on the hunt crazy. But maybe not for long, as seemingly extirpated species have reappeared in the past Opines McKenna-Foster, "[M]aybe it's here, but maybe it's been extirpated, maybe it's gone now. There are only [about] two records around 1965 and 1993. And the last record was way before that time. Both [newer] records are from Madequecham Valley. So the question is: are there other populations on the island that we just missed? Are the populations still in Madequecham Valley? So there are little mysteries."

4. Smyers was impressed with the DNA marker research in which O'Dell and her partner at Wheaton College were involved, but from his perspective, a DNA marker doesn't signify much. Smyers puts more store in actual physical differences, morphology of the turtles, their behavior and life history variability between populations—such divergence as female egg-laying frequency, egg incubation at varying temperatures, the time it takes juveniles to reach sexual maturity, longevity and maturity size, and length of reproductive activity. Even if no difference in DNA is found between mainland and Nantucket populations of spotted turtles, these characteristics have been proven "to vary in some of our more common, successful species on a relatively short geographic separation," according to Smyers.

IT'S A BUG'S ISLAND

1. At the molecular level, chitin is a polysaccharide, similar in consistency to cellulose, that is composed of blocks of a glucose derivative, N-acetyl-D-glucosamine, forming a long chain. The resulting material provides a tough protective shell, called an exoskeleton, for arthropods. This shell doesn't grow but molts when a new shell is created by a secretion from the interior skin of the animal, allowing the creature to grow.

2. The Nantucket Conservation Foundation hires commercial apiarists to truck in hives of honeybees to pollinate their cranberry plants each season, but in the area there are also

amateur beekeepers' bees looking for nectar and other species, including certain wasp species, bumblebees and hummingbirds, that do a large portion of this pollinating work for Nantucket's cranberry crops. And it's a good thing that honeybees have help; as the Maria Mitchell Association's Director of Natural Science, Andrew McKenna-Foster explains, "Honeybees are being hit by various things causing the colonies to collapse. . . . The whole pollination issue is big one right now."

3 Since recorded history began, thousands of years after the 27 outer islands of Southeastern Massachusetts already had their complement of plants and animals, entomologists and biologists in general, seeking to paint a picture of the species of arthropods that existed on the coastal plain, have had to rely on fossil evidence. Plant pollen, Paul Goldstein says, is a solid clue toward ancient insects, because at least entomologists know what species relied on which plants. Stevens's thesis holds that an admixture or mosaic of plant communities, containing many of the floral elements (species) we see today, hosted herbivorous insects. But, (Goldstein continues), evaluating the structural composition of Pleistocene plant communities is difficult and controversial enough without superimposing assumptions about which insects may have been around or when they arrived. There are species that appear to be Pleistocene relicts, species whose origins probably lay in their having been isolated in the wake of the glaciers. One such is the Water Willow stem-borer *Papaipema sulphurata*, perhaps the only insect known to be endemic to Massachusetts, which is found only in the Cape and Islands region.

4 For the four deer tick infections to exist in a given area, a blood meal source must share the same habitat as the ticks. Telford and Tiffney theorized that the infections within this archipelago might have been maintained by ticks surviving on white-footed mice that lived on Muskeget and Coatue after Native Americans and European settlers killed off all the deer.

5 Mello said he couldn't explain the decline of and eventual disappearance of the regal fritillary from Nantucket, because its primary food plants are still growing on Nantucket. In his 1930 book, *A List of Insect Fauna of Nantucket, Massachusetts,* Johnson reported that Samuel H. Scudder recorded in his own book, *Butterflies of New England,* published in 1889, that he surveyed butterflies during several seasons on Nantucket in the 1880s and found the regal fritillary in abundance, along with the little sulfur butterfly and a few others west and southwest of Gibbs Pond.

6 The existence of island arthropod species over Nantucket's entire span of history is an educated guess based on fossil and pollen records, and entomologists believe they may have been on our portion of the coastal plain prior to the arrival of the glacier and after it retreated northward grounded in climate tolerability. Johnson and Kimball's insect and arachnid survey results and those of modern day entomologists are then only painting a small corner of the arthropod historical canvas. As Goldstein elaborates, "The furthest back we have any direct evidence is only about a century, but we can still point to the fact that the moth (and butterfly) fauna seems to have tracked changes in the landscape associated with shrinking open areas and a return of more forested habitat types. When we compare the faunas of Nantucket with those of Martha's Vineyard, we can make more inferences about what might have been on Nantucket prior to European colonization and subsequent removal of forest for agriculture. We know that the Vineyard has a greater complement of forest Lepidoptera than Nantucket, for example, and we've seen the appearance on both islands of many moth species typically associated with forested habitats during the last century since the shrinkage of open, post-agricultural landscapes."

7 Purseweb spiders get their name from the webs of silk they build to catch their food. Weaving a cylindrical, purse-like tube of silk about six inches long that descends from the base of woody plants or deciduous trees down through grass or leaf litter into the ground, the purse web spider hides in its silk "purse," and when an insect or worm passes over it, the spider sinks its fangs into its victim from within the purse and pulls it in close to kill and eat it.

8 Although the reintroduction participants buried the dead quails containing these beetles in the ground, the beetles preserve their animal of choice with anal and oral secretions. They then lay eggs that hatch in 12 to 14 days. The 25 to 30 enormous larvae that emerge also pupate in the animal carcass and then dig themselves out of the ground in the fall to eat what they can find. The pupae then hibernate during the winter and begin the process all over again as adults in the spring. During their larval and pupal stages, their parents actually feed their young by putting food in their mouths.

WATER: SALT AND FRESH

1 Curley says that eelgrass is an indicator species: like coral and frogs, they are species that react quickly to their environment. Eelgrass, she says, will begin to thin out and may disappear altogether as water quality and light availability begin and continue to downgrade. Eelgrass has a low tolerance for nutrients in the water, such as nitrogen and heavy metals from road runoff. It also requires abundant sunshine to thrive and, to certain extent, a density of plants. Hence, large boats, many boats closely moored together, boat docks and piers can shade eelgrass from the sun. Too many nutrients in the water will cause algae blooms; combined with increased sediments, they can increase turbidity, further cutting out sunlight. Boat moorings, with their tackle chains dragging on the bottom of the harbor, can scour entire sections of eelgrass from the sandy floor. And epiphytes, opportunistic plants that attach to eelgrass blades to live, also decrease the eelgrass plant's surface area for light absorption, as well as the surface area available for scallop larvae to attach. Curley is a bit skeptical of these factors, because eelgrass blades grow from their bottom up. However, all of these variables together contribute to decreased eelgrass densities in the harbor.

2 Oldale reasoned that Nantucket and Tuckernuck's south shore valleys and ponds were created by the churning waters of the glacial water, and his theory appears to explain what Shaler calls the "most peculiar feature of the southern plains." In his report, Shaler couldn't discern the origin of what he called "broad channels," but he recognized Hither, Broad, Narrow and Further Creeks to be the remains of such channels, similar to those that filled in with fresh water to create Miacomet, Hummock and Long Ponds, as well as the valleys that once contained ponds, such as Forked, Toupshue, Madequecham, Nobadeer and Weweeder Ponds, Great and Little Mioxes Ponds, and the Slough on Tuckernuck's east end. The outwash valleys that became the four creeks would have been cut deeper than these, and when the ocean flooded Nantucket Sound, they would have filled in with water. By the time Shaler did his survey, all that remained of them were short indentations on the inside of Smith's Point. All in all, Shaler counted 23 of these channels, depressions or troughs (he used the terms interchangeably) along the south shores of Nantucket and Tuckernuck.

3 Horseshoe crabs, survivors of more than 400 million years of evolution, most certainly were some of the first animals to wander in from Nantucket Sound and colonize Nantucket's harbors. Once so abundant that they were used as fertilizer in 1930s, their population was depleted by that practice, which forced the closing of the fishery. Between the 1940s and

1970s, the species rebounded significantly. Although whelk and eel fishermen now swear by horseshoe crabs as bait, prizing them above all others because the scent of their eggs is a powerful attractant, these crabs are most famous for the use of their blood in detecting poisonous endotoxins before they enter the body through injections and other medical procedures. Johns Hopkins researcher Dr. Frederik Bang and Dr. Jack Levin at the Marine Biological Laboratory in Woods Hole, Massachusetts, found amebocytes in the blue blood of horseshoe crabs in the 1960s. The extract this pair discovered, Limulus Amebocyte Lysate, led to an endotoxin test that is now required by the U.S. Food and Drug Administration on all human and animal injectables, medical devices used to deliver these injectables, many implantable devices, and artificial kidneys used for renal dialysis. The extract costs $15,000 a pint, fueling a multi-million-dollar industry. However, the crabs are not killed for the blood but drained just enough to continue to live, and then they are released. They are also the main "roadside" food of migratory shorebirds flying north to Arctic breeding areas. The red knot, ruddy turnstone, semipalmated plover, least sandpiper, pectoral sandpiper, black-bellied sandpiper, sanderling and dowitcher all dine on horseshoe crab eggs in the Delaware Bay estuary.

4 Halliwell, Hartel and Launer detail in their book, *Inland Fishes of Massachusetts*, southern and northern routes that freshwater fish species used to find their way back into Massachusetts and the rest of Northern New England. They theorize that most of Nantucket's pond fish moved back in from the south and possibly from the east from Georges Bank. Estimate this trio, "The current distribution pattern of fishes along the Atlantic coastal plain indicates that the majority of Massachusetts freshwater fish species survived the glacier in refugia along the coast, probably as far south as North Carolina (Schmidt 1986), or in areas off the present Connecticut coast (Whitworth 1996). A northern coastal refugium in the vicinity of Georges Bank has also been suggested, and this area might account for some of the forms found on Cape Cod and the Islands."

5 An upland area after the glacier receded, the three Nantucket islands were isolated from the major waterways on the mainland, and this has meant that human intervention has played a large role in determining which fish have found their way into island ponds. At one time or another existing in the island's freshwater and brackish ponds, these are Nantucket's pond fish: white perch, yellow perch, pumpkin seed (sunfish), white crappie, black crappie, catfish, Northern pike, chain pickerel, swamp darter, golden shiner, blueback herring, American eel, small-mouth bass, large-mouth bass, striped bass, pipefish, mummichugs, killifish, Atlantic silversides, smelt, mullet and sticklebacks. As with any Nantucket list, however, any given Nantucket fisherman will probably have several species to add to this list and several from this list to refute.

6 In Appendix No. 2 of "A Report of The Committee on Long Pond Madaket Ditch" submitted to Town Meeting on March 20, 1882, the following excerpts from the minutes of various municipal meetings shed light on the creation of the Madaket Ditch and the management of its and Long Pond's resources: "The first action taken by the Proprietors is without date, the last previous record being dated Oct. 1665: At a meeting at Nantucket the Inhabitants agree to dig a Trench to drean the Long Pond forthwith with regard to a Ware for taking fish and also for making Meadow the work to be carried on thus the one half of the work is to be done by the Indians the other half by the English Inhabitants or owners the Indians to have one half the fish so long as they tend to the Weare carefully. Jan. 4th, 1674.—Voted by the Town that Mr. Thomas Macy shall have the benefit of the fish

ENDNOTES

in Long Pond if he lets it out. Feb. 9th, 1676.—At a Legal Town Meeting Granted Thomas Macy and Peter Coffin their heirs and assigns Sole liberty for fishing in Creek at Little Neck and Weare near Madaket on condition that they Set down their Weares or Nets 12 months and furnish Such as they catch to the town on reasonable terms as two Indifferent men shall judge if they do not agree themselves this Grant to Stand for ten years provided they improve it as opportunity presents. May 22nd, 1730.—Voted that the Proprietry will dig a Trench through Mattaket to drean the same in order to make feed for Cattle and for taking Alewives and other fish Committee chosen to carry the above Vote into effect Proprietors to suitably reward said Committee."

7 In trying to find a permanent way through the Nantucket Bar, despite the surveying help, funding and engineers from the U.S. Government, plus privately funded dredging projects—the camels and the pier and rock breakwater musings—the island community beached itself in this endeavor because its citizens couldn't agree on which method to employ. Stackpole noted this in his 1940 *Historic Nantucket* article: "Thus the year 1829 saw the last attempt at cutting a channel through Nantucket Bar, until the jetties were built more than half a century later. It is a curious fact that during the period from 1820 to 1830 Nantucket approached its zenith as the leading whaling port of the world, and its interests were duly recognized by merchants and politicians alike—and yet the island merchants could not concentrate their desires for adequate channels into the harbor so as to present a single voice for a single plan." Instead of trying to solve this problem, which ultimately hastened the decline of Nantucket whaling, the ship owners, merchants and captains were much more interested in exploring the new whaling grounds around the globe.

8 In Andrews's chapter on quahogs, he wrote that, in 1955, Massachusetts effectively shut down the commercial quahog fishery in Nantucket Sound because it sensed that the dredgers had fished this population down to such a low level that it couldn't recover. They did a survey of the Sound by hiring a hydraulic quahog dredger to dredge the principal beds and discovered a scarcity of this mollusk. Because it could not find any quahogs reproducing, the state ruled that it should end this fishery by dredging up the remaining adult quahogs. But it didn't let any Nantucket fishermen share in this final catch. As Andrews remembers, "The State hired a fleet of Rhode Island boats, whose owner had a market for the quahogs, to come down into the Sound to fish. Their dredges caught large numbers, in some cases filling the vessels in two days. They fished two summers and then the quahogs really were gone."

9 After spawning in the Sargasso Sea, female American eels lay up to four million eggs and then promptly die. From the eggs hatch the larval eels, which metamorphose into juvenile "glass" eels that have no pigmentation as they migrate from salt water into rivers, estuaries, and freshwater lakes and ponds, where their pigmentation changes. Now known as yellow eels, these still-immature American eels can stay in this stage for a few years before migrating from their freshwater habitat and out to the Sargasso Sea, evolving for the last time into sexually mature eels and taking on their adult colors of silver or bronze, a process that begins shortly before they begin migrating to their ocean spawning grounds.

10 Two years after the Harbor and Shellfish Advisory Board was formed by the town, the Marine and Coastal Resources Department began keeping track of the total number of bushels harvested by commercial scallopers fishing Nantucket's waters. The Marine Department logged the bushels taken, the numbers of commercial licenses sold, the average boat price per pound and the total monetary value of each season's catch. This data is presented

in that order. Each year represents the starting year of each season; the commercial scalloping season runs from November 1 to March 31. (The totals for 2011 are as of November 29, 2011.)

Year	Licenses	Bushels	Avg. price/lb.	Value in $$$
1978	329	59,000	$5.22	$2,000,000
1979	435	96,000	$5.34	$3,400,000
1980	379	117,000	$4.70	$3,700,000
1981	331	77,900	$5.20	$2,700,000
1982	304	50,000	$7.10	$2,400,000
1983	294	48,300	$6.13	$2,000,000
1984	326	36,600	$6.74	$1,660,000
1985	300	38,000	$7.80	$2,000,000
1986	240	No data available for this year.		
1987	260	23,000	$5.34	$830,000
1988	280	25,000	$6.68	$1,100,000
1989	252	48,000	$5.50	$2,000,000
1990	440	44,000	$6.29	$1,800,000
1991	330	27,000	$6.00	$1,300,000
1992	340	24,000	$7.00	$1,260,000
1993	320	13,000	$8.75	$853,000
1994	260	28,000	$9.25	$1,940,000
1995	240	13,391	$9.50	$954,108
1996	250	11,100	$10.00	$957,375
1997	270	8,000	$11.50	$577,875
1998	239	5,800	$12.75	$267,750
1999	137	14,000	$13.00	$1,400,000
2000	117	15,000	$13.00	$1,462,500
2001	197	14,500	$10.50	$1,141,800
2002	195	13,900	$10.00	$1,042,500
2003	157	15,600	$10.50	$1,228,500
2004	150	32,500	$9.50	$2,315,625
2005	179	5,500	$12.50	$515,625
2006	147	3,800	$14.50	$413,250
2007	161	16,800	$12.50	$1,575,000
2008	153	8,900	$11.50	$767,625
2009	156	13,800	$9.50	$721,050
2010	164	7,000	$11.50	$644,000
2011	N/A	11,500	$11.50	$1,079,925

11. Unlike a lot of the perceived privileges of living on Nantucket, the islanders held on to their pond rights. In 1684 and 1687, the government of the Province of New York granted the 20 original purchasers of the island, the Trustees of the Freeholders and Commonality of the Town of Sherburne, later incorporated as the Proprietors of the Common and Undivided Lands of Nantucket in 1716, the original patents and grants along with a manor form of government, the right purchase land from the Indians and the right to fishing, hunting, hawking and fowling. In 1691, New York transferred its jurisdiction over the islands of Southeastern Massachusetts to Massachusetts, and these rights were ratified in a special act of the Massachusetts Bay General Court in 1693, essentially preserving intact Nantucket's rights of ownership of its ponds. In 1841, Proprietors voted to convey Long Pond, Madaket Ditch and Madaket Harbor to the town, giving the town total and sole control over these bodies of water, and then in May 1855, a special act of the Massachusetts General Court granted the County of Nantucket the power to make and enforce laws governing the fisheries in all island ponds. At annual Town Meetings in 1856 and 1857, Nantucket voters adopted bylaws and penalties for the governance of its ponds. Nantucket's sovereignty over its ponds was tested in 1954 when Nantucket District Court blocked the state from prosecuting 20-year-old Arthur Styojack and 17-year-old John Cabral for fishing in Long Pond without a license based on the legislation above. To this day, no fishing license is required for pond fishing on Nantucket. Further securing their ownership and rights over Nantucket's ponds, in 1957 Town Meeting voters adopted an article authorizing the two to purchase the remaining 8,700 sheep common shares left over from the 19,440 first created, which "represented the remaining property of the common and undivided real estate on the Island including Great ponds, proprietors roads, etc." on the island owned by the estate of Franklin E. Smith and the Nantucket Cranberry Co. In doing so, the town essentially acquired sole governance of this island property. On June 4, 1957 the state confirmed Nantucket's purchase in a special act of the legislature.

12. Eutrophication is a marine biologist's or limnologist's word for over-enrichment of a body of water by the input of such nutrients as nitrogen, phosphorous, heavy metals and petroleum products from the air by atmospheric deposition—around 70 percent of total pollution—runoff from roads and over land, from over-fertilized lawns and gardens and leaky septic systems contaminating groundwater, which leaches into the pond or harbor, and from sediments beneath the bottom. While low levels of nitrogen, phosphorus and other naturally occurring compounds help marine and freshwater plants grow, when a pond or harbor is overloaded with these—nitrogen in salt water and phosphorus in fresh—growth of various forms of algae explode. While alive, the more microscopic ones kill or stunt shellfish by clogging their gills, which for some, like the bay scallop, also filter out food, and the larger ones smother other plants by blocking out sunlight and starving them of vital energy from photosynthesis. When the algae die, as they decompose, they use up dissolved oxygen in the water, depriving pond and harbor fauna of this food. Add to this potion of contaminants poor circulation—shoaling in the harbors and infrequent and short openings in the ponds—and it's easy to understand how our ponds and harbors get so dirty and are hard to clean up quickly.

A BACKYARD OCEAN

1. The gray seal population in the North Atlantic is expanding because the two largest colonies on earth, found on Sable Island, Nova Scotia, and in the Gulf of St. Lawrence, have grown so large that the competition for food and mates is fierce. Brault and Wood say that, in 2008, 55,400 pups were born on Sable Island and 13,000 in the Gulf of St. Lawrence. Add

the same number of adult females that gave birth to these pups, and that's 136,800 gray seals, not counting the adult males that mated with the females. That's a huge number of seals all competing for mates; for sand lance, which is half of their diet; and for other groundfish in just two areas. Since they range as far south as Long Island, New York, it was just a matter of time before gray seals started a breeding colony on Muskeget, which in 2008 produced 2,000 pups, making the gray seal population there at least 4,000 or more. With Muskeget designated a National Natural Landmark in 1980, largely because it's the only known home of the Muskeget vole, Massachusetts's only endemic species, and the island no longer inhabited year-round, it was just a matter of time before gray seals set up housekeeping on this island.

2 Cold water contains more oxygen than warm water because of Brownian motion, which dictates that molecules in all substances vibrate. Because cold water molecules vibrate slowly, oxygen has more space to dissolve among them, whereas the molecules of warmer water are vibrating faster, leaving less room for oxygen to dissolve.

BIBLIOGRAPHY

Alden, Peter, and Brian Cassie. *Field Guide to New England*. New York: Knopf, 1998. Print.

Allen, Edward. "Curley Orders Deer Slaughter Halted; 84 Slain in Day on Nantucket Island." *The Boston Herald* 12 Feb. 1935. Print.

Amos, William H. *Wildlife of the Islands*. New York: Harry N. Abrams. Print.

Andrew, Jennifer C., and Inga M. Fredland. *A Field Guide to the Marine Life of Nantucket*. Nantucket: The Maria Mitchell Association, 2001. Print.

Andrews, Clinton J. *An Annotated List of the Saltwater Fishes of Nantucket*. Nantucket: The Maria Mitchell Association, 1973. Print.

Andrews, Clinton J. *Fishing Around Nantucket*. Nantucket: The Maria Mitchell Association, 1990. Print.

Andrews, Clinton J. "Indian Fish and Fishing Off Coastal Massachusetts." *Bulletin of the Massachusetts Archeological Society* (1986). Spec. issue of *Historic Nantucket* (1994). Print.

Andrews, Clinton J., and Mark B. Epstein. "Mammals of Nantucket County." Nantucket: The Maria Mitchell Association, 1980. Print.

Andrews, Clinton J., and Wesley N. Tiffney, Jr. "Sesachacha & Sankaty: Pond Opening and Erosion on Nantucket's Eastern Shore." *Historic Nantucket* Spring 1990. Print.

"Atlantic Cod." *FishWatch*. National Marine Fisheries Service, 29 Sept. 2011. Web.

"Atlantic Walrus." *Fisheries and Oceans Canada*. Fisheries and Oceans Canada, 6 Sept. 2008. Web.

Barney, William, Alfred Folger, Alexander Macy and Shubael Worth. *Report of the Committee on Long Pond and Madaket Ditch*. Office of the Town Clerk, Nantucket, 28 Mar. 1882. Print.

Beattie, Karen. Personal interview. 5 Nov. 2010.

Beecroft, Willey Ingraham, Edward Howe Forbush and Herbert Keightley Job. *A History of the Game Birds, Wildfowl and Shore-birds of Massachusetts and Adjacent States*: Massachusetts State Board of Agriculture, 1912. Print.

Belding, David L. *The Works of David L. Belding, M.D., Biologist: Quahaug and Oyster Fisheries, The Scallop Fishery, The Soft-Shell Clam Fishery*. Barnstable County, MA: Cape Cod Cooperative Extension Service, 2004. Print.

Benchley, Rob, and Robert D. Felch. *Keeping the Light: The Epic Move and Preservation of Nantucket's Sankaty Head Lighthouse*. Siasconset, MA: The 'Sconset Trust, 2009. Print.

Benchley, Robert, III, and Wesley N. Tiffney, Jr. "Nantucket's Broad Creek Opening." *Proceedings of the Fifth Symposium on Coastal and Ocean Management, Seattle, WA, May 26–29, 1987*. Ed. Orville T. Magoon. New York: American Society of Civil Engineers, 1987. Print.

Blieler, John, and Peter W. Dunwiddie. "Bogs of Nantucket." Nantucket: The Maria Mitchell Association, 1988. Print.

Blackshaw, Kenneth Turner. "Nantucket's Birding Natural History." *Yesterday's Island*. 23 Nov. 2009, 10 Jan. 2010. Print.

Blount, Bill. Personal interview. 10 Feb. 2012.

Bohne, Catherine L. "Changes in Above Ground Biomass Along a Successional Gradient of Heathland, Nantucket, Massachusetts, or Frolicking with Flora." Sr. Proj. Bard College, 1989. Print.

Brace, Peter B. *Our Natural World*. Nantucket: The Nantucket Independent. 30 Aug. 2006. Print.

Brace, Peter B. "Under the Eaves: Tashama Farm." *The Nantucket Independent*. 20 Oct. 2004. Print.

Brace, Peter B. *Walking Nantucket: A Walker's Guide to Exploring Nantucket on Foot*. Nantucket: Faraway Publishing, 2003. Print.

Bradley, W. H., and Joshua I. Tracey, Jr. "Nantucket Harbor and the Proposed Cut at Chatham Bend." *U.S. Geological Survey* 1949. Print.

Brannen, Peter. "Oughta Know Where Otters Go, So Scientists Map Weasel Tracks." *The Vineyard Gazette* [Edgartown, MA] 7 Jan. 2011. Print.

Brault, Solange. Personal interview. 2 Oct. 2011.

Brown, Francesca D., Michael J. Goetz, Michael L. Gutman, James F. Lentowski and Wesley N. Tiffney, Jr. *Nantucket Shoreline Survey: An Analysis of Nantucket Shoreline Erosion and Accretion Trends Since 1846*. Nantucket: Nantucket Conservation Foundation, 1979. Print.

Burdick, David. Personal interview. 1 Dec. 2011.

Carlisle, Henry Coffin. "The Haulover: A 'Conversation' between Henry C. Carlisle and Arthur McCleave." *Historic Nantucket* Apr. 1967: 7. Print.

Carlquist, Sherwin. *Island Life: A Natural History of the Islands of the World*. New York: The Natural History Press, 1965. Print.

Chadwick, Alcon. "Reminiscences of Old Podpis." *Historic Nantucket* Summer 1994. Print.

Chamberlain, Barbara Blau. *These Fragile Outposts: A Geologic Look at Cape Cod, Martha's Vineyard, and Nantucket*. Garden City, NY: The Natural History Press, 1964. Print.

Christensen, Sonja. Personal interview. 4 Apr. 2011.

Coffin, Edward Wayman. *Nantucket's Forgotten Island: Muskeget*. Rockland, ME: Lakeside Printing, 1996. Print.

Coffin, Edward Wayman. *Tuckernuck Island: A Pictorial Review of the Island with Facts and Misinformation for the Uninformed*. Rockland, ME: Lakeside Printing, 2000. Print.

Coffin, Marie M. "Orange and Union Streets Neighborhood Study: Elisha Green House." *Historic American Buildings Survey* (HABS Publication No. MASS-1056). The Library of Congress, June 1970. Web.

Cokinos, Christopher. *Hope is the Thing with Feathers: A Personal Chronicle of Vanished Birds*. New York: Jeremy P. Tarcher/Putnam, 2000. Print.

Collier, Cormac. *A Walk in Squam: Notes on a Special Nantucket Place*. Nantucket: Nantucket Land Council, 2001. Print.

Collier, Cormac. Personal interview. 28 Apr. 2011.

Coope, G.R. "Several Million Years of Stability among Insect Species Because of, or in Spite of, Ice Age Climatic Instability?" *Philosophical Transactions of the Royal Society B: Biological Sciences* Jan. 2004. Web.

Coppinger, Raymond P., and David K. Wetherbee. *Time Lapse Ecology: Muskeget Island, Nantucket, Massachusetts*. New York: MSS Educational Publishing Company, 1972. Print.

Costello, Charles T., and William Judson Kensworthy. "Twelve-Year Mapping and Change Analysis of Eelgrass (Zostera marina) Areal Abundance in Massachusetts (USA) Identifies Statewide Declines." Massachusetts Department of Environmental Protection 2010. Print.

Cromidas, Dan. "Wasting Disease in Nantucket Harbor Eelgrass Populations: What's Ailing the Eelgrass?" Nantucket: UMass Boston Nantucket Field Station, 1997. Print.

Curley, Tracy. Personal interview. 14 Sept. 2011.

Cushman, Joseph Augustine. *The Pleistocene Deposits of Sankaty Head, Nantucket, and Their Fossils*. Nantucket: The Nantucket Maria Mitchell Association, 1906. Print.

Dathe, David, and Carla W. Montgomery. *Earth: Then and Now*. Dubuque, IA: Wm. C. Brown, 1996. Print.

de Crèvecoeur, J. Hector St. John. *Letters from an American Farmer: Describing Certain Provincial Situations, Manners, and Customs, Not Generally Known; and Conveying Some Idea of the Late and Present Interior Circumstances of the British Colonies of North America*. 1782. Print.

Diamond, Jared. *Guns, Germs, and Steel: The Fates of Human Societies*. New York: Norton, 2005. Print.

Doughty, Elaine D., Edward K. Faison, David R. Foster, Barbara C. S. Hansen and Wyatt W. Oswald. "A Climatic Driver for Abrupt Mid-Holocene Vegetation Dynamics and the Hemlock Decline in New England." *Ecology* June 2006. Print.

Dubock, Deborah. "Glacial Formation of Nantucket." *Historic Nantucket* Apr. 1969. Print.

Dunwiddie, Peter W. "Forest and Heath: The Shaping of the Vegetation of Nantucket Island." *Journal of Forest History* July 1989. Print.

Dunwiddie, Peter W. Personal interview. 2 Feb. 2010.

Dunwiddie, Peter W. "Postglacial Vegetation History of Coastal Islands in Southeastern New England." *National Geographic Research* 6 (1990). Print.

Dunwiddie, Peter W., and Bruce A. Sorrie. *The Vascular and Non-Vascular Flora of Nantucket, Tuckernuck, and Muskeget Islands*. Nantucket: The Massachusetts Audubon Society, Massachusetts Natural Heritage and Endangered Species Program, Nantucket Maria Mitchell Association and the Nature Conservancy, 1996. Print.

Dunwiddie, Peter W., and Peter D. Vickery, eds. *Grasslands of Northeastern North America: Ecology and Conservation of Native and Agricultural Landscapes*. Lincoln, MA: The Massachusetts Audubon Society, 1997. Print.

Erichsen, Thomas. Personal interview. 16 Mar. 2008

Facey, Douglas E., and Michael J. Van Den Avyle. "Species Profiles: Life Histories and Environmental Requirements of Coastal Fishes and Invertebrates (North Atlantic), American Eel." *U.S. Fish and Wildlife Service Biological Report* Aug. 1987. Print.

Folger, Edith V., and Ludlow Griscom. *The Birds of Nantucket*. Cambridge, MA: Harvard University Press, 1948. Print.

Foster, David R., and John O'Keefe. "Dynamics In The Postglacial Era." *Arnoldia: The Magazine of the Arnold Arboretum* [Jamaica Plain, MA] Spring 1998. Print.

French, Thomas. Personal interview. 18 Feb. 2011.

Fronzuto, David. Personal interview. 18 Jan. 2012.

Gambee, Robert, and Elizabeth Heard. *Impressions of Nantucket*, 2001. Print.

Goodman, David. Personal interview. 13 Oct. 2011.

Green, Ariana. "Move to Redefine New England Fishing." *New York Times* 30 May 2009. Print.

Green, Eugene, and William Sachse. *Names of the Land: Cape Cod, Nantucket, Martha's Vineyard, and the Elizabeth Islands: A Compendium of Cape Area Proper Names with Derivations.* Chester, CT: Globe Pequot Press, 1932. Print.

Guba, Emil Frederick. "Government of the Fisheries of the Great Ponds of Nantucket Island." *Historic Nantucket* April 1967. Print.

Guba, Emil Frederick. "The Sheep Commons Fight." *Historic Nantucket* July 1964. Print.

Gutman, Andrew L., Michael J. Geotz, Francesca D. Brown, James F. Lentowski and Wesley N. Tiffney, Jr. *Nantucket Shoreline Survey: An Analysis of Nantucket Shoreline Erosion and Accretion Trends Since 1846.* Cambridge, MA: University of Massachusetts Cooperative Extension Service and Massachusetts Institute of Technology Sea Grant Program, 1979. Print.

Hartel, Karsten E., David B. Halliwell and Alan E. Launer. *Inland Fishes of Massachusetts.* Lincoln, MA: Massachusetts Audubon Society, 2002. Print.

Iwata, Sunao. *Corticolous Lichens in Nantucket Town: Dyeing Decorators or Dying Detectors?* Nantucket: UMass Boston Nantucket Field Station, 1995–2001. Print.

Jenkins, Jerry. *Checklist of the Vascular Plants of Nantucket.* Rev. ed. White Creek, NY: Maria Mitchell Association, July 1979. Print.

Johnson, Charles Willison. *A List of the Insect Fauna of Nantucket, Massachusetts.* Nantucket: The Nantucket Maria Mitchell Association, 1930. Print.

Johnson, Luanne. Personal interview. 7 Jan. 2011.

Jones, Bassett. "Was Nantucket Ever Forested?" *Historic Nantucket* April 1965. Print.

Kelley, Kenneth M. *The Nantucket Bay Scallop Fishery: The Resource and its Management.* Nantucket: Town of Nantucket, 1981. Print.

Kennedy, Robert. Personal interview. 1 Jul. 2010.

Kimball, Charles P., and Charles Morton Jones. *The Lepidoptera of Nantucket and Martha's Vineyard Islands, Massachusetts*. Nantucket: Maria Mitchell Association, 1943. Print.

Knieper, Elizabeth. Emailed response to questions. 5 Oct. 2011.

Kurlansky, Mark. *Cod: A Biography of the Fish that Changed the World*. New York: Walker Publishing Company, 1997. Print.

LaFarge, Bam. Personal communication.

Lamb, Jane. *Wauwinet*. Nantucket: Jane Lamb, 1990. Print.

Lancaster, Clay. *Nantucket in the Nineteenth Century*. New York: Dover, 1979. Print.

Largy, Tonya. Personal interview. 2 Jan. 2011.

Lazell, James D., Jr. *This Broken Archipelago: Cape Cod and the Islands, Amphibians and Reptiles*. New York: Quadrangle, 1976. Print.

Little, Elizabeth A. "Nantucket Algonquian Studies #6: Essay on Nantucket Timber." *Historic Nantucket* 1981. Print.

Lovette, Irby. Personal interview. 2 Dec. 2010.

Ludlum, David M. *The Nantucket Weather Book*. Boston: Nimrod Press, 1986. Print.

Mackay, George Henry. *Shooting Journal of George Henry Mackay, 1865–1922*. Cambridge, MA: Cosmos Press (for John C. Phillips), 1929. Print.

Macy, Obed. *A History of Nantucket: Being a Compendious Account of the First Settlement off the Island by the English, Together With the Rise and Progress of the Whale Fishery; and other Historical Facts Relative to Said Island and its Inhabitants*. St. Petersburg, FL: Hailer Publishing, 2006. Print.

McKenna-Foster, Andrew. Personal interview. 21 Mar. 2011.

McManis, Debra A. *Town Farms & Country Commons: Farming on Nantucket*. Nantucket: Mill Hill Press, 2010. Print.

Mehrhoff, Leslie J. "Thoughts on the Biogeography of Grassland Plants in New England." Dunwiddie and Vickery.

Mello, Mark J. Personal interview. 9 May 2011.

Miller, Gerrit S., Jr. *The Beach Mouse of Muskeget Island*. Boston: Boston Society of Natural History, 1896. Print.

"Natural Habitats of Nantucket." *Nantucket Conservation*. Nantucket Conservation Foundation. Web.

Niering, W.A., and R.S. Warren. "Vegetation Patterns and Processes in New England Salt Marshes." *Bioscience* [West Sussex, U.K.] 1980. Print.

O'Boyle, Robert, and Michael Sinclair. "Seal-cod interactions on the Eastern Scotian Shelf: Reconsideration of Modeling Assumptions." *Fisheries Research* 115–116 (March 2012). Web.

O'Brien, John. *Codium Fragile, Drift, Density and Distribution in Nantucket Harbor*. Nantucket: UMass Boston Nantucket Field Station, 1973. Print.

O'Dell, Danielle. Personal interview. 13 Mar. 2011.

Oktay, Sarah D. "Restoring Our Marshes." *Yesterday's Island* 38:14 (July 31–August 2008). Web.

Oktay, Sarah D. Emailed response to question. 22 Aug. 2009.

Oktay, Sarah D., and James W. Sutherland. *Hummock Pond Water Quality 2009: A Summary of Physical, Chemical and Biological Monitoring*. Nantucket: The Nantucket Land Council, 2009. Print.

Oktay, Sarah D., and James W. Sutherland. *Miacomet Pond Water Quality 2009: A Summary of Physical, Chemical and Biological Monitoring*. Nantucket: The Nantucket Land Council, 2009. Print.

Oldale, Robert N. *Cape Cod, Martha's Vineyard and Nantucket: The Geologic Story*. Yarmouth Port, MA: On Cape Publications, 1992. Print.

Oldale, Robert N. *Freshwater*. Print.

Patrick, James E., and Robert Benchley III. *Scallop Season: A Nantucket Chronicle*. Nantucket: Autopscot Press, 2002. Print.

Perkins, Blair. Personal interview. 1 Dec. 2011.

Peteet, Dorothy. Personal interview. 27 Jan. 2010.

Pew, Bill. Personal interview. 5 Oct. 2011.

Philbrick, Nathaniel. *Away Offshore*. Nantucket: Mill Hill Press, 1994. Print.

Philbrick, Nathaniel. *Abram's Eyes: The Native American Legacy of Nantucket Island*. Nantucket. Mill Hill Press. 1998. Print.

Pielou, E. C. *After the Ice Age: The Return of Life to Glaciated North America*. Chicago: University of Chicago Press, 1991. Print.

Pochman, Kitty Kish. Personal interview. 15 Oct. 2009.

Rainey, Mary Lynne. "The Archeology of the Polpis Road Bike Path: A Landmark in the Study of Native American Lifeways on Nantucket." *Historic Nantucket* Summer 2004. Print.

Raleigh, Lloyd. *The Natural History of the Coatue-Coskata Wildlife Refuge*. Vineyard Haven, MA: Trustees of Reservations, 1998. Print.

Reithof, George. Aerial Photographs of Nantucket. n.d. Nantucket, MA.

Rice, Mabel A. *Trees and Shrubs of Nantucket*. Nantucket: Maria Mitchell Association, 1946. Print.

Riley, Tara. Personal interview. 18 Oct. 2011.

Robinson, Charles T. *Native New England: The Long Journey*. North Attleboro, MA: Covered Bridge Press, 1962. Print.

Rosen, Peter S. "Origin and Processes of Cuspate Spit Shorelines." *Estuarine Research, Vol. II: Geology and Engineering*. New York: Academic Press, 1975. Print.

Rosenberg, Steven A. "New report could tighten cod fishing regulations." *Boston Globe*. Boston Globe, 11 Dec. 2011. Web.

Russell, Howard S. *Indian New England Before the Mayflower*. Hanover, NH: University Press of New England, 1980. Print.

Scannell, Steve. "Island Regains Power to Open Great Ponds." *The Nantucket Beacon* (27 Oct. 1993). Print.

Shaler, Nathaniel S. "The Geology of Nantucket." United States Geological Survey (1889). Washington, DC: U.S. Government Printing Office. Print.

Sibley, David Allen. *The Sibley Guide to Bird Life & Behavior*. New York: Knopf, 2001. Print.

Sibley, David Allen. *The Sibley Guide to Birds*. New York: Knopf, 2000. Print.

Sjolund, Carl. Personal interview. 15 Nov. 2011.

Skomal, Greg. Personal interview. 29 Dec. 2011.

Smith, Doug. Personal interview. 11 Mar. 2011.

Smyers, Scott. Personal interview. 11 Apr. 2011.

Stackpole, Eduoard A. "Nantucket Bar." *Historic Nantucket* Apr. 1940. Print.

Sterling, Dorothy. *The Outer Lands: A Natural History Guide to Cape Cod, Martha's Vineyard, Nantucket, Block Island and Long Island*. New York: Norton, 1978. Print.

Stockley, Bernard H. "An Introduction to the Prehistory of Nantucket." *Historic Nantucket* Jan. 1968. Print.

Stockley, Bernard H. "The Prehistory of Nantucket, Part II: Early Man." *Historic Nantucket* Apr. 1968. Print.

Stockley, Bernard H. "The Prehistory of Nantucket, Part III: Early Villagers." *Historic Nantucket* Oct. 1969. Print.

Strahler, Arthur N. *A Geologist's View of Cape Cod*. New York: Natural History Press, 1966. Print.

Tamarin, Robert H., and Thomas H. Kunz. "Microtus breweri." *Mammalian Species* 45 (June 1974). Print.

Tamarin, Robert H., and Thomas H. Kunz. "Microtus breweri," *The American Journal of Mammalogists* (28 June 1978). Print.

Teal, John and Mildred. *Life and Death of the Salt Marsh.* Boston: Little, Brown, 1977. Print.

Telford, Sam R., III. Personal interview. 15 Jul. 2011.

Tiffney, Wesley N., Jr. *Sea Level Rise, Coastal Retreat, and the Demise of Nantucket Island, Massachusetts.* Nantucket: UMass Boston Nantucket Field Station. Print.

Tiffney, Wesley N., Jr., and Doug E. Eveleigh. *Nantucket's Endangered Maritime Heaths.* Nantucket: UMass Boston Nantucket Field Station, 1985. Print.

Town of Nantucket. (1949). *Town Report.* Nantucket. Print.

Town of Nantucket. (1952). *Town Report.* Nantucket. Print.

Town of Nantucket. (1957). *Town Report.* Nantucket. Print.

Town of Nantucket. (1969). *Town Report.* Nantucket. Print.

Tudge, Colin. *The Bird: A Natural History of Who Birds Are, Where They Came From, and How They Live.* New York: Crown, 2008. Print.

Walker, Eugene. Water Resources of Nantucket Island, Massachusetts. Reston, Va. United States Geological Survey, 1980. Map and print.

Ward, Peter D. *The Call of Distant Mammoths: Why the Ice Age Mammals Disappeared.* New York: Copernicus Springer-Verlag, 1998. Print.

Wood, Stephanie. Personal interview. 30 Sept. 2011.

Yee, Vivian. "Shark fatality still hits home." *Boston Globe.* Boston Globe, 25 July 2011. Web.

Young, Louise B. *Islands: Portraits of Miniature Worlds.* New York: Freeman, 2000. Print.

Zube, Ervin H., and Carl A. Carlozzi. *An Inventory and Interpretation: Selected Resources of the Island of Nantucket.* Nantucket: Cooperative Extension Service, 1966. Print.

GLOSSARY

Accretion—Slow addition to land by deposition of water-borne sediment.

Anadromous—Fish that spend most of their lives in saltwater but swim into freshwater streams, rivers and ponds to spawn.

Anthropogenic—Human-influenced impacts on the natural world, such as the grazing of sheep related to plant succession; erosion control structures; and endangered species protection laws.

Archaic Period—The period of time, beginning roughly 8,000 to 11,000 years ago, in which the Early and Late Archaic Indians came to North America at the end of the Ice Age, when they were transitioning from being solely hunter-gatherers to focusing as well on foraging locally.

Arthropod—Invertebrate animal without a backbone, including insects, arachnids, centipedes and crustaceans. Instead of an interior skeleton, arthropods have an exoskeleton made of chitin; in addition, their bodies are broken up into segmented sections and their arms and legs jointed.

Austral—Pertaining to southern regions of the planet.

Bathymetry—Depth measurements of bodies of water.

Beach Nourishment—Essentially, replenishing sand on a beach depleted by erosion, in an effort to rebuild the beach and to fortify against continued erosive wave action.

Browsing—The effort of whitetail deer to eat vegetation.

Biomass—A volume of living things in a given area, measured in weight per unit of area.

Capelin—A small edible marine fish of the smelt family, found in the northern and Arctic seas.

Catadromous—Fish that spend their lives in freshwater but swim into saltwater to spawn.

Cetacean—The noun form of Cetacea, the name for the order of large marine mammals, including whales and dolphins, defined as having a streamlined body with forelimbs that evolved into pectoral flippers; flukes; no rear flippers; and a blowhole on top of its head for respiration.

Chitin—A nitrogen-containing polysaccharide that forms the hard, resilient exoskeleton of arthropods.

Chord of the Bay—The portion of Nantucket Sound southeast of an imaginary line connecting the north end of the east jetty and Great Point.

Climax forest—Also called climax vegetation, it is a state of near equilibrium reached when a plant species in a given zone becomes the dominant species. For Nantucket and the rest of the Cape and Islands region, American beech trees fill this role.

ConCom—Local parlance for Nantucket's wetlands regulatory board, the Conservation Commission.

DDT—Dichlorodiphenyltrichloroethane, a chlorine-based pesticide used in the U.S. from the late 1930s to the late 1960s to kill various insects, including, on Nantucket, moths.

Delta—A plain at the mouth of a river or tidal inlet, low in elevation and composed of a mixture of sediments.

Diatoms—One-celled microscopic algae in the class Bacillariophyceae, Division Chromophyta, also known as plankton, that serve as food for many marine creatures.

Dinoflagellate—A form of plankton, mostly protozoans, that live in seawater and sport two swimmers, called flagella, extending from their bodies.

Drainage (or **drainage basin**)—An area of land drained by a system of rivers, streams and other interconnected waterways.

Ebb tide—The outgoing tide.

Embayment—A harbor, large cove, estuary or bay along an ocean or lake coastline.

GLOSSARY

Endemic—A species of life that is native to just one region, such as a state, county, town or—as in the case of Nantucket—island.

Entomologist—A biologist who studies insects.

Enzyme—A protein operating as a biochemical catalyst.

Epiphyte—A plant that relies on another plant for structural support, but not for food, and typically attaches itself to the host plant.

Erosion—In the case of Nantucket's beaches, the wearing of sand by waves, tidal currents and wind.

Eutrophication—The breakdown of the life-sustaining abilities of estuaries, bays, harbors, lakes and ponds, precipitated by excessive input of nutrients, including nitrogen and phosphorous. This results in the growth of algae and other plants whose blooms block sunlight from reaching aquatic plants, and they, in turn, deplete a water body's dissolved oxygen when they die and decompose.

Eutrophic—Condition of an estuary, bay, harbor, lake or pond whose vegetation has taken over the body of water, due to excessive amounts of nutrients—phosphates and nitrates—entering their water from surrounding watersheds.

Extirpate—To exterminate a species completely from a given region or area.

Fetch—The distance a wave travels from its creation point to where it breaks on a shoreline.

Flood tide—The incoming tide.

Floristic—Related to the study of the number, distribution, and relationships of plant species in one or more areas.

Fluke—Summer flounder. This alternative name, coined by commercial fishermen, derives from the unusual placement of the summer flounder's eyes on the left side of their bodies, rather than the right, as is common to other flounder.

Gabion—A wicker basket up to four feet in height. As used in this book, the same concept, but made of high-strength plastic.

Geo-Grid—A form of high-tensile-strength plastic caging or mesh used to hold soils in place.

Great pond—A pond larger than 20 acres, as determined by the Commonwealth of Massachusetts.

Great salt pond—A salt or brackish pond 20 acres or larger, as determined by the Commonwealth of Massachusetts.

Groin—A rock wall, similar to a jetty, built perpendicular to a beach and designed to be above the high tide mark to prevent sand from eroding from a beach.

Groundfish—Fish caught on the traditional New England fishing grounds, including Nantucket Shoals, Georges Bank, Stellwagen Bank and the Grand Banks.

Haulout—A section of coastline, usually a beach or smooth rock shoreline, used as a resting, feeding and sometimes breeding area by marine mammals, including seals, sea lions and walruses. Also called a hauling-out.

Historic Nantucket—The quarterly publication of the Nantucket Historical Association highlighting the island's history.

Home rule petition—The legislative vehicle Massachusetts municipalities use to request that the state legislature pass a bill creating a local law. The petition is generated by a positive two-thirds vote on an article containing the home rule petition at Town Meeting, and the law is enacted by the governor through his signing of the bill after it is approved by both the house and senate.

Hydrostatic pressure—The pressure applied by a liquid, such as the pressure exerted by the salt water around Nantucket against the island's sole-source aquifer because of the force of gravity.

Hyper-eutrophic—Devoid of all plant and animal life, except algae, as in the extreme case of a water body that is overloaded with nutrients, including nitrogen, phosphorous and fecal coliform bacteria and possibly heavy metals and petroleum products from road runoff.

Ichthyologist—A biologist who studies fish.

Krill—A shrimp-like marine crustacean living in the ocean that is a chief source of food for both marine mammals, such as baleen, right and humpback whales, and seabirds, including gulls, jaegers and shearwaters.

Limnologist—One who specializes in the study of the biological, chemical and physical features of freshwater lakes and ponds.

GLOSSARY

Middens—In archeological terms, a trash dump created and used by Native Americans for the disposal of shellfish shells, bones from animals on which they dined and anything else they discarded. Such sites, typically mounds unearthed near villages, are troves of valuable historic artifacts.

Millinery—The design and production of ladies' hats, hairpins and other fashion adornments and accessories. Bird feathers were widely employed in millinery; sometimes, whole birds were used.

Nautical miles—Distance measurement at sea over the curvature of the earth equal to one minute of its arc of latitude along any line between the north and south poles or one minute of arc of longitude at the equator. A nautical mile is roughly 796 feet longer than a land mile of 5,280 feet.

Paleo—An archeological term that means early, first, or oldest when applied to all lifeforms.

Pelagic—An adjective used to describe creatures that live in deeper waters of an ocean. In Nantucket's case, that includes anything living beyond the 1,000-fathom line, which falls about 12 miles east of the island.

Phosphorus mobilization—Phosphorous, held in soils beneath ponds, which is released into the water when iron levels are reduced.

Photosynthesis—The process by which green plants and other organisms produce simple carbohydrates from carbon dioxide and hydrogen, using energy that chlorophyll or other organic cellular pigments absorb from radiant sources.

Plant succession—The slow dynamic of plant species' evolution within their various habitats.

Primary forest—[See Climax forest.]

Proprietors—In Nantucket history: the original 27 European settlers who first moved to Nantucket with their families from Amesbury and became the first landowners of the island after purchasing it from the Archaic Indians.

Reagent—Substance that is part of a chemical reaction used to measure, detect, examine or produce another substance.

Refugium (plural: refugia)—An area that has escaped ecological changes occurring elsewhere, such as flora and fauna erased, or driven southward, by advancing glaciers, which therefore provides a suitable habitat for species to exist until the area they fled returns to a habitable condition to their liking.

Rhizosphere—A cramped region of the soil where microbes feed on root secretions and protozoa and nematodes dine on bacteria, and where nutrient cycling and disease control for the plant happen.

Rookery—A group nesting area for birds and animals, including great blue herons, various egret and stork species, seals and walruses, that become permanent breeding colonies for these creatures—the birds nesting in the tops of trees and marine mammals on shorelines. The term originates from a Central Asian and Northern European cousin of the crow called a rook.

Scarp—A steep cliff or slope, which for Nantucket and other coastal areas is called a marine scarp or beach scarp.

Serology—A diagnosis; identifies antibodies in blood serum that doctors use to prove the presence of certain diseases.

Smack—Another name for a small, typically sail-powered fishing boat rigged in a variety of ways. Many have built-in fish wells for moving live fish to market.

Spirochetes—Spiral-shaped bacteria.

Staging—Generally, preparation for a long trip; locally, the feeding and resting activities of seasonal birds on Nantucket readying themselves for migrations north and south of the islands.

Substrate—A substance that is acted upon, especially by an enzyme, in a biochemical reaction; or the surface from which plants grow.

Swampscott dory—A 14- to 18-foot fishing boat used in the mid-1800s in coastal Massachusetts waters. Built by fishermen to be beach-launched and rowed by one or two people. A hybrid of the Wherry design and newer dory-building techniques employed in bank dory construction, it handled better than a bank dory because of its rounded sides and diminished bow and stern overhang.

Tombolo—A small island just off of a main, larger island, sometimes connected with it by a sand spit or barrier beach.

Turbidity—A measure of water clarity based on the amount of particulate matter, such as sediments in a body of water.

Upwelling—The movement of currents of water up to the surface of an ocean from the bottom; likewise, the movement of currents of air mass from lower atmospheric levels to upper.

Vascular—Relating to or having fluid-carrying vessels; for example, blood vessels in animals or the sap-carrying vessels in plants.

Wampanoag—A tribe of Native Americans that inhabited Nantucket's islands from the 17th century well into the 19th century and were the last Native Americans to live on Nantucket.

Water column—Conceptual in nature: an area of water from the surface to the bottom.

Watershed—An area of land from which groundwater drains into a harbor, ocean, bay, pond, lake, river or stream.

Weir—Essentially a maze made of netting or brush held in place by posts placed at right angles to the shore, ending in a center enclosure with an opening on one side or the other or both. Because fish can't look behind them, once they venture inside the center enclosure, they are trapped. Native Americans and European settlers using these fish traps either waited for the tide to drop to collect their catch or speared them in the water.

Weto—A traditional Wampanoag dwelling.

Zoologist—A biologist who studies animal life: their structure, development, physiology and classification.

INDEX

A

Abram's Point, 25
After the Ice Age: The Return of Life to Glaciated North America, 110
Alden, Peter, 139
Almanac Pond, 14, 68, 70
Almanac Pond Road, 48
Altar Rock, 1–2, 8, 9, 15, 65
Altocid, larval-killing donuts, 174
American beach grass, 53–54, 57, 69
American burying beetles, 147–148, 164
American crows, 97
American herring, 98
American Journal of Mammalogists, 105
American kestrels, 86
American Ornithologists Union, 88
American Ornithology, 87
American oyster catchers, 31, 79, 97, 99, 108
Amphibians, 131
Anadromous species, 185, 186, 191
Andrews, Clinton, 90, 92, 126–127, 131, 189, 191, 204, 245
Andrews, Edith, 90
Anoplura (lice), 149
Antonia (ship), 116, 157
Aquifer, 7–8
Archaic Indians, 36–37, 104, 239
   Late, 36, 37, 113, 191–192, 239, 242
   Early, 36, 191

Archaic Period, 36–37
Arthropods
   classification, 148–149
   diseases from, 150
   diversity factors, 168
   migration, 173–174
Anthropogenic changes, 152, 187, 223, 235
Asian land bridge, 33
Aster, 61
Atlantic Flyway, 77
Audubon, John James, 94
Auk, 88, 91
Avian
   adaptation, 92–93
   birding season, 31, 75, 95
   Bigelow Point and, 77
   Carolina wren, 99
   classification of, 93
   ducks, 99
   Eskimo Curlew, 91
   evolution, 81–82
   falcons, 76
   food sources, 96–97
   genocide of, 91
   global warming effect on, 99–101
   Golden Plover, 91
   great auk, 86–87
   Greater prairie-chickens, 83
   ground-nesting water birds, 76

Guinea hens, 85–86
gull species, 76
harriers, 76, 97–98
hawks, 76
heath hen, 83–85
herring, 76
history of, 77–83
jet stream fall out, 97
land developers and, 91–92
long-tail ducks, 75, 76, 82
micro-habitats, 95–96
migration of species, 82, 97–98
migration routes, 77–78
owls, 31, 98–99
permanent species of, 93–94
poultry birds, 85–86
predators, 76–77, 86
red-bellied woodpecker, 99
refuge for, 75–76
seed dispersal, 58–59
shore birds, 97
species of, 37
tufted titmouse, 99
tundra birds, 82
See also Hunters; Hunting; Marker gunners
Away Offshore: Nantucket Island and its People, 1602–1890, 240

B

Babesiosis, 153, 158, 161
Baffin Bay, 238
Baffin Island, 238
Baird, S. F., 105
Ballou, F. K., 198
Bangs, Outram, 106
Barn owls, 97
Barnard Valley Road, 13
Barrens, 66
Bartlett's Ocean View Farms, 173
Bass Rip shoal, 270
Batchelder, Charles, 106
Batrachochytrium dendrobatidi, 143
Bats, 120

Baxter Road, 266
Baxter Road Bluff, 271
Bayberry, 61, 69
Beach dewatering, 267, 268, 269, 276
Beach grass, 53, 104, 105. *See also* American beach grass
Beach Mouse of Muskeget Island, 106
Beach nourishment projects, 264, 265, 269, 268, 270, 276
Beach plants, 54
Beach plum, 54
Beach woods, 47, 49, 50
Beak-rush, 61
Bean Hill, 9, 12, 15
Bearberry, 61
Beattie, Karen, 108–109, 112, 120, 121–122
Beach nourishment, 264, 265, 269, 268, 270, 276
Bedrock, 1, 3, 6
Beeches, 48, 50, 51
Beecroft, Willey I., 88
Beetles, 164, 171–172
Beinecke, Walter Jr., 72
Belding, David L., 200
Benchley, Peter, 256
Bering Sea, 36
Bering Strait, 36
Beryllium-10 dating method, 44, 45
Bettie, Karen, 28, 29
Betts's Sheep Pond Road, 272
Bigelow Point, 25, 37, 53, 278–279
Bigelow, Jacob, 76
Biodiversity, 23–24, 28, 30, 31
  initiative, 31, 33
  species range expansion, 171
Biomass, 148, 253, 258
Biopolymers, 39–40
Birds. *See* Avian
Birds of Nantucket, 86, 89, 93, 118
Birds of prey, DDT and, 130
Biting spiders, 148
Bivalve filters, 224

INDEX

Black-and-white sea ducks, 75, 97
Black-backed gulls, 98
Black-capped chickadees, 98
Black cherry, 54
Black-chinned hummingbird, 78
Black ducks, 76, 97
Black-headed gulls, 76
Black huckleberry, 61, 62, 63
Black oaks, 48, 54
Black rail, 37, 78
Black skimmers, 78
Black tupelo, 48, 69
Black widows, 170–171
Blizzard of 1978, 213
Block island, 2, 5, 172
Blount, 249, 250–251
Blueberry, 69, 72
Blue jays, 97
Boat moorings, 218, 228
Bobolinks, 97
Bog rosemary, 72
Bogs, defined 71
Bonaparte's gulls, 76
Boreal chickadees, 82
Boreal forest species, 46
Boston Herald, 115, 117, 126
Boulders, 4, 5
Box turtle, 138
Brannen, Peter, 123
Brault, Solange, 230, 257
Brewer, Thomas, 105
Broadwood (hardwood) forests, 50, 139
Broad Woods, 47
Browsing, 63, 66, 118, 162
Bulletin of the Massachusetts Archeological Society (1986), 192
Bullfrogs, 141
Bumblebees, 168
Burdick, David, 180, 181
Burnt Swamp, 69
Bushy rockrose, 61
Butterflies. *See* Lepidoptera (moths and butterflies)
Butterfly-weed, 61

C

California Gold rush, 65, 121, 203
Cambridge Street, 267
Camels, 197
Canada geese, 97
Canada jays, 82
Canada's Department of Fisheries & Oceans (DFO), 254
Canadian Arctic, 238
Canadian Species at Risk Act, 238
Capaum Pond, 192
Cape Cod, history of, 3–4
Cape Cod Bay, 3, 10
Cape Cod Bay Lobe, 4, 5–6, 11, 13
Cape Cod, Martha's Vineyard & Nantucket: The Geologic Story, 5
Cape Hatteras, 238
Capelin, 238
Cape Wind Associates, 91
Cardinals, 79
Carlson, Jeff, 271
Carnivorous bog plants, 71–72
Carolina wrens, 79, 99
Carrion beetle, 172
Carson, Rachel, 130
Cassin's sparrow, 100, 101
Catadromous, 186
Centers for Disease Control and Prevention, 161
Cetacean, 239
Chaffseed, 63
Chain pickerel, 188
Chapman, Frank M., 90
Chase, Tom, 171
Chicken Hill, 4
Chitin, 148
Choral tree frogs, 135
Chord of the Bay, 18, 190, 191
Christensen, Sonja, 124
Christmas Bird Count, 31, 80, 90, 130
description of, 94–95
Chukchi Sea, 36
Cisco Beach, 43
Cisco Estates, 267

Civil War (1816), 65, 87, 121
Clark Cove, 26, 213, 267
Clay, 45, 69
Clean Water and Clean Air acts, 222
Climax forest, 50
Clovis people. 111
Coastal plain highlands, 25
Coastal Stabilization, Inc., 269
Coatue, 16, 18, 19
   beach plants, 54
   evolution of, 18, 25
Cob weaver family (Theridiidae), 170
Cod, 243–245
   Canadian stocks, collapse of, 254
   decline, 246–247
   fishery, 253–254
   fishing, 18–19
   study of, 249
Coffin, Edward Wayman, 19
Cokinos, Christopher, 83
Coleoptera. *See* Beetles
Collier, 131–134
Colt Valley, 4
Comeau-Beaton, Cheryl, 33, 171
Commercial fishermen, 250–253
Commercial fishing trawlers, 110
Committee for the Protection of North American Birds, 88
Common bearberry, 62
Common eider ducks, 81, 82
Common hairgrass, 62
Comprehensive Wastewater Management Plan, 225
Computational Laboratory in the Department of Geology & Geophysics, 8
Conch meat, 250
ConCom, 269, 271, 272, 273, 277
Concord Grape, 72
Conrad's broom crowberry, 61, 62
Conservation
   DDT and, 129–131
   history of, 130
   marker hunters and, 87, 90–91

   protection methods, 29, 30, 60, 63, 66, 73
   state and federal protection laws, 94
   See also Erosion; specific groups
Consue Springs, 225
Continental Shelf, 3, 36, 46, 110, 266
Coope, G. R., 152
Cooper's hawks, 76
Cord grass, 56–57, 69
Cordilleran ice sheets, 111
Coskata, 54
Coskata-Coatue Wildlife Refuge, 17
Coskata Pond, 16–17, 19
Coskata Woods, 10, 16
Cottontails, 114–115, 122
Coyotes, 86, 109, 113, 122
Cranberry, 72
Cranberry bogs, 9, 71–73
Creeping St. John's wort, 61
Cretaceous Period, 6
Crèvecoeur, J. Hector St. John, 188
Crossbills, 82
Crows 82
Cuckoos, 97
Curley, James Michael, 117, 220
Curley, Tracy, 178
Cuspate spits, 18, 53
Cyanobacteria (blue-green algae), 224
Cypress, 50

D

Dammin, Dr., 162
Damminix mousetraps, 162
Damselflies (Odonata), 168–159, 174
Danish Geotechnical Institute, 268–269
Danish North Sea Research Center, 268
Davis Strait, 238
DDT, 149
   ban of, 223
   effects of, 130–131
   habitat tolerance, 139, 145
   insects and, 142
   regal fritillary and, 165
   report on, 130

snakes and, 142
spadefoot toad and, 133–134, 138
tussock moth and, 129, 165
Dead Horse Valley, 4
Dean, Arthur, 72
Deer, 109, 116–117
    habitats, 124–127
    herd size, 124–125
    hunting season, 116–118, 125–126
    Lyme disease and, 120, 159
    MassWildlife-sanctioned February deer hunt (2004), 174
    "park", 124–127, 160
    White tail, 109, 116–117, 120
Deer flies, 148
Deer tick, 152–163
    development, 152–153, 159
    epidemic, 162
    eradication plans, 174
    food sources, 156
    human-deer-tick contact, 158
    introduction of, 153–156, 157–158
    prevalence of, 156
    Tick Advisory Committee, 162–163
    See also Lyme disease; specific species
Delta, 11, 12
Dennis, John, 90
DEP. *See* Department of Environmental Protection (DEP)
Department of Conservation, 129
Department of Environmental Protection (DEP), 273
Dewatering, beaches, 268
Diatoms, 179
Dionis, 15, 133
Dinoflagellates, 179
Diptera (flies), 149
Division of Marine Fisheries (DMF), 232
Dog ticks, 156–157
Dolphins, 242
Donut Ponds, 14, 40, 43, 70–71
Dough bird, 87
Dowitchers, 97

Dragonflies (Odonata), 168–159, 174
Drainage (or drainage basin), 132–133, 185, 187
Draney, Michael J., 171
Dreamland property, 193
Ducks Unlimited, 88
Ducks, 99. *See also* specific types
Dunes
    erosion control, 268
    foredune, 189
    longshore drift, 274
    oldest, 17
    plants of, 52, 57
Dunlins, 97
Dunwiddie, Peter, 35, 40, 42, 59, 65
Dwarf chestnut oak, 63

E

Early sweet blueberry, 62
Earthworms, 37
East-west long shore drift, 19
Eastern Equine Encephalitis, 150
Eastern gray squirrel, 27, 119
Eastern pitch pine, 63, 65, 66–67
Eastern red bats, 120
Eastern red cedar, 48, 54
Eat Fire Spring, 7, 8
Ebb tide, 112, 174, 198
Eel Point, 19, 25
Eelgrass, 177–182
    loss of, 217–218
    restoration, 227
    wasting disease, 206–207
Effectiveness of Sheep Grazing as a Management Tool on Nantucket Island, MA., 61
Ehrlichiosis, 150, 153, 161
Eilert property, 33
Elgar, Steve, 275
Elizabeth Islands, 26
Embayment, 217, 226
Endangered Species Act, 139
Endemic species, 29, 63, 104, 118
Entomologists, 149, 153, 154, 160, 170

Environmental Protection Agency, 227
Enzymes, 39, 72, 162
Epiphyte, 179, 218
Era to the Mesozoic Era, 1–2, 7
Erichsen, Tom, 273, 278
Erosion, 259–279
   -accretion dynamic, 21, 43, 113, 260, 263, 266, 274
   annual data, 266–267
   beach armoring, 26
   cliff face, 9
   control innovations, 268–272, 276
   control structures, 274
   future outlook, 266–268
   group combat tactics, 266
   high-energy, 267
   kettle holes and, 54
   lifespan for Nantucket, 260
   Madaket and, 273, 275
   Muskeget and, 105
   North Shore and, 263–264
   ocean-inundated valleys and, 54
   overview, 259–260, 276–279, 281
   preservation actions, 262
   rates of, 54, 260–262, 264, 266–267
   resistant clays, gravel and sand, 16
   Siasconset and, 260–263
   Smith's Point neighborhood, 273, 276
   soil detail, 262
   Tom Nevers Head and, 260–263
   viewpoints on, 274
   wave-driven, 19, 272
   West End, 264–266
   Western End, 272–276
   WhisprWave control technology, 271
   wind, 10
Eskimo Curlew, 87, 90, 91
Essay on Nantucket Timber, 46–47
Esther Island, 12, 264, 267
Estuaries, 58, 177, 206
   report on, 214, 224, 226
Estuaries Project, 178, 214, 224, 226
Ethical Treatment of Animals (PETA), 161, 162

European settlers, 28–29
Eutrophic, 216
Eutrophication, 214, 216–217
Eveleigh, Doug E., 61
Evolution of Processes of Coatue Beach, Nantucket Island, Massachusetts: A Cuspate Spit Shoreline, 18
Ewer, Peter, 197
Extirpate, 27, 84, 116, 122, 165

F

Falcons, 76
Falmouth family, 156
False gromwell, 63
Farms, decline of, 120
Farrell, Joe Jr., 274–275, 276
Feral cat, 107–109
   Coyotes, 109, 113, 122
   Neutering program, 108
   Willie, 107
Ferns, 69
Ferrets, 86
Fetch, 263
Field Guide to New England, 139
Filters, 221, 224, 225
Fish, 184–189
   eels, 202–203
   fish varieties, 186, 188–189
   freshwater fish, 185
   scallops, 203–210
   stocking, 188–189
   See also Ponds
Fisher, John, 263–264
Fisher's Island, 5
Fisheries and Game Commission, 84
Fisheries Research, 254
Fishing Around Nantucket, 189
Fishing practices 189–192
   codfish decline, 246–247
   evolution of, 246–247
   harvesting, 200–202
   industry, 247–250
   regulations, 250–253
   stream-powered vessels, 202

INDEX

Flax, 61
Flounder, 246
Folger, Edith V., 86, 89, 91, 118
Folger's Hill, 2, 11, 65
Folger's Marsh, 7, 25, 31, 54
Forbes family, 156
Forbush, Edward H., 88
Forest and Stream, 94
Forested swamps, 69
Forests, 47–50
Forked Pond, 14, 25, 68
40th Pole, 15
Four-toed salamander, 26, 37, 135, 136, 139
Fowler's toad, 131–132
Fox-tail club-moss, 63
Foxes, 86, 113
French, Tom, 82, 83, 106, 118–119, 123
Freshwater, 56, 216
    boat-washing detergents and, 218–219
    boats, damage by, 218
    cleanup programs, 225–228
    eelgrass and, 177–182
    ice industry, 204
    microbes and, 180–181
    oxygen, 177
    pollution, 178
    quality, 178–179
    salinity, 177
    See also Ponds
Freshwater fish species, 188
Freshwater marsh, 69
Freshwater swamps, 142
Frogs, 142
    Batrachochytrium dendrobatidi, 143
Fronzutol Dave, 178, 220
Fukushima I Daiichi Nuclear Power Plant, 250
Fungi, 37, 163

G

Gabion, 271, 276
Game Birds: Wildfowl and Shore-birds of Massachusetts and Adjacent States, 88
Gardner's Island, 5
Garter snakes, 137, 141
Genthner, Marc, 234
Geogrid, 271, 276
Georges Bank, 33, 110
Gerardia, 63
Gibbs Pond, 11, 14–15
Gibbs Pond kettle, 11
Glacial erratics, 4, 5
Glacial Lake Cape Cod, 11
Glacial Lake Sesachacha, 10, 11, 12
Glacial stage, 2–6
    aquifer, 7–8
    Bean Hill, 15
    Cape Cod Lobe, 5–6, 11
    dating, 44–45
    Gibbs Pond, 14–15
    Great Neck, 20
    melting, 34, 71
    Muskeget, 6
    New England, 6
    outwash plains, 11–14
    Sangamonian Interglacial, 10
    Sankaty Head Lighthouse, 9–10
    Siasconset, 11–12
    splash pools, 34
    terminal moraine, 5
    timeline, 37
    Tuckernuck, 19–20
    warming trends, 25–26
    Wisconsin Glacial Stage, 3–5, 10, 33
Glacial Till, 3, 4, 10, 15
Glades, 17
Glaucous gulls, 76
Global warming, 99–101, 278–279
Godfrey, Joyce, 26–27
Gold rush, 65, 121, 203
Golden heather, 62
Golden Plover, 91
Good-night green-briar, 63
Goodman, David, 213, 188
Google Earth, 263

Goshawks, 86
Gosnold, Bartholomew, 86
Grass species, 59
Grasses, 56–57
Gravelly Islands, 20, 25
Gray catbirds, 97
Gray seals, 37, 230, 255–256
Gray squirrels, 27
Great auk, 86–87
Great blue herons, 76
Great Depression, 174–175
Great Drought of 1874, 8
Great Harbor Yacht Club, 194
Great Neck, 20
Great Point, 6, 9, 16–20, 25
   erosion of, 263–264
   gray seals of, 255
   island highpoints of, 17
   sharks of, 255–256
Great Point lighthouse, 20
Great ponds, 142, 186, 217
Great Rock, 5
Great salt pond, 186, 192, 203, 211, 212
Great South Channel, 3, 10
Great South Channel Lobe, 4, 10
Great South Point, 25
Great South Pond, 20
Great white sharks, 232–235
Greater prairie-chickens, 83
Green snake, 134, 135, 136, 141–142
Greenhead flies, 129, 148, 149–150
Greenland, 238
Grey Lady, 6, 264
Grinnell, George Bird, 94
Griscom, Ludlow, 86, 89, 91, 118
Groins, 264, 268, 274
Groundfish, 248
Ground-nesting water birds, 76–77
Guinea hens, 85–86
Gulf of Mexico, 238
Gulf Stream, 23, 79, 96, 238, 239
Gull species, 76

H

Habitat preservation, 63
Habitats
   development of, 139–141
   evolution, 92–93
   island, 66–67
   melting glaciers and, 34–35
   reptiles, 139–141
   types of, 29, 31
Haddock, 244
Halliwell, David B., 184
Harbors
   camels, 197
   channels, 199–200
   dredging, 18, 195, 198–199, 200, 202, 204, 205
   evolution of, 192–200
   jetties, 197–199, 226–227
   Nantucket Bar, 197
   nutrient overload, 218, 221
   seafood ad, 200–201
   whale oil and, 194
Harbor watersheds, 217–218, 223, 226
Hardwood forests, 50, 139
Harriers, 76, 97–98
Hartel, Karsten E., 184
Haulouts, seal, 255
Haulover cut, 16, 19, 20
   beach plants, 54
   closure, 37, 201
   evolution of, 25
Hawks, 76
Head of Hummock, 13
Heath hen, 83–85
Heathlands, 34, 24–25, 61
   burning of, 89
   plants, 35, 58, 64, 65
Heathlands Partnership, 167
Herring, 76
Hickey, Michael, J., 221
Hickories, 50
Hidden Forest, 49

INDEX

Historic Nantucket (1967), 50, 197
History of Nantucket, 1–2
History of Nantucket: Being a Compendious Account of the First Settlement of the Island by the English, Together With the Rise and Progress of the Whale Fishery; and Other Historical Facts Relative to Said Island and its Inhabitants, 63, 64
History of the Game Birds: Wildfowl and Shore-birds of Massachusetts and Adjacent States, 88
Hither Creek, 14, 267
Hoary bats, 120, 127
Hoicks Hollow, 13
Holland, Linda, 131, 222
Hollings, Donald, 261
Holocene Epochs, 33, 35, 58, 81
Home rule petition, 118, 212
Homoptera (leaf hoppers), 149
Honeybees (Apis mellifera), 168
Hope Is the Thing With Feathers: A Personal Chronicle of Vanished Birds, 83, 84
Horse flies, 148
Horse Shed, 207
Horsehoe crab, 32
House sparrows, 98
Howes, Brian, 214, 218
Howland, John, 83–84
Hudsonian curlews, 98
Human occupation, 32
  bird species, impact on, 85, 94
  sandplain grassland plants and, 60
  species introduction and, 27, 104, 115
  landscape alteration, 24, 32, 60, 65, 73, 191
  mammals and, 127
  terminal moraines and, 24
  timber harvesting and, 76
  See also Deer; DDT; Paleo-Indians; specific species
Hummingbirds, 97
Hummock Pond, 13, 25, 43, 267
Hummock Pond Homeowners Association, 224
Hummock Pond Road, 266
Hunters, 87–90
  MassWildlife-sanctioned February deer hunt (2004), 174
Hunting, 87–91
  season, 116–118, 125–126
  shooting journal, 88, 89
Hurricane Esther, 183, 200
Hurricane Gloria, 182, 200
Hurricane Noel, 278
Hussey Shoal, 207
Huyser, Henry, 133
Hydrostatic pressure, 8
Hymenoptera (wasps and bees), 149
Hyper-eutrophic, 216
Hypsithermal, 58

I

Ice industry, 204
Icelandic gulls, 76
Ichthyologist, 184, 187, 237
Illinoian, 3
Illinoian Glacial Stage, 9
Inland Fishes of Massachusetts, 184, 185
Insects, 37, 142, 148, 173–175
  benefits from, 150–151, 163–164
  bias toward, 149–150
  classification, 148
  deer tick, 152–163
  description, 148
  hunting and, 158
  origins and adaptability, 151–152
  prosperity factors, 168
Interconnectivity, ocean, 235–237
  coastal plains and, 235
  Continental Shelf, 235
  Nantucket Archipelago, 243
  Nantucket Sound, 236, 237
  Nantucket waters, 238–239
  Vineyard Sound, 237

333

Interlobal moraine, 10
International Chimney of Buffalo, 270–271
Invasive species control, 28
   brush cutting as, 73
   burning and mowing methods, 67, 167
   management of, 60
   protection, 29
   sheep as, 64–65, 119
Isoptera (termites), 149

J

Jack pine, 46
Jackrabbits, 27, 115–116
Jackson Point, 27, 267
Japanese black pine, 63, 67
Jaws (movie), 256
Jersey Shore, 2, 5
Jet stream fall out, 97
Jetties, 197–199, 226–227
Jetties Beach, 8, 16
Jewel Ponds, 14, 70
Job, Herbert K., 88
Johnson, Charles Willison, 155
Johnson, Luanne, 123, 166
Jones, Bassett, 50, 166
Justice, William V., 115

K

Kafer, Lester, 20–21
Kafer, Peter, 21
Kelley, Ken, 217
Kennedy, Bob, 30, 142
Kenny, Raymond J., 117
Kestrels, 76
Kettle hole pond plants, 68
Kettle holes, 34, 40, 68
Kettle ponds, 70, 71, 80
Killen, John, 204
Kimball, 166
Knieper, Elizabeth, 42
Krill, 238

Krogh, 232
Kunz, Thomas H., 105

L

Labrador Current, 238
Labryrinthula zosterae, 206
LaFarge, Bam, 119
LaHaye, Don "Clambo", 212
Land clearing, 91–92, 121
Land developers, 91–92, 121, 125
Land formation, 52–53
Larsen, Roy, 72
Late sweet blueberry, 62
Launer, Alan E., 184
Laurentide ice sheet, 2, 3, 5, 110, 111
   climatological impact of, 46, 99–100
   final advance of, 25
   glaciation, 35
   islands and, 110
   mass extinction and, 111
   melting of, 58
   New England and, 153
   ocean elevation and, 33, 55
   retreat of, 44, 152
Laux, E. Vernon, 95, 147
Laws
   bird hunting, 89–90, 94, 230
   Canadian species act, 238
   environmental protection, 73, 134, 139–140, 2211, 35
   fishing, 234
   hunting season, 109
   mammal protection, 230–231, 234, 254–255, 256, 257
   oak groves, 156
   ponds, 211–212, 213
Lazell, James "Skip", 130, 137
Least sandpipers, 97
Leatherleaf, 72
Lepidoptera (moths and butterflies), 37, 147, 149, 164–168
   butterflies, comparisons, 165–166
   migration, 173

Monarch migration, 173
   suppression, 165, 149
   tussock, 165
Lepidoptera of Nantucket and Martha's Vineyard Islands, Massachusetts, 166
Lesser golden plover, 87, 90–91
Lesser yellowlegs, 97
Letters from an American Farmer, 188
Lichens, 41–43, 163
Life and Death of the Salt Marsh, 56
Lighthouses
   Sankaty Head Lighthouse, 2, 9, 260, 269, 271
   Great Point lighthouse, 20
Lily Pond, 192
Limnologist, 216
Linda Loring Nature Foundation, 30, 95, 147
List of Insect Fauna of Nantucket, Massachusetts, 155
Lithic Period, 36, 46, 62
Little blue-eyed grass, 61
Little bluestem grass, 61
Little gulls, 76
Little Neck, 267
Little, Elizabeth, 46–47
Littoral drift, 15, 16, 17, 19, 267
Lobstermen, 250
   limits for, 253
Long Pond, 14, 25, 267
Long woods, 47
Long-billed curlew, 87, 90
Long-tail ducks, 75–76, 81, 82, 97
LORAN station, 12
Lowbush blueberry, 61
Lyme disease, 120, 159–160
   Baltic amber tick and, 153
   first Nantucket case, 37, 152
   identification, 159, 161
   mice and, 157
   prevention, 161, 120
   spirochetes, 157
   tracking of, 160–161

M

Mackay, George Henry, 88–90
Mackerel, 245–246
Macrofossils, 43
Macy, Obed, 64
Macy, Thomas, 113
Macy's Hill, 2
Madaket Beach, 43
Madaket Harbor, 19
Madaket Harbors Action Plan, 227
Madaket Road, 5, 12
Madequecham Valley, 13, 25
Madequecham, 68
Maglathlin, Fred, 72
Main Street, 12
Malaria, 150
Mallard ducks, 76, 97
Mammals, 28, 35–36, 37, 109–111
   as predators, 76–77
   habitats, 122
   history of, 103–104
   mass extinction, 111–112
   movement of, 113–114
   random selection, 112
   reintroduction of, 122
   species of, 28, 127
   See also specific species
Mammoths, 110
Maple, Bill, 133
Maples, 50
Maria Mitchell Association (MMA), 30, 37, 80, 90, 147, 172, 227
Marine life, species of, 37
Marine Coastal Resources Department, 187
Marine Mammal Protection Act (MMPA) of 1972, 230, 231, 257
Marine Mammal Stranding Team, 234–235
Market gunners and, 86–87, 90–91. *See also* Hunters
Martha's Vineyard, 2, 5, 26, 32
Martha's Vineyard family, 156

Mass extinction, 111–112
Massachusetts Audubon Society, 30, 63, 67, 172
Massachusetts Coastal Zone Management, 260
Massachusetts Department of Environmental Protection, 139, 211, 274
Massachusetts Environmental Protection Act, 211
Massachusetts Estuaries Project, 178
MassWildlife, 122–123, 124, 127
   -sanctioned February deer hunt (2004), 174
Mastodons, 110, 111, 112
Maxey Pond, 204
McAtee, W. L., 42
Mcblair Shoals, 239
McCandless, Andrew, 27
McCarthy, Jerry, 248
McKenna-Foster, Andrew, 26, 33, 121, 142, 147–148, 171, 172
McManis, Debra A., 72
Mehrhoff, Leslie, J., 58–59
Mello, Mark J., 165, 166–167
Mesozoic Era, 7
Miacomet Creeks, 13
Miacomet Pond, 12, 13, 25, 217, 267
Miacomit tribe, 37
Mice, 103
Microbes, 180–181
Microtus breweri, 105
Middens, 131, 235
   local food and, 191
   Native American currency and, 201
   turtles and, 136, 188
   vertebrae, as ornaments, 192
Middle Moors, 9
Midwestern
   agrarian cargo, 59
   arthropod species, 155
   insects, 155
   migrations, 90

Migration, 59
   bird species, 75, 77, 78, 82, 83, 91, 96, 97–98
   deer, 27
   dune, 17
   faunal, 136
   insect, 173–175
   reptiles, 137–143
   seed, 59
Milestone, 71, 72–73
Milestone bog, 33
Milestone Cranberry, 71
Milestone Cranberry Bogs, 8, 9, 11
Milestone Road, 12, 61, 67
Milk snakes, 141
Mill Hill, 4
Miller, Gerrit S. Jr., 106
Millinery, 86, 89, 94
Minks, 86
Mioxes Pond, 14
Mitchell, Maria, 26, 174
MMM. See Maria Mitchell Association (MMA)
MMPA. See Marine Mammal Protection Act (MMPA) (1972)
Mockingbirds, 98
Monarch migration, 173
Monarch Watch, 172
Mundus, Frank, 256
Monomoy, 7
Moors, 24, 50, 61–62
Moors End, 173
Moraines, 5, 11–13, 14, 16, 52
Morrison, Todd, 275
Mosquito control, 174–175
Moth Suppression Department, 165
Moth Suppression Reports, 129
Mothball Way, 66, 267
Moths. See Lepidoptera (moths and butterflies)
Muskeget, 4, 6
Muskeget Island, 2, 6, 12, 13
Muskeget vole, 29–30, 104–107, 112

INDEX

Muskellunge, 188
Muskrats, 112

N

Nantucket Anglers Club, 188
Nantucket Bar, 197
Nantucket Beacon, 213, 261
Nantucket Biodiversity Initiative (NBI), 30, 38
Nantucket Birding Club, 80
Nantucket Boat Basin, 210, 219
Nantucket Cat Trap's 108
Nantucket Conservation Foundation, 23, 30, 66, 69, 71, 114, 172
Nantucket Fever (Babesiosis), 153, 158–159
Nantucket Fire Department, 60
Nantucket Garden Club, 30
Nantucket Harbor, 16–17
  cuspate spits, 18
  dredging, 18, 195, 198–199, 200, 202, 204, 205
  evolution, 181–184, 195
  formation, 16–17
Nantucket Heathlands Partnership, 60
Nantucket Hunt Club, 27, 116
Nantucket Independent, 115, 265, 273, 278
Nantucket Island School of Design & the Arts, 7
Nantucket Islands Land Bank, 23, 30, 63, 67
Nantucket land council, 223–228
  bivalve filters, 224
  eelgrass restoration, 227
  environmental consciousness, 223
  harbor watershed protection districts, 223
  salt and fresh water cleanup programs, 225–228
  water quality testing, 223
  water restoration, 224
  wellhead protection district, 223
Nantucket Shadbush, 61, 62–64

Nantucket Shellfish Association, 227
Nantucket Shoreline Survey: An Analysis of Nantucket Shoreline Erosion and Accretion Trends, 260, 263, 264, 267, 273, 274
Nantucket tribe, 37
Nantucket Wildflowers, 66
Nantucket's Board of Selectmen, 271
Nantucket's Endangered Maritime Heaths, 61
Nantucket's Forgotten Island: Muskeget, 19
National Marine Fisheries Service (NMFS), 231, 250–251, 252, 253
National Oceanic and Atmospheric Administration (NOAA), 231, 253, 257–258, 278
Native Americans, 28–29, 37, 113
  along-shore whaling, 241
  eels and, 202
  environmental adaption, 191
  fishing encampments, 192–193
  fuel useage, 92
  impact on wild life, 86, 87, 136–137, 155, 191, 192
  land burning, 28
  movement of, 113
  nomadics, 137
  Old Saul, 4
  plants used by, 60
  population, 113
  population, 113–114
  relocation, 191
  sachem rights, 239
  settlement, 60
  sharks and, 235
  subtribes, 37
  turtles and, 136
  white-tail deer and, 27
Natural Heritage & Endangered Species Program (Massachusetts Division of Fisheries & Wildlife), 30, 82, 106, 107
Nature Conservancy, 88
Naushon Island, 50–51

Nayhew, Thomas, 46–47
NBI. *See* Nantucket Biodiversity Initiative
Needlegrass, 63
New England, 2, 3, 4, 6, 33
New England Fisheries Management Council, 251
New Jersey, 2
New York, 2
Nighthawks, 97
1986 Bulletin of the Massachusetts Archeological Society article, 192
NMFS. *See* National Marine Fisheries Service (NMFS)
NOAA. *See* National Oceanic and Atmospheric Administration (NOAA)
No Bottom Pond, 66
Nomans Land, 26
Norcross, Arthur, 20
North Monomoy Island, 112–113
Northern conifers, 46
Northern flickers, 98
Northern harriers, 28, 76, 83, 97–98
Northern shrikes, 82
North Shore, 263–264
Northwest Atlantic walrus population, 238
Nova Scotia, 238
Nub scallops, 219–221
Nut-rush, 63
Nutrient-deprived soils, 72
Nutrient overload, 214, 216, 218, 221

O

O'Boyle, Robert, 254
O'Dell, Danielle, 144–145
Oaks, 50
Occupy Great Point movement, 234
Oceanographic & Atmospheric Administration, cod study, 249
Oktay, Sarah, 23–24
Old Buck (deer), 27
Old Saul, 4
Oldale, Robert N., 5, 6, 7, 10, 12, 13, 17, 41, 44, 56, 182
Opossums, 86
Orion Shoals, 239
Osprey, 96, 97, 130, 222
Otters, 109, 123–124
Outwash plains, 11–14, 25
Owls, 31, 98–99
Oxygen, 18, 177, 199, 224, 238
Oystercatchers, 31
Oysters, 186, 200, 210–211, 224

P

Paddock, Ichabod, 241
Paddock, Love, 193
Paleo-Indians, 36, 46, 62, 86, 190
Peepers, 135, 137
Pennsylvania, 2
Pennsylvania sedge, 62
Pelagic fish, 245
People for the Ethical Treatment of Animals (PETA), 161, 162
Peregrine falcons, 76, 86
Perkins, Blair, 239
Perry, Bruce, 63
Person, Mark, 8
Peteet, Dorothy, 43–44, 45
Pew, Bill, 188
Philbrick, Nat, 240
Phillips Run, 14
Phillips, John C., 89
Philosophical Transactions of the Royal Society B: Biological Sciences, 152
Phosphorus mobilization, 224
Photosynthesis, 42, 239
Pielou, E. C., 110, 111
Pitch pines, 51, 54, 66
Pitcher plant, 71
Plant species
 early vegetation, 40–41
 growth, 41, 45, 46, 52, 53 54
 moors and, 61–62
 nutrient-deprived soils and, 72

post-glacial vegetation, 34–35, 40–41, 43–45, 51–52
  soil profile, 41, 43
  statistics, 52
  transition zone, 7, 57
  varieties of, 35, 52, 56–57
  vascular plants, 37
  wetland, 14
  See also Sporopollenin; specific types
Plant succession, 66, 71, 73, 165, 167
Pleistocene, 6, 9, 33, 35, 81, 82
Pochman, Kitty, 31
Pocomo, 10
Podzol, 41
Poison ivy, 69
Pollen, 43
Polpis Harbor, 10, 25, 182
Polpis Road, 4, 7, 12, 13, 27, 61
Polpis tribe, 37
Pond plants, 68
Ponds, 184–189
  clean up of, 217
  defined, 71
  fish varieties, 186, 188–189
  freshwater fish, introduction into, 185
  loss of eelgrass, 216
  management of, 211–212
  Miacomet Pond, 216
  opening of, 186–188
  salt, 211–219
  stocking, 188–189
  See also Salt ponds
Possums, 113
Post-glacial marine deposits, 25
Post-glacial vegetation, 34–35, 40–41, 43–45, 51–52
Poultry birds, 32, 85–86
Pout Ponds, 14, 68, 70–71
Prairie dogs, 119
Prairie peninsula, 58, 155
Prairie plants, 59–60, 155
Pre-Illinoian, 3

Precambrian, 1
Predators, 86, 96
Prickly pear, 61
Primary forest, 156, 157
Proceedings of the Boston Society of Natural History, 106
Proprietors of the Common and Undivided Lands of Nantucket, 47, 64, 212
Prospect Hill, 4
Pumpkin seed, 188
Purple cudweed, 61
Purseweb spider, 171

Q

Quahogs, 200–202, 210–211
Quaise, 10
Quanaty Bank, 192, 195
Quarter Mile Hill, 2, 4–5, 11, 66
Quidnet, 4, 10

R

Rabbits, 113–116
  cottontails, 122
  habitats, 122
  jackrabbits, 115–116
Raccoons, 86, 113, 119
Ram Pasture, 12, 13, 267
Rare plants, 65
Ratner, Gene, 273
Rats, 103
Ray, Edie, 79–80, 96–97
Razorbills, 97
Reagents, 39
Red cedar, 48
Red fescue, 62
Red maple, 69
Red-bellied woodpecker, 99
Red-breasted robins 79
Red-tail hawks, 76, 97–98
Redback salamanders, 137
Refugium, 154
Regal fritillary, 167–1268

Reinhard, Allen, 2–3
Reintroduction process
    burying beetle, 171–172
    insects, 148
    river otters, 123
    white-tail deer, 37
Reithof, George, 278
Reproductive cycles, 100
Reptiles, 131–137–143
    choral tree frogs, 135
    habitats, 139–141
    peepers, 135, 137
    salamanders, 135–136
    snakes, 134–135, 136, 141–142
    turtles, 131, 135–137, 143–145
    See also specific species
Rhizosphere, 180
Ribbon snakes, 141
Riley, Tara Anne, 221
Ring-necked pheasants, 98
Ring-necked snakes, 141
River otter, 109, 113
Rock doves, 98
Roger Williams Zoo, 147
Rookery, 133, 237, 255
Rose mallow, 69
Rosen, Peter, 17, 18
Rough-legged hawks, 76
Rounsville, Martland "Red", 72
Ruddy turnstones, 97
Rust tide, 214, 221–222

S

SAC. *See* Seal Abatement Coalition
Sachems Spring, 8
Sangamonian layers, 10
Salamanders (Urodela), 26, 37, 139, 135–136, 142
Salinity, 177, 213, 238, 239
Salt marsh ecosystem, 55–59
    areas of, 55
    evolution of, 34
    grasses, 56–57
    seed dispersal, 58–59

Salt meadow grass, 69
Salt ponds, 211–219
    environmental impact on, 211–212
    management of, 211–212
    nutrient overload of, 214, 221–222
    openings, 213–214
    study, 216
    See also Ponds
Salt water
    cleanup programs, 225–228
    eelgrass and, 177–182, 206
    microbes and, 180–181
    oxygen, 177
    pollution, 178
    quality, 178–179
    salinity, 177
    See also Ponds
Saltwater mosquitoes, 149–150, 174–175
Sand deposits, 259
Sanderlings, 97
Sandplain grasslands, 31, 59–60
Sanford Farm, 12, 13, 23, 267
Sangamonian Interglacial stage, 10
Sankaty Bluff, 3, 4, 10
Sankaty Head, 10
Sankaty Head Lighthouse, 9–10, 11, 260, 269, 271
Sasacaskeh tribe, 37
Sassafras, 69
Saul's Hills, 4, 80
SBPF. *See* Siasconset Beach Preservation Fund (SBPF)
Scallops, 203–210
    algae and, 221
    catboats, 205–206, 208
    codium fragile, 208
    decline in, 209–210
    environmental factors, 208–209
    green crabs and, 208
    harvesting, 204–205, 210–211
    Nantucket's, 236
    nub, 219–221
    wasting disease, 206–207

Scannell, Steve, 212–213
Scarp, 9, 10, 262
School of Marine Science and Technology (SMAST), 214–215
Science Department of Nantucket High School, 30
'Sconset, 157
Scoters, 81, 82, 97
Scrub oak, 63, 66, 67
Sea
   Gulf stream, 23, 32, 79, 93, 96, 238–239, 243
   Labrador Abyssal, 3
   Labrador current, 238–239, 243
Sea level rise, 113–114, 282
Seal Abatement Coalition (SAC), 230–232, 254, 257
Seals, 230–232
   Marine Mammal Protection Act (MMPA), 231
   National Marine Fisheries Service (NMFS), 231
   National Oceanic and Atmospheric Administration (NOAA), 231
   population statistics, 230
   rescue team, 234–235
   Seal Abatement Coalition (SAC), 230
   sharks versus, 254–258
Sears, Kathryn, 45
Sedges, 68
Seed dispersal, 58–59
Semipalmated plovers, 97
Septic Management Plan, 225
Serology, Lyme disease and, 161
Sesachacha Pond, 10, 11, 12, 14
Several Million Years of Stability among Insect Species Because of, or in Spite of, Ice Age Climatic Instability?, 152
Shaler, 182
Shallow wetland, 69
Sharks, 232–235, 255–256
   attacks on humans, 256
   evolution, 234
   great white, 232–235

meat protection act, 234
seals versus, 254–258
species of, 37
varieties of, 234, 237
seals versus, 254–258
Sharp-shinned hawks, 76
Shaukimmo tribe, 37
Shawkemo Hills, 2, 4, 25
Shawkemo Spring, 7
Sheep
   as invasive species control, 64–65
   as management tool, 61
   statistics, 65
Sheep laurel, 72
Sheep Pond Road dwellers, 266, 267, 275
Shell-Fish Management Plan, 227
Sherburne, 192, 193, 194
Shimmo area, 4, 54
Shoal modules, 275
Shoals, 52, 86, 197
   Bass Rip, 270
   cleaning, 199
   erosion, 264
   fishing around, 244, 248
   flounders and, 246
   moving, 255, 267
   wave-breaking, 266
Shorebirds, 97
Short-eared owls, 98
Shrews, 103, 112
Shrub swamps, 69
Siasconset, 11–12
   erosion of, 260–263
Siasconset Beach Preservation Fund (SBPF) 262, 269–272, 277
Siasconset outwash, 11–12
Siasconset Sewage Treatment Plant, 12
Siasconset tribe, 37
Side Hunt, 90
Silent Spring, 130
Silt, 69
Silver-haired bats, 120
Sinclair, Michael, 254
Sjolund, Carl, 198

Sjolund, Karl, 198
Skomal, Greg, 232–233
Skunks, 86
Smack, 245
SMAST. *See* School of Marine Science and Technology (SMAST)
Smith Point, 19, 25, 275, 277–278
Smith, Doug "Smitty", 124–125, 126
Smith's Island, 20, 264, 267
Smith's Point, 266, 273–274
Smyers, 137–138, 140
Snails, 179, 183, 208, 249
Snakes (Squamata), 37, 134–135, 136, 141–142
Snow geese, 97
Soil profile, 41, 43
Sorrie, Bruce A., 42
South Monomoy Island, 112–113
South Shore, 43
Southern flying squirrel, 119
Sovereignty, over ponds, 37, 212
Spadefoot toad, 131–133, 140
Sphagnum bogs, 69, 71–72
Sphagnum moss, 69
Sphagnum moss swamp, 26
Spiders (arachnids), 33, 37
    bias toward, 149–150
    bites, 150
    black widows, 170–171
    cob weaver family (Theridiidae), 170
    purseweb, 171
Spirochetes, 153, 157
Sporopollenin, 39
Spotted turtle, 143–145
Spring peepers, 137
Spruce grouse, 82
Squam Swamp, 33, 34, 48, 69, 142
Squam tribe, 37
Squibnocket Pond, 123
Squirrels, 118–120
    Eastern gray, 119
    Southern flying, 119
St. Andrew's cross, 61
St. Johns wort, 68

St. Lawrence Region, 2
Sta-Beach dewatering system, 269
Stackpole, Edouard A., 197, 198
Staging, 31, 173
Starbuck, Maria Mitchell, 88
Starlings, 98
State and federal protection laws, 94
Steamship Authority ferries, 119
Stump pond, 33
Stump Swamp, 69
Sturgis, Josias, 66–67
Substrates, 41
Sundews, 68
Surfside, 267
Sutherland, Jim, 216
Swallows, 97
Swamp azalea, 68–69
Swampscott dories, 201
Swamp variations, 69
Swans, 97
Sweet pepperbush, 69

T

Talhanio tribe, 37
Tamarin, Robert H., 105
Tanagers, 97
Tashama Farm, 115
Taylor, Orley R., 173
Teal, John, 56
Teal, Mildred, 56, 57
Telford, Sam R. III, 120
Tent caterpillars 148
Terminal moraine, 3, 4–5, 11, 15, 25
    biological safe zones in, 184
    human-altered, 24
    Peteet's study, 44
    places to view, 9, 13
Tertiary Period, 6
Tetaukimmo Island tribe, 37
This Broken Archipelago: Cape Cod and the Islands, Amphibians and Reptiles, 131, 139
Thoughts on the Biogeography of Grassland Plants in New England, 58–59
Tick-borne Encephalitis, 150, 153

Tick-trefoil, 63
Tiffney, Wes Jr., 61, 268, 273
Till, 3, 4, 10, 15
Timber records, 46–48, 50
Toads, 131–133
Tombolo, 16, 17, 55–56
Tom Nevers, erosion of, 260–263
Tom Nevers Head, 11, 12, 14
Tom Nevers Pond, 12, 14, 267
Tom Nevers Road, 9
Toupshue, 25, 68
Toupshue Pond, 14
Town Farms & Country Commons: Farming on Nantucket, 72
Triassic Period. 6–7
Trichoptera (caddis flies), 149
Trot's Swamp. 69
Trott's Hills, 5
Trout, 188
Trout Unlimited, 88
Troy, Joseph Jr., 233
Trustees of Reservations, 15, 30
Tuckernuck, 19–20, 32
Tuckernuck Island, 2, 5, 6, 12, 13, 20
Tuckernuck Land Trust, 30
Tufted titmouse, 99
Tundra birds, 82
Tundra plant communities, 24
Tupelo, 40, 46, 49
Turbidity, 179, 222
Turkey vultures, 79
Turkeys, 26–27
Turtles (Testudinata), 37, 131, 135–137, 143–145
Tussock moth, 129, 165
2010 Section Allocation, of fish, 252

U

United States Coast and Geodetic Survey, 260
University of Massachusetts at Boston, 172
   Nantucket Field Station, 30
Upwelling underwater, 238

U.S. Army Corps of Engineers, 213, 226
   Beach Erosion Board, 260
U.S. Fisheries and Wildlife Service (USFW), 122, 147, 172
U.S. Geological Survey (1975), 6, 7

V

Vascular and Non-Vascular Plants on Nantucket, Tuckernuck and Muskeget Islands, 42
Vascular plants, 37, 42, 52, 59
Veit, Dick, 77, 85
Vineyard Gazette, 123
Vireos, 97
Voles, 29–30, 104–107, 112

W

Walruses, 237–238
Wampanoags, 37, 64, 113
   as fishermen, 191–192
   subtribes of, 37
Wannacomet Water Company, 7
Warblers, 82, 97
Washing Pond 188
Water birds, ground-nesting, 76–77
Water columns, 238
Waterman, Cameron, 205
Water quality, 96, 178–179, 222
   atmospheric pollutants and, 209
   decline, 218
   eelgrass and, 217
   fish, lack of and, 222
   forum, 215
   scallops and, 208, 220
   testing, 223–224, 227
   watershed overdevelopment, 217
Water snakes, 141
Watersheds, 68, 189, 214, 217, 225
   fertilizers and, 214
   flood control and cleaning, 214, 226
   overdevelopment, 217
   protection districts, 223
   residential development within, 209, 211, 217

Water Tower Beach, 193
Wauwinet, 17, 21, 54, 140, 218
Wauwinet Road, 7, 16
Wave Dispersion Technologies, Inc.
  See WDT
WDT (Wave Dispersion Technologies, Inc.), 271–272
Weirs, 191, 192
Weld, William, 212–213
Wesko Landing, 192
West End, 264–266
West Nile Virus, 150
Western end, 272–276
  erosion, 273
  erosion control structures, 274
  ocean-current measuring meter (MAVS-3), 275
  property owners, 274–276
  storms and, 272
Wet meadows, 69
Wetland vegetation, 67–68
Wetlands, 69–70, 129–145
  bullfrogs and, 141
  clay and sand of the, 140
  as developable land, 139
  evolution of, 70
  habitats, 28, 121–122
  peat, 70
  plants, 13, 14, 67–72
  protection of, 63, 215, 276
  spadefoot toad, 132
  sphagnum moss, 71, 72
  varieties of, 140
Wetlands Protection Act, 139
Weweeder Ponds, 14
Whale Island, 20, 25, 53
Whale oil, 194
Whales, 239–243
  scrag, 240
  species of, 37
  sperm, 242
  whaling, 239–242

Whimbrels, 97
WhisprWave wave attenuation installation, 271–272
White-and red-breasted nuthatches, 99
White-footed mouse, 112
White oaks, 48
White perch, 123, 188, 192
White-tailed deer. See Deer
Wigwam Pond, 14, 68, 70
Willets, 97
Willett, Jeff, 174
Williams, Sandy, 275
Wilson, Alexander, 86
Windswept, 70, 71
Windswept bog, 33
Windswept Cranberry Bog, 71
Winter Flora of Muskeget Island, Massachusetts, 50, 52
Winterberry, 69
Wiregrass, 62
Wisconsinan Glacial Stage, 3–5, 10, 33
Wolves, 86
Wood frog, 139
Wood, Stephanie, 230
Woodcocks, 98
Woodland rodents, 118–120
Woodman's hardwood, deliveries, 119–120
Woody shrubs, 72
Woolly mammoths, 110, 111, 112
Woolman, John, 48

X

Xerothermic Period, 58

Y

Yellow perch, 123, 188, 192, 213

Z

Zoologists, 38, 184